CURRENT LEGAL PROBLEMS 1987

Volume 40

AUSTRALIA AND NEW ZEALAND
The Law Book Company Ltd.
Sydney : Melbourne : Perth

CANADA AND U.S.A.
The Carswell Company Ltd.
Agincourt, Ontario

INDIA
N.M. Tripathi Private Ltd.
Bombay
and
Eastern Law House Private Ltd.
Calcutta and Delhi
M.P.P. House
Bangalore

ISRAEL
Steimatzky's Agency Ltd.
Jerusalem : Tel Aviv : Haifa

MALAYSIA : SINGAPORE : BRUNEI
Malayan Law Journal (Pte.) Ltd.
Singapore

CURRENT LEGAL PROBLEMS 1987

Edited by
ROGER RIDEOUT and JEFFREY JOWELL
with
BEN PETTET as Assistant Editor

On behalf of
THE FACULTY OF LAWS
UNIVERSITY COLLEGE LONDON

Editorial Committee

Volume 40

LONDON
STEVENS and SONS
1987

Published in 1987
by Stevens & Sons Ltd.
of 11, New Fetter Lane, London
Computerset by Promenade Graphics Ltd., Cheltenham
Printed in Great Britain
by Page Bros. (Norwich) Ltd.

British Library Cataloguing in Publication Data
Current Legal Problems.—Vol. 40 (1987)
1. Law—Periodicals—Great Britain
340'.05   K3
ISBN 0–420–47790–X

All editorial communications should be addressed to:
The Editors,
"CURRENT LEGAL PROBLEMS,"
Faculty of Laws,
University College London,
4–8 Endsleigh Gardens, London, WC1

PREFACE

In the Preface to the first volume, the editors (Professor G.W. Keeton and Dr. Schwarzenberger, as he then was) disclosed that that volume had sprung from requests to publish public lectures delivered at University College London. This concept of published lectures survives. The editors continue to regard the presentation of a series of public lectures as a valuable aspect of the work of the Faculty and their presentation in published form as a valuable contribution to legal scholarship. It has been suggested in the past that it is difficult to combine the qualities of a good public lecture with those of a learned paper. The editors have no hesitation in asserting that, if such a difficulty exists, it has been overcome by each of the seven contributors to this volume who have accepted the double challenge. We are, indeed, proud to present the twelve contributions that make up this, the fortieth, annual volume of this journal which, as usual, provide a diverse and wide range of surveys of legal issues.

As one would expect, Sir John Vinelott provides a masterly survey of the new law relating to Insolvency containing such a quantity of information that we continue to be surprised that it could be compressed into a single lecture. Gavin Lightman Q.C., expert in the fields of receivership and sequestration, had been closely involved in their application in relation to the National Union of Mineworkers and, with the dispassion that only a master can command, provides us with a powerful exposition of the strengths and weaknesses of that application.

The pleasure of listening to Adrian Zuckerman's discussion of the legal and ethical problems of reliance upon illegally obtained evidence conveys itself in this paper, wasting no words to make a forceful criticism of inflexible admissibility and inadmissibility rules. Jack Beatson provides an excellent example of how to present in so short a space an unusually wide range of critical analysis of a difficult subject. Despite the unfamiliarity of his large audience with the actual practice of gratuitously emptying overflowing sewers, this lecture, and so the paper in which it finds expression, is another fine example of concise comprehensibility.

Sir Roger Ormrod, the latest in the line of distinguished Bentham Club Presidents, expressed a feeling of inadequacy in competing with his predecessor. No support for this is to be found in his learned and detailed research into the startling change in attitude towards the exercise of judicial discretion.

It has, for some time, been the practice of the editors to approach distinguished practitioners with a request to contribute leaving the choice of subject open to them, albeit with a fairly settled expectation of what will be offfered. Not entirely surprisingly, Michael Beloff Q.C. chose, in his systematically structured discussion of the legal problems of dealing with minority language rights, to shatter those expectations. This paper will, undoubtedly, be ranked as a leader in the study of this developing issue. Malcolm Grant, recently appointed to a post in this Faculty is, for the first time, alone among our immediate colleagues in performing the double of delivering a lecture and writing the subsequent paper. His account of the law of co-ownership, which might be regarded as one of the common law's least successful developments, will add considerably to the understanding of that topic.

Finally, but so far as this College is concerned, first in time, Robert Stevens, in May 1986, fascinated us by opening long closed doors in the Lord Chancellor's Office. Like us, the reader may well wish to return to see more of the personal attitudes and policies which have shaped the work of this office.

There is, however, yet one further paper arising from a lecture to be accounted for. Although it is the first time we will have published a lecture not delivered in this College we read William Twining's account of the history of 150 years of law teaching in the University of London with great pleasure, discovering that that which might so easily have been a list of dates and people was, in fact, an illuminating work of the highest academic standard. We do not regard the University of London as a current legal problem, but we are sure our readers will find this account amusing and instructive.

One of the new found pleasures of editing this publication derives from the submission of papers for which we have not contracted in advance. We can only publish a small proportion of these and some we have to reject simply because they do not seem to fit in to the traditional areas covered by this series. The paper by Professor Peiris, however, picks up a theme we pursued in 1986 and we are delighted to offer it.

The once dominant aspect of internal contributions from members of the staff of this Faculty has been deliberately reduced over the past 15 years but remains an important part of a publication so closely linked to the Faculty as this. We have already noted one such contribution and we would like to express our gratitude to two other members of the staff who have contributed papers to this volume. The range and interest of David Nelken's sociological research in law is well demonstrated in his study of social work contracts. Toni Williams is one of the masters of the art of law in its economic context. She reveals this mastery fully in her closely reasoned discussion of reservation of title in the construction industry. It is no surprise to us that we have already been asked for permission for this paper to be published elsewhere.

It is expected that this year will see the publication of three more volumes in the series of special issues containing four or five papers in a particular area which we undertook two years ago. Ben Pettet, our assistant editor to whom our thanks are again due for his hard work in producing this volume, has edited an issue on Company Law. Francis Rose a previous assistant editor, has presented a volume on the Law of Insurance and Dawn Oliver and Jeffrey Jowell will edit, towards the end of the year, the fifth in the series which will cover current developments in judicial review.

A fourth, edited by Professor Freeman on medical ethics and the law, will appear in 1988.

THE EDITORS

CONTENTS

TABLE OF CASES

TABLE OF STATUTES

Individual Insolvency—The Insolvency Acts 1985 and 1986

SIR JOHN VINELOTT

I do not propose to attempt to review the whole field of insolvency law. I shall confine myself to individual insolvency; within that field I shall endeavour to bring into closer focus the main features of the revolutionary change in the law brought about by the Insolvency Acts of 1985 and 1986.

The two terms "bankruptcy" and "insolvency" need some initial clarification. Blackstone in his Commentaries defined bankruptcy as a proceeding by which the State takes possession of the property of a debtor by an officer appointed for that purpose who is charged with the realisation of that property and its distribution amongst the persons to whom the debtor owes money or to whom he has incurred pecuniary liabilities.[1] That definition directs attention to the coercive disposition of the property of the debtor. Any developed system of bankruptcy law must include provision for the discharge and release of the debtor from debts due at the time of his bankruptcy so that he can re-enter commerce. Both these aspects of bankruptcy are comprehended in the classic definition of bankruptcy given in *Re Reimann* a decision of the Federal Courts of the United States of America as "a system of law for the benefit and the relief of creditors and debtors in cases where the latter are unable [I would add or unwilling] to pay their debts."[2] Bankruptcy in either of these senses describes a process of law. Insolvency describes a state of affairs. In many legal contexts it is used in a narrow but precise sense to describe the situation of a debtor who is unable to meet his debts as they fall due. In other contexts and, I think most often in business contexts it is used in a wider sense—to describe the situation of one whose assets are insufficient to enable him to meet all his liabilities. In that wider sense the concept of insolvency is not a precise one. It prompts a number of questions. How are the assets—in particular business assets—to be valued? Is the business to be valued as a going-concern? Are other assets (or business assets which cannot or should not be sold as part of the going concern) to be valued as under a forced sale or over a longer period of time? How far are future and contingent liabilities to be taken into account and valued and how are they to be weighed against assets which may have no present but a considerable potential value, over the period during which the future and contingent liabilities will fall due? These are questions which are likely to become increasingly important under the new legislation. However they lie outside the scope of this talk. For the present the point I would stress is that the scope of bankruptcy and of insolvency (in whatever sense that word is used) is not coterminous. A man may be made bankrupt although he is not insolvent on any test; I need only instance the individual deserving the full vigour of the bankruptcy law who decamps with his assets to a more hospitable clime. The purpose of the process of bankruptcy is to give the creditors a remedy against the assets of one who is unable *or unwilling* to pay his debts (my emphasis). Then in the past there has been no means of invoking the bankruptcy law against one whose means may be adequate to enable him to pay his debts as they fall due but who is plainly insolvent if his future liabilities are taken into account and who may indeed be intent, possibly from motives of spite, on depleting his assets in order to avoid meeting a future liability. In saying this I do not overlook section 4(1)(*b*) of the Bankruptcy Act 1914 which gave a creditor with a debt owed at a future time the right to present a bankruptcy petition. The creditor was given standing to present his petition but to succeed on it he had to show that there had been an antecedent available act of bankruptcy. One of the objects of the new legislation is to bring bankruptcy and insolvency into greater conformity by allowing a remedy to a creditor faced with a debtor who is insolvent in any realistic sense of the word but who is nonetheless able to meet his current liabilities as they fall due (See *e.g.* The 1986 Act, ss.267(2)(*c*) and 268(2)). That is not of course the only object. In the past bankruptcy procedures have for all practical purposes been the only proceedings available to or against an insolvent debtor. One of the purposes of the new legislation is to provide other means by which a debtor, individual or corporate whose affairs are temporarily embarrassed but who may with time and skilled assistance be able to meet all his obligations may escape being enmeshed unnecessarily in the expensive and damaging processes of bankruptcy or compulsory winding-up, and to ensure that whenever possible viable businesses and the jobs of those employed in them are preserved. Lastly, the legislation is designed to free bankruptcy procedures from the excessive technicalities with which they been entangled in the past. To understand these far reaching changes the new legislation must be placed in its historical setting.

Historical Background

English law was late in adopting any system of bankruptcy law. Lord Coke saw the absence of a bankruptcy law as one of the ancient liberties enjoyed by Englishmen in a past golden age. In former times he said, "as the name of a bankrupt so was the the offence itself a stranger to an Englishman who of all nations was freest of bankruptcy." It was a sign of the depravity of later times "that we have fetched as well the name as the wickedness of bankrupts from foreign nations."[3] This language may bring a smile to the lips of modern readers. But I draw attention to it with a serious purpose. Lord Coke's view of the bankrupt as one who has transgressed the moral code and broken his contract with society is one which has dominated and I think distorted our bankruptcy laws until the present time. As I shall later show, his view of bankruptcy is echoed by liberal and progressive thinkers in the late nineteenth century and is reflected in the Bankruptcy Act of 1883 which was in turn modified only in minor respects by the Act of 1914. Lord Coke ascribed the introduction of bankruptcy law to an enactment in the reign of Henry VIII passed in 1542. The Irish Bankruptcy Law Committee which reported in 1972 found an earlier origin in an Act passed in the reign of Edward III in 1357 which was directed against three Lombard banking firms the Recardi of Lucca, the Frescobaldi and the Bardi and Peruzzi. However the Act of 1542 was the first Bankruptcy Act of general application. The situation when it was passed was very shortly this. The dissolution of the monasteries, like the discovery of oil in the North Sea, brought a habit of conspicuous consumption by the new middle classes which excited envy and in turn led to some spectacular commercial collapses. The preamble to this Act stresses the wickedness of those who "suddenly flee to parts unknown or keep their houses not minding to pay or restore to any of their creditors their duties but at their own wills and pleasures consume debts and the substance obtained by credit of other men for their own pleasures and delicate living against all reason, equity and good conscience." The quaint expression "keep their houses" has been repeated in every Act up to and including the 1914 Act and describes the conduct of one who withdraws to the inner parts of his house to avoid service, a ruse which must be as common today as then and at every level of society. The 1542 Act provided for the appointment of Lords Commissioners who had power by proclamation to require the debtor to appear before them and answer the charge. If the debtor failed to answer the proclamation or to satisfy his creditors his goods and land were to be realised and applied rateably in satisfaction of his debts. Two points should be noted. In contrast with later Bankruptcy Acts the 1542 Act was not confined to traders. And it contained no provision for the release or discharge of the debtor. It remained in force for 28 years but surprisingly there is no reported case upon its construction and effect and it is difficult now to discover how far it was used. It was superseded by the great Elizabethan Statute of 1570, parts of which (those relating to fraudulent conveyances) were repealed and re-enacted as recently as 1925. Like the earlier statute it contained no provision for the release or discharge of the bankrupt until his debts were fully paid. Provision for the release of a bankrupt before payment in full of all his debts was first introduced by an Act of the reign of Queen Anne in 1705. The release and discharge and, pending release, an allowance to the bankrupt out of the estate for his maintenance, were introduced, not out of humanity to the debtor, but as a reward to those who co-operated fully in discovering and surrendering all their property. The co-operative bankrupt was given a certificate by his creditors to that effect. The stick, and a very heavy stick was the death penalty. In 1732 the death penalty was imposed on all bankrupts who failed to surrender themselves within 42 days of the issue of the commission and in 1755 it was imposed for the bankrupt's failure to deliver a schedule of his estate and effects.

It was thus not until 1705 that England had a developed system of bankruptcy law—that is a system for the benefit of creditors and for the relief of the bankrupt. And in 1705 the bankruptcy law was confined to traders. For the non-trader there was no relief and equally no machinery for the administration of his estate for the benefit of his creditors. The debtor was exposed to the threat of imprisonment until the debt was paid; the creditors' only other remedy against the contumacious debtor lay in the cumbersome, expensive and often inadequate machinery for the execution of his judgment. That was not remedied until 1813. By an Act of that year a Court for the Relief of Insolvent Debtors was established. It adopted a very different and more modern approach though it was available only to the small debtor. The debtor could present a petition for protection from process. It was then open to the Court to stay all proceedings against him until the hearing of the petition. If he made out a prima facie case for relief—if the Court was satisfied that his debts were not contracted by fraud, or at a time when he had no reasonable expectation of being able to pay his debts—the Court might make an order vesting his property in a trustee and making provision for the payment of his debts in whole or in part out of after-acquired income or earnings. This humane Act which was the ancestor of the administration order procedure in the County Court ran alongside the Bankruptcy Acts until 1861 when the two streams were merged. Then the ordinary bankruptcy law became available to and against the non-trader. The provisions of the 1813 Act continued to apply to the small debtor and as I have said were in time embodied in the administration order in the County Court.

Until the eighteenth century the system of bankruptcy law was largely creditor controlled. There was a right of appeal from Commissioners in Bankruptcy to the Lord Chancellor, but in other respects the system operated outside the control of the Courts. The nineteenth century saw a move towards the greater involvement of the State in the administration of the bankrupt's estate. New bankruptcy courts were established, and in 1831 the office of the official assignee charged with the collection and administration of the bankrupt's estate was created. The progress was one of slow growth—of patchwork and not of radical reform. During the first 60 years of the nineteenth century there were no fewer than 50 Bankruptcy Acts. Nor did the tide flow always in the same direction. An Act of 1869 marked a temporary reverter to the old system of creditor control or, in modern jargon, the privatisation of bankruptcy law. It also introduced a short lived experiment, a new procedure for initiating bankruptcy. That was the debtor's summons, a summons issued by the Court upon the application of the creditor who had not obtained a judgment but who claimed that a sum was due to him and that he had failed to obtain payment after using reasonable efforts to do so. The new procedure was severely criticized in a series of cases in the Court of Appeal. I shall come back to examine it later. The judgment summons bears a superficial resemblance to the statutory demand introduced by the 1986 Act. The changes introduced by the 1869 Act were reversed by the Act of 1883 which was in all but minor details re-enacted in the Act of 1914.

Before turning to the 1883 Act and to the system it introduced, it may be worth delaying for a moment to consider how the bankruptcy laws were perceived by the educated public at the time. In retrospect they seem oppressive, and in the punishment meted out to the fraudulent or recalcitrant bankrupt, barbarous and inhumane. That is not how they were perceived at the time. The imposition of the death penalty for the bankrupt who concealed or who contumaciously refused to reveal his assets must be seen in the context of a criminal code which imposed the death penalty for over 300 offences. Contemporary research suggests that the reality was not as harsh as would appear from a reading of the Statute book. After we acquired a large scale open prison in New South Wales the death sentence was only executed in the case of the severer crimes.

However, apart from the barbarity of the penal system which came under increasing attack in the early nineteenth century there was the scandal of the debtors prison brought vividly to public attention by Charles Dickens. That was the consequence not of a defect in the system of bankruptcy law but of the absence of any system of bankruptcy applicable to the non-trader. So far as my researches go there seems to have been remarkably little dissatisfaction with the basic framework of the bankruptcy laws. Indeed such dissatisfaction as was expressed seems to have been directed as much to their laxity as to their severity. Lord Eldon in 1805 declared that "there can be no stronger proof of the good nature and humanity of the British character than the readiness with which creditors sign a certificate without any thought, even previously to the third meeting, when full disclosure is to be made, although at the time of signing there has been no examination." See *Re King*[4] Mr. Christian in his famous work in 1818 adds this footnote: "This unthinking eagerness to show compassion to the unfortunate debtor Lord Eldon thought it his duty to restrain." There are those here whose instinctive response will be—well of course, Lord Eldon would say that wouldn't he. But Lord Eldon was not alone. Jeremy Bentham of course, was the leader with Sir Samuel Romilly in the reform of the system of criminal justice and in the reduction of the number of offences attracting the death penalty. He criticized caustically the scandal of the debtors' prison. But I have not myself been able to discover in his voluminous writings any blueprint for an ideal system of bankruptcy law. His great disciple John Stuart Mill was entirely of Lord Eldon's opinion. His work on the Principles of Political Economy was, I suppose, part of the intellectual furniture of every educated and liberal Englishman in the latter half of the nineteenth century and beyond. He quoted with approval the testimony of one of the official assignees to the bankruptcy court that "by far the greater part of insolvencies arise from notorious misconduct. The records of the Insolvent Debtors Court and of the Bankruptcy Court will prove it." The witness went on to say:

> "many insolvencies are produced by tradesmen's indolence; they keep no books or at least imperfect ones which they never balance; they never take stock; they employ servants, if their trade be extensive, whom they are too indolent even to supervise, and then become insolvent. It is not too much to

say, that one half of all the persons engaged in trade, even in London, never take stock at all; they go on year after year without knowing how their affairs stand, and at last, like the child at school, they find to their surprise, but one half penny left in their pocket. I will venture to say that not one fourth of all the persons in the provinces, either manufacturers, tradesmen, or farmers, ever take stock; nor in fact does one half of them keep account books deserving of any other name than memorandum books."[5]

Reading that passage I wonder how many of us take stock year by year, see that our books balance and are never surprised by the discovery that we have but one halfpenny left in our pocket? J. S. Mill's conclusions are of some interest because they form the background to the 1883 Act and were, I suspect the foundation of the famous speech of Joseph Chamberlain introducing that Act which is cited in the Cork Report. For Mill the first principle underlying the bankruptcy law was public morality, the preservation of pecuniary integrity. Next was the economic domino effect of bad debt, first because it destroyed trust and secondly because of the cost of bad debt "every saving in which is a diminution in the cost of production." For those who favoured the relaxation of the bankruptcy laws he had little sympathy:

> "the reform of them like that of the criminal law generally has been taken in hand as an affair of humanity only, not of justice; and the modish humanity of the present time, which is essentially a thing of one idea (and is indeed little better than a timid shrinking from the infliction of anything like pain, next neighbour to the cowardice which shrinks from the unnecessary endurance of it) has in this, as in other cases, gone into a violent reaction against the ancient severity, and might almost be supposed to see in the fact of having lost or squandered other people's property, a peculiar title to indulgence."

The doctrine that the sole object of bankruptcy law should be to get at the property of the bankrupt and to distribute it amongst the creditors was to him "a totally inadmissible piece of spurious humanity. It is the business of the law to prevent wrong-doing and not simply to patch up the consequences of it when it has been committed." He criticized even the 1813 Act. "Imprisonment at the discretion of a creditor was really a powerful engine for extracting from the debtor any property which he had concealed or otherwise made away with."[5]

The 1883 Act

I have cited these passages at some length because Mill reflected and did much to form contemporary educated and liberal opinion. The attitude expressed in them forms the essential background to the 1883 Act. I do not propose to attempt to summarize all the provisions of that Act. Instead I shall draw attention to those features which have caused or contributed to the undue technicality of the law and have made it unacceptable to contemporary society.

(1) The 1883 Act was founded as every preceding Act had been upon an act of bankruptcy. That was the corner-stone of the structure. Some—departing the realm or keeping house with intent to defraud creditors—descend in direct line from the Act of 1542. With one exception all the acts of bankruptcy later added (conveying property to trustees for creditors, making a fraudulent conveyance, creating a fraudulent preference or suffering execution) were, in essence, public sign-posts signalling to others an inability on the part of the debtor to pay or a determination not to pay all his creditors. One (the failure to comply with a bankruptcy notice served by a judgment creditor) is in a different category. Though it might be relied upon by other creditors it was in effect an additional remedy given to the judgment creditor. However, in all cases, the bankruptcy laws unlike the laws of any jurisdiction not derived from English law required the creditor to jump two hurdles: to establish an act of bankruptcy as well as the failure of the bankrupt to pay the debt on which the Petition was founded. This two-tier system had two main disadvantages which led to its universal condemnation by those who gave evidence to the Cork Committee. First it focused attention upon a past date and on past events with which the petitioner might have had nothing to do. It diverted attention from the real issue which should be the debtor's current insolvency. Secondly, taken together with the strictness with which bankruptcy proceedings have been regarded by the Courts it introduced an undesirable technicality in the law which enabled many unscrupulous bankrupts to escape. I have known experienced practitioners to claim that few petitions could not be faulted upon some technical ground.

(2) The theme of the 1869 Act was creditor control. Following some scandalous bankruptcies in the ensuing 14 years the

pendulum swung the other way. Under the 1883 Act the conduct of the bankruptcy, the investigation of its causes and the public examination of the debtor were entrusted to the Official Receiver; given the absence of any organised or reputable body of insolvency practitioners at the time this feature was probably unavoidable. But it had the consequence that following a receiving order the bankrupt was enmeshed in an official proceeding which might be wholly disproportionate to his offence and to the scale of the bankruptcy. Many bankrupts were ultimately crushed not by the weight of their debts but by the expense and delay of the bankruptcy proceedings.

(3) There was under the 1883 legislation no realistic alternative to the full process of bankruptcy leading, after much expense and delay, to, at best, a discharge. The bankruptcy legislation ran parallel with another procedure which was codified in the Deeds of Arrangement Act 1914—that is, an arrangement between the debtor and his creditors for the partial or delayed payment of his debts. But that procedure became virtually a dead letter. The execution of the deed was itself an act of bankruptcy which could be relied on by any creditor not himself a party or privy to the deed, or by any creditor if the deed became void. The Bankruptcy Act itself also provided for the extrication of the debtor by a composition or scheme of arrangement approved by a majority in number and by a three-quarters majority in value of his creditors. However, the machinery proved too complex and too cumbersome. I understand that since the last war only one or two debtors have successfully taken his course in any year. The major stumbling block was that the composition or scheme required the approval of the Court and any creditor might oppose it. The application could not be heard until the public examination had been concluded. Moreover, as interpreted by the Courts, the scheme had to give the creditors some advantage they would not have received in bankruptcy before it could be approved. The practical impossibility for the bankrupt even with the concurrence of a majority of his creditors to escape from the expensive regime of bankruptcy became I think, the major weakness in the bankruptcy law.

(4) The last point I have already touched on. The bankrupt was seen in 1883 as one who had transgressed the moral code. He was therefore required to explain in a public examination the causes of his bankruptcy. He had, as it were, to

make a public confession of his transgressions before he could be forgiven. Of course in many cases a public examination is a necessary and healthy feature of any system of bankruptcy law; no-one has suggested its total abolition. The public has a legitimate interest in seeing that if there is fault, on the part of the bankrupt or others, those faults are suitably punished, and in seeing also that where the bankruptcy is not the result of mis-fortune the activities of the bankrupt are suitably curtailed. But the full panoply of a public examination is not necessary in all cases. Moreover a dangerous imbalance developed between the treatment meted out to the individual insolvent and the situation in an insolvent winding-up where public examination of directors fell into desuetude.

The New Law

That is in broad outline the background to the new legislation. Over the two past decades the public perception of the causes of individual insolvency and of the ends which a system of bankruptcy law should be designed to achieve has radically changed. In a credit orientated society the consumer debtor is seen more often as the victim than as a wrong-doer. The villain is not the lavish spender pictured in the preamble to the Act of 1542 or even the indolent trader who keeps no adequate books but lives from hand to mouth who called down the wrath of J. S. Mill. The villains are those who entrap the unwary with promises of credit and those who shelter behind and manipulate phoenix-like companies which perish in the flames of insolvency and are magically re-born. The old edifice therefore had to be pulled down and rebuilt. The aims which the new structure is designed to achieve are to ensure that a state of insolvency is diagnosed early, that the individual insolvent is encouraged to reach a sensible accommodation with his creditors without invoking the expensive machinery required to achieve a full liquidation and a rateable distribution of his assets and that, if insolvency ensues, then at least for those made bankrupt for the first time discharge and restoration to health will follow reasonably quickly. The legislature has also been anxious to simplify procedures for the inception of insolvency proceedings which had become excessively technical. In this last respect the legislature (and the Cork Committee) has been much influenced by the model of company law. The limited liability company is of course of comparatively recent creation. The Companies Consolidation Act 1862 which can for practical purposes be taken as its birth date contained provision for the winding-up of an insolvent company. Its affairs were to be wound up in the same way as an insolvent estate. Later Acts incorporated much of the technical machinery of the bankruptcy laws governing for instance the rights of secured and unsecured creditors the debts provable and the valuation of future and contingent liabilities. But the machinery for instituting insolvency procedures has always been far simpler. The Companies Court has been seen in this respect at least as a model of efficiency. So, in formulating new procedures for making the individual bankrupt, the procedure for the winding-up of an insolvent company has been taken as a guide. However there are profound and irreconcilable differences between a corporate and an individual insolvent which must be taken into account in any attempt to assimilate the two systems. They can be grouped under three heads:

(1) A company, like a good soldier has a name, a number and a place. A company must have a registered office at which it can be served. Of course, many companies do not but if as a result a company becomes enmeshed unnecessarily in a winding-up the directors have no one but themselves, or sometimes, their professional advisers, to blame. The individual insolvent has an untidy habit of moving from place to place and on occasions changing his name. There is a paramount need to ensure that an individual is given full notice of steps which may lead to insolvency proceedings. A system requiring no more than service of a demand at an individual's last known address as proof of his inability or unwillingness to pay a debt would not meet that need.

(2) A company is like a money box. Some of the contents may have been improperly extracted by its owner and his friends. Any effective winding-up code must contain adequate means for ensuring that contents improperly abstracted are restored. But at the end of this process there will be an identifiable fund to be shared amongst its creditors. The situation of the individual insolvent is quite different. He has a capacity to earn money which must be preserved not only for the benefit of his creditors (there is to that extent an analogy with the company) but also to ensure that when the insolvency procedures have been exhausted he will not be a burden on his fellow citizens. The end of the insolvency process is, for the company, almost invariably dissolution. It has not yet been suggested that the death penalty should be re-introduced for bank-

rupts in order to simplify the administration of their affairs
as insolvent estates.

(3) One of the main aims of individual insolvency legislation
must be the rehabilitation of the individual. There is an
analogy here with the company. Among the most valuable
innovations of the new legislation have been the introduction of voluntary arrangements between a company and its
creditors and for the administration of a company under the
supervision of the Court so long as there is a prospect that
the company or its undertaking can be preserved as a going-
concern and the jobs of its work-force preserved. Examination of this part of the new legislation and of the novel
jurisdiction conferred on the Courts by the making of an
administration order lie outside the ambit of this paper.
There are parallel provisions applicable to insolvent individuals which I shall mention briefly in a moment. However, the main difference between a company and the
individual remains. If the company or its undertaking cannot be preserved by a voluntary arrangement or by an
administration order the process of winding-up must take
its course. A system of individual insolvency on the other
hand must be designed to ensure that at every stage in the
process the individual is in a position to bring the process to
a halt if he is able to persuade a sufficient majority of his
creditors that some sensible alternative exists.

My purpose in the remainder of this paper is to examine the way in
which these differences between individual and company insolvencies are reconciled in an Act designed to assimilate the two procedures and in the Rules which give effect to that Act.

The statutory demand

I start with the statutory demand. This is, of course, a familiar
phrase in the field of company law. The relevant ground for winding-up a company is that the company is unable to pay its debts.
Under the Company Act 1948, s.223 a company was to be deemed
to be unable to pay its debts if first (paragraph (*a*)) a creditor had
served on the company a demand requiring the company to pay a
sum due and the company had for three weeks neglected to pay it
or to secure or compound for it to the reasonable satisfaction of
the creditor or, secondly (paragraph (*b*)) in England and Wales if
execution had issued on a judgment and had been returned unsatisfied in whole or in part or, thirdly (paragraph (*d*)) "if it is proved
to the satisfaction of the Court that the company is unable to pay

its debts and in determining whether a company is unable to pay its debts the Court will take into account the contingent and prospective liabilities of the company."

I have summarized these provisions fully because they can be seen on analysis to contain a curious and unremarked mingling of two very dissimilar concepts. The first two heads are designed to provide a convenient way of demonstrating that a company is unable to pay its debts as they fall due. As was pointed out by Mr. Justice Slade in *Re Capital Annuities*.[6]

> "Neglect in payment of a sum as to which a statutory notice has been given is only one of several ways of showing inability to pay debts which may be shown in any other way; see *Re Globe New Patent Iron and Steel Company* (1875) LR20 Equity 337 and *Re Flagstaffe Silver Mining Company of Utah* (1875) LR20 Equity 268. A failure by the company to pay an admitted creditor within a reasonable time after demand would be likely to provide ample evidence of such inability."

And equally, service of a statutory demand for a debt which has not been paid or compounded for is not conclusive evidence that the company is unable to pay its debts; the company may rebut the prima facie presumption by proof that it can in fact do so (see *Re Bradford Tramways Company*).[7] More importantly the debt may be disputed. I shall return to this point later. These observations apply equally to the return unsatisfied of execution on a judgment debt. In both cases the satisfaction of the legislative criteria deeming a company to be unable to pay its debts is not a necessary and in some circumstances is not a sufficient ground for a winding-up order. However, the purpose of the last of these three tests is quite distinct. It is not directed to evidence. A provision that a company is to be deemed to be unable to pay its debts if it is proved to the satisfaction of the Court that the company is unable to pay its debts would be vacuous. The purpose of sub-paragraph (*d*) is to be found in its second limb; in determining whether a company is unable to pay its debts the Court "shall take into account the contingent and prospective liabilities of the company." This provision is not directed to the means by which insolvency may be proved; it enlarges the meaning of insolvency to comprehend what is sometimes called balance sheet insolvency.

The difference of function between on the one hand paragraphs (*a*) and (*b*) and on the other hand paragraph (*d*) is recognised by the Insolvency Act 1986. Section 123(1) provides that a company is to be deemed to be unable to pay its debts in the circumstances envisaged in paragraphs (*a*) and (*b*) of section 223 and also "if it is proved to the satisfaction of the Court that the company is unable to pay its debts as they fall due.'' The section thus makes it clear that the tests in paragraphs (*a*) and (*b*) of section 223 are only convenient and not exhaustive ways of establishing insolvency. Balance sheet insolvency is a separate ground; under subsection (2) a company is to be deemed to be unable to pay its debts if it is proved to the satisfaction of the Court that the value of its assets is less than the amount of its liabilities taking into account contingent and perspective liabilities.

The new insolvency procedure for individuals is also founded upon a statutory demand. A creditor who wishes to present a petition must be able to show (amongst other things) that the debt is one which the debtor appears to be unable to pay or to have no reasonable prospect of paying (section 267(2)(*c*)). To satisfy this condition the creditor must show, if the debt is one payable immediately, either that he has served a demand requiring the creditor to pay the debt or to secure or compound it to the satisfaction of the creditor and that three weeks has passed without the demand being satisfied, or, alternatively, that execution has issued on a judgment debt due to him and has been returned unsatisfied in whole or in part. In the case of a debt not immediately payable he must prove that he has served a statutory demand requiring the debtor to establish to his satisfaction that there is a reasonable prospect that he will be able to pay the debt when it falls due and again that three weeks have passed without it having been complied with. The procedure for founding a petition on a debt which is not immediately due is an innovation of the greatest importance. It introduces the wider test of insolvency for the first time into the field of individual insolvency and enables a creditor to start insolvency proceedings against a debtor who is or is likely to become commercially insolvent before his debt is due, but who is in the meantime able to stave off his other creditors. However my present concern is with the common feature—the statutory demand. It is quite unlike a statutory demand in the field of company law. It is not simply evidence of insolvency. Save in the case of a judgment creditor, when execution has issued and has been returned unsatisfied, it is the straight and narrow gateway. Moreover, the time of service of the statutory demand is of critical importance. The bankruptcy petition can only be presented (subject to a power for the Court to abridge the period) when 21 days have elapsed from the service of the demand.

Proof of service and of the date of service of the statutory demand is thus central to the new system. How is the statutory demand to be served? The legislation is silent on this question which is left to be resolved by the Rules. The Cork Committee proposed that the statutory demand should be served personally or that in appropriate cases an order for substituted service should be obtained. The proposed Rules have not adopted this solution. A statutory demand is not a judicial proceeding. To involve the Court in directing substituted service would be to impose on the Court a heavy burden and, more importantly, might give to the debtor a wholly misleading impression. In rejecting this proposal the Insolvency Rules Advisory Committee was very much influenced by the experience of the Courts following the enactment of the 1869 Act. I have already described the machinery introduced by that Act—the service of a debtor's summons on the application of a creditor who had not obtained a judgment and who was only required to allege that he had failed to obtain payment of his debt after using reasonable efforts to do so. The summons was required to be in a prescribed form resembling as near as circumstances would admit a Writ issued by one of Her Majesty's superior Courts. It must have looked to the ordinary debtor much like the initiation of an action or even execution though founded on mere allegation that a debt was due. The new procedure was castigated in a series of judgments in the ensuing years. In 1886 Lord Justice Bowen commented: "what was the consequence of enabling creditors to put in force this summary process. There was a crop of abuses. The process was commonly used for the purpose of extortion, and, just as companies are often wrecked by unfounded winding-up petitions, so many debtors were assailed by an abuse of this process of the law." (See *ex parte Blanchett*).[8]

An order for substituted service might be equally pernicious in its effect and a debtor would not even have the protection of a statement by the creditor on oath that he had made more than one application for payment of the debt. In an extreme case the Court might find itself making an order for substituted service of a statutory demand which on its face was extortionate. At the same time the system would be hamstrung if every statutory demand has to be personally served. Some debtors have been known in the quaint language of the old legislation to "keep house" when they see a process server in the offing.

The solution to these difficulties adopted in the Rules is shortly as follows. Where a petition is not founded on a judgment debt the rule is personal service. If personal service is impracticable and if service has not been acknowledged by the debtor the creditor when he presents his petition must state the means by which it was sought to bring the demand to the attention of the debtor and specify the last date on which he claims it must have come to his attention. The petition will only be allowed to proceed if the Court is satisfied that the circumstances are such as would have justified an order for substituted service and that the creditor has done all that is reasonable to bring the demand to the debtor's attention. Subject to one exception advertisement is not permitted. It would be intolerable that, for instance, a debt collection agency should be permitted to advertise the names of those alleged to be indebted to it or to its clients.

These requirements are, and are intended to be strict. It must be borne in mind that the creditor has the alternative of establishing his debt by judgment and seeking to recover his debt by execution. If the execution is returned unsatisfied the route to a bankruptcy petition is clear. At first sight there would seem no reason why a creditor who cannot satisfy the statutory requirements as to service of a statutory demand should not be left to obtain a judgment and levy execution. But here there is a practical difficulty. A common situation which must be covered by the Rules is that of the debtor who absconds leaving no assets on which execution can be levied. The creditor may nonetheless wish to invoke insolvency proceedings in order to attack some antecedent transaction. The proposed rule therefore allows an exception to the strict rules I have described in the case of a judgment creditor who seeks relief against a debtor who has absconded and who is avoiding service and where there is no real prospect of the debt being recovered by execution. In that case and in that case only the demand may be advertised. The time for compliance runs from the date of the advertisement.

The disputed debt

A petition for the winding-up of a company cannot be founded on a debt which is disputed in good faith and on some substantial ground. No order will be made on such a petition even if the company is otherwise shown to be insolvent. There has been considerable debate in the cases as to the proper foundation of this sensible and salutory rule. It has been suggested that if the debt is disputed, then unless the Court itself tries the dispute or stands the petition over to await its resolution elsewhere—a course which was often taken in the earlier years—the petition must be dismissed because, pending resolution of the dispute, the petitioner has not shown that he has *locus standi* to present the petition. The Court therefore lacks jurisdiction to make the Order (see *Mann* v. *Goldstein*).[9] I suggest that the explanation is simpler and more pragmatic. An unsatisfied demand is no more than evidence of a company's inability to pay its debts as they fall due. If the debt is disputed in good faith on substantial grounds the failure of the company to pay goes no way to establish that fact. That in itself would not prevent the Court from making an order on the petition if supported by other evidence of insolvency. The basis of the rule that the Court will not entertain a petition founded on a disputed debt even if there is other evidence to show that the company is commercially insolvent is that the winding-up procedure should not be used as a means of putting pressure on a company to pay a disputed debt; as was pointed by Bowen L.J. in the passage I have cited, a company can easily be wrecked by the advertisement of an unfounded winding-up petition.

It is a curious fact that the Insolvency Bill when first introduced contained no machinery for ensuring that a petition could not be founded on a disputed debt. Of course, such a petition unlike a winding-up petition is not advertised. But the service of it might have a traumatic effect on the individual served, and news of its presentation might easily leak out. The Act does however contain a machinery added by amendment to the Bill designed to avoid this mischief. A petition may only be presented (save in the case of a judgment debt) if a statutory demand has been served and if it has neither been complied with nor set aside in accordance with the Rules. Once application is made to set it aside the position is frozen.

The procedure for setting aside a statutory demand is therefore of critical importance. The Rules provide for application to be made within 18 days from the service or advertisement of the statutory demand; that leaves a margin of three days before the petition can be presented. The effect on the debtor's right to apply to set aside a statutory demand will have to be carefully considered if an application is made to abridge the 21 day period for presentation of a petition. If an application to set aside a statutory demand is made the Court may accede to the application: (a) if the debtor appears to have a counter-claim, set-off or cross-demand which would exceed the debt; or (b) if it is disputed on some substantial ground; or (c) if the creditor holds some security which equals or exceeds the debt. The statutory demand procedure is only available to the unsecured creditor or to one whose security is inadequate; a creditor who has security is expected to enforce it first without recourse to the insolvency procedures.

The procedure envisaged by the Rules is thus analogous to that which has evolved in practice in the field of corporate insolvency.

Substitution

Insolvency proceedings are collective in nature. The creditor who institutes the proceedings becomes in effect the representative of all the creditors; they will share rateably in the assets of the debtor if a winding-up or bankruptcy order is made. The debtor cannot be allowed to pay off the petitioning creditor leaving the other creditors to share in a smaller pool of assets. Equally the petitioning creditor if he is paid cannot be allowed to retain what he has taken out of the pool to the detriment of the other creditors. How is this to be avoided?

In the field of corporate insolvency this abuse of a winding-up petition—its use, that is, to put pressure on an insolvent company to pay the petitioning creditor in priority to other creditors—has been avoided by a procedure developed by the Courts and later embodied in the Winding-up Rules. A winding-up petition and the date fixed for hearing must be advertised. Any creditor is then entitled to appear at the hearing to support or oppose the petition. If the petitioning creditor does not proceed with his petition or consents to it being dismissed any other creditor who could have presented a petition may ask to be substituted as petitioner. If an order for substitution is made the petition is treated as if it had been made in its amended form. So, if a winding-up order is made on the amended petition the winding-up relates back to the presentation of the petition. Any disposition of property made after the presentation of the petition is void unless the Court otherwise orders. Thus, the petitioner who accepts payment of his debt runs the risk that if another creditor is substituted and a winding-up order is made he will be bound to repay what he has been paid by the company.

The Rules made under the 1914 Act also provided for the substitution of another creditor for the petitioning creditor. In practise such orders were very rare indeed. None have been made in recent years. The reason is that under the 1914 Act if a receiving order was made the proceedings related back to the act of bankruptcy on which the petition was founded. So, if the petitioner accepted payment of his debt and did not proceed with his petition he ran the risk that another creditor would present a petition and that he would be liable to repay the trustee what he had received from the debtor. However, under the 1986 Act a petitioning creditor no longer has to allege and prove the commission of an act of bankruptcy. If a bankruptcy order is made on his petition it will relate back, as in the case of an insolvent company, to the presentation of the petition. How then is the potential mischief which I have described to be avoided?

At first sight it might seem that the practical solution adopted in the Companies Court should be equally applicable in the field of individual insolvency. But the analogy is in fact a superficial one. I have already described the difference in the function of a statutory demand in corporate and individual insolvency. In the case of a company any creditor can apply to be substituted whether he has served a statutory demand or not provided, of course, that he can produce sufficient evidence that an undisputed debt was owed to him at the date of the petition. In the case of an individual debtor the creditor must prove service of a statutory demand more than three weeks before the petition was presented or the return unsatisfied of execution on a judgment debt. In practice it is unlikely that a creditor who learns of pending bankruptcy proceedings will be able to satisfy these conditions. If he cannot then the Court will have no jurisdiction to make a substitution order.

It is provided by the 1986 Act that a petition once presented cannot be withdrawn without the leave of the Court. But it is also provided that the Court is not to make a bankruptcy order unless satisfied that the debt in respect of which it was presented is one which has been neither paid or compounded for (Section 271(1)(*a*)). Is the Court then bound to give leave to withdraw his petition to any creditor who has been paid his debt unless some other creditor can show that he had himself satisfied the statutory requirements for the presentation of a petition at the time when the creditor who is being paid off presented his petition so that an order for substitution can be made? If the Court is bound to give leave then bankruptcy proceedings will in effect cease to be a collective remedy. The first creditor who presents his petition will be paid; others will be left to share in a diminished pool. There are those who see in this a welcome recognition that the law of the survival of the fittest should prevail. To others, myself included, it would be a reversion to the law of the jungle and would often penalise both the small and the responsible creditor at the expense of the unscrupulous. As I have said, bankruptcy proceedings have always been regarded as collective in their nature. However, if the Court refuses leave in the circumstances I have described, will not the petition then be left suspended in mid-air like the smile on the face of the Cheshire cat—a perpetual reminder of the inability of the Court to make an order which, in justice to other creditors, the Court clearly ought to make?

The answer to this conundrum is, I suggest to be found in the decision of Pennycuick J. in *Re Bostels Limited*.[10] There, an order for substitution was made on a petition for the winding-up of a company. The question was whether the petitioning creditor was entitled to his costs or (as Pennycuick J. held) only to that part of his costs which contributed to the making of the winding-up order obtained by the substituted creditor—that is, in effect, the cost of the presentation and advertisement of the petition. One question which troubled Pennycuick J. was whether a petitioner offered payment of his costs in full is not bound to accept the offer. If he is then, as Pennycuick J. observed, a real injustice might result. The petitioning creditor would be bound to accept payment of his debt and costs but would have to recoup them if a winding-up order were made in the petition. The answer Pennycuick J. gave to this conundrum is important:

> "I was troubled during the argument by one consideration. Could it be said that if the company offers to the petitioner payment in full of his debt and costs, the petitioner is bound to accept that offer? If so, a real injustice might be involved. Mr. Heyman gave what seemed to me a satisfactory answer to this difficulty. In such circumstances, the offer by the company although in form unconditional, would in fact carry the detriment that in the event of a winding-up order being made at the instance of a substituted petitioner the original petitioner would lose his prospective right to receive his costs already incurred. That being so, the original petitioner, on the offer of payment, has, I think, a real choice. He may accept the payment, give up his role as petitioner and take the risk of having to restore not only the debt but the costs, with no right of proof as to the latter. Or he may refuse the payment, maintain his role as petitioner and take no risk of losing his costs. He may choose whichever of those courses he thinks fit. If he chooses the former course and the gamble does not come off, I think no injustice is involved."

Thus the offer by the company is not an offer of payment which the petitioner is bound to accept; for the offer is not an offer of unconditional payment. If that is right then it would seem that the Court is not precluded by the 1986 Act, section 271(1)(*a*) from making an order on a petition if the debt on which the petition was founded has been paid by the debtor out of his own monies—that is out of monies which the creditor by availing himself of the collective remedy of a bankruptcy petition has in effect sought to have realised and applied for the benefit of all the creditors.

The Rules are framed upon this view as to the effect of section 271(1)(*a*). The Rules provide for the substitution of a creditor if the petitioner is found not to be entitled to petition or if he consents to the dismissal of the petition or fails to take appropriate steps to obtain a bankruptcy order. As I have said, it is likely to be uncommon in practice for another creditor to be in a position to apply for an order for substitution. The Rules also provide that if it

appears that a petitioning creditor intends to secure the postpone-
ment or withdrawal of the petition or that he does not intend to
prosecute it diligently, the carriage of the petition may be given to
another creditor even though he is not in a position to apply to be
substituted as petitioner. However, no order giving the carriage of
the proceedings is to be made if it appears that the petitioning
creditor's debt was paid or compounded for either by third party
money or by a disposition made with the leave of the Court or rati-
fied by the Court. The collective nature of the petition is thus preserved if, but only if, the creditor was paid out of the fund which
ought to be distributed amongst the creditors as a class. If an application is made for leave to withdraw the petition the application
must be supported by evidence showing whether the petitioning
creditor has been paid and, if he has been paid, from what source
he was paid.

The interim order

I have so far concentrated upon the machinery created by the
1986 Act for subjecting the affairs of an insolvent debtor to the collective remedy of a bankruptcy order. But the Act contains new
and important provisions designed to ensure that this machinery,
which can be expensive and in some cases oppressive, is not
unnecessarily resorted to. A debtor whose affairs are embarrassed
and who is faced with the risk of a bankruptcy petition or who has
even been served with one may apply to the Court for an interim
order staying these and all other proceedings. He may do so only
upon the ground that he intends to make a proposal to his creditors for a scheme of arrangement. Those proposals must provide
for the appointment of an experienced independent adviser (a
licensed insolvency practitioner) to supervise the arrangement. If
an interim order is made and so long as it is in force the insolvency
practitioner is required to consider the scheme and whether it
should be put to the creditors. If he decides that it should, he must
summon the necessary meetings. Once the interim order has been
made the Court is in control and if the necessary report is not
forthcoming the Court may order that the insolvency practitioner
nominated be replaced by another. If, following a creditors meeting the scheme is approved by a three quarters majority in value it
is binding on all the creditors unless one of them can satisfy the
Court that he is unfairly prejudiced by the scheme or that there
was some material irregularity in relation to the meeting at which
it was approved. To this there are two important exceptions. No
scheme can be approved if it adversely affects the rights of a
secured creditor or the amount or the priority of a preferential

debt without the consent of the secured or preferential creditor concerned. If the scheme is approved and is not successfully attacked it must be carried out by the insolvency practitioner who prepared it, or by one appointed in his place, under the supervision of the Court, which has power on the application of any person affected [1] to review any act or decision of the insolvency practitioner.

These provisions differ radically from the provisions to which I have referred in the 1914 Act. The first difference lies in the early introduction of an insolvency practitioner to advise on the practicability of the scheme and to report on it to the creditors and the Court. The success of the new scheme will depend upon the integrity, experience and professional skill of those who are licensed to act as insolvency practitioners. Secondly, the scheme or arrangement may be prepared at any stage in anticipation of or after the commencement of bankruptcy proceedings. By contrast under the old system a scheme could only be approved after the completion of the public examination. Thirdly, if approved by a sufficient majority of the creditors the scheme can only be upset by a creditor who can show that he is unfairly prejudiced. The burden is shifted from the debtor and the creditors who support the scheme to an opposing creditor. The scheme is no longer liable to be upset by the Court if the debtor cannot show that the creditors obtain an advantage under the scheme which they would not obtain in bankruptcy. The Act thus provides the machinery for the resolution of a state of insolvency otherwise than by bankruptcy proceedings. It is creditor controlled in that a decision to accept or reject the scheme rests with the creditors. But in the initiation and in the working out of the scheme the Court remains in control.

An Insolvency Court

I turn to one last point. One of the proposals made by the Cork Committee was that there should be a single Court exercising jurisdiction over all insolvency matters corporate and individual and that concurrent jurisdictions should be abolished. The new legislation does not in form adopt these proposals. However, the provisions of the 1986 Act and of the Rules taken together with recent changes in the organisation of the work of Chancery Division have pragmatically achieved substantially that end. Under the 1986 Act, section 375 an appeal from a County Court or from a Registrar in bankruptcy lies to the High Court and with leave of the Judge or of the Court of Appeal to the Court of Appeal. There is no similar provision in the Act dealing with appeals from County Courts in winding-up cases. However, the provisions capable of being included in the company insolvency rules expressly include provisions applying in relation to the winding-up of companies any enactment contained in those parts of the 1986 Act relating to individual insolvency. The proposed rules accordingly provide that appeals in relation to the winding-up of companies whether from the Registrar of the Companies Court or from the County Court shall be to the High Court. Appeals under both these provisions will be heard in the Chancery Division. Heretofore the Judges of that Division have been assigned on appointment to one of two groups one of which staffed the Companies Court and the other the Divisional Court in bankruptcy. These groups have now been abolished. In the future all the Judges of the Chancery Division will hear indifferently (and I use the word in its old-fashioned sense), cases arising under the initial jurisdiction of the High Court and the Companies Court or as the first tier of appeal in both the corporate and the individual fields. To that extent the Chancery Division will be the Insolvency Court envisaged by the Cork Committee.

Notes

[1] 2 Bl.Comm. 472.
[2] 20 Fed.Cas. 490, 494 (1874).
[3] 4 Inst. p. 277.
[4] 11 Ves. 42.
[5] *Principles of Political Economy* (3rd ed., 1852), pp. 909–912.
[6] [1979] 1 W.L.R. 170, 187.
[7] (1876) 4 Ch.D. 18, 22.
[8] (1886) 17 Q.B.D. 303, 307.
[9] [1968] 1 W.L.R. 1099.
[10] [1968] Ch. 346.

A Trade Union in Chains: Scargill Unbound—The Legal Constraints of Receivership and Sequestration[1]

GAVIN LIGHTMAN Q.C.

Introduction

The miners strike began on March 13, 1984 and continued until March 4, 1985. The strike was not unlawful or illegal in any sense other than that it was (or may have been) called in breach of the rules of the National Union of Miners ("NUM") and was accordingly unofficial.[2] This long acrimonious dispute spawned litigation and gave rise to legal questions not previously addressed. Few can be of greater interest or significance than the effects of sequestration and receivership on the continued functioning of a trade union. Notwithstanding these draconian measures, the Union never ceased its activities. This fact induced some to whom it was both unpalatable and unexpected to cry "contempt" to all those concerned, and to argue that the NUM should be treated as a pariah by the courts until the orders for sequestration and receivership had been discharged. The validity of this charge is a serious current legal problem and it is the purpose of this paper to examine this question.

This paper will first briefly deal with four preliminary matters, namely A. the history of the proceedings leading to the appointment of the sequestrators and the receiver; B. the distinction between civil and criminal contempt; C. the nature of sequestration and receivership; and D. the identity of the appointees as sequestrators and receiver. The paper will then consider in greater detail six main topics namely: A. the duty of a union subject to a sequestration or receivership order and its officers to co-operate with the sequestrators and receiver; B. the right of the union to be heard in court, C. the privileged access to the Court of the sequestrators and receiver; D. the scope of the doctrine of contempt and the effect of orders of sequestration and receivership on the continued functioning of the union, and the risks undertaken by those providing the union with assistance and advice; E. title to foreign assets; and F. the discharge of the sequestration and receivership orders and the conditions to be satisfied before such discharge can be obtained.

Preliminary Matters

A. *History*

In the action *Taylor* v. *NUM, (Yorkshire Area)*, (which I shall call "the Taylor Action") by an order dated October 10, 1984, Nicholls J. fined Mr. Scargill and the union respectively £1,000 and £200,000 for disregarding orders made earlier in that action.[3] The fine imposed on the union not having been paid, on October 25, 1984 the same judge gave leave to the Plaintiffs to issue a writ of sequestration to sequestrate the property of the Union. The four sequestrators appointed were partners in the firm of Price Waterhouse.

On November 8, 1984, 16 members of the NUM commenced proceedings (entitled *Clarke* v. *Heathfield*) against the trustees of the Union's assets, and various officers of the Union, seeking orders for the removal of the trustees on the ground that the assets of the Union were in jeopardy whilst in their hands. I shall call this the Clarke Action. On November 30, 1984 an opposed *ex parte* application came before Mervyn Davies J. for interim relief over until December 6, 1984. On that application he made an order for the removal of the trustees and the appointment of Mr. Brewer as receiver of the income and assets of the Union (save in so far as the same might be in the possession or control of the sequestrators). On Saturday December 1, 1984, the Court of Appeal dismissed an appeal from this Order.[4]

The *inter partes* hearing of the application for interlocutory relief came before the judge on December 6, 1984. Before this date, objection having been taken to the fitness of Mr. Brewer to act as receiver, the Plaintiffs in his place sought to appoint a Mr. Arnold, a partner in Arthur Young & Co. The learned judge granted the application.[5] He held that there was jurisdiction to order the removal of the trustees and the appointment of a receiver of a trade union on a motion; that on an application of this character, the guidelines of *American Cyanimid Co.* v. *Ethicon Ltd.*[6] applied; and that the order should be made, in particular because the trustees had actively sought to place trust property abroad out of the reach of the sequestrators. He also held that jeopardy to the trust assets of the union likewise required the appointment of the receiver to be made. " . . . the trustees activities have placed the [union's] funds in jeopardy by subjecting the funds to obligations to pay a substantial fine and by leaving no conclusion but that their conduct, if now unchecked, may lead to further fines." In concluding his judgment, he said "Since I am removing the trustees, there will be an appointment of a receiver to act for the time being until new trustees are appointed, or, on a change of heart, the removed trustees are restored." The hopes of an early discharge of the receivership order engendered by these words, so pregnant with reassurance for the Union, proved misplaced.

B. *Civil and criminal contempt*[7]

Few areas of law are in greater confusion than that distinguishing between criminal and civil contempt and the significance of the distinction between the two types of contempt. Since the liberty of the subject is involved, this would appear to be a priority area for action. The distinction may have significant consequences in the field of sequestration.

The classic distinction between the two types of contempt is that a criminal contempt involves words or acts obstructing, or tending to obstruct or interfere with, the administration of justice; whilst a civil contempt involves disobedience to an order of the court involving a private injury.[8] (The distinction is however somewhat blurred by the fact that a civil contempt in the form of a breach of an injunction or undertaking is a common law misdemeanour).[9] The critical problem may be posed in this way: when does a civil contempt, *i.e.* a disobedience to an order of the court, also involve an obstruction of the administration of justice and therefore a criminal contempt?[10] The authorities indicate that the answer is whenever the disobedience is "contumacious,"[11] and a disobedience is contumacious when the disobedience involves deliberate defiance of the Court, or an intention "to flout the order of the Court without regard to the seriousness of the matter."[12] Such a breach involves an interference with the administration of justice because it challenges the authority of the court and the supremacy of the law, and is meant to and will (unless punished) shake confidence in the administration of justice.[13]

There has been a process of assimilating the law of civil and criminal contempt, *e.g.* as to burden of proof and as to double jeopardy, but the process is not yet complete. Thus:—

(a) For the commission of a civil contempt, whilst proof of notice of the injunction is necessary, no "*mens rea*" (in the sense of an intention to disobey) is required,[14] but such *mens rea* is a constituent of a criminal contempt[15];

(b) A third party can only be in contempt of an order made

against a party if he "aids and abets" the disobedience by the party of the court order. Such a contempt is probably a civil (and not a criminal) contempt unless contumacious,[16] but nonetheless a third party cannot be guilty of such contempt unless he has *"mens rea," i.e.* he knows that, or is recklessly indifferent whether, his actions aid and abet the disobedience.[17]

(c) A criminal contempt cannot be waived by the parties. There is authority for the proposition that a civil contempt may be waived by the parties,[18] but it is thought that such a waiver is only possible in the case of non-compliance with procedural orders. In the case of such orders, the direction of the Court may readily be read as subject to the implicit condition "unless waived by the other party." In the case of all other orders, it is difficult to see how a party can waive another's "common law misdemeanour,"[19] and the Industrial Relations court on a number of occasions ruled against the right of a party to waive a contempt of the Court's orders.[20]

(d) The remedies, *e.g.* sequestration, in case of civil contempt are primarily coercive, *i.e.* designed to secure the enforcement of the party's rights, although they may also be used to vindicate the authority of the court,[21] whilst the remedies in the case of criminal contempt are primarily punitive,[22] though they may also be coercive in the sense of being designed to secure public acknowledgment of the Rule of Law and the enforcement of the underlying rights of the other party.

The distinction between the punitive and coercive functions of the remedies may have significance when the issue arises whether actions taken by third parties to alleviate the consequences of the order on the contemnor are contrary to the policy of the law or the spirit of the order and therefore may themselves constitute contempt. The character of the contempt (whether civil or criminal) giving rise to the remedies may afford but little assistance in determining the function of the remedy. Indeed in none of the judgments in the various NUM proceedings in England did the Court advert to the question whether the contempt was civil or criminal. The contempt was apparently contumacious and accordingly (on the analysis of contempt adopted in this paper) criminal.[23]

C. *Nature of sequestration and receivership*

Sequestration and receivership are each in their respective ambits remedies of last resort, to be used only when the more orthodox and less oppressive means of achieving the court's wishes have proved, or are bound to prove, ineffective.

The writ of sequestration is a process of civil contempt by proceeding against the property of the contemnor. It is coercive in character depriving the contemnor of the use of his assets until the will of the court is complied with.[24] Before the court can order this writ to issue, it will require to be satisfied beyond reasonable doubt[25] that a contempt has been committed, and before the court will in its discretion make such order, it will wish to be satisfied that no lesser order will be effective.[26] The court will be particularly slow to order this relief if innocent third parties will be prejudiced, *e.g.* employees will lose their livelihood.[27] Sequestration lies at the top end of the scale of severity of financial penalties which the court can impose to enforce its order.[28] Indeed it appears to be deliberately designed to occasion the greatest possible financial cost to the contemnor, for what other justification can there be today for requiring that in all cases the writ must issue to not less than four commissioners, called sequestrators, albeit that only two must act? The contemnor of course at the end of the day must pick up the bill.[28a] The sequestrators are chosen by the persons obtaining the order. They need not be professional persons but in practice are accountants, and they are not required to provide security.

The order binds the property of the contemnor from the date of the writ: the writ vests in the sequestrators the right to possession of all the contemnor's assets within the jurisdiction (excluding assets vested in the contemnor as trustee).[29] The Writ in no way vests title in the sequestrators or divests the contemnor of it. In the ordinary course, if a litigant obtains a court order and the other party does not comply with the order, the court will only enforce the order at the instance of the litigant or (if there is a public element involved) on an intervention by the Attorney General. In exceptional cases of a clear contempt, which cannot wait to be dealt with, however, the Court may act of its own volition to punish contempt.[30] In the field of industrial relations, (a field where this rare and antique process has been given a new lease of life) the circumstances may peculiarly call for this jurisdiction to be exercised, and a writ of sequestration to be issued by the court of its own motion.[31] If the court is minded to proceed of its own motion, it may issue subpoenas in order to find out the true facts, on the basis of which it may act.[32] But since this procedure involves the judge appearing to be both prosecutor and judge, "a role which does not become him well"[33] and since this procedure is rough justice and contrary to natural justice,[34] it can only be justified if nothing else will do. Rarely (if ever) will this condition be satisfied in the case of an alleged breach of an injunction.[35]

A receiver may be appointed of any property to secure that property from misapplication or dissipation. In the field of private trusts, it is available only in cases where application is made by a beneficiary and the court considers that the trust property is in jeopardy.[36] The prime jeopardy is the risk of misapplication in breach of trust. The court cannot foist a receiver upon a private trust against the will of the beneficiaries. In accordance with this principle, a receiver can only be appointed of the assets of a trade union on the basis that its assets are held on trusts for the union itself or for its members, and that the assets are in jeopardy. A receiver will not be appointed if a declaration or an injunction will prove an adequate remedy. In the case of such an appointment, the order of the court may extend to all the property of the trade union in question, including property situate abroad. The order will specify the receiver's duties, which will ordinarily require him to collect and take possession of all property. Again his entitlement is to possession, not legal title.

D. *Identity of appointee as sequestrator and receiver*

A contemnor has no voice as to the identity of the sequestrators appointed any more than a prisoner has a voice as to the identity of his warders. " . . . the sequestrators are named by the Plaintiff, or the party who applies for the sequestrations; the court hath no concern in the propriety of the nomination; and they do not give security for what they receive."[37]

The sequestrators have a choice whether to be selected. The office is scarcely enviable, and few would seek office for its own sake. A high profile does not necessarily mean good publicity. The appointment as sequestrator of a trade union can imperil relationships with other unions and so colour the reputation and prejudice the acceptability of the sequestrator's firm as to disqualify the firm (at least temporarily) from some other assignments. The Rule of Law requires that suitable appointees are available and willing to accept appointment, since only if this is the case will this legal weapon continue to be available in the judicial armoury. A sense of public duty is thought to be the impelling factor in acceptance of this office. But even a sense of public duty cannot be expected to be enough if there is no assurance that the sequestrated assets will be sufficient to pay their costs and remuneration. A guarantee may be required from the party seeking the appointment. The court has no power or funds with which to underwrite their costs. In the Taylor action, the sequestrators were close to seeking their discharge because of the problem over their funding. To overcome this problem, the Attorney-General (who was committed to the success of the sequestration) volunteered to underwrite their costs.[38] The Attorney-General later announced that he would do the same in any case in the future where the party in contempt had squirrelled abroad his funds prior to and in order to defeat the sequestration.

By contrast, the subject of a receivership order does have a voice as to the identity of his receiver.

In the Clarke Action, after the *ex parte* appointment of the receiver of the assets of the NUM had been confirmed by the Court of Appeal, the NUM objected to the identity of the receiver. The appointment of a known supporter of the Conservative Party as receiver of a left wing trade union was attacked as being as appropriate as the appointment of Mr. Scargill as Treasurer of the Conservative Party. The general rule of practice is clear that, when the court appoints a receiver, "some entirely indifferent person ought to be appointed."[39] The objection was never put to the test, for on objection being made, another candidate was substituted to whom no objection could be made. In this way, the rule requiring impartiality was vindicated.

It should not be thought that the appointment as a receiver of a trade union is lightly assumed. It is not merely that the Court's remuneration of its officers may not be as generous as the remuneration available to a receiver appointed out of court, *e.g.* under a debenture.[40] As with sequestrators, there may also be a question whether the union assets will be sufficient to meet the expenses and remuneration.[41] It is thought that the office of a receiver, like the office of a sequestrator, is genuinely accepted as a public duty rather than as a source of profit.

The Main Topic

A. *Co-operation with the sequestrator and receiver*

After the indignity of a sequestration order or receivership order made against a trade union, there comes the ultimate in unpalatability, namely the requirement of co-operation with the sequestrator and receiver. Co-operation is required of the sequestrator and receiver if any of the assets of the Union are to be available to enable the Union to continue to function. I am however presently concerned with the co-operation which may be required by the sequestrator and receiver in the form of assistance in securing and recovering assets and indeed in obtaining information to enable the court officer to commence proceedings based on the information, on occasion against the informant himself.

I shall consider first the extent of the legal right of the sequestrator, and then of the receiver, to such co-operation from union officers, employees and others.

a. *Co-operation with sequestrator* A sequestrator by the Order appointing him is required to seize the assets of the body in respect of which he is appointed. He must search them out, find and secure them, and deal with them thereafter as directed by the Court.

In the case of *Eckman* v. *Midland Bank*,[42] after the A.U.E.W. had been fined £5,000 for contempt which it had failed to pay, the National Industrial Relations Court ordered that writs of sequestration should issue and that the sequestrators should seize sufficient of the unions funds to pay the fine and the costs of execution. The sequestrators wrote to the union's bankers requesting them to pay the fine, but they refused to do so without a specific order of the court. The sequestrators accordingly applied for orders that (1) the Banks verify by affidavit the balances of the union's funds and all other assets held by them on the union's behalf and (2) pay a sum sufficient to cover their costs.

Sir John Donaldson (President) held that, whilst the order for sequestration (like an injunction) only binds the parties to the action, (again like in the case of an injunction) all members of the public are under a duty to refrain both from knowingly assisting a party to the action to break the order of the court and from knowingly taking any action which will obstruct compliance by the sequestrator with the terms of the writ of sequestration, which requires him to take possession of the assets. This public duty requires all third parties, not merely to refrain from any action the object of which is the frustration of the writ; but also (overriding any ordinary obligation of confidence) to disclose promptly, accurately and fully what (if any) property is held of the contemnor's (and to transfer the same to the sequestrator on request); and if property has at some time past been held, but is no longer held, to reveal when, in what manner and to whom it was disposed of. If there is a real doubt whether any particular property is the property of the contemnor or is liable to sequestration, the full facts should be explained to the sequestrator, who may then decide whether to apply to the court for a specific order for their delivery up. The court accordingly held in the *Eckman case* that the Bank ought to have furnished the affidavit and (since there was no dispute of the contemnor's entitlement to the funds) paid the money without requiring any recourse by the sequestrator to an order of the court: this conduct in law constituted a contempt.

It is to be noted that the statement of principle in *Eckman's case* was expressed in terms of a duty to disclose assets held by the third party. The question whether the duty was so limited arose in the case of *Messenger Newspapers Group* v. *National Graphical Association*.[43] In that case, the sequestrators appointed when the Union failed to pay a fine requested the Union's auditor to disclose information regarding the Union's assets. The auditor refused on the grounds that (1) the union had not consented and (2) since the auditors did not hold any property belonging to the union, they were not obliged to comply with the request. Sir John Donaldson M.R. dismissed both grounds as excuses and held that the duty of disclosure was not limited to assets held by the informant. For the auditors (or anyone else) to refuse to divulge information as to the whereabouts of assets was "a very clear obstruction of the sequestrators."

The assets of the contemnor include choses in action, *e.g.* a bank facility.[44] They will include all causes of action, including causes of action against the officers of a trade union in contempt for any loss occasioned by any breach of duty involved in causing the contempt of court to be committed. How far can the sequestrators require such officers to provide information which will incriminate themselves in such proceedings or any other proceedings? It is thought that, for the purpose of ascertaining and taking possession of the contemnor's assets, the sequestrators can require full disclosure of all dealings with assets, though such disclosure may involve admissions of breach of trust or other irregularity, for inquiries in this regard are necessarily incidental to the duty of the sequestrators to seize the property of the union. But the sequestrators cannot properly demand information required, not for this purpose, but to further a claim against the officer. The power to obtain information would in this case be exercised for an improper purpose or oppressively. Rather, however, than simply refusing to answer, the (potential) informant should apply to the court for a direction that he need not answer. It is established that the court may order that the sequestrators should not inspect confidential documents.[45] This would suggest that the court can, and indeed should control any search for information which is not strictly necessary for the discharge of the sequestrators duties.[46]

b. *Co-operation with receiver* Throughout the receivership of the NUM, there was a lively, indeed acrimonious, but unresolved, dispute, whether anyone whom the receiver approached for information was under a duty to assist and co-operate with him as an officer of the court and whether failure in this regard constituted contempt of court. The anxiety whether this sanction was available reflected the uncertainty of the law in this regard. Is the effect of the appointment of a receiver in this respect the same as that of a sequestrator? It is tempting to equate the two kinds of court officers.[47] Their respective duties under the terms of their orders of appointment are not materially different. The appointment of a receiver (like the appointment of a sequestrator) has an effect, not merely as between the parties to the action, but also touching third parties.[48] But nonetheless it is suggested that there is a distinction between the duty of co-operation owed to a sequestrator and the duty owed to a receiver, at least by third parties.

The principle is stated in Halsburys Laws of England[49]: "Any interference with the possession of a receiver appointed by the court is a contempt of court and renders the offending party liable to committal." All the instances given are of positive acts of interference. Halsbury later states that: "A receiver appointed by the court is an officer of the court, and to interfere with him or disturb him in his capacity as such is a contempt."[50] Only one (unreported) authority has come to my attention where the court gave any consideration to the duty of cooperation owed to a court appointed receiver. In that case, where a receiver was appointed of a "quasi partnership" company, the Court of Appeal spoke of the duty of the two partners to cooperate with and furnish information to the receiver.[51] No authority so far as I am aware has held that there is any duty on non-parties to cooperate with the receiver if under no duty to the parties to do so. Indeed the authorities have drawn the clearest distinction between parties and non-parties. Parties are bound from the moment the receivership order is pronounced to put the receiver into possession of all assets[52] and are guilty of contempt if they seek to steal a march on him by dealing with assets before the receiver can obtain possession.[53] But the duty of non-parties is limited to not interfering with the assets after the order has been perfected and after the receiver has taken possession of them.[54] Until such date, third parties may compete with the receiver in a race to gain possession.

This distinction between sequestrator and receiver may rest on their distinct roles. The receiver has the duties of a caretaker, to protect and hold a balance between the interests of the parties to the action. He can have no greater right to information from third parties than that to which the parties themselves would be entitled.[55] The sequestrator is a representative of the State: his role is to assist and secure the Rule of Law. To this end his powers and duties must be equal to his task and cannot be seen to fail or be frustrated.

B. *Right to be heard*

a. *Sequestration* The NUM were held to be in contempt of court in one set of proceedings (the Taylor Action) and the receiver was later appointed in another (the Clarke Action).

On the original application for the appointment of the receiver, and repeatedly thereafter on applications to the court in the receivership, the Court insisted that the NUM had no right to be heard because it was in contempt of court and had not yet purged its contempt. In the Court of Appeal, on appeal from the *ex parte* order for the appointment of the receiver, the matter received some attention in the judgment.[56]

Stephenson L.J. said: "the position of a party in open and continuing contempt who comes to the court whose orders he has disobeyed for any form of relief is of course well known. Generally speaking the court will not listen to him until his contempt is purged. It is exceptional for the court to hear an appeal by a contemnor from any order, however exceptional . . . We have however decided to hear it, because the defendants, or most of them, are sued as trustees and therefore the interests of all the members of the union as beneficiaries are involved in this dispute."[57]

O'Connor L.J. said: "We have the NUM and its chief officers before the court and they are admittedly in contempt of court. In the ordinary course of events, as Stephenson L.J. has said, a court will not entertain an application at their suit and this appeal is such an application. The authority for that proposition is best found in *Hadkinson* v. *Hadkinson*.[58] There is always a discretion in the court to consider even a person in contempt in suit when he comes before the court, and sometimes it is convenient for the court to hear the person before deciding whether he should have been heard or not. For my part I would not wish it to be thought that, because in the exceptional circumstances of this case this court has listened to this appeal today, we are in any way departing from the law as laid down in *Hadkinson* v. *Hadkinson*[59] and, were it necessary, for my part I would rule that we ought not to have heard the appeal. But it would have been wrong in the exceptional circumstances of this case to have come to that decision without hearing the defendants."[60]

Slade L.J. merely agreed that the appeal should be dismissed for the reasons given by Stephenson and O'Connor L.JJ.

It is to be noted that this was a "Saturday morning" appeal. Enquiries of counsel involved reveal that there was in fact no argument on the issue, for the court made it clear that in view of the importance of the case the appeal should be decided on its merits. The fact was that the finding of contempt had been made in other proceedings, and most certainly the significance of this fact, was not adverted to.

On the hearing *inter partes* of the application for the appointment of the receiver, the issue again arose whether counsel was entitled to address the court. The matter is dealt with thus in the judgment of Mervyn Davies J.:

> "[Counsel] addressed me on behalf of the defendants. I informed counsel that I was not satisfied that he had any right to address me on behalf of any defendants who might be in contempt of this court while that contempt was not purged, but that, in my discretion, I was willing to hear him. [Counsel] asserted his right to address me in any event, but, since I had decided to hear him, I was not called upon to consider [counsel's] assertion. I should say that I think it would be wrong to hear an application of this kind without hearing, as of discretion if not of right, counsel desiring to address me, albeit on behalf of persons who may have been active in causing orders of the court to be disregarded."[61]

Counsel did not, therefore, have the opportunity to argue that the exclusionary rule was inapplicable because (1) the contempt was in separate proceedings: and (2) the NUM was not making any application (whether originally or by way of appeal) but merely resisting an application.

The judicial view that the NUM had no right of audience was to be heard on numerous occasions thereafter. Whenever the NUM sought to put the issue to the test, it was told that it should not do so because the court in its discretion would in any event allow the NUM to be heard. This was unsatisfactory for the NUM, for the belief is easy to engender that, if the court is only listening as a matter of indulgence, it does not listen with the same attentiveness. This was also unsatisfactory for the law, for the reports of the decisions give credence to the view that a party in contempt (*i.e.* against whom an order for committal or the equivalent has been made, which order has not been discharged) is a legal leper until the contempt is discharged.

The rule that a party in contempt will not be heard was a rule of canon law adopted by the ecclesiastical and chancery courts as a means of getting the parties to obey their orders. The common law courts had no need for such a sanction, and accordingly did not adopt any equivalent rule. In 1618, Lord Bacon stated the rule in

Chancery thus: "They that are in contempt . . . are not to be [heard] neither in that suit, nor any other, except the court of special grace suspend the contempt." But the rule came to be much restricted in scope and the disability of the defaulter was confined to applications made by him to the Court in the same cause as that in which the contempt occurs, other than applications to purge the contempt or to appeal against the order in which the contempt is found[62] or to appeal against or resist proceedings taken subsequently to his contempt on the ground of want of jurisdiction or irregularity.[63] There is no bar against a party who is in contempt until an order for committal or its equivalent is made, and thereafter the bar in no way precludes him from defending any application in the same cause or making any application in any other cause. In the unreported case of *NUM* v. *NUM*, (*Nottingham Area*)[64] Warner J. reaffirmed the principle that a party in contempt in one set of proceedings is entitled to apply to the court for relief in another, even if they arise out of the same dispute. In the *Clarke Action*, accordingly, because the sequestration order was made in different proceedings, the rule had no scope for application at any of the various hearings in the receivership proceedings or on the hearing of the appeal against the *ex parte* order appointing the receiver. In any case in the future where the committal order is made in the proceedings in which the defaulter wishes to take some part, the limitations on the scope of the rule require to be strictly observed. For, however heinous it may be to commit a contempt, the relic of times when the ecclesiastical and chancery courts felt the need in this way to vindicate their authority over those who denied it has little relevance today after their integration with the common law courts, which never had any need or place for such sanctions.[65] The guide to the future lies in the unreported case rather than in the reported.[66]

b. *Receivership* There was a recurrent objection taken on the various applications before the court in the *Clarke Action* and other related actions that, once the receivership order was made, the NUM could not be represented in court otherwise than by or with the consent of the receiver. This issue was never resolved: counsel for the NUM was always heard, if only as a matter of discretion.

It is thought that this challenge to the right of a body in respect of whose assets a receivership order has been made to instruct its own legal representative, *a fortiori* in disputes with the receiver, is ill-founded. When the court merely constitutes the court officer a receiver of the assets of an incorporated or unincorporated body, and does not authorise the officer to manage or carry on the body's

business or activities, the executive authority of that body continues to be vested with the right and power to manage its affairs
(and hence to authorise its representation in court), albeit it may
not be able to deal with its assets and accordingly pay its representative without the consent of the receiver or the court.[67] Fortunately the legal representatives of trade unions in trouble are used
to acting with no expectation of payment.

C. *Applications by receiver and sequestrator to court*

Under Order 30 rule 8 of the Rules of the Supreme Court, a
receiver is entitled to have direct access to the court for its directions and guidance on matters relating to the due performance of
his duties. In accordance with this practice a receiver appointed by
the court can see the judge who appointed him or has the conduct
of the receivership privately in the judge's room to express his
wishes and concern and obtain the judge's directions. Sequestrators have a like right of access to the judge appointing them or having the conduct of the sequestration.

The existence and exercise of the right of private access is in the
ordinary case unobjectionable. No prejudice can result to anyone.
But this course may be objectionable in a case where the same
judge, who is approached in this way, has at the same time or subsequently to adjudicate upon applications by or against the
defendant and in particular on applications for the discharge of the
sequestration or receivership orders. Exchanges may have taken
place between the judge and his officer on the matters in issue, and
the judge may have committed himself in advance or received
communications which may affect his decision. In respect of all
these matters the defendant may be and indeed is likely to be in
the dark. If the adoption of the course of receiving representations
from one party in the absence of the other is in any ordinary case
regarded as totally objectionable and a ground for vitiating a
decision, it is difficult to see why it should not be so in this case.[68]

It is doubtful if the existence of an established practice affords
any justification, for the practice may only indicate that no objection has been taken in any previous case (it may be) for under-
standable reasons. A challenge alleging disqualification is hardly a
passport to judicial favour if the challenge does not succeed. It
may be argued that support for this procedure may be found in the
majority decision of the Court of Appeal in *Bahai* v. *Rashidian*.[69]
In that case, a trial judge in the course of his judgment made the
most serious findings of misconduct against the plaintiff's solicitor
and indeed made a complaint in respect of his behaviour to the
Law Society. Subsequently the successful defendants sought an

order for costs against the solicitor personally. The solicitor objected to the same trial judge determining this issue on the ground that the trial judge was reasonably to be considered to be biased against him. The majority held that the fact that the judge had expressed highly critical views did not constitute bias or the appearance of bias in the action. Balcombe L.J. stated as follows:

"A judge properly exercising his judicial function, *e.g.* by criticising the conduct of a party's solicitor in the course of his judgment on a matter which he considers relevant to his decision, cannot by that process be said to be biased. Bias is the antithesis of the proper exercise of a judicial function."

The conduct of private conversations with the receiver or sequestrators is no doubt the proper exercise of a judicial function, but there must surely be a difference between the expression by the judge in open court of views on admissible evidence and the reception of representations and discussion of merits other than in the presence of all parties to the proceedings. A litigant can be excused feeling a real sense of grievance if he knows that communications have taken place with the judge to which neither he nor his representative have been a party. There must be a concern whether matters have not been "tied up" before the judge enters the court.

For these reasons, even if the current practice is not legally objectionable, it is thought that as a matter of judicial discretion it should not be followed blindly, and the initiative should not always be left to the defendant to take this point. There are cases (and cases of the appointment of a receiver or sequestrator of a trade union are of this class) where the concept of the fallibility of the judiciary should be countenanced.[70] The practice is adopted in cases where trustees seek the directions of the court whether to take or defend legal proceedings, for the trustees' application for directions to be made to a judge other than the judge who is to try the action in question. This analogy can surely be adopted. Applications by the sequestrator and receiver could likewise be heard by a judge other than the judge who determines whether or not the sequestration or receivership should be discharged. As Hodson L.J. said in *Schlesinger* v. *Schlesinger*[71] when emphasising the need to limit access of counsel to the judge in his private room in the course of a trial: "nothing should be done to impair public confidence by even giving room for suspicion that any part of a public trial is being conducted behind closed doors."

D. *The scope of the doctrine of contempt*

Three questions arose in the NUM litigation relating to the scope of the doctrine of contempt which are of far-reaching significance, but none of which was finally resolved. The first was whether pre-emptive action taken prior to and in anticipation of orders appointing receivers or sequestrators may constitute contempt. The second was whether the provision of assistance in functioning to the contemnor after the date of the orders constitutes contempt. The third was how far professional and other advisers are at risk in acting for a client where the adviser believes that the conduct of the client involves no contempt, but the court subsequently holds that it does.

a. *Pre-emptive action* A person fearing or anticipating orders of sequestration or receivership may "squirrel away" his assets so as to protect them from seizure. Such action may be unlawful, *e.g.* as a breach of trust. The question to be addressed is whether such action can constitute a contempt on the ground that its purpose and effect is to set at nought the processes of the Court if and when subsequently brought into play.

In his judgment discharging the sequestration order in the Taylor Action, Nicholls J. said: "those who assist others to take steps intended to thwart orders which it is anticipated that a court may thereafter make should not regard themselves as necessarily unassailable."[72] Implicit was the warning that such conduct may constitute a contempt. If such conduct may constitute contempt, the further question immediately arises whether such conduct will constitute contempt only if an order is subsequently made and the steps taken do thwart that order; or whether the mere taking of the action with the requisite intention is sufficient irrespective of its effect and irrespective whether the order is made. Both of these concepts are objectionable. The former involves judging the character of a man's actions, whether lawful or criminal, by reference to the subsequent actions of others, *i.e.* the making by the other party in the action of an application for, and by the judge on such application of, the order of sequestration; and as regards the latter, if the making of preparations to commit a contempt, and possibly even an attempt to commit a contempt, do not themselves constitute contempt,[73] it is difficult to see why this conduct should either.

It is thought that, on principle, pre-emptive action cannot constitute contempt. To forestall a court order is legitimate unless the conduct in question by reason of some applicable rule of law constitutes a crime, a tort, a breach of trust or other civil wrong, and even then is not a contempt. Indeed this is often the rationale for the grant of *ex parte* injunctions, in particular of the Mareva and Anton Piller variety. The ambit of the law of contempt should not be extended. The Courts have no power to create new offences or so to widen existing offences as to make punishable conduct of a type hitherto not subject to punishment.[79] As we have seen, contempt is an indictable misdemeanour. It is enough that the making of the sequestration order imposes on the participant in the prior scheme to thwart the order a duty to unravel what has previously been done, to recall assets within reach and to make full disclosure, and that the sanction for breach of this duty may be contempt.

b. *Assistance in functioning* The critical question arises whether the appointment of a sequestrator or receiver requires a trade union to cease to function and whether cooperation afforded by outsiders to its continuation to function constitutes a contempt.

It is of course open to the court to order that a trade union cease to function (though this would be a remarkable order to make in an open society) or to direct that the sequestrators or receiver take the management of the trade union into their own hands, *i.e.* appoint the receiver or sequestrators to act as manager of the union as well as receiver and sequestrators of its assets. This order would be equally remarkable. But in the absence of any such order, it is thought that the continuation of functioning of the trade union is in no way forbidden or a contempt, though the trade union must of course only function so as fully to respect the rights of the receiver and sequestrators. This limitation means that the trade union, its officials and servants, must not interfere with the receiver's or sequestrators' possession or right to possession of the union's assets without the consent of the court officer or the court. It is open to the court in making the receivership or sequestration order specifically to exempt from the order monies required by the union to carry on its lawful activities.[75] Such is scarcely feasible, save when the court is concerned only to seize sufficient funds to pay some fine or other liability and there are plainly adequate funds to meet this purpose and allow the union to function. It is necessary therefore to review the law's application in cases where "common form" sequestration or receivership orders are made, containing provisions neither for management by the sequestrators or receiver nor for exemption of any funds.

So long as a sequestration or receivership order is in force, the trade union cannot draw on, expend, deal with or realise the union's assets without the consent of the court officer or the court.

To function, the union must therefore operate without making any payments, and it can normally only do so if either it can lawfully borrow or obtain credit; or if outsiders can lawfully finance or support it. This accordingly leads to two critical questions:

(1) Can the union borrow or obtain credit without the consent of the court or the court's officer?[76]
(2) Can outsiders finance or support the union in its efforts to continue to function without committing a contempt?

It is thought that the answer to both these questions ought on principle to be in the affirmative, but it is necessary to say that the stance adopted by the courts during the miners' strike raises serious doubts.

(i) *Precedent*

(a) It is clear that a third party may pay the contemnor's fine with his consent, or without it, and thereby incur no risk of contempt.[77] Indeed Mr. Scargill's fine of £1,000 was so paid. This is explicable on the dual grounds (a) that the fine is a punishment for contempt, and not the coercive means of securing obedience to the will of the Court[78]; and (b) that the means are in this way available to prevent a contemnor achieving martyrdom by refusing to pay and courting prolonged imprisonment without loss of face by the Court.

(b) In *Hopkins* v. *N.U.S.*[79] Scott J. held that a third party could not make any donation to the NUM as it was in contempt: any payment would have to be made to the sequestrators. But he recognised that it was not illicit to provide indirect assistance to the contemnor by setting up trusts to alleviate hardship amongst miners' families. The sequestrators had no claim to such trust funds. No challenge was made during the strike to the action of the T.U.C. in setting up a Miners Solidarity Fund and a Hardship Fund to relieve the hardship of miners and their families. No action was taken or threatened against the T.U.C. when it amended its rules to defer payment by the N.U.M. of its affiliation fees—fees for payment of which the receiver refused to release funds.

(c) There was a threat of contempt proceedings when the T.U.C. sought to clear with the receiver and sequestrators a scheme for setting up a trust to pay staff and outside creditors of the NUM. It would have been naive to have expected the go-ahead from the receiver or sequestrators or indeed any response other than that which they received. The correctness or otherwise of the response was not tested, as it might have been on an application to the court, but the response effectively deterred (or excused) implementation of the scheme.[80]

Some credence is lent to the view that such a scheme would constitute a contempt by the observations made by Nicholls J. in his judgment in the Taylor action on the occasion of his discharge of the sequestration order. After giving his reasons for doing so, he said "I add the two general observations. I am aware[81] that during the sequestration area unions of the NUM and others have provided financial assistance to the NUM. The identity of at least some of these bodies is known to me. Although I propose to take no action with regard to these activities at this stage, those concerned and others should not conclude that, if such activities should take place in the context of another sequestration, they will be treated with similar leniency. On the contrary those who wilfully obstruct sequestrators in the discharge of their duties should understand that they themselves are in contempt of court."[82] The weight of the observations of Nicholls J. is somewhat reduced by the fact that there was no argument or citation of authority before him on this issue any more than on the issue of the exposure to liability of an adviser,[83] as which see (iii) below.

(ii) *Principle.* The reason why on principle the answers to both questions should be in the affirmative is as follows. The order of the court making the appointment of sequestrators and receiver is directed at collecting and seizing the assets of the contemnor. Unless the order making the appointment gives the sequestrators or receiver the conduct or management of the undertaking of the contemnor, it is not directed at preventing the contemnor obtaining credit. Obviously any prospective creditor should be informed of the court order and that he can expect no discharge of his debt out of the assets of the contemnor until discharge of the court order or an earlier direction for payment by the court. But it is another matter to say that the outsider is barred from giving credit with his eyes open. If the outsider agrees to sell some seizable asset to the union, the asset must of course be handed to the court officer. But if he merely agrees to discharge a liability, *e.g.* to pay the union employees or to continue to provide telephones or other services at the union's premises, this course may be "uncommercial" but can scarcely be described as a contempt. If the contemnor is an individual, can he not be sold "bed and board" or provided with accommodation? Is a Good Samaritan (in the eyes of the contemnor and his sympathisers anyway) at risk of committal?

The alternative thus postulates that there can be no Good Samaritan. At least in the case of a trade union in contempt, any Samaritan must by definition be bad. The orders are supposed to hurt, and any person who eases their pain is frustrating the processes of the court.

This thesis found expression on a number of occasions during the strike, and the threat of contempt was a formidable bar to well wishers. Of contempt they had no need in their lives.

The bed rock for this approach is the judgment of Lindley L.J. in *Seaward* v. *Patterson*.[84] In that case, the Court of Appeal upheld an order to commit for contempt a person who aided and abetted a breach of an injunction restraining others from holding boxing matches. The Court was concerned only to establish that jurisdiction extended to punish third parties for such acts. The jurisdiction was held to rest on the inherent jurisdiction of the court to prevent its process being set at nought and treated with contempt.

Two problems arise. The first is whether a third party is guilty of contempt if he does an act which sets at nought (in the sense of negating the affectiveness of) a court order made against a party to the action, or whether he is only guilty if he aids or abets the party in a breach of the order. In 1986 the principle that the court will not allow its orders to be bye-passed or thwarted was extended so as to render punishable for contempt the acting third parties in doing or causing to be done acts forbidden by injunctions to be done by the defendants in the action—in that case interfering with a statutory right of access to land.[85] This extension has however rightly been repudiated by Sir Nicholas Browne-Wilkinson V-C in *Attorney General* v. *Newspaper Publishing plc.*[85a] He held that one newspaper does not commit a contempt by publishing what another newspaper has been banned from publishing. The Vice Chancellor reaffirmed the principle that third parties can only be liable for contempt if they aid and abet the party injuncted to breach the terms of the injunction. If this is correct, the answer to both questions must be in the affirmative there is no "aiding or abetting" of a breach of any court order. If however I am wrong, and a third party is guilty of contempt if (independently of any aiding or abetting of a breach) his action sets the Court's process at nought, this second problem has to be decided, namely whether the court's process is being set at nought or treated with contempt if the trade union is assisted in continuing to function.

The argument in favour of this proposition is that the court intends by its order to place the maximum pressure on the union to submit and any action by a third party which operates to ease this pressure is thwarting the will of the court and therefore amounts to contempt. The answer to this argument is, I suggest, that the intendment of the Court in all cases of contempt must surely be found on the face of the order or by necessary implication. If the order on its face leaves open to question whether some action is forbidden, proceedings for contempt cannot be appropriate.

Thus whilst the order for sequestration may ordinarily result in the contemnor ceasing to function, such cesser is not necessarily the case, and may not be the clear and unambiguous purpose of the court order. The reality is that assistance by third parties softens the blow, lessens the pain, allows life to continue. But it is thought that the achievement of these results, sidestepping certain adverse consequences of the Order, cannot constitute contempt. Contempt of court is a serious charge, and an order should not be read as forbidding (let alone with this sanction) conduct which on its face it does not clearly state to be forbidden. If the court wishes the union to be treated as a pariah, let it say so in the order: if it wishes to stop it functioning, let it order this result; if the order for contempt is intended to hurt and no palliatives are allowed, the court should face up to drafting and making an order in these terms rather than subsequently finding a third party guilty of an offence for action contrary to the imputed spirit rather than the clear language of its order. As Eveleigh L.J. said in *Z Ltd*. v. *A-Z*[86] "If a person to whom an injunction is addressed is entitled to certainty, how much more so should this apply to a person who is not even a party to the proceedings."

(iii) *Professional and other advisers* Nicholls J. in *Taylor* v. *NUM* went on to give a warning to advisers of contemnors and prospective contemnors.

> "Secondly, those who give professional or other advice to a person against whom an injunction has been granted or whose assets are the subject of a sequestration order must be vigilant to see that they are not assisting in a breach of the injunction or an interference with the sequestrators. Solicitors as officers of this court have a particularly heavy responsibility in this regard. Giving legal advice on the legal implications of particular conduct which they know is or may be a contempt of court is entirely different."

Nicholls J. did not define "assistance." Clearly the giving of bad legal advice is not enough.[87] The adviser must have counselled, actively participated in or been privy to the unlawful action.[88] But suppose the client instructs a solicitor to draft a document or complete a transaction when the solicitor appreciates that there is a risk of contempt but bona fide believes (if necessary on the advice of counsel) that the matter falls within the permissible rather than the impermissible side of the line? Surely in such a case the solicitor should be free of risk, and the client should be entitled to his conscientious services in the transaction without the solicitor being required throughout to guard his own position.[89] There must be established on the part of the adviser before any question of contempt on his part can arise, not merely carelessness or recklessness, but some lack of good faith or contumacious indifference whether the actions advised or furthered constitute contempt by the client.[90]

E. *Foreign assets*

One of the tasks assumed by the receiver and sequestrators of the NUM was to seek the recovery of the union's assets situated abroad. On November 3, 1984, Nicholls J. expressly authorised the sequestrators to commence and prosecute proceedings in the High Court of Ireland, seeking the recovery of funds belonging to the NUM in a bank account in Ireland. Such proceedings were duly commenced and an injunction was obtained freezing the money pending trial. Shortly before trial, the receiver applied to be joined as co-Plaintiff and this application was acceded to. On December 20, 1984, counsel for the NUM applied for an order that his costs should be paid out of the monies in the bank account on the ground that the sequestrators costs were being underwritten by H.M. Government whilst the NUM's funds were frozen by the sequestration and receivership orders, and that such an order of the Irish Court was required if the NUM was to have a fair opportunity of defending the proceedings. Barrington J. acceded to the application.

At the trial in June 1985 Barrington J. held that the sequestration order granted on the conviction of the NUM of a contumacious contempt was in effect essentially a penal process, and that such order could not under established principles of Private International Law be recognised or given effect to in Ireland.[91] Accordingly the claim of the sequestration failed.

Barrington J. also refused to accede to the claim of the receiver. He held that, having regard to the interlocutory nature of the order making the appointment and his view that the application was opposed by the Executive Committee of the NUM, the monies should remain frozen in Ireland until new permanent trustees of the union's properly had been appointed.[92]

In fact the assets were later voluntarily repatriated and returned within the jurisdiction. The lesson of this experience is that it is essential if there is to be a real prospect of recovering assets of a union abroad that the court appoint, not merely sequestrators or receivers, but new trustees compliant with the courts wishes. Their title to foreign assets, it is conceived, could not be successfully challenged.

F. *Discharge of order*

a. *Sequestration order and need for apology.* Once the subject of a sequestration order, a party must purge his contempt before the episode can be called closed. The order required discharges the defaulter from further punishment.

Purging contempt has traditionally been regarded as analogous to confession, requiring the defaulter to acknowledge the error of his way, apologise and undertake to behave better in the future.

This approach has, however, proved inappropriate in many cases where the defaulter is not prepared to undertake this exercise in humiliation for reasons of conscience or otherwise.

Fortunately the Courts have been willing to recognise that the insistence on any particular requirement for purging contempt may prove counterproductive and expose rather the ineffectiveness of the law's processes to impel the necessary change of heart, and may create public sympathy for the defaulter as a victim.

What the Court is concerned to ensure is that the offender and the public know that the law must be obeyed and will be enforced. For this purpose, the Judge may require that the offender, and, in the case of a union, its principal officers, attend Court on the application for discharge and hear personally a warning from him as regards their future conduct.

In *Richard Read (Transport) Ltd.* v. *NUM (S. Wales Area)*,[93] application for discharge of a sequestration order was made by the contemnor without any apology or assurance of his intention in the future to abide by the terms of the injunction. Nonetheless Scott J. granted the discharge on the ground that the writs of sequestration had served their function and accordingly the contempt should be treated as cleared. It was sufficient that the Union had recognised the authority of the Court. He "was not troubled by the absence of a formal apology, since the courts dignity did not depend upon or require an expressed public recantation, the sincerity of which, if offered, might in the circumstances be open to question."

In the Taylor Action, after payment of the £200,000 fine by the Receiver, the receiver (no doubt with the authority of the Judge having the conduct of the receivership proceedings) applied to the Judge having the conduct of the sequestration proceedings to discharge the sequestration order. This application on February 18, 1985 Nicholls J. refused, no doubt on the ground that something more than this was required if the authority of the law was to be seen to be upheld. On November 14, 1985, the NUM itself applied for discharge of the sequestration order. The three principal officers attended the hearing voluntarily—a wise precaution, for there can be no doubt that, if they had not done so, their attendance would have been ordered by the Court. They swore an affidavit described by the judge as perfunctory. They tendered a formal apology, but gave no assurance thereafter to comply with orders of the court. Nonetheless, having regard in particular to the detrimental effects of the sequestration order on innocent members of the NUM, he ordered the discharge of the sequestration order. He said " . . . the authority of the law has now been sufficiently upheld, and seen to be so."

b. *Discharge of receivership and the courts jurisdiction to refuse or delay.* I have already referred to the passage in the judgment of Mervyn Davies J. when appointing the receiver which indicated that the receivership would continue only until the existing trustees relented or new trustees were appointed. New trustees were appointed on September 1, 1985; and were on October 21, 1985 paraded before the court to establish under sustained cross-examination their fitness and independence. They passed with flying colours, the judge expressing his satisfaction in this regard. Yet despite repeated applications, the NUM only finally succeeded in securing the discharge of the receiver on an appeal to the Court of Appeal on June 27, 1986. The court had previously successively refused to countenance the discharge of the order until after (1) the discharge of the sequestration order; (2) the cooperation of the past trustees and officers of the union with the receiver; (3) the resolution to the satisfaction of the receiver of all outstanding matters of account; and (4) the provision of the information by the former officers and trustees required by the receiver, though this stopped short of information required for the purpose of arming the receiver with material required only to sue them (and others) in the name of the union.

When these hurdles had been surmounted, the receiver invited the Court to continue the receivership in an attenuated form, namely limited to the continued conduct of the action commenced by the receiver in the name of the Union against the former trustees and officers and others for damages for breach of trust. All parties to the action sought the complete discharge. Mervyn Davies J. acceded to the receiver's invitation, saying in his judgment on May 20, 1986 " . . . I see great difficulty in the new trustees and new solicitors and indeed perhaps new counsel taking over the action . . . I think that the prospect of success in the action is better if there is no change." Reaffirming this decision in a judgment delivered on June 11, 1986, he said: "I am satisfied from my own knowledge over the months[94] that the prosecution of this claim is best handled by the receiver. It is in the interests of the Trust Fund that the amounts to be recovered are the largest possible."

On June 27, 1986, the Court of Appeal reversed this decision, holding that the prospects of success in the breach of trust action with the receiver in the saddle was not a relevant factor in a determination whether to discharge the receiver. Since new trustees had been appointed, undertakings had been given by the executive of the union not to interfere with the conduct of the breach of trust proceedings by the new trustees and no member of the union sought to justify the continuation of the receivership, the receivership should be discharged. The Court left open the question whether the Court had jurisdiction against the wishes of all parties to the action to continue the receivership, but held that (assuming such jurisdiction to exist) the circumstances justifying the court's exercise of its discretion in this way must be exceptional and did not exist in this case.

It is thought that the receivership order ought to have been discharged as soon as the new trustees passed muster. The order was made to preserve assets in jeopardy, and once that purpose had been achieved it was wrong to continue the order as leverage to achieve collateral objects, however desirable, or to teach the "wrongdoers" a lesson. Further in a case where the judge when making an order expressly stated that its duration would be limited, the court should itself respect this statement, if the litigants (and the public) are to respect other statements of the court. As regards the point left open by the Court of Appeal, the court indeed has surely no jurisdiction to continue relief which no party to the action wants, even if the court believes that such relief will secure substantial benefits for the parties. Where all parties are of full age and capacity, it is for the parties, and not the courts, to decide how their best interests are served, and the Judge should not be seen to enter the arena.[95]

c. *Legacy* With the judgment of the Court of Appeal, the fetters on the NUM were finally removed. But what were these fetters? Did the union during the periods of the sequestration and receivership continue to function in breach or in accordance with the law? Was the union living in sin?

The legal legacy of the strike is a body of authority all decided in the highly charged atmosphere of the strike and much without argument or full (or on occasion any) citation of authority. Some of these decisions (like the decision in *Liversidge* v. *Anderson*[96]) may require careful reconsideration in peacetime conditions. A conflict between a powerful trade union and the law may happen again. It is as well that the legal consequences of any order for sequestration or receivership should be examined and clarified ahead of time. This paper is intended as very much a first step in that direction.

NOTES

[1] For an illuminating review of the legal history of the strike, see Lord Wedderburn's *The Worker and The Law* 3rd ed., p. 730. The author acknowledges his debt to Lord Wedderburn, Mr. John Whittaker, Mr. Jack Beatson and Mrs. Eve Barfield for their advice and assistance.

[2] *Hopkins* v. *N.U.S.* [1985] I.C.R. 268. But *cf. Fettes* v. *NUM* (Scottish Area) September 25, 1984. As a consequence, the Union funds could not be used to support strikers: *Taylor* v. *NUM* (Derbyshire Area) [1985] I.R.L.R. 99.

[3] For the circumstances in which the Orders breached were made, see [1984] 1 R.L.R. 445.

[4] [1985] I.C.R. 203.

[5] [1985] I.C.R. 606.

[6] [1975] A.C. 396.

[7] See the Note in 1974 M.L.R. 187 by Lord Wedderburn on *Con-Mech (Engineers) Ltd.* v. *A.U.E.W.* [1973] I.C.R. 620.

[8] Halsbury's *Laws of England* (4th ed.), Vol. 9, para. 2. The order breached must be coercive, and not merely declaratory: *Webster* v. *Southwark L.B.C.* [1983] Q.B. 698.

[9] *Jelson (Estates)* v. *Harvey* [1984] 1 All E.R. 12 at p. 20, and see *Balogh* v. *Crown Court* [1975] Q.B. 73. A criminal prosecution, rather than proceedings for contempt, is only appropriate in a case where the conduct in question "is so bad that an ordinary right-thinking person would immediately and without hesitation regard it as criminal in nature" *per* Lord Brandon in *Reg.* v. *D.* [1984] A.C. 778 at 806 (a case of kidnapping by a parent of his own child in breach of a court order).

[10] Halsbury, *supra* in n. 2 says that it does in all cases.

[11] *Express & Star* v. *N.G.A.* [1986] I.C.R. 589 at p. 595; *Poje* v. *A-G for British Columbia* (1953) 2 D.L.R. 705; *Re New Brunswick* (1977) 73 D.L.R. (3d) 94; contra *Larkins* v. *NUM infra* where the distinction was drawn between mere civil and contumacious civil contempts, adopting a passage in Arlidge and Eady on Contempt of Court at p. 57.

[12] *Per* Skinner J. in *TDK Tape Distributors (U.K.)* v. *Videochoice* [1986] 1 W.L.R. 141; *Z* v. *A-Z* [1982] Q.B. 55 at pp. 579–584, *per* Eveleigh L.J.; *Express & Star* v. *N.G.A.* [1986] I.C.R. 589 at p. 595. Contumacy would appear to involve something more than "*mens rea,*" *i.e.* a knowing breach of an injunction: there must be an intention to set the law at nought.

[13] *Badry* v. *DPP* [1983] 2 A.C. 297.

[14] *Knight* v. *Clifton* [1971] Ch. 700.

[15] *Z* v. *A.-Z.* [1982] Q.B. 558 at pp. 579–584, *per* Eveleigh L.J.

[16] *Scott* v. *Scott* [1913] A.C. 417 at p. 458. It is thought that if contumacy (*i.e.* something more than *mens rea*) is required to render a party to the action guilty of criminal (as opposed to civil) contempt, a third party should likewise only be guilty of criminal (as opposed to civil) contempt if he is contumacious. The decision in *Seaward* v. *Patterson* [1897] 1 Ch. 545 is usually cited in support of the proposition that "aiding and abetting" by a third party constitutes a criminal contempt, but it does not in fact decide this and on the facts the court clearly regarded the third party's action as contumacious: see *Webster* v. *Southwark L.B.C.* [1983] 1 Q.B. 698 at 706–7.

[17] *Z* v. *A-Z* [1982] Q.B. 558 at p. 583 *per* Eveleigh L.J. In *TDK* v. *Videochoice* [1986] 1 W.L.R. 141, a solicitor was held guilty of contempt where he received and expended his clients money in breach of a Mareva injunction. The solicitor knew of the injunction but did not apply his mind to the question whether the particular application of the money constituted a breach. Counsel for the solicitor had, however, conceded that a breach which with the exercise of reasonable care would have been avoided was a contempt, particularly if committed by a practising solicitor (see p. 348f).

[18] *Yianni* v. *Yianni* [1966] 1 W.L.R. 120 at p. 124.

[19] See n. 9 *supra.*

[20] See n. 7 *supra.*

[21] *Re Barrell* [1972] 3 All E.R. 63 at p. 639; *Jennison* v. *Baker* [1972] 2 Q.B. 52 at pp. 64–65.

[22] *A-G* v. *Times Newspapers* [1974] A.C. 273 at p. 308.

[23] The character of the contempt was analysed by Barrington J. in the proceedings in Ireland, as a civil contumacious contempt: see also footnotes 11 and 73.

[24] *Con-Mech (Engineering) Ltd.* v. *A.U.E.W.* [1973] I.C.R. 620 at p. 627.

[25] *Dean* v. *Dean*, The Times, November 13, 1986.

[26] Halsbury's *Laws of England* (4th Ed.), Vol. 17, para. 505 *et seq.*

[27] See *Steiner Products* v. *Willey Steiner* [1966] 1 WL.R. 986.

[28] *Howitt Transport Ltd.* v. *T.G.W.U.* [1973] I.C.R. at p. 11: see also *Showerings Ltd.* v. *Fern Vale Brewery* [1958] R.P.C. 462 at p. 463.

[28a] Because of the high costs involved, the mere threat of a sequestration Order is an effective deterrent to trade union action and *e.g.* was the decisive factor in the capitulation of Sogat 1982 on February 5, 1987 after a long strike action against Times Newspapers.

[29] Halsbury's *Laws of England* (4th Ed.), Vol. 17 para. 511.

[30] *Clarke* v. *Chadburn* [1985] 1 W.L.R. 78.

[31] See Sir John Donaldson M.R. in *Con-Mec (Engineers) Ltd.* v. *A.U.E.W.* [1973] I.C.R. 620 at p. 626. The Industrial Relations Court, no doubt at least in part in reaction to the persistent challenges to its authority, required parties to whom it granted injunctions to report to the Court whether such orders had been complied with (see n. 7). The special need and procedures of the court to secure respect for its orders placed a premium on the court's jurisdiction to take the initiative in contempt proceedings. Sir Jack Jacob in Sequestration for Contempt of Court 1986 Current Legal Problems p. 221 denies this power of the Court, arguing that R.S.C. Order 46 Rule 5 lays down as mandatory requirements for the issue of writs of sequestration a notice of motion and affidavit. But surely these mandatory requirements are applicable on applications for leave to issue the writ by litigants, and not intended to preclude orders by the court of its own motion: see also *Balogh* v. *Crown Court* [1975] Q.B. 73.

[32] *Yianni* v. *Yianni* [1966] 1 W.L.R. 120 at p. 124 (Cross J.).

[33] *Balogh* v. *Crown Court* [1975] Q.B. 73 at p. 85, *per* Lord Denning M.R.

[34] *Ibid* at p. 292, *per* Stephenson L.J.

[35] Lawton L.J. *ibid* at p. 295 said:

"In my judgment, this summary and draconian jurisdiction should only be used for the purpose of ensuring that a trial in progress or about to start can be brought to a proper and dignified end without disturbance and with a fair chance of a just verdict or judgment. Contempts which are not likely to disturb the trial or affect the verdict or judgment can be dealt with by a motion to commit under R.S.C. Order 52 by indictment."

[36] See Halsbury's *Laws of England* (4th Ed.), Vol. 48 para. 924 and 949. In the case of a public or charitable trust, a receiver may be appointed on the application of the Attorney-General, see *A-G* v. *Schonfeld* [1980] 3 All E.R. 1.

[37] *Rowley* v. *Ridley* Dickens 621, which reports that the application for relief was made at the rising of the court "when it was scarcely possible to hear, much less to understand."

[38] See [1984] New L.J. 1097, the statement of the Attorney-General to the House of Commons on December 11, 1984 in Hansard; and the account of this episode given in the judgment of Barrington J. in *Larkins* v. *NUM* (unreported) in June 1985.

[39] *Per* Page Wood V-C in *Fripp* v. *Chard Ry.* (1853) 11 Hare 241 at p. 261.

[40] *Cf. Re Potters Oils Ltd.* [1986] 1 W.L.R. 201.

⁴¹ *Cf. Evans* v. *Clayhope Properties Ltd.*, [1987] 1 W.L.R. 225.
⁴² [1973] 1 Q.B. 519.
⁴³ [1984] 1 All E.R. 293.
⁴⁴ See *Eckman's Case* at p. 529.
⁴⁵ *Re Suarez* (1918) 88 L.J.Ch.10.
⁴⁶ Mervyn Davies J. did indicate in the course of the Clarke Action, when objection was made to the receiver's demand for such incriminating evidence, that he would not require it to be provided.

⁴⁷ Both sequestrators and receivers are liable for negligence, and similar principles govern the exercise of the court's jurisdiction to grant relief from such liability: see *I.R.C.* v. *Hoogstraten* [1985] Q.B. 1077 and the judgment of the Court of Appeal in the Clarke Action delivered on June 27, 1986.

⁴⁸ See Meagher Gummow & Lehane, *Equity Doctrine & Remedies* (2nd ed.), para. 2878.
⁴⁹ (4th ed.), Vol. 39, para. 890.
⁵⁰ *Ibid.* Vol. 9, para. 34.
⁵¹ *Parsons* v. *Mather & Platt* December 9, 1976, cited in Lightman and Moss, *The Law of Receivers of Companies* para. 22.04.
⁵² *Levasseur* v. *Mason & Barry Ltd.* [1891] 2 Q.B. 73.
⁵³ *Skip* v. *Harwood* (1747) 3 E.R. 564.
⁵⁴ See *Re Maudsley* (1900) 1 Ch. 602 at pp. 611–612.
⁵⁵ The court has jurisdiction, in order to protect preserve and trace trust funds, to order any person to provide information as to their whereabouts, see *Bekhor* v. *Bilton* [1981] Q.B. 923 at p. 937.
⁵⁶ *Clarke* v. *Heathfield* [1985] I.C.R. 203.
⁵⁷ At p. 205.
⁵⁸ [1952] p. 285.
⁵⁹ See n. 58 *supra.*
⁶⁰ At p. 207.
⁶¹ *Clarke* v. *Heathfield* (No. 2) [1985] I.C.R. 606 at p. 613.
⁶² See *Hadkinson* v. *Hadkinson* [1951] p. 285 at pp. 295–296 and *Bettinson* v. *Bettinson* [1965] Ch. 465.
⁶³ See *Oswald on Contempt* (3rd ed.), p. 247–248.
⁶⁴ December 19, 1984. Warner J. rejected the argument based on a passage in Daniell's *Chancery Practice* (cited by Plowman J. in *Bettinson* v. *Bettinson*, *supra*) that the application in the two causes had to relate to distinct matters if the party in contempt was to be heard. He acknowledged the artificiality of the principle under which the outcome depended upon whether the vehicle for the application to the court was the same or different proceedings, but held that this was not a sufficient reason to depart from the authorities. This artificiality is not likely to have practical consequences in many cases, for (a) even when the rule barring access to the court applies, the court has a discretion to override it; and (b) in any case where there is scope for exercise of discretion, the existence of the contempt must be a relevant (and often the deciding) consideration.

⁶⁵ The retention of the rule of exclusion in judicial proceedings may be contrasted with the extension of the right to be heard in non-judicial proceedings. It may be questionable whether the rule can be enforced consistently with the provisions of the European Convention on Human Rights.

⁶⁶ This state of affairs emphasises how quixotic are the decisions as to what cases should be reported and the role of editors of the law reports as law makers.

⁶⁷ See Lightman & Moss, *supra*, para. 2.08. In the field of Company Law, the distinction between the effect of the appointment of a receiver and of a receiver and manager (or administrative receiver) on the powers of the directors is well established. The appointment of a receiver and manager of a trade union is theoretically

possible but in practice highly improbable and indeed undesirable in view of the political and economic roles and activities of unions.

[68] For examples where the judgment apparently reveals the existence of relevant knowledge so acquired, see notes 81 and 94.

[69] [1985] 1 W.L.R. 1337. This decision is in stark contrast with the developments in the field of natural justice where the Court has been astute to detect vitiating bias in other tribunals.

[70] The presumed immunity of judges from normal human frailties and infirmities (*e.g.* the immunity, implicit in the judicial retirement age of 75 years, of their faculties from normal aging processes) should not be extended to stretch the credulity of litigants or the public too far.

[71] [1959] 1 All E.R. 155 at p. 160.

[72] *The Times*, November 20, 1985.

[73] See *Balogh* v. *Crown Court* [1975] Q.B. 73 at 87B per Stephenson L.J. See also *R.* v. *Smith* [1975] A.C. 560 for the requirements of the common law crime of attempt.

[74] *D.P.P.* v. *Withers* [1974] 3 All E.R. 984.

[75] See Sir John Donaldson M.R. in *Messenger Newspapers Group* v. *National Graphical Association* [1984] 1 All E.R. 293 at p. 295.

[76] This question is of critical importance to persons dealing with the union, for if the dealing constitutes a contempt, it may be held unlawful and accordingly give rise to no legal rights (*Clarke* v. *Chadburn* [1985] 1 W.L.R. 78); it is also important to members of the Union who might ordinarily be entitled to an indemnity in respect of costs from the union (see *Bourne* v. *Colodonse Ltd.* [1985] I.C.R. 291). It is thought that if the union can borrow or obtain credit without the consent of the court or its officers, it must fully inform the lender or creditor of the limitations upon its ability to pay in due course and that payment cannot be made prior to discharge of the court order without the consent of the court or its officer, see *D.P.P.* v. *Ray* [1974] A.C. 370.

[77] This rule is a departure from the general principle that a stranger cannot by payment discharge another's debt without his prior authority or subsequent ratification: see Goff & Jones, *The Law of Restitution* (3rd ed.), p. 17.

[78] See Wedderburn, *The Worker and the Law* (3rd ed.), p. 715.

[79] [1985] I.C.R. 268 at p. 277.

[80] See T.U.C. General Council, Annual Report 1985, pp. 40–62 and Wedderburn *supra* at p. 742.

[81] This awareness would appear to have been obtained in the course of applications in Chambers to the judge by the sequestrators.

[82] *Taylor* v. *NUM, The Times*, November 20, 1985.

[83] It is not fashionable today to adopt the vigorous approach of Jessel M.R. who said "I do not pay much attention to the dicta of modern judges" (*Quilter* v. *Heatly* (1883) 33 Ch.D. 42 at p. 49).

[84] [1897] 1 Ch. 545 at pp. 555–556.

[85] See *U.K. Mirex Ltd.* v. *Barton, Times* L.R. October 14, 1986.

[85a] *The Times* L.R. June 3, 1987.

[86] [1982] Q.B. 558 at p. 582.

[87] See *Re Plant* (1881) 45 L.T. 326.

[88] Consider *The Jay Linn* [1965] 3 All E.R. 36.

[89] *Compare Orchard* v. *S.E. Electricity Board, The Times* November 14, 1986.

[90] See Eveleigh L.J. in *Z Ltd.* v. *A-Z* [1982] Q.B. 558 at p. 583. But see *TDK* v. *Videochoice* [1985] 3 All E.R. 345 where the solicitor conceded that his negligent assistance in the breach of an injunction by his client constituted a contempt. The requirement for actual as opposed to constructive notice is analogous in this context to the requirement of actual notice in the case of the tort of wrongful interference with contract.

[91] Following *Buchanan* v. *McVey* [1954] I.R. 89.

[92] A full account of the proceedings is given in the judgment of Barrington J. in *Larkins* v. *NUM* (1984) No. 8465P.

[93] *The Times*, March 19, 1985.

[94] This would appear to be the knowledge acquired in the course of consultations with the receiver during the receivership when directions were given relating to this action.

[95] *Robinson* v. *Duleep Singh* 11 Ch.D. 798.

[96] [1942] A.C. 206. Like reconsideration may have to be given to certain decisions of the Industrial Relations Court which adopted a novel procedure in monitoring compliance with its own orders, see n. 26.

Illegally-Obtained Evidence—Discretion as a Guardian of Legitimacy

ADRIAN A. S. ZUCKERMAN

This paper is concerned with a simple and age-old question: should a court give judgment on the basis of evidence that has been procured by illegal or immoral means? Simple though it is, the question is far from settled in Anglo-American jurisprudence. I shall argue that this is due to two principal causes. The first is a failure to come to terms with the nature of the problem. The second is a refusal to accept that the problem has a constitutional dimension that transcends the boundaries of the law of evidence.

The first failure is apparent in the disingenuous justification that supports the traditional principle. The original position—common throughout the Anglo-American system—was that relevant and reliable evidence was admissible irrespective of its provenance.[1] The logic of this principle has a pseudo-deductive attraction: the object of the trial is to ascertain the facts in issue, the proferred evidence helps ascertain these facts, ergo it is admissible. But an appeal to relevance is hardly sufficient when many a type of relevant evidence is excluded. Supporters of this position, such as Wigmore, therefore add that the trial is an unsuitable forum for trying violations of legality which are unconnected with the issue in the case and an investigation of the alleged illegality could confuse and delay adjudication on the main issue. With characteristic vigour Wigmore said:

> " . . . a judge does not hold court in a street-car to do summary justice upon a fellow passenger who fraudulently evades payment of his fare; and, upon the same principle, he does not attempt, in the course of a specific litigation, to investigate and punish all offences which incidentally cross the path of that litigation. Such a practice might be consistent with the primitive system of justice under an Arabian sheik; but it does not comport with our own system of law."[2]

This perception presupposes that the issue of illegality is strictly one of evidence, straddling civil and criminal proceedings alike. In fact the problem assumes a wholly different nature in criminal trials. The criminal trial has a special moral dimension. It is concerned with the determination of moral blame, as well as of legal liability, which may in turn justify the infliction of suffering and humiliation on an individual. The willingness of the public to accept the authority of the criminal court as a dispenser of punishment depends on the extent to which the public believes in the moral legitimacy of the system. The morality or fairness of a system of adjudication hinges on many factors, such as the impartiality and incorruptibility of the judiciary. Amongst these must also be numbered a publicly acceptable judicial attitude towards breaches of the law. A judicial community that is seen to condone, or even encourage, violations of the law can hardly demand compliance with its own edicts.[3]

Generally speaking, it is practical to dissociate the admissibility of evidence from its legality where incidents of illegality are not recurrent or where they emanate from individuals whose actions do not reflect on the judicial institution as a whole.[4] Criminal judges last century may even have been right when they divorced admissibility from illegality, so long as they felt that the trial process was so detached from the police investigation as to be insulated from any illegalities that occurred in police stations.[5] However, today the investigative process is seen as *part* of the administration of justice which is why the debate regarding illegally-obtained evidence has assumed such importance.[6]

The moral dimension is not the only distinguishing feature of the criminal trial. The public demands satisfaction of its sense of being protected from crime as well as of its moral sentiment. Suppose that evidence conclusively implicating the accused in murder has been obtained by illegal means. If the court turns up its nose at the illegality and excludes the evidence, the public would feel that the court has betrayed its duty to protect the community from crime.[7]

There is an uncanny symmetry between the consequences of an admissibility and an inadmissibility rule. If applied consistently, each of these rules will undermine public confidence in the criminal process. If the court always admits illegally-obtained evidence, it will be seen to condone the malpractice of the law enforcement agencies. If it always excludes it, it will be seen to abandon its duty to protect us from crime. The first thing that we must therefore accept is that the criminal trial presents a dilemma which cannot be solved by an inflexible rule. An unwillingness to grasp the intractability of this dilemma has contributed more than anything else to the backwardness of the law on illegally-obtained evidence.

The second cause of this backwardness lies in a failure to appreciate that any attempt to solve the dilemma must take into account the law in related areas. Granted that we cannot do without some exclusionary jurisdiction, two theoretical bases for the jurisdiction are current. The first is the vindication or remedial theory holding that the object of an exclusionary rule is to vindicate the accused for the infringement of his rights. The second is the deterrent theory, suggesting that the object of exclusion is to deter the law enforcement agencies from future abuses. I shall deal with each of these in turn.

A person has a right not to have his person and premises illegally searched, not to have his possessions illegally seized and not to be unlawfully arrested. It is suggested that by imposing these restrictions the state has staked out the boundaries for lawful access to evidence and has indicated that beyond these limits it is *willing* to forego evidence of crime in *defence* to individual freedom.[8] Consequently, it is said, exclusion of evidence secured through illegal search, seizure and arrest puts the prosecution in the position where the constitution, or the legislature, meant to put it when it imposed those restrictions: without the evidence.

This argument ignores a crucial factor in the circumstances that we are considering. The evidence has been obtained, is now available and does tend to prove the accused's guilt. In devising the powers of search and seizure the lawmaker laid down that an individual, who must be presumed innocent, should not be disturbed without probable cause. Here, whether we like it or not, we are no longer concerned with the question of whether we should disturb an individual against whom there is no probable cause but with the question of whether a person, in relation to whom evidence of guilt is now available, should be treated as if there were no increased probability of his guilt. The increased probability of guilt creates the need to protect the public from the crime, which makes a return to the *status quo ante* rather awkward.

The perception of the problem as purely one of admissibility of evidence at the trial has diverted attention from other areas in which a similar conflict of interests and rights takes place. If we look beyond the confines of the law of evidence we discover that the situation of *ex post facto* calculation is quite normal in relation to civil liberties. The Police and Criminal Evidence Act 1984, s.24(5), lays down:

> "Where an arrestable offence has been committed, any person may arrest without warrant—(a) anyone who is guilty of the offence; (b) anyone whom he has reasonable grounds for suspecting to be guilty of it."

This means that an otherwise groundless arrest is excused if it should turn out that the arrested person has in fact committed an arrestable offence.[9] This constitutes a choice of policy about the protection of civil liberties. A similar choice was made in relation to seizure when Horridge J. held that:

> " . . . the interests of the State must excuse the seizure of documents, which seizure would otherwise be unlawful, if it appears in fact that such documents were evidence of a crime committed by anyone . . . "[10]

Moreover, in the fight against crime our institutions are prepared at times to forgive a lesser crime in order to punish a more serious one, as the practice of immunity given to state witnesses shows.

If we then turn to the law of tort we find that there too the tension between legality and just deserts has been resolved, to some extent, in favour of the latter. Under the American Civil Rights Act a person may sue for damages for infringement of his constitutional rights.[11] However, if as a result of an infringement of rights, evidence is found that leads to the aggrieved person's conviction, that person loses his claim. The reason given is that immunity from action will encourage bolder and more efficient police action in combating crime.[12] While there is no direct English authority on the point, it is difficult to believe that, in practice, the guilty would secure any better remedies under English tort law.[13]

It would be odd if the consideration of *ex post facto* guilt were completely absent from the law of evidence when it is so potent in the law of arrest, search and seizure and in the law of tort. Yet the law of evidence would have to be completely insulated from such considerations if the vindication theory were to sustain the general exclusion of illegally-obtained evidence. It is said in support of this theory that exclusion is a necessary remedy because tort remedies are unlikely to be taken seriously by the civil courts who would have little sympathy for convicted plaintiffs.[14] However, the practical preferences that prevent an effective civil remedy cannot be neutralised merely because we deal with a question of exclusion rather than one of damages.

Furthermore, the vindication theory runs up against the difficulty of maintaining a satisfactory balance between illegality and its remedy. In a criminal trial exclusion of evidence of guilt amounts to a contribution towards the acquittal of a person who may be guilty. It is by no means self-evident that acquittal of the guilty is an appropriate response to earlier police transgressions. Nor is a blanket exclusion capable of achieving a balance between the seriousness of the infringement and the benefit to the accused.[15]

Given these difficulties, the justification for the exclusion of illegally-obtained evidence shifts to the second theory: the argument that exclusion is necessary not so much to vindicate the accused, as to deter the police from unauthorised searches and thus protect the peace and privacy of individuals against whom there is no probable cause.[16] Quite apart from the question of efficiency this strategy suffers from a prominent weakness because it flies in the face of the general willingness, that I have just illustrated, to detract from constitutional liberties in order to further crime control. In the absence of widespread resentment of the police, citizens are unlikely to feel that they require protection from the police by means which let guilty persons go free.[17]

From a practical point of view there are a number of reasons for doubting whether a general exclusionary rule would have significant deterrent effects.[18] First, police officers are subject to influences that may well outweigh the sanction of exclusion; *e.g.* considerations of personal safety, the expectations of peers and supervisors and public pressure to apprehend offenders. Secondly, the violation of search rules would involve, at most, exclusion at some distant date and is therefore unlikely to constitute a serious break on illegal searches.[19] Thirdly, even if officers were inclined to comply, it may be that the provisions of the search and seizure rules are not communicated to them effectively enough to secure compliance. Finally, if objections to unauthorised search turn out to be rare, or if police officers stand a good chance of concealing the breaches, the efficacy of an exclusion rule as a deterrent will be limited.

The manifest weaknesses of a pure vindication theory and of a pure deterrent one in justifying a rule of exclusion, and the shortcomings of an inclusionary rule, leave us with only one possible policy to pursue, that of safeguarding the judicial process against the undesirable consequences of an absolute commitment to either exclusion or inclusion.[20] I shall refer to this as the principle of judicial integrity or the principle of legitimacy.[21] This principle has been criticised for lack of clarity.[22] It is, however, a mistake to assume that because individual decisions cannot be derived mechanically from rules the principle has no guiding force. The social need to balance two conflicting constitutional requirements is in itself a powerful engine. Indeed, it is important that the courts should be seen to exercise a balancing jurisdiction, for this will inform the public of the difficulty of choosing between admissibility and inadmissibility and will secure support even from those who might have preferred a different result in an individual case.

That this is the direction in which a solution should be sought is demonstrated by the recent fluctuation of the American law and the clamour for discretion in the Commonwealth.[22a]

By 1961 the old rule of universal admissibility was completely replaced in the United States by a new rule of universal exclusion.[23] Within a decade the United States Supreme Court began to appreciate that total exclusion was socially unacceptable and ever since then the Supreme Court has been searching for ways to limit the scope of the exclusionary rule.[24] Contemporary American decisions indicate that both the remedial and deterrent policies have a part to play in the judicial strategy. The remedial idea may be seen at work in decisions holding that the exclusionary rule does not apply in situations where search and seizure violations were directed against a third party and not the accused.[25] At the same time the American courts have distanced themselves from any commitment to the idea that exclusion is a remedy to which the accused is entitled as a matter of right.[26] Simultaneously considerations of deterrence brought about the principle that exclusion is appropriate only where it is likely to lead, in the long run, to some incremental deterrence.[27]

The legitimacy principle has found its clearest statement in the new Canadian Constitution which provides:

> "Where . . . a court concludes that evidence was obtained in a manner that infringed or denied any rights or freedoms guaranteed by this Charter, the evidence shall be excluded if it is established that, [having regard to all the circumstances,] the admission of it in the proceedings would bring the administration of justice into disrepute."[28]

Even in England there was a last minute addition to the Police and Criminal Evidence Act 1984 on this subject. Section 78 empowers the court to exclude prosecution evidence if its admission "would have such an adverse effect on the fairness of the proceedings that the court ought not to admit it." Unfortunately, the notion of "fairness" is unhelpful since it can refer to a multitude of aspects and merely furnishes an excuse for achieving whatever result is wanted without rigorous justification. Worse still, the record of the English judiciary leaves little hope that this jurisdiction will be exercised to advantage.

This state of affairs is the result of a legal methodology, fast becoming the exclusive preserve of the English profession, according to which major problems of principle receive the kind of treatment that is more appropriate to the interpretation of technical tax provisions. *Sang*[29] is a case in point. On the issue of exclusionary discretion five Law Lords devoted their energies to reconciling dicta in previous cases, while leaving untouched the questions of principle: should there be discretion and, if so, what role might it fulfill? In the event the decision only succeeded in throwing doubt on the very existence of discretion.[30] Given the rudimentary discussion of these questions it is not surprising that subsequent case law has been equally unsatisfactory.

The most recent House of Lords pronouncement is to be found in *Fox* v. *Chief Constable of Gwent*.[31] On finding a car at the scene of an accident, the police unlawfully entered the driver's house and asked him to provide a specimen of breath. When the accused refused, he was arrested and taken to a police station where he was made to provide a breath specimen which showed that the amount of alcohol in his breath exceeded the prescribed limit. The accused was convicted, first, of failing to provide a breath specimen contrary to the Road Traffic Act 1972, s.7(4), and, second, of driving with excess alcohol contrary to s.6(1) of the same Act.

The first conviction was quashed because, according to *Morris* v. *Beardmore*,[32] as trespassers, the police could not make a legally valid request for a breath specimen. Against the second conviction the accused argued that, since the specimen had been obtained as a result of a wrongful arrest, it should have been excluded as matter of discretion. Rejecting this argument Lord Fraser said:

> " . . . the Divisional Court was . . . right in treating the fact that the appellant was in the police station because he had been unlawfully arrested merely as a historical fact, with which the court was not concerned. The duty of the court is to decide whether the appellant has committed the offence with which he is charged, and not to discipline the police for exceeding their powers. I note in passing that there were several reasons any one of which might have accounted for the appellant's being in the police station perfectly lawfully. He might have been there because he had been lawfully arrested. Or he might have gone there voluntarily etc."[33]

This extraordinary reasoning bodes ill for the section 78 jurisdiction; if followed, hardly any evidence would be excludable because it would almost always be possible to postulate hypothetical circumstances in which the evidence could have been obtained otherwise than by the impropriety in question.[34] Turning a blind eye to proven acts of illegality and pretending that the evidence might have been obtained with propriety is unlikely to enhance respect for the administration of justice.

There was nevertheless a glimmer of appreciation of the problem when Lord Fraser remarked that:

"Of course, if the appellant had been lured to the police station by some trick or deception, or if the police officers had behaved oppressively towards the appellant, the justices' jurisdiction to exclude otherwise admissible evidence . . . might have come into play."[35]

Yet the terms used here are not self-explanatory and one might wish to know why, if the accused was made to go to the police station by being falsely told that he was under lawful arrest, this did not amount to a trick, or a deception? Similarly, why does not false imprisonment amount to oppression? These were the real issues in the case, but they went unanswered.[36]

Courts in the United States of America, Australia, Canada and other common law jurisdictions are by contrast addressing themselves to the very issues that our courts decline to take seriously. Much can be learnt from their decisions.[37] The High Court of Australia, for instance, has been developing an exclusionary theory by setting out the type of considerations that have to be taken into account.[38] They include the following: whether the transgression was mistaken or intentional, whether the illegality affected the probative value of the evidence, the ease with which the law might have been complied with in order to obtain the evidence and the nature of the offence charged.[39]

It would be wrong to claim that these considerations present simple choices. Indeed, some of them point at once in different directions. On the one hand, it could be said that if an officer acted under a mistaken belief in the lawfulness of his action, the reception of the evidence would not undermine legitimacy since the court would not be perceived as condoning intentional violations of legality. Nor, it could be argued, is exclusion necessary for deterrence since an innocent officer would not be deterred by the knowledge that illegality may result in exclusion. But the opposite case could also be made, for if ignorance were to excuse infringement of individual rights, the police would have no incentive to inform officers of the limits of their powers.[40]

A similar ambiguity is involved in the consideration that the evidence could have been lawfully secured. It might be said that, since the evidence could have been obtained in any event, the accused has not lost much by the illegality; but if this is accepted, the police would have no incentive to conform with the legal requirements.

The consideration relating to the seriousness of the offence might also be a source of conflicting conclusions. On the one hand, the more serious the offence, the more difficult it is to justify exclusion and thereby risk acquittal of a guilty and possibly dangerous person. On the other hand, the more serious the consequences of conviction the higher should be the moral rectitude of the means by which it is achieved.

This takes us back to Wigmore's objection, mentioned at the outset. How, it may be asked, can the trial judge be expected to address difficult questions of policy while having to conduct criminal proceedings efficiently and expeditiously? It must be realised from the outset that an exclusionary jurisdiction cannot have satisfactory results without a willingness on the part of the superior courts to develop suitable principles. Once policies and priorities have been clarified by these courts, the jurisdiction would be exercisable along well charted paths. Yet we must not delude ourselves into believing, as do those seekers after rule-based solutions, that in this area policy can be satisfactorily shaped once and for all. A defensible attitude towards illegality requires the continuing development of the legal and moral limits of police investigation.

This brings out the most salutary aspect of the jurisdiction: the subjection of police practices to judicial scrutiny. A jurisdiction to exclude illegally-obtained evidence makes investigative practices subject to judicial scrutiny in much the same way as other executive activities. Indeed, the very fact of scrutiny is as important as decisions on individual instance of admissibility because the existence of judicial scrutiny gives public notice that the police are not above the law. Moreover, it brings out the constitutional dimension involved and advances its development.[41] The concept of reasonableness, for instance, is fundamental in defining the constitutional powers of search, seizure and arrest. The same parameters have important implications to the admissibility of evidence. The admissibility stage seems particularly suitable for dealing with the constitutional issues involved here because it makes scrutiny much more likely than it would be if the matter were left to the sidelines of civil litigation.[42]

Since an adequate exclusionary theory will have to be worked out by courts and commentators over a period, I do not propose to embark here on a comprehensive discussion of its elements, except to draw attention to a number of tricky points.

First, the exclusionary jurisdiction will have to concern itself with violations of moral standards, as well as with those of express legal prohibitions, and the superior courts will have to develop criteria to identify those police measures that are considered morally unacceptable. English courts have decided, for instance, that evidence obtained by an agent provocateur is not excludable.[43] In America the Supreme Court devoted much thought to evidence obtained by means of surreptitious listening devices and other infringements of privacy.[44] But the theory of immorality is still very rudimentary and much more has to be done.

Secondly, a warning needs to be sounded about the burden of proof in the present context. It sometimes happens that an impossible burden is imposed on a party in order to resolve the issue against that party without seeming to do so.[45] This might happen here if it were held, for instance, that an accused objecting to illegally-obtained evidence must prove that the police make a practice of conducting unlawful searches.[46] Since the object of the jurisdiction is to seek justification from the law enforcement agencies for their practices it should be for them to satisfy the courts.[47]

A third and related point concerns the distinction between what is and what is not provable. We have seen that in formulating guiding principles the courts will have to have regard to the consequences of their decisions. Sometimes these consequences will be empirically discoverable, but not always. If the courts adopt a vigorous policy of exclusion because of widespread transgressions by the police, prosecuting authorities should be free to show that the bad practices have ceased. But considerations such as the likely effect of admissibility or inadmissibility on public sentiment are not capable of proof in the ordinary sense.[48] In relation to such issues the courts will have to make a judgment that combines social and moral considerations. They will have to consider what, in a society with high moral standards, should be the public reaction to institutional violations. In other words, decisions will be taken by reference to a normative model as well as a factual one.

The reader who accepts my criticism of inflexible admissibility and inadmissibility rules and who is persuaded by my criticism of the deterrent and vindication theories may still remain sceptical about the benefits of the discretionary jurisdiction which I have argued is necessary. He may feel that this jurisdiction is too tortuous and indirect a method for securing our social and constitutional goals. These are, as will have become clear, to deter the police from infringing our constitutional rights, to compensate individuals whose rights have been infringed adequately (especially when they are innocent) and, lastly, to convict the guilty. It has been suggested that it would be more effective to attempt to achieve each of these goals by independent steps.[49] First, it is said, we could set up an effective disciplinary court, under judicial supervision, to try and punish infringements of individual rights by the police. Secondly, the law could explicitly provide for compensation in respect of such infringements and establish a cheap and easy procedure that would encourage aggrieved persons to sue. These two measures, it is suggested, would make any further action during the criminal trial redundant; evidence will be admissible and the guilty punished.

I doubt that independent procedural devices of this kind could avoid the need for developing constitutional mechanisms for dealing with the ubiquitous conflict between individual rights and community's interest in the protection from crime. A disciplinary court would still have to devise an adequate compromise to this conflict and to draw an imperfect line between failure to comply strictly with the rules and unacceptable conduct.[50] Furthermore, since we want to prevent not only violations of explicit rules but also immoral methods of investigation, a disciplinary court would still have to evolve a normative theory of police behaviour. Similarly, compensatory civil procedures would have to have regard to the normative problems that now beset admissibility. It is unlikely that a substantive law of damages could solve these problems at a stroke, as the American case law on civil rights violations shows.[51]

I am not suggesting that present disciplinary procedures could not be improved. Nor am I saying that civil remedies are satisfactory at the moment. Much can be improved, quite apart from the question of illegal police action. For instance, if the police detain the goods of an innocent person on reasonable suspicion that they were stolen, the lawfulness of the detention prevents the owner from obtaining compensation.[52] While police action in such circumstances may be supported, it does not follow that the loss should fall on the individual rather than be borne by the public.[53] However, I do not think that improvements in these respects could possibly obviate the need for developing criteria of legitimacy.

The tension between strict observance of constitutional rights and the protection from crime is ever present and there are only two alternative approaches for reaching a compromise. One is to sweep manifestations of police transgression under the carpet. In a moment of candour Lord Denning hinted at this strategy when, commenting on the law as it then stood, he said:

> "No magistrate . . . has the power to issue a search warrant for murder. . . . The police have to get the consent of the house holder to enter if they can; or, if not, to do it by stealth or by force. Somehow they seem to manage. No decent person refuses them permission. If he does, he is probably implicated in some way or other. So the police risk an action for trespass. It is not much risk."[54]

The trouble with this method is that in the long run it is likely to cast doubt on the impartiality of the judiciary. If a compromise has to be found it is better to do so in a publicly accountable fashion rather than by wink and nod. The other alternative is, therefore, to bring into the open the conflict and develop a suitable constitutional theory for underpinning the legitimacy of the administration of justice. This is the course taken by most Anglo-American systems and sooner or later English law will have to follow.

Notes

[1] *R.* v. *Leatham* (1861) 8 Cox C.C. 498. *Wigmore on Evidence* (3rd ed., 1940), vol. 8, s.2183.

[2] *Wigmore on Evidence*, (3rd ed., 1940), vol. 8 s.2183, p. 5. See also quotation from *Fox* v. *Chief Constable of Gwent* [1985] 1 W.L.R. 1133 referred to in n. 33 below, where the English version of the same argument takes the simpler form that it is not the courts' function to discipline the police.

[3] Holmes and Brandeis stressed this in their dissenting judgment in *Olmstead* v. *U.S.* 277 U.S. 438, 484–485 (1928): "Our government is the potent, the omnipresent teacher. For good or for ill, it teaches . . . by its example . . . If the government becomes a law breaker, it breeds contempt for law; it invites every man to become a law unto himself; it invites anarchy." The need to keep a distance from illegitimate activities has produced an entire body of law in relation to illegal contracts.

[4] It is thus possible to justify the admissibility of illegally-obtained evidence in civil litigation, where the transgressors are private citizens. See *Calcraft* v. *Guest* [1898] 1 Q.B. 758; *Ashburton* v. *Pape* [1913] 2 Ch. 466. Even in civil proceedings the illegality of the means is not always kept out of consideration; *e.g.* in relation to illegal contracts.

[5] *Warwickshall* (1783) 1 Leach 263; *Griffin* (1809) Russ & Ry 151; *Gould* (1840) 9 C. & P. 364; *Leatham* (1861) 8 Cox C.C. 498; *Berriman* (1864) 6 Cox C.C. 388. By 1955 even Lord Goddard C.J. felt obliged to make some concession to this consideration when he declared the existence of a judicial discretion to exclude otherwise admissible evidence where it would "operate unfairly against the accused"; *Kuruma* v. *R.* [1955] A.C. 197 at p. 204. Justice Brennan has recently observed that " . . . by admitting unlawfully seized evidence, the judiciary becomes a party of what is in fact a single governmental action . . . " *U.S.* v. *Leon* 104 S.C.T. 3430, 3432 (1984).

[6] See the Police and Criminal Evidence Act 1984, s.78. The American Supreme Court held that the Fourteenth Amendment provides protection only against "the activities of sovereign authority"; *Burdeau* v. *McDowell* 256 U.S. 465 (1921); *Walter* v. *U.S.* 447 U.S. 649 (1980). Problems of illegality could of course arise in civil cases but there they are of a different dimension and I do not propose to deal with them here.

[7] As Mellor J. observed: "It would be a dangerous obstacle to the administration of justice if we were to hold, because evidence was obtained by illegal means, it could not be used against a party charged with an offence." *Jones* v. *Owen* (1870) 34 J.P. 759.

[8] Loewy, *The Warren Court as Defender of State and Federal Criminal Law etc.*, 37 Geo.Wash.L.Rev. 1218, 1236 (1969). See also dissent of Justice Brennan in *U.S.* v. *Leon* 104 S.Ct. 3430, 3431–6 (1984).

[9] Similarly, under s.24(4), (7).

[10] *Elias* v. *Pasmore* [1934] 2 K.B. 164, 173. It was criticised by Lord Denning in *Ghani* v. *Jones* [1969] 3 All E.R. 1700, 1703, but the same sentiment was present in Lord Denning's own judgment. See also Lord MacDermott C.J.'s dictum in *Murphy* [1965] N.I. 138, 187–8: "The appellant was . . . a serious security risk; this was revealed by the trick of misrepresentation practiced by the police . . . and no other way of obtaining this revelation has been demonstrated or suggested."

[11] 42 U.S.C.A. s.1983.

[12] *Pouncey* v. *Ryan* 396 F.Supp. 126 (1975); Harper and James, *The Law of Torts* (1956), s.4.12, p. 347. Alternatively, a conviction could reduce the damges: *Long* v. *Mann* 65 So.(2d) 500 (1953); *Massantonio* v. *People* 236 P. 1019 (1925).

[13] See L. Lustgarten, *The Governance of the Police* (1986), pp. 133–4, 138.

[14] For American discussion see: *Bivens* v. *Six Unknown Named Agents of Federal Bureau of Narcotics* 403 U.S. 388, 421–2 (1971); Comment, "The Tort Alternative to the Exclusionary Rule" 63 J.Crim.L., C. & P.S. 256 (1972); Foote, "Tort Remedies for Police Violations of Individual Rights 39 Minn.L.R. 493 (1955); Plumb, "Illegal Enforcement of the Law" 24 Cornell.L.Q. 337, 385–91 (1939); Loewy, "The Fourth Amendment as Device for Protecting the Innocent" 81 Mich.L.R. 1229, 1265–6 (1983). Loewy also makes the point that if the civil remedy is taken seriously it might deter policeman from pursuing legal searches in cases where legality might be controversial or where the crime seems to them not serious enough to justify the risk of civil litigation. For the position in Australia see Australian Law Reform commission, Rep. No. 2 Criminal Investigation, (1975), paras. 287–302; and in Canada, Oakes, "Studying the Exclusionary Rule in Search and Seizure" 37 U.Chi.L.R. 665, 701–6 (1970). See also Lustgarten, n. 13, p. 135 n. 33.

[15] As Chief Justice Burger said, " . . . society has [at least as much] a right to expect rationally graded responses from judges in place of the universal 'capital punishment' we inflict on all evidence when police error is shown in its acquisition." *Bivens* v. *Six Unknown Named Agents* 403 U.S. 388, 419 (1971).

[16] R. B. Dworkin, "Fact Style Adjudication and the Forth Amendment etc" 48 Indiana L.J. 329 (1973).

[17] The situation is somewhat analagous to the enforcement of the privilege against-self incrimination; the innocent do not feel particularly disturbed by breaches because they are unlikely to wish to refuse to co-operate with interrogation.

[18] For a thorough examination of the deterrent argument in theory and in practice see: Oaks, "Studying the Exclusionary Rule in Search and Seizure." 36 Univ. of Chi.L.R. 665 (1970).

[19] Besides, the gathering of admissible evidence may not be a paramount objective in violating the search rules.

[20] In the U.S. the argument from judicial integrity is some times used as providing support for an absolute exclusionary rule. I am not using it in that way.

[21] It should be noted that the appeal to judicial integrity has been used in the United States as a justification for a strict exclusionary rule. My argument takes a different form and the use of the term "legitimacy" will perhaps cause less confusion.

[22] *McCormick on Evidence* (3rd ed., 1984), p. 462. See also *Stone* v. *Powell* 428 U.S. 465, 485 (1976). Judicial integrity has even been equated with deterrence: *Janis* v. *U.S.* 428 U.S. 874, 458 n (1976).

[22a] The problem of illegally obtained evidence is not confined to the common law systems. For a survey of the position in the major European legal systems see: W. Pakter, "Eclusionary rules in France, Germany, and Italy", in *Hastings International and Comparative Law Rev.* 1 (1985).

[23] In the landmark decision of *Mapp* v. *Ohio* 367 U.S. 643 (1961) the Supreme Court ruled that all evidence obtained by illegal searches and seizures was inadmissible in a criminal trial. The origins of the rule are in *Weeks* v. *U.S.* 232 U.S. 383

(1914). The rule applies to illegalities involving violation of the Federal Constitution, mainly violation of the Fourth Amendment which provides: "The right of people to be secure in their persons, houses, papers, and effects, against unreasonable searches and seizures, shall not be violated, and no warrants shall issue, but upon probable cause, supported by oath or affirmation, and particularly describing the place to be searched, and the persons or things to be seized."

²⁴ Justice Cardozo foresaw this development back in 1926 in *People* v. *Defore* 242 N.Y. 13, 150 N.E. 585. The exclusionary rule has been cut down by decisions to sanction exclusion only where the benefit, in greater future observance of legality by the police, outweighs the disadvantage of loss of relevant evidence; *McCormick on Evidence* (3rd ed., 1984), p. 465. It has been held, for example, that the exclusion of illegally-obtained evidence would not provide sufficient incremental benefit where the evidence is merely used for impeaching an accused who is giving evidence; *Harris* v. *New York* 401 U.S. 222 (1971). For similar reasons it has been decided that the exclusionary rule does not apply to grand jury proceedings; *Calandra* v. *U.S.* 338 (1974); or in situations where the police made an excusable mistake about the legality of search or seizure; *U.S.* v. *Leon* 104 S.Ct. 3405 (1984). Finally, the court has categorically stated that "an assessment of the flagrancy of the police misconduct constitutes an important step in the calculus," and that "suppression of evidence obtained pursuant to a warrant should be ordered only on a case-by-case basis and only in those unusual cases in which exclusion will further the purposes of the exclusionary rule." *U.S.* v. *Leon* 104 S.Ct. 3405, 3415, 3419 (1984).

²⁵ *McCormick on Evidence* (3rd ed., 1984), 514.

²⁶ *Elkins* v. *U.S.* 364 U.S. 206 (1960); Notes, 12 Am.Crim.L.R. 507, 508–10 (1975).

²⁷ For instance, it has been held that little will be gained from excluding illegally-obtained evidence used by the prosecution solely for the purpose of impeachment and such evidence is therefore admissible: *Harris* v. *NY* 401 U.S. 222 (1971). See also n. 24 above.

²⁸ Constitution Act 1982, s.24(2). Armed with this jurisdiction the Supreme Court lost no time in discarding the old common law doctrine that was embodied in *R.* v. *Wray* [1971] S.C.R. 272, 11 D.L.R. (3d) 673, and began to evolve principles for the exercise of discretion: *Rotham* v. *R.* (1981) 59 C.C.C. (2d) 30; *R* v. *Therens* [1985] 4 W.W.R. 286. See review by McCrimmon, 8 Supreme Court L.R.

²⁹ [1980] A.C. 402.

³⁰ See Polyviou, "Illegally-obtained evidence and *R.* v. *Sang*" in *Crime Proof and Punishment*, Tapper, ed., 1981), 175.

³¹ [1985] 1 W.L.R. 1126 decided before s.78 came into force.

³² [1981] A.C. 446.

³³ [1985] 1 W.L.R. 1126 at p. 1132.

³⁴ Why not, after all, also draw a "historical" divide between the police entry and their subsequent request and thus uphold their initial request as valid? Indeed, that was the very point that the House of Lords in *Morris* v. *Beardmore* refused to accept. There the prosecution tried to draw a veil between the constables' entry as trespassers and their request for the specimen, claiming that the former was a fact of the past leaving the subsequent request unaffected. Rejecting this approach Lord Diplock said: "I find it quite impossible to suppose that Parliament intended that a person whose common law right to keep his home free from unauthorised intruders had been violated in this way should be bound under penal sanctions to comply with a demand which only the violation of that common law right had enabled the constable to make to him." [1981] A.C. 446 at p. 456.

³⁵ [1985] 1 W.L.R. at p. 1133.

³⁶ There is a serious risk that the new exclusionary jurisdiction will suffer the fate of the discretion to exclude confessions which proved negligible. Although the

Judges' Rules were designed to protect the privilege against self-incrimination, English judges hardly ever exercised their discretion to exclude confessions obtained in clear violation of the rules. This has been due, as I have explained elsewhere, to the moral weakness of the privilege ("The right against self-incrimination: an obstacle to the supervision of interrogation." (1986) 102 L.Q.R. 43). By contrast, the rights, such as the right to privacy and security in the home and the right not to be degraded by those in power, which are threatened by illegal search, seizure and arrest are indisputably important rights.

[37] *Welsh* v. *Wisconsin* 104 S.Ct. 2091 (1984), which deals with a situation identical to that of *Fox* v. *Chief Constable of Gwent*, stands in stark contrast to the English decision. The American Supreme Court showed no reluctance to face the real point of difficulty: the conflict between the right to privacy in one's own home and the public interest in being protected from drunken drivers.

[38] *Bunning* v. *Cross* (1977) 141 D.L.R. 54 78–80. See also J. Hunter, "Tainted Proceedings: Censuring Police Illegalities" (1985) 59 Australian L.J. 709.

[39] In Canada too the courts have been refining the balancing strategy; *R.* v. *Therens* [1985] 4 W.W.R. 286.

[40] A premium will thereby be placed on the ignorance of the police officer, as the McDonald Report in Canada pointed out; Commission of Inquiry Concerning Certain Activities of the Royal Canadian Mounted Police. Second Report: Freedom and Security Under the Law, 1981, 1046. See also Kaplan, *op. cit.*, 26 Stan.L.R. 1027, 1044.

[41] By its very nature, scrutiny has to be continually asserted and its principles periodically reviewed in response to institutional and social changes. As Justice Blackmum observed in *U.S.* v. *Leon* 104 S.Ct. 3405, 3424: " . . . the scope of the exclusionary rule is subject to change in the light of changing judicial understanding about the effects of the rule outside the confines of the courtroom."

[42] Lustgarten, n. 13, 145–6.

[43] *Sang* [1980] A.C. 402. Though one suspects that it would be as difficult to maintain unconditional admissibility here as it is in relation to other kinds of questionable methods.

[44] See *Katz* v. *U.S.* 389 U.S. 347 (1967); *U.S.* v. *Karo* 104 S.Ct. 3296 (1984) and discussion in *McCormick on Evidence* (3rd ed., 1984), 466–472.

[45] *e.g.*, according *Air Canada* v. *Secretary of State for Trade (No. 2)* [1983] 2 A.C. 394, where the government claims public interest immunity in respect of relevant documents in its possession, the courts will not inspect them unless the litigant seeking disclosure proves that they can materially help his case. Since the documents are in the government's hands the litigant is not in a position to prove their content and this rule effectively denies discovery. See [1983] All E.R.R. 205.

[46] *Cf. U.S.* v. *Leon* 104 S.Ct. 3430, 3437–8.

[47] The original proposal for the Police and Criminal Evidence Act 1984, s.78, imposed an onus on the prosecution to justify admissibility of illegally-obtained evidence. Lustgarten, n. 13, at p. 145.

[48] *Cf.* McCrimmon, "Developments in the law of evidence: the 1984–85 Term." 8 Supreme Court L.R.Z.Z.Z.; *U.S.* v. *Leon* 104 S.Ct. 3430, 3437.

[49] See S. R. Schlesinger, *Exclusionary Injustice* (New York, 1977.)

[50] Justice Renquist observed in *Michigan* v. *Tucker* 417 U.S. 433, 446 (1974): "Just as the law does not require that a defendant receive a perfect trial, only a fair one, it cannot realistically require that a policeman investigating serious crimes make no errors whatsoever. The pressure of law enforcement and the vagaries of human nature would make such an expectation unrealistic. Before we penalize police errors, therefore, we must consider whether the sanction serves a valid and useful purpose." See also *Scheurer* v. *Rohdes* 41 U.S. 232, 241–2 (1974), *per* Chief Justice Burger.

[51] See n. 12 above. It is to be noted that a compensatory jurisdiction already exists in English law. An aggrieved person can sue for trespass to person or property and may even be able to obtain exemplary damages. See *George* v. *Metropolitan Police Commissioner The Times*, March 31, 1984; *Connor* v. *Chief Constable of Cambridgshire, The Times*, April 11, 1984.

[52] *Chic Fashions* v. *Jones* [1968] 2 Q.B. 299.

[53] See Weir [1968] C.L.J. 193, 195.

[54] In *Ghani* v. *Jones* [1970] 1 Q.B. 693, at p. 705. Today a magistrate may issue a search warrant in the circumstances described: Police and Criminal Evidence Act 1984, s.8.

Benefit, Reliance and the Structure of Unjust Enrichment

J. BEATSON[1]

I. Introduction

There is a danger that we tend to overuse our favourite concepts, particularly once we have left the familiar territory of contract and tort. For restitution lawyers (including myself[2]) the temptation is artificially to enlarge the category of obligations which are based on the defendant's unjust enrichment at the expense of the plaintiff by an overinclusive concept of enrichment. Restitution scholars have encouraged a broad approach to "enrichment" and argued that the subject's boundaries should be limited by the grounds of relief (the question of 'unjustness') and the meaning of 'at the expense of."[3] One consequence of a broad approach to enrichment may be to marginalize the concept of "reliance."[4] It is perhaps no accident that neither of the English books on Restitution[5] refers to "reliance" in the index. In so far as reliance is considered in the text it is treated as a factor in the determination of whether something is enriching and, if so, whether it is "at the expense of" the intervener/plaintiff. In effect reliance is treated as a sub-category of enrichment.

There is, however, an equal tendency on the part of others less enthusiastic about restitution to marginalize the role of "unjust enrichment' as a source of obligations. This is either done by reintegrating part of quasi-contract into a new broad conception of contract[6] or by emphasising reliance as a source of obligation. Under the second, the fact that a plaintiff has relied on a defendant's words or conduct (especially where the reliance is detrimental) justifies imposing an obligation whether or not the defendant has gained a benefit or an enrichment. The restitution interest, where such a benefit or enrichment is gained is, on this approach, treated as a sub-category of the reliance interest. The classic example of such reasoning is Fuller and Purdue's seminal article on the reliance interest where it is said that: " . . . all of the cases coming under the restitution interest will be covered by the reliance interest."[7] Even Professor Atiyah, who accepts that the trend in modern law is to recognise benefit based obligations,

71

appears to question the theoretical case for treating benefit as a source of obligation unless there has also been reliance.[8]

In other words the danger is that either reliance is made a sub-category of benefit/enrichment, or that benefit/enrichment is made a sub-category of reliance. Both may marginalize obligations based on "consent." My purpose is to question the first type of reductionism which is present in both the English books on Restitution:[9] I shall also seek to indicate how one might map out the appropriate territory for the concepts of "enrichment," "reliance" and "consent." I do this with some trepidation because, although present in Goff and Jones, this form of reductionism is most clearly evident in the important and illuminating contribution to our understanding of restitution by Professor Birks who, first as a teacher and later as a colleague, stimulated my interest in the subject, and the foundations of whose book are to be found in six contributions to this series.[10] The question is not a new one. Thus, Fuller and Purdue point out that:

> "The inescapable flexibility of the concept 'benefit' means that drawing the line between the reliance and the restitution interests is in the end rather an arbitrary affair. By substituting for 'benefit' a stricter term like 'enrichment' we shift the line in one direction; by substituting a looser term like 'performance received by the promisor' we shift it in the other."[11]

My concern is with services and the extent to which remedies given in respect of services rendered or received should be seen as based on the unjust enrichment of the defendant. Services may take a number of forms;

(i) those that *result* in improvements to property or in a marketable residuum in the hands of the defendant;

(ii) those where, although there is no marketable residuum, a necessary expense of the defendant is anticipated or avoided[12] (as where a debt is paid or other obligation met by the plaintiff);

(iii) those with no marketable residuum in the hands of the recipient but an increase in his human capital (as where a teacher gives a lesson to an able pupil),[13] and;

(iv) those where there is neither marketable residuum nor increase in human capital (as where an actor or a musician performs his art or where the teacher's lesson falls on deaf ears).

I shall concentrate on (iii) and (iv) which are forms of "pure" service. Both Birks and Goff and Jones treat certain pure services as within the category of enrichment. According to Birks the function of conceptual analysis, definition and differentiation is to reveal the skeleton of principle which holds a subject together.[14] Once this is done it can be subjected to critical review and the complex adjustments and refinements which are an inevitable feature of a mature legal subject. "The key [he says] is a sensible balance between conceptual purity and convenience."[15] Is the treatment of services justified by these criteria? I hope that what follows will not be dismissed as an arid exercise in categorisation for it is my belief, as I shall illustrate, that there are important practical consequences for the types of rules adopted, the arguments that will be relevant in a given case and the relationship of obligations in respect of services with rules of contract and tort law.

But the theory comes first. At the outset something needs to be said about two relationships; that between "restitution" and "unjust enrichment" and that between "restitution"/"unjust enrichment" and other legal categories. There are basically two approaches to these relationships. As far as the relationship between restitution and unjust enrichment is concerned, the first approach equates the two and states that the law of Restitution is the law relating to all claims which are founded on the principle of unjust enrichment.[16] Its adherents recognise that the principle of unjust enrichment may also operate within other categories, for instance contract and tort,[17] but this corrective or subordinate role is distinct from the independent and primary right to restitution based on unjust enrichment. The second approach does not accept the equation between unjust enrichment and restitution for one of two reasons. One is that while unjust enrichment exerts interstitial influence over many areas it is not a complete explanation of any and there is not therefore a coherent law of Restitution.[18] The other is that in a number of situations commonly treated as "Restitutionary" there is no *enrichment* in any ordinary sense of the word[19] and that restitutionary remedies in fact may operate as loss-splitting devices, aids to the unwinding of a contract, deterrents against unfair conduct or methods of protecting certain relationships of dependence.

The division between those who favour the equation of restitution and unjust enrichment and those who recognise the importance of benefit-based liabilities but do not believe in a Law of Restitution based on such liabilities obviously influences the approaches to the second relationship, that between restitution/ unjust enrichment and other legal categories. Professor Dawson (and probably Professor Atiyah) consider that unjust enrichment contributes insight and corrects doctrines framed without primary reference to it and its remedies.[20] In other words it is a supplementary or parasitic principle to be deployed to ensure "equity" where other principles do not. Lord Goff and Professors Jones and Birks, on the other hand, see it as an independent category of claim.[21] These differences appear to reflect different views of the utility of conceptualising legal principles rather than different views as to whether there should be a remedy (and if so its extent) on the facts of any given case.

II. Purity of Concept

(a) Independent and dependent restitutionary claims

For Birks restitution is "the response which consists in causing one person to give up to another an enrichment received at his expense or its value in money."[22] It is a *measure* of relief (like compensation and punishment[23]) generated by one of two types of enrichment; enrichment by subtraction[24] and enrichment by wrongdoing.[25] The first type of enrichment, enrichment by subtraction from the plaintiff, occurs where value passes to the defendant from the plaintiff, as where he makes a payment to the defendant, and this gives rise to independent and primary rights. The second, where the only way of showing that an enrichment is at the expense of the plaintiff is by showing that it was acquired by breach of a legal duty such as tort or breach of contract, is a dependent claim—a remedial alternative to other responses more usually associated with breaches of duty, such as compensation. Birks's purpose in distinguishing independent and dependent restitutionary claims is to make it clear that prima facie the former are not affected by the rules and policies of other categories whereas the latter are normally subject to the rules of the primary claim.

In this paper I shall only consider the treatment of what I have termed "pure" services as an example of the independent claim. Both Birks and Goff and Jones treat them as such and, as will be seen, there are no fundamental differences between the two although Goff and Jones do not make the distinction between independent and dependent claims.

(b) Enrichment equated with "wealth"

The starting point is the concept of enrichment. The question "was the defendant enriched?" is the first of the stable set of "large questions" seen as necessary for the development of a pattern of analysis.[26] In his chapter on definition Birks equates enrichment with wealth; "the law of restitution is not concerned with attributes and interests which are not wealth."[27] He concedes that it is very difficult to say which things count as wealth and which things do not but the only clue he gives is the reference in the third adjustment to his basic definition adding to "specific restitution" of the thing received "pecuniary restitution" of its value in money. He states:

> "Restitution is usually effected in money. Claims which cannot be valued in money are necessarily outside the range of such pecuniary restitution. . . . Admittedly not much can be said for evicting them from the subject as a whole, except that the necessarily blurred restriction to wealth promotes homogeneity."[28]

In view of the range and variety of interests to which courts give or have given money value (including disappointment, reputation, pain, opportunity and enjoyment of life's amenities), a requirement that wealth be capable of monetary valuation does not in fact narrow the category of "enrichment" and is not particularly conducive to its homogeneity. But two factors show that he does not regard capacity to be valued in money as *sufficient* in English law for an interest to constitute wealth. First there is his treatment of "reputation," which clearly does satisfy that test, as a borderline case. Secondly, there is his acceptance of the fact that in English law the existence of a market in the subject-matter of a non-monetary intervention, such as the rendering of a service, does not (as a general rule) mean that the recipient of that intervention is enriched. This is so even though the existence of a market makes it possible to give the intervention an objective value. The reason is English law's premiss that "benefits in kind have value to a particular individual only so far as he chooses to give them value," and that if he does not so choose he can "subjectively devalue" them.[29]

What then is wealth? It is not a term that has attracted much discussion in legal writing and such references as there are in legal dictionaries are to Adam Smith and John Stuart Mill.[30] It has sometimes been used as a synonym for "property."[31] For Lawson & Rudden[32] the contrast within property is between different ways of dealing with "things" (whether tangible or intangible). Thus, there are things with a use value, *i.e.* with an entitlement to *in specie* enjoyment, and things with only an exchange-value, *i.e.* those investments of which the entitlement is to money value alone. The latter are termed wealth. Value, moreover, should be distinguished from cost. Value "refers to the advantage that is expected to result from the ownership of a given object of wealth (or to the market price that this advantage will command) whereas [cost] refers to the sacrifice involved in acquiring the object."[33]

Even for those with a wider, less mercantilist,[34] view of wealth, however, the notion of exchange-value and transferability is important. Thus it has been said that wealth is the possession or ownership of such *means of* property as would reasonably entitle one to expect and receive credit.[35] This approach to wealth is similar to that of economists[36] although in more recent times the tendency has been for economists to emphasise wealth as something with an income-producing capacity rather than solely as something with exchange-value.[37] The dominant form of wealth has thus become the expectation of revenue. As Berle and Means put it the "wealth [of a person] consists . . . of a bundle of expectations which have a market value and which, if held, may bring him income and, if sold in the market, may give him power to obtain some other form of wealth.[38]

(c) Services as enrichment

If exchange-value, transferability and capacity to produce income are the hallmarks of wealth it is difficult to see how pure services qualify, at any rate when one is asking whether they are wealth in the hands of the recipient. Services may be the *source* of wealth[39] or they may be its *product*. Services may be a source of wealth where they result in an end-product or an improvement to property, as where a tailor makes a suit or a builder constructs a house. Services may also be the product of wealth; in the above examples the services are products of the skills constituting the human capital of the tailor and the builder. These are very different items of wealth from that which may result from the service. A service can be the product but not the source of wealth as where a physician treats a patient or a lawyer advises a client without success. The *right to a service* may in some sense be a form of wealth,[40] although the non-assignability of rights to personal services[41] means that even this proposition requires qualification. But the service itself does not fit comfortably into this notion of wealth; it ceases to exist when it has been rendered and cannot be exchanged, transferred or turned to account in any other way. According to Alfred Marshall, "services and other goods, which pass out of existence in the same instant that they come into it, are of course, not part of the stock of wealth."[42]

For Birks and Goff and Jones, however, the receipt of services can constitute a clear example of enrichment; *i.e.* of the receipt of wealth. Why is this? They have two primary tests of enrichment; incontrovertible benefit and "free acceptance."[43] In the context of non-monetary enrichment, incontrovertible benefit is either the anticipation of *necessary* expenditure or the realization in money of a benefit.[44] Necessary expenditure is anticipated where, for instance, the plaintiff pays the defendant's debt to a third party. A non-monetary benefit which does not anticipate a necessary expenditure may nevertheless become "incontrovertible" by its realization in money, for instance, where the defendant sells the property the plaintiff has improved. The second test of enrichment, free acceptance, is satisfied "where a recipient knows that a benefit is being offered to him non–gratuitously and where he, having the opportunity to reject, elects to accept." The person who, seeing a window-cleaner beginning to clean the windows of his house, hangs back unseen till the window-cleaner has finished the job has freely accepted the service and cannot maintain that he does not have to pay for work which he never ordered. On this approach showing that a defendant has freely accepted an intervention establishes both that he has been "enriched" and that there is a ground for restitution; *i.e.* that the enrichment is "unjust."[45]

The two cases of incontrovertible benefit are not problematic. The "realization in money" category satisfies the exchange-value test by treating as the enrichment/wealth not the pure service itself but its product. Interventions in anticipation or avoidance of necessary expenditure, termed "negative" enrichments,[46] also satisfy the exchange-value test. This is clearly so where the plaintiff pays the defendant's debt to a third party and it may also be so even where the intervention is a service rendered, as where the plaintiff clears the defendant's overflowing drains, abating his nuisance.[47] But for the intervention, the defendant's assets ("wealth") would necessarily have been reduced and, as the intervention has prevented this it has enhanced his stock of assets with exchange-value, *i.e.* his wealth. The one case in which this might not be so is where the defendant would have abated the nuisance by his own labour and, in this case, it is arguable that the test of anticipation of necessary *expenditure* is not satisfied.[48] It should be noted that the exchange-value test would not be satisfied by loose use of the word "necessary," for instance to include expenditure which the defendant *might* have incurred.

So far, therefore, the treatment of enrichment/wealth is consistent with the exchange-value test. The difficulty arises with the second test of enrichment; "free acceptance." This test establishes that there is an enrichment (a benefit, a receipt of wealth) by reference to the consent or acquiescence of the defendant to an act of injurious reliance on the part of the plaintiff. There is no concern with the utility of the intervention (*i.e.* objective benefit) or with its realizability. On this test of enrichment, a pure service would count as an enriching intervention whether or not it results in any physical or human capital in the hands of the recipient.[49] Viewed from the perspective of the renderer of services and prospectively, it may be plausible to argue that the ability to render service has exchange value.[50] Physicians, lawyers and other professionals can after all agree to exchange their services for payment and are (subject to professional etiquette) free to refuse to do so. But to look at the matter this way is in effect to make the opportunity-loss of the unrequested renderer of services the source of the obligation whereas the hallmark of a restitutionary claim is the gain to the receiver. Viewed from the perspective of the receiver of the service (the patient or the client) and retrospectively there is no question of pure service satisfying the exchange-value test.

It is clear that a person who has rendered services requested, accepted or acquiesced in by the defendant is entitled to recompense whether or not the defendant gained from the services. Thus, recompense has been given in respect of plans prepared in the anticipation of the conclusion of a contract by a developer but rendered useless when the landowner decided not to proceed.[51] Recompense has also been given in respect of alterations to property effected by the owner at the request of prospective tenants when the negotiations for a lease broke down.[52] The second case, *Brewer Street Investments* v. *Barclays Woollen Co. Ltd.*, is particularly striking since the work was done on the *plaintiff's* property. The basis of the obligation in these cases is the request and the reliance. The same reasoning is used even where the services do lead to an increase in the defendant's assets. Thus, in *British Steel Corporation* v. *Cleveland Bridge & Engineering Co. Ltd.*[53] where B.S.C. manufactured and delivered cast–steel nodes to Cleveland pursuant to a letter of intent but in anticipation of a contract, the basis of the obligation was said to be Cleveland's *request* that B.S.C. undertake the work and B.S.C.'s *compliance* with that request, rather than the receipt and use of the nodes by Cleveland. These cases are all seen by Birks as examples of unjust enrichment by free acceptance. The irrelevance of the exchange-value test in these cases is also illustrated by *Planché* v. *Colburn*, a case which uses identical reasoning but which is classified by Birks as enrichment by reason of "limited" as opposed to "free" acceptance.[54] In *Planché* v. *Colburn* an author had contracted to write a book on Costume and Ancient Armour for The Juvenile Library, a series to be published by the defendant. The series was abandoned after the plaintiff had started to work and the publisher was obliged to recompense him by a *quantum meruit* for the work he had done, even though the manuscript had not been completed or tendered.

These cases are concerned with "consent," "acquiescence," "reliance," "fault" and "risk" rather than "enrichment" or "benefit."

The concept of free acceptance as enrichment is therefore a wide one. How well does it succeed in grouping together most "like" cases and separating most "unlike" cases?[55] In other words how does it measure up to the test of homogeneity and conceptual purity which is, according to Birks, one of the roles of definition and differentiation? It is submitted, with respect, that it does not.

The paradigm case of enrichment is an intervention which produces exchange-value (in the wide sense used above and including for this purpose any increase in the defendant's human capital) in the hands of a defendant. The inclusion of all requested, accepted, consented-to and acquiesced-in services destroys the homogeneity of the category because it includes not only (i) capital items, and (ii) income-sources[56] but also, (iii) all acquiesced-in interventions whether or not they result in something with exchange-value and indeed whether or not they result in anything of any use to the defendant. Given his equation of "enrichment" with "wealth" and the meaning of "wealth" in other contexts, the inclusion of that which, in the hands of the defendant, has neither exchange-value (in the extended sense used above) nor even utility seems somewhat artificial.

It might be objected that if pure services are not regarded as an enrichment because they do not satisfy the exchange-value test, why should the use of another's property which has been treated (by myself amongst others) as the basis of an independent restitutionary claim. The exchange-value test is in fact wider than the much criticised "appropriation" test propounded in *Phillips* v. *Homfray*.[57] Further, although in some ways I may have put the matter more broadly in my earlier work than I would now, the cases on waiver of conversion do satisfy the exchange-value test by requiring for the restitutionary claim that the goods be turned into money.[58] Other cases on the use of property satisfy the "negative" enrichment aspect of the test (*i.e.* where the use of the property is *necessary* to the defendant's enterprise).[59] The "waiver of tort" cases that do not satisfy the test are those in which assumpsit for work and labour was granted against one who wrongly induced an apprentice to work for him.[60] The doubts of Lord Mansfield and Lord Ellenborough in those cases about whether the principles in the use of property cases were applicable support the arguments made above and suggest that these cases should not, in modern terms, be seen as examples of unjust enrichment. Birks states that "no rational distinction can be taken between knowingly usurping

enjoyment of land and knowingly seducing the labour of someone
else's articled servant. In both cases there is a free acceptance of a
benefit in kind."[61] Although there are differences—a person's
right to dispose of his services is not a property right[62] and therefore the defendant is invading a different sort of interest, I would
not want to take this rather technical point. Where the only basis
of "enrichment" is free acceptance I would make no distinction
between services and the use of property and argue that neither
qualify as "enrichment." To the extent that my earlier work suggests otherwise, it needs modification. However, where property is
used it is likely that the exchange-value test (and the test of enrichment by incontrovertible benefit) will be satisfied. If so, the use of
the property of another will give rise to a restitutionary claim
because that use has led to the enrichment of the defendant.

The wide approach to enrichment also appears less useful as a
method of dividing up the law of obligations because, unlike one
based on exchange-value, it does not make a sharp distinction
between "enrichment" and either "reliance" or "consent" and is
indeed founded on a factual basis in which those two concepts play
an important role. It is wider than Fuller and Purdue's "restitution
interest," *i.e.* that interest in which there is *reliance* by the plaintiff
and a *resultant gain* to the defendant,[63] and, in effect, includes virtually all cases within their reliance interest.[64] Considerable overlap is also produced with obligations based upon agreement or
promise, *i.e.* with contractual obligations, by including all
requested or consented-to interventions. In fact, arguably the
enrichment by "free acceptance" is only established by showing
either reliance or consent or a mixture of the two and is therefore
dependant on *another* source of obligation; *i.e.* consent or injurious reliance. In Birks's classification this would make such a claim
a dependent rather than an independent restitutionary claim.[65]

How might Birks deal with the argument that such claims are
not independent restitutionary claims? He appears to have two
possible replies. First, there is no dependence on contractual
notions because "there is all the difference in the world between
wanting something and agreeing to pay for it."[66] In view of the use
of objective tests to determine whether a contract has been
entered into and the widespread use of terms implied in law or by
custom in contracts, the sharpness of this difference may be questioned. This excessively subjectivist view of contract enables him
to separate "free acceptance" and contract and to reject the view
that *all* examples of free acceptance can be analysed in terms of
genuine implied contract. While recognising that *some* examples
are susceptible of contractual analysis, he states that *all* can be

understood independently of contract as examples of unjust enrichment.[67] He argues that contractual explanations for the obligation to pay may be either fictitious or obstructed by technical requirements. Often the defendant meant to have the benefit for nothing and "the inference of a promise to pay was drawn more on the basis of what good men ought to intend than by genuine interpretation of what this defendant did intend or what the generality of mankind would have intended."[68] The implications of this for the law of contract and, in particular, for the objective view of contract, which judges the will of a person by outward manifestations, are startling. The criticism puts into question the contractual nature of implied terms and other doctrines which are normally treated as part of the modern law of contract. This is not the place for an extended treatment of objectivity in contract.[69] It is, however, clear that the question of whether words and acts constitute a contract are judged by reference to what reasonable people would intend.[70] It is also clear that vagueness is resolved by reference to this standard and that where terms have not been stated the court will establish what the contract is[71] having regard to the type of relationship between the parties (landlord/tenant; consumer/supplier). The court treats the obligation as flowing from what the law prescribes and what is reasonable in view of the nature of the relationship, rather than based on the intentions of the parties. Unlike Professor Fried, however, who sees that the objective standard of interpretation is inconsistent with his view of "Contract as Promise"[72] and concedes that this central contract doctrine can only be explained by non-promissory principles, Birks denies that he is engaged in a radical re-grouping of the bases of civil liability.[73]

His subjective view of contract is also the basis of the second possible reply to the argument that the claim is not an independent restitutionary claim. He states that "the facts which constitute an unjust enrichment never include, unless fortuitously, a promise to make restitution."[74] His reason is that it is "the merest accident" that the content of the promise happens to be measured by the amount of the promisee's receipt[75] whereas "a restitutionary right is definitively and necessarily measured by the amount of the enrichment at the plaintiff's expense."[76] But in cases of "free acceptance" of the sort we have considered there is no *real* receipt (*i.e.* enrichment) apart from the defendant's consent or acquiescence.[77] Not even a relatively broad use of "enrichment"/"receipt" justifies the treatment of the remedy in cases such as *Planché* v. *Colburn, Brewer St. Investments* and *Sabemo* v. *North Sydney M.C.* as based on the defendant's "receipt" or "enrichment." The requisite manifestation of will ("consent," "request," "acquiescence") necessarily *and non-fortuitously* establishes the existence and the extent of the remedy. It is not possible to treat the remedy as based on "receipt" or "enrichment" independently of such manifestation of will except by wholly fictitious reasoning.

For these reasons it is submitted that the inclusion of pure services as enrichments is not justified by conceptual purity. In my view it also leads to a number of practical disadvantages.

The argument that freely accepted pure services are not enrichments should not, however, be taken to exclude the notion of free acceptance/acquiescence from any role in the law of unjust enrichment. Where there is an enrichment that satisfies the exchange-value test no remedy will be given unless there is a ground for restitution; *i.e.* a ground establishing the "unjustness" of the enrichment. One such ground is that the defendant freely accepted the enrichment. Free acceptance may also affect the nature of the relief and the availability of defences. Thus it is not clear that change of position should ever be a defence to a freely accepted enrichment. But this is not the place to consider that aspect of free acceptance; the concern of this paper is with enrichment.

III. Practical Disadvantages of Regarding "Pure" Services as Enrichments

I shall seek to show that there are strong reasons of convenience for not treating pure services as enrichments. But I face an initial and formidable difficulty in the judgment of Robert Goff J. (as he then was) in *B.P. Exploration Co. (Libya) Ltd.* v. *Hunt (No. 2)*.[78] The issue was whether B.P. was entitled to an award under the Law Reform (Frustrated Contracts) Act 1943, s.1(3). This provides for a remedy in respect of pre-frustration performance by a party to a contract which performance confers a "valuable [non-monetary] benefit" on the other party. The judge held that as a matter of construction "benefit" in section 1(3) normally meant the end product of services rather than the services themselves.[79] However, the difficulty I face is that he would have preferred the legislature to have treated the services themselves as the benefit.[80] Although he recognised that, at common law, the identity and value of any benefit to the recipient of services may be debatable and the problem of restitution therefore more complex, there are not, in his view, insuperable difficulties in treating pure services as benefits within the principle of unjust enrichment.[81] Even under the 1943 Act he held that pure services *may* be benefits. There would therefore seem to be a stable pattern of analysis sanctified by statute recognising the fact that pure services can be "benefits" or "enrichments."

Three reasons suggest that we should either not accept this pattern, or at least recognise that it in fact conceals two patterns. First, the language of benefit may be positively misleading in situations in which the part-performance is useless or is destroyed as in *Appleby* v. *Myers*[82] where partially built machinery was destroyed by a fire which frustrated the contract to supply and erect the machinery. Most commentators[83] believe that where a contract has been frustrated a remedy should be given for partial performance even where the part-performance was destroyed by the frustrating event. Now while restitution *cognoscenti* may appreciate that uselessness and destruction do not necessarily affect the matter, others might be forgiven for taking the view that they preclude a finding of benefit. It has, indeed, been held that, in such a case no remedy is available because at the statutorily relevant time there is no benefit.[84] Such decisions would be avoided if the legal doctrine's formulation were to make explicit the fact that part performance by one party will justify adjustment whether or not the other has received a real benefit. The trend of modern Commonwealth proposals for reform and legislation on adjustments of rights and liabilities following the frustration of a contract is to do this.[85]

Secondly, the pattern promotes fictions. Thus, the British Columbia Frustrated Contracts Act,[86] s.5(4) states that "a 'benefit' means something done in the fulfilment of contractual obligations whether or not the person for whose benefit it was done received the benefit" and the Restatement of Restitution states that benefit includes the rendering of services at the request of another.[87] Chief Justice Traynor of California has said[88] that:

> "If in fact the performance of services has conferred no benefit on the person requesting them, it is pure fiction to base restitution on a benefit conferred."

He said that recompense in respect of such services is based on the performing party's justified reliance on the request. Robert Goff J.'s judgment is also open to question on this ground. He states that the 1943 Act (and inferentially the law of Restitution) is not designed to apportion losses between the parties.[89] He also states that expenditure by a contracting party under the contract *does not necessarily* confer a benefit on the other party.[90] But his approach to "benefit" in fact negates both statements. While he recognises that expenditure may be incurred under a contract without conferring a benefit on the other party, his view that pure services are "benefits" is justified on the ground that "the services in question have been requested by the defendant who normally takes the risk that they may prove worthless, from whatever cause."[91] It is difficult to see how any direct act in performance "done under a contract" is not "requested" by the other party and therefore a benefit to that party. If so, in principle, a remedy will be available for all such acts "done under a contract." How does this differ from loss-apportionment?

Thirdly, insofar as the pattern treats situations in which part-performance leads to a realizable benefit in the hands of the defendant as governed by the same principle, "benefit," as those in which it does not, it may lead to an identity of adjustment of rights and liabilities; *i.e.* to identity of remedy in the two situations. The inappropriateness of this is, however, shown by the New South Wales Frustrated Contracts Act 1978, ss.11 and 13 which make a sharp distinction between recompense for realizable benefits (called "received performance") and recompense for costs incurred in performing the contract. The recompense for realizable benefits is the appropriate proportion ("attributable value") of the contract price (the "proportionate allowance") less any diminution in value because of the frustrating event (the "lost value" of the performance) but recompense for costs incurred is fair compensation for the burden incurred for the purpose of giving the performance.

Robert Goff J.'s approach may be justified on pragmatic grounds where, as under the Law Reform (Frustrated Contracts) Act, adjustment is only possible where there is a "benefit," *i.e.* "unjust enrichment." But this should not be the case at common law, granted the growing recognition of reliance as a source of obligation. Once it is recognised that, at common law, either benefit or reliance justify adjustment, the pragmatic reasons cut the other way.

There are two further reasons of convenience for not treating pure services as benefits. The first is that in cases, such as *Planché* v. *Colburn*, in which a *quantum meruit* is sought in respect of services rendered under a contract which is discharged before completion, most commentators, including Birks and Goff and Jones,[92] believe that a contracting party should not be able to get more than a proration of the contract price because to do otherwise would subvert bargains. In other words the contractual price should control the *quantum meruit* which should not be allowed to save a person from a bad bargain. If the claim is regarded as based on reliance or as a dependent restitutionary claim the relevance of the contract price as a limit is obvious.[93] If, on the other hand, the claim is regarded as an instance of an independent restitutionary claim—as it would if the pure services were regarded as a benefit—the contract price would prima facie be irrelevant.

So neither Birks nor Goff and Jones apply one of the normal incidents of the independent claim to these cases. They explain this by reference to the policy favouring the upholding of bargains. What they do not explain is why claims for the recovery of money paid under contracts on the ground that there has been a total failure of consideration, where the exchange-value test of benefit is clearly satisfied, are *not* also subject to this policy. In such cases the objection that recovery will reverse a contractual allocation of risks has not been taken. Indeed it has been expressly held that it is no objection to a claim for the recovery of money that it will rescue the plaintiff from an unprofitable bargain.[94] The different treatment of recompense for services rendered is difficult to justify except on the basis that claims for services are either dependent restitutionary claims or directly based on reliance or consent (with the limits of those categories) whereas claims for the recovery of money are independent claims.

The position taken by Birks and Goff and Jones treats both recovery of money and recompense for services as "independent" restitutionary claims but nevertheless distinguishes recompense for services and subjects it to the restrictions that are incidents of the dependent claim. If both are independent then why is the argument from the reallocation of risks not equally relevant (or irrelevant) to both? The view advanced in this paper, that pure services are an example of the dependent claim, because there is no enrichment independent of the defendant's will (consent/request/acquiescence), explains the difference. The desired practical result would harmonise rather than clash with the underlying theory.

Finally, there is the position of services rendered in the anticipation of a contract. The restitutionary approach in cases such as *British Steel Corporation* v. *Cleveland Bridge & Engineering Co. Ltd.*[95] to the problems of performance in the anticipation of a contract has been criticised by Mr. Ball[96] as inimical to the fine tuning of the details of a relationship. In particular it is said that suppliers of goods and services freely accepted will get paid at the going rate but expectations of the recipient (in relation to, for instance, quality or delivery dates) are given no protection. Receipts but not expectations are protected. This criticism, of course, applies to cases which satisfy the exchange-value test but it is particularly compelling where the test is not satisfied. In such cases, the expectations of one party but not of the other are protected. If, rather than "benefit" or "enrichment," the elements of "consent," "reliance," "risk" and "fault" upon which the cases were decided are emphasised, it is submitted that this form of criticism can be met.

IV. Conclusion

In his book on *Unjust Enrichment*, the late Professor Dawson said of this area of the law; "when anyone ventures to construct a system, we all set cheerfully to work to destroy it."[97] This paper has not in fact sought to put into question the utility of restitution or unjust enrichment as a separate category of the law of obligations.

It has, however, been argued that the concept of "enrichment" or "benefit" by free acceptance developed by Birks and Goff and Jones is overinclusive. The consequent lack of conceptual purity and functional homogeneity leads either to inappropriate rules or to the development of fictions. These might be tolerated on a subjective view of contractual consent and in the absence of a developed principle of injurious reliance. But English law does not have a subjective view of contract and is increasingly recognising the principle of injurious reliance. Once that principle is recognised we should not permit an overinclusive concept of "unjust enrichment" to marginalize it; just as we should not allow the imperial claims of the reliance principle to marginalize unjust enrichment. Another consequence is that the distinction between independent and dependent claims becomes very difficult to sustain if freely accepted services constitute "enrichment." It is submitted that the exchange-value test of enrichment developed in this paper is a theoretically attractive and practical method of identifying the ambit of the principle of unjust enrichment, that freely accepted pure services do not satisfy it and, Birks and Goff and Jones must therefore give up a small part of the territory they claim for that principle.

Notes

[1] I am grateful to P. S. Atiyah, C. H. Beatson, A. S. Burrows, G. O. A. Elias and G. H. Treitel for their comments which have much improved this paper.

[2] See the criticism by Birks in (1982) 35 C.L.P. 53, of earlier work of mine; (1978/79) 17 U. W. Ont. L.R. 1 for failure to recognise that some restitutionary claims are "dependant." See further, below *II(a)*.

[3] Dawson, *Unjust Enrichment*, p. 23; Birks, *An Introduction to the Law of Restitution* (hereafter *Introduction*), pp. 23–40–44, 313–314, 347–355.

[4] This familiar term is used although it has been criticised; see Burrows, (1983)

Benefit, Reliance and the Structure of Unjust Enrichment 87

99 L.Q.R. 217, 219–220 who describes the interest concerned with compensation for harm as the "status quo" interest.

⁵ Birks, *Introduction*; Goff and Jones, *The Law of Restitution* (3rd ed., 1986), (hereafter Goff & Jones). There is a change of approach in the 3rd edition of Goff and Jones. In the second edition it was recognised that recompense for services rendered in an emergency might not be based on benefit to or enrichment of the defendant but now, reflecting Jones, (1980) 18 U.W.Ont. L.R. 447, it is also recognised that recompense for services rendered in anticipation of a contract which does not materialise may also not always be based on benefit or enrichment; see pp. 22, 341–343 (emergency) and Chap. 24 (anticipated contracts). But the implications of this for the structure of the subject are not considered, *e.g.* in the section (pp. 16–22) on the character of the benefit.

⁶ See P. S. Atiyah, *The Rise and Fall of Freedom of Contract* (1979), hereafter *Rise and Fall; Promises, Morals and the Law* (1981), hereafter *Promises*; S. Levmore, "Explaining Restitution" (1985) 71 Va. L.Rev. 65; Hugh Collins, *The Law of Contract* (1986), pp. 51–52.

⁷ "The Reliance Interest in Contract Damages" (1936) 46 Yale L.J. 52, 55.

⁸ *Promises*, pp. 34–36.

⁹ Reductionism is not inevitable; it is avoided by Stoljar, *The Law of Quasi-Contract* (1964) where, albeit in language which is not particularly clear ("proprietary" and "contractual") the different strands of liability are kept separate. See also Childres & Garamella, (1969) 64 Nw.U.L.R. 433.

¹⁰ *An Introduction to the Law of Restitution*. The lectures are; (1971) 24 C.L.P. 110, (1972) 25 C.L.P. 179; (1974) 27 C.L.P. 13; (1980) 33 C.L.P. 191; (1982) 35 C.L.P. 53; (1983) 36 C.L.P. 178.

¹¹ (1936) 46 Yale L.J. 52, 72; Jones, above n. 5.

¹² See the discussion in Beatson, (1981) 97 L.Q.R. 389, 408–409, 414–416.

¹³ Mill distinguished (iii) and (iv) because in the second, the only utility is in the mere service rendered; it is not fixed or embodied in any object (material or human): *Principles of Political Economy* (2nd ed., 1849), vol. 1, pp. 57–58. Both are distinguished from services that result in utilities fixed and embodied in external objects. Only services that result in such utilities are treated by Mill as wealth although he does recognise that where the service results in human capital it might be (although it is not usually) spoken of as wealth; *ibid.* pp. 59–61. For the significance of this see below.

¹⁴ *Introduction*, p. 1.

¹⁵ *Ibid.* p. 72.

¹⁶ Goff & Jones, pp. 3, 5, n. 9; Lord Wright in *Fibrosa* [1943] A.C., at 61; Birks, *Introduction*, pp. 23, 26, 40–41, 133. For Dawson the fact that unjust enrichment as an independent motive for judicial action is apt to be recognised late in any legal system means that it is unlikely to have much territory that is exclusively its own since many of the problems are dealt with by other motives already expressed in doctrine; *Unjust Enrichment*, pp. 39–40.

¹⁷ This is, in effect, the point of Birks's second category of enrichment (see below n. 25), enrichment by wrongdoing, which seeks to explain when and how it can do this.

¹⁸ P. S. Atiyah, *Rise and Fall* (1979) pp. 764 *et seq.* (equating the principle of unjust enrichment and the concept of benefit-based liability); S. Hedley, "Unjust enrichment as the basis of Restitution—an overworked concept" (1981) 5 Leg. Stud. 56, 57–58, 60, 61–62, 66.

¹⁹ J. P. Dawson, "Restitution without Enrichment" [1981] Boston U. L.Rev. 563; S. J. Stoljar, "Negotiorum Gestio" Chap. 17 of *Int. Encycl. of Comparative Law*, vol. X, pp. 11–13, 17; S. Hedley, above n. 18.

[20] Dawson, *Unjust Enrichment* (1951) pp. 116–117; Atiyah, above note 6.

[21] Although *n.b.* Goff & Jones's refusal (p. 13) to engage in the *definition of concepts*.

[22] *Introduction*, p. 13. For him, (a) restitution is the mechanism for *reversing* unjust enrichment, other mechanisms are concerned with its prevention and anticipation (p. 25) and, (b) restitution can be triggered by events other than unjust enrichment by subtraction, in particular wrongs (p. 39, *et seq.*).

[23] *Introduction*, p. 26.

[24] *Ibid.* pp. 23, 132–133.

[25] *Ibid.* pp. 40–41, 326, *et. seq.*; [1982] 35 C.L.P. 53.

[26] *Ibid.* p. 7.

[27] *Ibid.* p. 13.

[28] *Ibid.* p. 13.

[29] *Ibid.* p. 109. Although he accepts the force of the argument from "subjective devaluation," he is attracted to an objective approach to value (see pp. 124–128). But an objective approach to value coupled with the view that anything which can be valued in money is an "enrichment" draws vast areas of law into the "enrichment" category. The homogeneity of the category is not achieved by the concept of enrichment but by using another ingredient in the definition, such as "at the expense of" as a control device. The very broad definition of enrichment appears to lead to a relatively narrow view of "at the expense of" (*Introduction*, pp. 132–139 *cf.* 129); a view which is not based on the way the caselaw has developed; see, *e.g.* *Mason* v. *N.S.W.* (1959) 102 C.L.R. 108, 146 (Windeyer J.); *Hydro Electric Commission of Nepean* v. *Ontario Hydro* [1982] S.C.R. 347.

[30] Smith, *Wealth of Nations*, vol. 1, p. 37; Mill, *op. cit.*, n. 13 above p. 10 referred to in Wharton's Law Lexicon (14th ed., 1938); Jowitt, (2nd ed., 1977).

[31] Salmond on Jurisprudence, (12th ed.), p. 238; Dias on Jurisprudence, (5th ed.), pp. 295–297.

[32] *The Law of Property* (2nd ed.), p. 16 "[A]ny valuable asset which is the object of commerce is properly treated as a thing . . . ," p. 226 "wealth" is such things (corporeal or incorporeal) as "are more likely to be thought of primarily, or even exclusively, in terms of their "money value" (also referred to as "exchange-value").

[33] Bonbright, *Valuation of Property* (1937) vol. 1 p. 19. (In respect of services Birks does not always clearly distinguish these two, see n. 50 below.)

[34] Mill, *op. cit.* n. 13 above, pp. 5–8.

[35] *Branham* v. *State* 22 S.E. 957 (1895) (Sup. Court of Georgia), interpreting "wealth" in the criminal code. See also Sir Fredrick Pollock, *Jurisprudence and Legal Essays*, p. 72 ("We must recognise as things, in fact, all objects of exchange and commerce which are recognised by the usage of mankind.")

[36] Smith, *Wealth of Nations*, (1828) (ed. McCulloch) vol. 1, p. 9n; Mill, *Principles of Political Economy* (2nd ed., 1849), pp. 10–11 (for his view of services see n. 13 above); Sidgwick, *The Principles of Political Economy* (3rd. ed., 1901), (ed. Keynes), p. 78; Marshall, *Principles of Economics* (8th ed., 1947), p. 54. Economists who include human capital within their concept of wealth (see, *e.g.* Alchian & Allen, *Exchange and Production: Competition, Co-ordination and Control* (2nd ed., 1977), pp. 424, *et seq.*) mean the *person* as a source of a future flow of services rather than the service itself (*i.e.* the service is the *product* of wealth); Alchian & Allen, *op. cit.* p. 162.

[37] Bannock, Baxter & Rees, *The Penguin Dictionary of Economics*, p. 460; Cairncross, *Introduction to Economics* (4th ed.), p. 61 ("wealth is a fund upon which we can draw in *consumption* . . . "); Hicks, *Capital and Time*, p. 1 ("A capital good . . . is one that can be used in any way to satisfy wants in subsequent

periods.") On interest and capital, see Samuelson, *Economics* (11th ed.), p. 558. On "income" see Hicks, *Value and Capital*, (1946) Chap. XIII. In a perfect market there may well be no difference between the "exchange-value" and "income source" formulations.

[38] *The Modern Corporation and Private Property*, p. 305 (this "passive" form of wealth is contrasted with a form which consists of the "control" of functioning enterprise). See also Macpherson, *Property* (1978), p. 8.

[39] Locke, *Two Treatises of Government* (Laslett ed., C.U.P., 1960), pp. 306, 314 (*Second Treatise*, Chap. V., paras. 27, 40).

[40] *Hill* v. *Parsons* [1972] Ch. 305, 321. The use of an injunction in *Lumley* v. *Wagner* (1852) 1 D.M. & G. 604 to restrain a singer from breaking her contract by singing for a rival theatre (and the liability of the rival for wrongful interference with contractual rights: *Lumley* v. *Gye* (1853) 2 E. & B. 216) may appear to give the right to services a proprietary flavour (and see *Warner Bros.* v. *Nelson* [1937] 1 K.B. 209) but there is no ability to *force* a person to render services or to exchange the right in the marketplace. On *Lumley* v. *Wagner* see Treitel, *The Law of Contract* (6th ed.), p. 780; Sharpe, *Injunctions and Specific Performance*, paras. 579–586, 689–698 (esp. 579 and 695) but for the view that arguments from personal freedom do not justify the refusal to grant specific performance see Kronman, (1978) 45 U. of Chi. L.R. 351; Schwartz, 89 Yale L.J. 271, 296.

[41] *Nokes* v. *Doncaster Amalgamated Collieries Ltd.* [1940] A.C. 1014 (employers right to employees services); *Griffith* v. *Tower Publishing Co.* (1897) 1 Ch. 21 (publishers right to author's services). *Cf.* the position under the Capital Gains Tax legislation where the right to an employees services is an "asset": *O'Brien* v. *Benson's Hosiery (Holdings) Ltd.* [1980] A.C. 562. In the U.S.A. the services of a company promoter have not been treated as corporate assets for the purposes of construing anti-stockwatering legislation: see Dodd, *Stockwatering* (1930) p. 42; Bonbright, *Valuation of Property* (1937), vol. 1, pp. 99, 795. See also *Government of Malaysia* v. *Selangor Pilot Association* [1978] A.C. 337 where the deprivation of rights to render services as pilots in a harbour area was held not to be a deprivation of a property right although those rights had previously been transferable.

[42] *Principles of Political Economy* (8th ed., 1947), p. 56.

[43] *Introduction*, pp. 114, *et seq.*, Goff and Jones, pp. 14–18. Birks states that there are *three* tests of enrichment but the third "others" is something of a miscellany (see p. 132) and will not be examined. For present purposes it suffices if it can be shown that his treatment of services in the first two is overinclusive.

[44] *Introduction*, p. 116, *et seq. Cf.* Goff and Jones, p. 19, 144, 148 who use a test of *realizability* rather than actual realization. For criticism of this see Beatson, (1981) 97 L.Q.R. 389, 410–411 but note that it, like Birks's test, presupposes something with exchange-value in the hands of the defendant.

[45] *Introduction*, pp. 107, 265 (definition of free acceptance), pp. 114, 266–267 (bivalence). This does not, however, explain all the cases and he also develops a category of "limited acceptance" (within his third miscellaneous category of enrichment, n. 43 above) to deal with some of them; see pp. 127, 232, 238–241 and n. 54 below.

[46] *Introduction*, p. 129, where, however, no distinction is made between "negative" enrichments that are incontrovertible benefits (where *necessary* expenditure is anticipated or avoided, p. 117, *et seq.*) and those that are only enrichments by virtue of "free acceptance." Only the former necessarily satisfy the exchange-value test.

[47] The exchange-value test is thus wider than the widely criticised "appropriation" or "accretion" test laid down in *Phillips* v. *Homfray* (1883) 24 Ch.D. 439 for

cases of "waiver or tort." On differences between "pure" services and the use of another's property as enrichments see below.

[48] *Quaere* whether this was the reason for non-recovery in *Macclesfield Corp.* v. *Great C. Ry.* [1911] 2 K.B. 528.

[49] See n. 13 and 36 above.

[50] Arguably Birks does do this; see the discussion of positive and negative enrichment (*Introduction*, p. 129): "Saving man's dignity, his work is the user or enjoyment obtainable from him over time. It is referred to as his 'time' and he 'markets' his time (time in himself) just as he hires out time in his corporeal property."

[51] *Sabemo* v. *N. Sydney Municipal Council* (1977) 2 N.S.W.L.R. 880; noted by Davies, (1981) 1 Ox. J.Leg. Stud. 300. *William Lacey (Hounslow) Ltd.* v. *Davis* [1957] 2 All E.R. 712 is another example although not unequivocally so because the defendant did use the estimates prepared by the plaintiff-builder in negotiating for compensation from the War Damage Commission. But this does not appear to have played a part in the decision, see p. 719. There is an important change of approach in the 3rd ed. of Goff and Jones (pp. 507–511) reflecting Jones, above n. 5 in that it is recognised that these cases and *Brewer St. Investments*, are not cases of "enriching" or "beneficial" services.

[52] *Brewer St. Investments Ltd.* v. *Barclays Woollen Co., Ltd.* [1953] 2 All E.R. 1330 (C.A.). In fact only Denning L.J. based his judgment on restitution, but the case is seen by Birks as an example of "free acceptance," *Introduction*, pp. 283–284. *Cf.* Goff & Jones, pp. 508–509 and *British Steel Corp.* v. *Cleveland Bridge & Engineering Co. Ltd.* [1984] 1 All E.R. 504, 511b-c.

[53] [1984] 1 All E.R. 504.

[54] (1831) 8 Bing. 14; 1 M. & Scott 51; 5 Car. & P. 58. *Cf.* Goff and Jones, pp. 466–467 who state that there was no benefit in *Planché*. But *n.b.* Robert Goff J.'s judgment in *B.P. Exploration Co. (Libya) Ltd.* v. *Hunt (No. 2)* [1979] 1 W.L.R. 783, 800, 802 where pure services are treated as beneficial; on this see further *III.* below. Birks states (pp. 232, 287) that it is not possible to explain this case as one of "free acceptance" because the publisher did not request or freely accept anything else than the complete manuscript but sees it as an example of "limited acceptance," see n. 45 above. But why is it not possible to say that where, as in *Planché*, the defendant has made it impossible to render the specified performance, he is prevented/"estopped" from relying on the specification; see Beatson, (1981) 97 L.Q.R. 389, 413 and the rule preventing a party to a contract from relying on self–induced frustration: Treitel, *The Law of Contract* (6th ed.), p. 682.

[55] Burrows, (1983) 99 L.Q.R. 217–218.

[56] (i) and (ii) include interventions (including services) which result in something with positive exchange-value in the hands of the defendant and those which do not, but anticipate or avoid necessary expenditure by the defendant ("negative enrichment" by preserving other assets).

[57] (1883) 24 Ch.D. 439, 471–471.

[58] Chitty, *Contracts*, para. 1978; (1978/79) 1 U. of W.Ont. L.R. 1, 22.

[59] Getting coal to the surface as on the facts of *Phillips* v. *Homfray* (1883) 24 Ch.D. 439 or getting one's luggage from Scarborough to Whitby as in *Rumsey* v. *N.E. Ry.* (1863) 14 C.B.(N.S.) 641.

[60] *Lightley* v. *Clouston* (1808) 1 Taunt. 112; *Foster* v. *Stewart* (1814) 3 M. & S. 191.

[61] *Introduction*, p. 324.

[62] See n. 40, 41 above. *Cf.* D. Friedmann, (1980) 80 Col. L.Rev. 504, 505–506.

[63] "The Reliance Interest in Contract Damages" (1936) 46 Yale L.J. 52, 54.

[64] Fuller & Purdue were aware of this consequence of a broad conception of "benefit"; *ibid.* p. 71.

[65] See above *II(a)*. Birks has argued that "*at the expense of*" is ambiguous (meaning either "by subtraction" or "by breach of duty") and that in certain cases where there is a clear enrichment it can only be shown to be "at the expense of" a plaintiff by pointing to a breach of duty, and is therefore a dependant claim. So also it can be argued that his concept of "enrichment" is ambiguous and can be established independently or by reference to other sources of obligation ("consent," "free acceptance" or "reliance").

[66] *Introduction*, p. 45.

[67] *Introduction*, p. 275.

[68] *Introduction*, p. 271. For an example of a fictitious contract see *Upton-on-Severn R.D.C.* v. *Powell* [1942] 1 All E.R. 220.

[69] See Treitel, n. 40 above, pp. 1–2; Howarth, (1984) 100 L.Q.R. 265; Collins, n. 6 above, pp. 89–92, 216–217.

[70] *Carlill* v. *Carbolic Smoke Ball* [1893] 1 Q.B. 256, 263, 264 (re. the argument that the offer was too vague); *Smith* v. *Hughes* (1876) L.R. 6 Q.B. 597, 607.

[71] *Liverpool C.C.* v. *Irwin* [1977] A.C. 239; *Shell U.K. Ltd.* v. *Lostock Garage Ltd.* [1977] 1 All E.R. 481.

[72] (Harv. U.P.) pp. 60–63. See Burrows, [1985] C.L.P. at 147.

[73] *Introduction*, pp. 6, 29.

[74] *Ibid.* p. 44.

[75] *Ibid.* p. 45.

[76] *Ibid.* p. 46.

[77] It clearly adds nothing to the coherence of the law to think of the rendering of the service as a "quasi-receipt" or a "constructive enrichment"; see *Introduction*, p. 22.

[78] [1979] 1 W.L.R. 783.

[79] *Ibid.* p. 801F, where he states that it should be so identified "in an appropriate case" and 801H–802A from which it appears that it will always be appropriate unless the services have no end-product.

[80] *Ibid.* p. 802E.

[81] See p. 799A where he states this to be the principle of recovery under the Act and 802A and E-F. And 799G for the difficulties in relation to identity and value of benefit.

[82] (1867) L.R. 2 C.P. 651.

[83] Cheshire, Fifoot & Furmston, *The Law of Contract* (11th ed.), p. 573; Cheshire & Fifoot's (4th Australian ed., 1980), p. 628; Treitel, *The Law of Contract* (6th ed.), p. 689; Waddams, *The Law of Contract* (2nd ed.) pp. 289–299; Law Reform Commission of New South Wales, *Report on Frustrated Contracts*, para. 6.5. For other Law reform proposals which take this position see n. 85 below.

[84] *Parsons* v. *Shea* (1966) 53 D.L.R. (2d.) 36 (a decision on the Newfoundland Act which is in similar but not identical terms to the English Act and which is in force in all but three of the Canadian provinces; but see the new recommended Uniform statute, n. 84 below). The Victorian and New Zealand statutes are in similar terms.

[85] British Columbia Frustrated Contracts Act (based on a B.C. Law Reform Commission report, also adopted in the Yukon and recommended as new Uniform Canadian Frustrated Contracts Act); Mullan, *Frustrated Contracts Law*, study paper for Nova Scotia Law Revision Advisory Commission (1976); Law Reform Commission of South Australia (71st rep., 1983); New South Wales Frustrated Contracts Act 1978 (based on a N.S.W. Law Reform Commission Report which contains the most sophisticated analysis of the problems).

[86] 1974 B.C. Statutes Ch. 37.

[87] p. 12 comments to para. 1.

[88] *Coleman Engineering* v. *N. American Aviation* 420 P2d 713, 729 (1966).

[89] *Ibid.* p. 799H.
[90] *Ibid.* p. 800A-B.
[91] *Ibid.* p. 802E-F. This statement about risk may be too broad. It is correct if the obligations under the contract are severable as opposed to entire because a *contractual* right to payment accrues incrementally as the services are rendered. But where a party has specified that complete performance is required, *i.e.* where the obligation is entire, it is difficult to accept that he should "normally" be seen as taking the risk that part-performance will prove worthless. See Treitel, *The Law of Contract* (6th ed.), pp. 589–592; Beatson, (1981) 97 L.Q.R. 389, 410–414.
[92] Goff & Jones, pp. 466–468 (criticising *Lodder* v. *Slowey* (1902) 20 N.Z.L.R. 321; [1904] A.C. 321); Birks, *Introduction*, p. 288; Treitel, p. 793 n. 37; Childres & Garamella, 64 Nw.U.L.R. 433 (1969). It is not easy to reconcile Goff and Jones's position here with their view (p. 456) that claims for a defendants profits from a breach of contract should be allowed because damage awards may not (because of difficulties of proof or the rules of remoteness) allow the plaintiff to recover his true loss. *Cf.* Palmer, *The Law of Restitution*, vol. 1, para. 4.4 who states that in the U.S.A. the remedy is not so limited (and should not be). For general discussion, see Chitty, *Contracts*, vol. 1, para. 2048.
[93] *C. & P. Haulage* v. *Middleton* [1983] 3 All E.R. 94; *C.C.C. Films* v. *Impact Quadrant* [1984] 3 W.L.R. 245; Palmer, *op. cit.* pp. 401–404.
[94] *Bush* v. *Canfield* 2 Conn. 485 (1818); *B.P. Exploration Co. (Libya) Ltd.* v. *Hunt (No. 2)* [1979] 1 W.L.R. 783, 800; Treitel, *The Law of Contract* (6th ed.), p. 708. Goff and Jones do not refer to such a limit in their discussion of the recovery of money paid under contracts discharged for breach and frustration (see pp. 369–371, 449–451, 458–465, 468–471) but in view of what is stated at pp. 455–456, in contrast to what they say about recompense for services, n. 92 above, do not appear to wish to impose such a limit.
[95] [1984] 1 All E.R. 504 considered above p. 78.
[96] *"Work Carried out in pursuance of letters of intent—Contract or Restitution?"* (1983) 99 L.Q.R. 572.
[97] p. 111.

The Gillick Case: Parental Authority, Teenage Independence and Public Policy

PROFESSOR G. L. PEIRIS*

I. Introduction

Litigation which has recently been engaged in almost with crusading zeal from the Queen's Bench Division[1] through the Court of Appeal[2] to the House of Lords,[3] has served as a catalyst for a searching examination of the response of modern English law to a well-nigh intractable moral problem.

The issue was whether doctors employed by an area health authority could lawfully give contraceptive advice or treatment to the plaintiff's daughters, who were under sixteen years of age, without her knowledge and consent. The area authority had received from the Department of Health and Social Security a memorandum of guidance on family planning which stated, *inter alia*, that to abandon the principle of confidentiality between doctor and patient in respect of children under sixteen years might cause some not to seek professional advice at all, thus exposing them to risks such as pregnancy and sexually transmitted diseases, and that in exceptional cases it was for a doctor exercising his clinical judgment to decide whether to prescribe contraception. The contention on the plaintiff's behalf was that the department, in issuing the memorandum, was exercising its discretion unlawfully. The deep cleavage of opinion with regard to the moral and ethical issues underlying the case is evident from the narrowness of the majority in the House of Lords upholding the legality of the department's action. Lord Fraser,[4] Lord Scarman[5] and Lord Bridge[6] recognised the entitlement of a doctor to give contraceptive advice and treatment to a girl under sixteen without her parents' knowledge and consent, in circumstances where she is very likely to begin or continue having sexual intercourse with or without contraceptive treatment, if the doctor is satisfied that her mental or physical health is likely to suffer unless she receives contraception. On the other hand, Lord Brandon[7] was convinced that to give such a child contraceptive treatment is to remove a powerful inhibition and, therefore, unlawfully to facilitate a sexual relationship. Lord Templeman concurred in the dissent on somewhat different grounds.[8]

All three courts, though with dramatically different results, came to grips with vexed moral and social problems in one of the most sensitive areas of the rapidly moving law of parent and child.

II. Parental Power

(a) General perspectives

The pivot of the case for Mrs. Gillick was that recognition of the competence of a child below sixteen years of age to give valid consent to contraceptive treatment amounted to an intolerable infringement of parental authority. In supporting her claim to a declaration that the advice contained in the revised circular issued by the department was unlawful and wrong, Mrs. Gillick's counsel contended vigorously that a parent has a fundamental right to be responsible for the educational, social and medical care of his or her minor children[9] and that the guidelines set out in the circular condone interference with the essential rights of parents to supervise, and to forbid intervention in, the moral upbringing of their children.[10]

Despite the precarious outcome of the litigation upholding the validity of the circular, the judgments in the Court of Appeal and the dissenting speeches in the House of Lords lend disquieting support to a conception of parental authority which is scarcely in line with modern ideas. The judgments in favour of Mrs. Gillick are marked by a pervasive emphasis on "a parcel of rights in relation to children in custody"[11] which is identified as the inalienable entitlement of a parent or guardian. The provision of contraceptive treatment for such children was characterised by Fox L.J. as "a serious interference with parental responsibility"[12] and as "an interference with the control of matters relative to the child and its person which the law gives to the parents."[13] The premise that "The parental rights at law are very wide"[14] sustains the judgment as a whole. Eveleigh L.J., having pointed out that a parent's freedom to decide may be curtailed by statute,[15] suggested that, where this is not so, the parent's right must be regarded as untrammelled.[16] The approach founded on a residue of parental rights entrenched by the common law is explicitly adopted by Lord Templeman, in his dissenting speech. Barring exceptional contingencies such as abandonment and abuse of parental rights which would make it necessary for a doctor to provide contraceptive facilities without parental consent, Lord Templeman was prepared to recognise a general duty in the doctor to inform the parent as soon as possible "in order that the parent might have the opportunity of exercising parental rights in such a manner as to deter or prevent the girl from indulging in sexual intercourse."[17] Lord Templeman felt no inhibition in asserting baldly that "A doctor is not entitled to decide whether a girl under the age of sixteen shall be provided with contraceptive facilities if a parent who is in charge of the girl is ready and willing to make that decision in exercise of parental rights."[18]

These propositions represent continuity with a line of authority which has been superseded by contrary developments in England and in most Commonwealth jurisdictions. The authoritative articulation of these ideas at the present day indicates an inflexibility of approach which has regrettable implications for social policy. Although extreme notions of parental power pervade judgments handed down by English courts in Victorian times,[19] the philosophy reinforcing these values is typically embodied in the concept of *patria potestas* in Roman law. The rigidity of pristine Roman legal principle in regard to the character and scope of parental power was attributable to the unity of personality between the father and his children *in potestate*.[20] Roman law developed this principle of *unitas* to remarkable lengths and had little difficulty in recognising that the father's personality could be assailed by a contumelious act directed against the person of his child subject to his *potestas*.[21]

Yet it is significant that modern legal systems founded upon the Roman law tradition which placed unique stress on the amplitude of parental power as an absolute postulate and characterised invasion of parental authority as an *injuria* which could be forestalled by interdict, have shown themselves capable of perceptive adaptation to a different social environment. A South African court applying Roman-Dutch law has declined to permit the father of a minor girl, by virtue of his parental authority, to prohibit a third person from contacting or associating with her against the wishes of the parent.[22] Among the primary elements of social policy underscored in the judgment are the Teutonic values favouring a freer and looser association among members of a family as part of the revamped body of Roman law received in the Netherlands,[23] the reciprocal quality of family obligations which have as their base mutual support and total confidence[24] and the gradually dwindling degree of the parental power with the advent of maturity in the child.[25] The South African court was keenly alive to the reality that a minor who had reached the age of discretion "would perhaps at this stage prefer the sound advice of (her father) given in a discussion between them to orders or prohibitions with which she is burdened indirectly by means of an order of court."[26] On another occasion a South African court, exercising

its discretion against the grant of an interdict in the light of changing social *mores*, observed: "It would be an order encroaching on
the domain of human passion, and enforcement thereof would
create practical problems. This is a case where human relationships must sort themselves out."[27] In the result, the father failed to
obtain an interdict prohibiting the respondent, a divorced woman,
the mother of two children and ten years older than the applicant's
minor unemancipated son, from communicating with the latter.

If so dramatic a transformation could take place in a modern
legal system deriving from incomparably less amorphous antecedents, the inevitability or even propriety of a continuing focus on
parental right or power, as part of the conceptual framework of
English law, is seriously open to question. A major assumption
which underlies discussion of the issues involved in the Gillick saga
is the intrinsically divisive nature of the fundamental moral problem. Lord Templeman effectively captures the volatile spirit of
conflicting moral and ethical approaches to the dilemma: "Some
doctors approve, and some doctors disapprove, of the idea that a
doctor may decide to provide contraception for a girl under sixteen
without the knowledge of the parent. Some parents agree, and
some parents disagree, with the proposition that the decision must
depend on the judgment of the doctor."[28] Nevertheless, despite
the uncompromising terms in which the views of the Court of
Appeal and the two dissenting Law Lords are expressed on this
point, the burden of the argument in this article is that overriding
importance attached to parental power does not serve as a convincing point of departure for the modern law.

(b) Arguments in support of parental right

In the Court of Appeal Fox L.J. identified, as one of the rele-
vent parcel of legal rights available to the father at common law, a
right to custody of his legitimate children during minority.[29] Moreover, a crucial component of custody was said to be control, in
that, while custody entails care of the child, "without control the
care may be hindered."[30] On this basis the view was taken that,
through the vehicle of custody, parental right, *vis-à-vis* minor
children, subsumes control which is unrestricted save by having
recourse to the jurisdiction of the courts. The paramountcy so
accorded to parental right has been skillfully buttressed by calling
in aid a variety of considerations.

(i) A powerful appeal was made to the order of nature, and to
natural relationship, as the source of parental right. Fox L.J. pre-
dicated "the principle of virtual supremacy of the parents'
wishes"[31] on the aspiration, regarded as sacrosanct in a judicial

utterance made more than a century ago, that "The father is the head of his house, he must have control of his family."[32] In keeping with the ideas of that time custody was denoted as "that sort of guardianship which the ordinary law of nature entrusts to the father till the age of infancy has completely passed and gone."[33] This was elevated to a "natural paternal jurisdiction"[34] which survived between the age of discretion and the age of majority. It was taken for granted that, founded on natural impulse and affection, "During infancy and over sixteen the right of the father still continues."[35] The heavy dependence on ideas derived from natural law shines through the typically Victorian comment by Bowen L.J.: "It is not the benefit to the infant as conceived by the court, but it must be the benefit to the infant having regard to the natural law which points out that the father knows far better as a rule what is good for his children than a court of justice can."[36]

(ii) The wide dimensions of parental power were said to be fortified impliedly by legislative provisions. The Court of Appeal made tentative use of a series of ambiguous provisions contained in the Family Law Reform Act[37] and in legislation dealing with mental health[38] and education.[39] But the main thrust of the appeal to indications supposedly contained in the statute law consisted of emphasis on the legislative bar preventing a parent from divesting himself of his rights and duties *qua* parent[40] and the definition of legal custody, in relation to a child, as connoting "so much of the parental rights and duties as relate to the person of the child, including the place and manner in which his time is spent."[41] On the strength of the latter provision Parker L.J. suggested: "If there is a right and duty to determine the place and manner in which a child's time is spent, such right or duty must cover the right and duty completely to control the child."[42] That this is a *non sequitur*, from the standpoint of the cardinal issues of policy involved as well as in terms of recurring patterns of judicial development in other countries of the Commonwealth, is apparent from the ensuing discussion.

(iii) The recognition of consent given by a minor child to medical treatment without the approval of the parent, it has been suggested, introduces a potentially insuperable obstacle to the discharge of parental duty. Parker L.J. pointed out that if a child could, without the parent's knowledge and consent, seek and receive contraceptive advice and treatment, he or she could, logically, also presumably do so in respect of other medical treatment. Parker L.J. stressed the dangers inherent in this conclusion: "A mother who, for example, does not know that her child has had some particular injection or is taking some form of drug may, if the child is in an accident and unconscious, assure the doctor that she has not had that injection and is not taking any drugs. This may have serious and possibly fatal consequences."[43] However, the relevance of this contingency to confirm or refute a well-considered rule in regard to the capacity of a minor who had attained the age of discretion, to consent to medical treatment in the generality of cases is, to say the least, doubtful.

(iv) A supportive argument in regard to the desirability of judicial detachment, in the light of an objectively established rule of the common law, has also been used. Parker L.J., while conceding that parental objection to competent contraceptive treatment may well be counterproductive, in that it could lead to pregnancy, or back street abortion and even death, nevertheless added: "Such matters are, however, matters for debate elsewhere. If it be the law that until a girl is sixteen no one may, save by the intervention of the court, afford advice or treatment without the parent's consent, then that law must be observed until it is altered by the legislature."[44]

This spirit of self-abnegation, imputing as it does to the law a certainty and stability it does not possess, is misplaced. What is called for, instead, is an aggressive judicial role committed to moulding the law in harmony with prevailing social priorities. From this point of view, there is particular value in the approach which commended itself to Lord Scarman in the House of Lords. Highlighting three dramatic features—contraception as a subject for medical advice and treatment, the increasing independence of young people and the changed status of women—which have transformed the character of modern society by heralding a degree of opportunity denied to previous generations, Lord Scarman rightly accepts that the condition of the law must accord with these developments if it is not to become obsolete.[45] He enjoins upon judges the creative task of discarding detail appropriate to earlier times in quest of vital legal principle which amply satisfies contemporary needs.[46] This requires a deliberate and discriminating exercise of judgment in adapting, by means of the case law technique, principles of the common law which had their origin in an age dominated by a wholly different social and cultural outlook. Judicial assessment, then, is the decisive factor in remodulating parental right, in regard to scope as well as duration.

(c) The opposing factors

The relegation of such an approach makes for the perpetuation of an inopportune attitude which unacceptably strains the law by sanctifying parental authority in a manner which suggests insufficient sensitivity to manifest realities and competing expectations. The antiquated common law premise was that, except in cases of misconduct, desertion or abandonment of parental right, the courts were not entitled to interfere with the rights of the parent or to consider "either what the wishes of the child may be, or what they might think to be most for its benefit."[47] Judicial authority illustrative of this trend stresses consistently that interference with the parental will is warranted only by utmost need and in the most extreme cases.[48] This attitude is grounded in a meretricious appeal to the sanctity of family life.[49] The appeal is unconvincing primarily because the bonds which join family members for mutual sustenance are of value only when they are marked by warmth and spontaneity,[50] and parental control assumes an oppressive quality if the *de facto* relationship with the child is inhibited by an irretrievable erosion of confidence.[51] However, potent vestiges of an outlook suited to a bygone age supply the impetus for the assertion by the Court of Appeal, in *Gillick*'s case, that "The father has a legal right of custody until the age of majority, and that right includes a right of control over the person."[52]

It is consistent with modern ideas that a frontal attack should be made against the proposition that a minor invariably remains in the custody of his parent until the attainment of majority or the death of the parent. A modern English court has considered it an essential element of such custody that the right to control the minor's life should be accompanied by "the capacity to exercise that control, whether arising from economic circumstances or otherwise."[53] The mere relationship between parent and child, bereft of this capacity for control, has been deemed insufficient to sustain the right to custody.[54] The emerging focus on the existence of circumstances which admit realistically of substantial control is incompatible with the view that custody is the inescapable consequence of rights conferred *a priori* by the law upon a parent in respect of his minor child.[55]

In any event, the absolute character of control as a necessary incident of custody sits uneasily with modern trends. The rigour of common law attitudes to the parental power of the father has been attenuated by the jurisdiction of the Court of Chancery, functioning as a delegate of the Crown as *parens patriae*, to exercise a supervisory power for the benefit of the minor child.[56] Departing radically from the common law premise that the father was absolutely entitled to the custody of his minor children, with all its attendant powers, unless he forfeited his right in consequence of grave misconduct,[57] Chancery, in its exercise of a benevolent jurisdiction,[58] did what, in the circumstances of the case, it was judici-

ally satisfied a wise parent acting in the true interests of the child
would or ought to do.[59] Although it was evident that this equitable
jurisdiction was resorted to, on the whole, during the last century
to reinforce the wishes of the father,[60] these judicial predilections
merely expressed the spirit of the age.[61] But the crucial development signified by the jurisdiction of the Court of Chancery was
that its power of intervention in the interest of the child was exercisable, notwithstanding that the natural parent had the desire to
assert his will and had not been found guilty of such misconduct as
entailed forfeiture of his common law right.[62]

The entrenchment of this benign principle was ensured by statutory initiatives which brought about the fusion of law and equity,
with the rules of equity prevailing.[63] It is of interest to note a
parallel development in American law, where the State is expected
to discharge a *parens patriae* function in protecting those who cannot take care of themselves.[64] The Supreme Court of the United
States has held that even parental rights protected by constitutional provisions are amenable to limitation by the State's interest in promoting the welfare of children, for example, by
prohibiting child labour.[65] The generality of the protective principle in Western legal systems today is indicated by the recurring
pattern in English[66] and Commonwealth[67] legislative provisions
which unequivocally accord primacy to the welfare of the child at
the expense of parental power. The House of Lords has recognised
that, in the setting of custodial disputes, unlike in such contexts as
serological examination with a view to establishing paternity, the
governing consideration is the child's welfare unencumbered by
any competing question of general public interest.[68] The legislative postulate of "paramountcy"[69] has received, at the hands of
Australian courts, the construction that the welfare of the child is,
if not the exclusive consideration,[70] at least the most important
among a number of relevant considerations.[71]

(d) Dominant trends in the law

The decisively changing focus from parental right to the welfare
principle emerges from a variety of interlocking strands in the
developing law, which cumulatively represent a significant transformation of core values in this branch of the law.

(i) Access to a child by a parent not having custody. The right of
periodical access to a child is looked upon by the common law as
"no more than the basic right of any parent."[72] The Federal Court
of Australia has accepted, as a general principle, that a parent has
"a very strong claim"[73] to access.

It is fitting, however, that modern courts should approach problems of access from a different standpoint, advisedly disavowing enforcement of parental right as the central issue. The reasoning of a South African court in a case where the matter for decision was whether a custody order should be varied so as to deprive the father, a Jehovah's Witness and a member of an actively proselytising group, of access to the divorced parties' minor children, who were being brought up according to the tenets of the Methodist Church, in keeping with the wishes of the mother, the custodian parent, offers a redeeming point of departure.[74] The problem might well have been approached from the point of view of the legal rights of the custodian parent. According to this approach, it was a compelling consideration that the father's efforts to proselytise on behalf of his religious group constituted an infringement of the custodian parent's right to determine the religion of the children. But the court was emphatic in its rejection of this approach and preferred to focus upon the right of the minor children to be allowed access to the non-custodian parent rather than upon the latter's right to obtain access to the children.[75] Admittedly, it is in general in the interest of the children, even where a family has broken up, for them to continue to have a wholesome and caring relationship with both parents. However, the courts today recognise, more frequently than in the past, that there are exceptional contexts in which the child's interests are best served by complete severance of ties with the non-custodian parent if exposure to his or her influence involves acute emotional distress for the child. Accordingly, the South African court withheld access from the father on the basis that subjection of the children to his proselytising influence in an environment where the religious bias in the schools they were attending was of an altogether different *milieu*, was likely to place them in a potential conflict situation which was detrimental to their welfare.[76]

This approach, which explicitly subordinates parental rights and claims to the overall welfare of the child, has evolved all the more readily in Commonwealth jurisdictions applying equitable principles derived from English law. A modern English court has declared: "The mere desire of a parent to have his child must be subordinate to the consideration of the welfare of the child, and can be effective only if it coincides with the welfare of the child."[77] The Court of Appeal of New Zealand has stated: "Our concern is with the welfare of the child as the first and paramount consideration, and not with the rights or desires of the parents, except as secondary or less important considerations."[78] Strengthened by the identification of priorities within the framework of the statutory régime applicable,[79] the Supreme Court of New Zealand has had no difficulty in considering the rival claims of parents to the custody of a child relevant as a subject distinct from the child's welfare, only on condition that these factors are always ancillary to the welfare consideration.[80] This principle, liberally construed so as to embrace moral and religious welfare apart from physical wellbeing and material considerations,[81] now indisputably holds sway in Canada,[82] the Irish Free State[83] and Northern Ireland.[84] "To this paramount consideration all others yield."[85]

(ii) Competing claims by spouses in respect of custody. An Australian court, capturing the spirit of the traditional common law, has stated: "The law which regarded husband and wife as one, which gave the husband's name to the wife, which regarded her property (with minor exceptions) as passing to him on marriage, naturally regarded the decision on disputed matters as resting with husband and father."[86] The harshness of this rule has been mitigated by legislative action as well as by judicial policy. Statutory changes in England throughout the last century substantially improved the legal condition of the mother of a minor child.[87]

Although there is no settled rule that a child of tender years must necessarily remain in the custody of the mother,[88] the "strong presumption"[89] founded less on law than on experience and the nature of ordinary human relationships is that a young child, especially a girl, should have the care and affection of the child's mother if it is not possible to secure for its upbringing the responsibility of both parents living together. The judicial preference for maternal custody in these circumstances has been put on the footing that, in the case of a young girl, the protection and care of the mother is likely to be more beneficial than that of the father who may be comparatively remote from vital areas of her growth and experience.[90] The presumption favouring the mother's custody in such a case, it has been pointed out in Australia, is capable of being displaced only by "the very strongest evidence"[91] that the custody of the mother is injurious to the wellbeing of the child. Moreover, the temptation to approach disputes surrounding custody and access as though they involve primarily a contest between spouses, and the inclination to accommodate the wishes of both parents whenever practicable in regard to the distribution of these rights, have been firmly discouraged in Australia.[92] The predominant consideration is that "The court is dealing with the lives of human beings, and these cannot be regulated by formulae."[93]

In the light of these developments it is hardly surprising that Lord Cave thought fit to comment, as early as 1925: "Some of the earlier judgments contain sentences in which, perhaps, greater stress is laid upon the father's wishes than would be placed upon them now."[94] The measure of judicial creativity in this area of the law is indicated by the willingness of South African courts today, modifying Roman and Roman-Dutch antecedents which considered it "beyond dispute"[95] that minor legitimate children are ruled according to the judgment of the father, to be guided, in the exercise of their jurisdiction as upper guardian of minors, by "one substantial norm"—namely, the predominant interests of the child.[96]

(iii) Moral turpitude and past neglect as bars in relation to custody. The unrelenting attitude of the ecclesiastical jurisdiction was that a wife who had been guilty of adultery was debarred, *ipso facto*, not only from custody but also from the right of access.[97] But so hypocritical a principle, assailed by Pollock M.R. over half a century ago as "cold and barren"[98] in its impact, has long since been eschewed by the common law. A more humane outlook has superseded the puritanical values of the pre-existing common law in Commonwealth jurisdictions as well. The established view in Commonwealth law is that the picture conjured up, by the past or even present lives of the spouses has a material bearing on the award of custody only in so far as the child's place in this picture needs to be envisaged by the court.[99] Consequently, although the conduct of the parents is not an entirely irrelevant circumstance,[1] the crucial factor is the long-term welfare of the child rather than moral evaluation of previous delinquent behaviour.[2] The fact that the mother had married her former companion in adultery, a New Zealand court has held, does not outweigh the vital consideration that the interests of very young children require that they should continue to have their mother's care.[3] To this extent, the competing claims of the spouses are relegated.

Changing social values are candidly acknowledged in the pronouncement, by the Court of Appeal of New Zealand, that "In modern times the fact that one of the spouses has been found to be guilty of some matrimonial wrong towards the other has not been regarded as having the same decisive influence as in days gone by."[4] It is clear, for instance, that the objections made by a father having custody of his minor children to their being brought into contact with the co-respondent cited in connection with a matrimonial offence alleged to have been committed by his wife, would be viewed in a different light today. A self-righteous attitude which purports to deny a parent access on the ground of past neglect or indifference has fallen into disfavour, since the child is likely to benefit from the availability of an opportunity to the repentant parent to make amends in the future.[5] The recurring idea is that the grant or refusal of custody or access cannot be exploited as a lever for the imposition of a deterrent or for the manifestation of approval of past or current conduct, for these considerations in their entirety must give way to the welfare principle.[6]

(iv) Custodial disputes between parents and strangers. The rule admits of no controversy today that there is no difference in principle between a contest between parents for the custody of a child and a contest between a parent and a stranger, the interest of the child being the dominant consideration in both cases.[7] This rule, however, is of comparatively recent origin. English and Commonwealth courts have felt a lingering reluctance to apply a uniform test in both contexts because of preoccupation with natural rights emanating from the blood tie. Influenced by conservative currents of opinion in the common law, Canadian courts, in the middle of the present century, have considered it "settled law"[8] that the natural parents of an infant have a right to its custody which, apart from statute, they can forfeit only by acts involving moral turpitude.[9]

Fortunately, this approach has been supplanted in recent years by a more discriminating and empirical principle which does not shrink from recognition that it is unsafe to proceed on the assumption that a child will receive greater love and more understanding upbringing if it is returned to a parent who did not want it than it would if left in the hands of those who sought it out for their love and care.[10] The only concession to legitimate parental claim which Australian courts are now disposed to make consists of a provisional presumption that, in a contest between parent and stranger, the interests of the child are likely to be better served, *ceteris paribus*, in the custody of its natural parent.[11] The qualification is important, for it is only where other considerations are equal that the court will give effect to the blood relationship and grant custody to a parent rather than to a stranger.[12] In keeping with emerging lines of authority in the modern law, no greater weight can be attached to parental right than is catered for by the principle that the course dictated by the child's welfare should always be chosen even if it is inconsistent with possession by the parents unless, from the point of view of the child's welfare, there is no difference between the two courses or the difference is negligible or speculative.[13] Accordingly, the House of Lords has declined to award custody to the natural parents, who were

Spanish nationals resident in Spain, in circumstances where the child, who was then ten years old, had spent almost the whole of his life with foster parents in England, spoke little Spanish and scarcely knew his parents.[14] The consideration uppermost in the minds of their Lordships was that the parents would probably be ill-equipped to cope with the problems of adjustment to a new environment which the child was certain to encounter[15] and that the child's sense of security should not, therefore, be disturbed in the circumstances by a change of custody.[16]

English law, expounded with admirable courage by the House, goes further than the current Australian approach in postulating "an end to any presumption of law respecting parental rights and wishes so far as the test of welfare is concerned."[17] The essence of the modern approach would seem to be that, where the tie between the child and its natural parent is taken into account by the law, this is done "not on the basis that the person concerned has a claim which he has a right to have satisfied, but to the extent that the conclusion can be drawn that the child will benefit from the recognition of this tie."[18] Recent Canadian decisions[19] are marked by trenchant criticism of judges at first instance who place "undue emphasis on the fact of paternity"[20] and give inadequate weight to factors addressing the best interests of the child.[21]

(v) Religious upbringing. This, too, is an area in which common law attitudes were characterised by extreme rigidity. Quite early in the present century, a New Zealand court felt able to assert uncompromisingly: "Now, whether the law relating to the religious education of children is good or bad, it is, at any rate, certain. It is beyond question that a father has the right to have his children brought up in the religion he professes."[22] Predictably, however, this spirit of inflexibility has appeared increasingly unattractive to contemporary judges.[23] It is now readily accepted that an infant who has reached the years of discretion may choose his religion without restraint.[24] Moreover, the House of Lords has upheld the view, in regard to religious education, that "The wishes of the father only prevail if they are not displaced by considerations relating to the welfare of the children themselves."[25] Thus a Queensland court has recognised that the indoctrination of certain religious beliefs may be harmful to the child[26]; and a court in Victoria has entertained no doubt that it is not in the interest of infants attending State schools and being brought up according to the conventions of the Presbyterian faith by their mother, the custodian parent, to be exposed, at their father's instance, to instruction in the beliefs of Jehovah's Witnesses.[27]

(vi) The parent's right to the services of the child. Legislative action in this field has been the major vehicle for giving expression to the values and outlook of the modern age.

At common law a child under the age of majority was deemed, constructively, to be a servant of the master of the house.[28] This doctrine has been applied to give a step-parent the benefit of the child's services.[29] The common law principle was that entitlement to the child's services was an attribute of the right to custody.[30] The foundations of the common law in this regard reflected, to some extent, a conception of the child as an economic asset.[31] Although the right to services was not capable of enforcement by direct action, it was the subject of oblique legal sanctions, in so far as acts of third parties which constituted wrongful interference with the right to services involved tortious liability.[32] Seduction and enticement could entail liability for loss of services, provided that the services were actually available to the plaintiff at the time the delinquent act was committed.[33]

This highlights the feature that the object of the action was ostensibly reipersecutory, in that the plaintiff's interest pertained to an anticipated economic gain of which he is unlawfully deprived. In reality, however, the predominant interest violation of which was sought to be compensated lay in the field of injury to feelings and self-esteem and, consequently, had to be seen as an inherent aspect of integrity of personality. This is borne out by the appreciably aggravated damages, out of all proportion to the monetary value of the services withheld, which in general attended a successful suit.[34] The underlying premise of liability suggests an imperfect parallel with the Roman law conception of *injuriae per consequentias*, the core of which is the invasion of the parent's personality by means of interference with the bodily integrity or dignity of his child.[35]

It was unmistakably clear that the common law cause of action was replete with anomalies which irreparably impaired its cohesive character.[36] Nevertheless, it is the repugnance of the cause of action to modern ideas relating to the relationship between parent and child, rather than the structural aberrations of the action, which prompted its abrogation by legislative action in England in 1982.[37]

(e) The status of parental claim in modern law

These developments, viewed in perspective, infuse the modern law with adequate resilience to forge on the anvil of contemporary policy an approach to the basis of parental claims which take into account sufficiently other countervailing elements central to the welfare consideration. The views of the majority of the House of Lords in *Gillick*'s case rest on a number of assumptions which impart to the law a pervading sense of relevance and immediacy. Chief among these is the assumption that parental right, to the extent that it receives legitimacy in the law, subserves essential purposes linked with the interest of the child. Buttressed by an innovative orientation of Blackstone's emphasis on the power of parents as an instrument for the fulfilment of their duty,[38] Lord Fraser of Tullybelton and Lord Scarman underscored the need for a perceptive refurbishing of the concept of parental right as a complement for other values which are part and parcel of modern legal culture. The point of depature adopted by the former is that "Parental rights exist for the benefit of the child, and they are justified only in so far as they enable the parent to perform his duties towards the child."[39] Lord Fraser approached the problem from the standpoint that, once the rule of absolute parental authority over minor children is abandoned, the solution depends in the final analysis on a judgment as to what is best for the welfare of the particular child.[40] Lord Scarman, similarly, placed stress on the consistent resolve of the common law, far from treating parental rights as "sovereign or beyond review and control,"[41] to look upon the child as a person invested with capacities and rights recognised by the law.[42] The emerging view, then, is that the parental right, in this setting, enjoys legal recognition only to the extent that it sustains a protective mechanism which complements, with progressively reduced intensity after the minor has attained years of discretion, the personality and wellbeing of the infant. The thrust of the development epitomised in these speeches is the growing judicial disinclination to regard parental right as subsuming interests which are worthy of recognition, intrinsically, as the pivot of a cause of action.

(f) American judicial approaches: a comparative dimension

A significantly different method of approach is inescapable in the United States of America because of the constitutional framework of the law which has generated a body of jurisprudence dominated by the philosophy of competing interests. The essential feature of American law is that "Numerous and significant interests compete when a minor decides whether or not to abort her pregnancy."[43]

Naturally, a cardinal interest, entrenched in American judicial attitudes, is that of the minor herself. The law of the United States concedes to a pregnant woman the fundamental right to choose whether to obtain an abortion or to carry the pregnancy to term.[44]

Her choice, in regard to deeply intimate decisions involving marriage,[45] procreation[46] and the use of contraceptives[47] is insulated from unwarranted State intervention by the right of privacy.[48] This is enveloped in American jurisprudence by "the right of every individual to the possession and control of his own person, free from all restraint or interference of others, unless by clear and unquestionable authority of law."[49] The suggestion has been made by an American court that the financial, psychological and social problems arising from teenage pregnancy and motherhood "argue for our recognition of the right of minors to privacy as being equal to that of adults."[50] Accordingly, the court struck down a prohibition embodied in State legislation against family planning assistance for minors without parental concurrence.[51]

In juxtaposition with the constitutional rights of the minor, American judicial attitudes are committed to the recognition of a substratum of parental rights. The Supreme Court of the United States has uniformly recognised, as a matter of constitutional interpretation, that "The parents' claim to authority in their own household to direct the rearing of their children is basic in the structure of our society."[52] This is seen as an aspect of the constitutional protection of the relationship between parent and child.[53] The seminal idea is that this relationship permeates a domain which is entitled under the legal régime to immunity from State intervention. The constitutional importance of demarcating the respective spheres of parental and State responsibility is spelt out in the comment that "It is cardinal with us that the custody, care and nurture of the child reside first in the parents, whose primary function and freedom include preparation for obligations the State can neither supply nor hinder."[54] American courts have accepted that parents have an indispensable "guiding role" to play in the upbringing of their children,[55] which presumptively includes counselling them on important decisions.[56]

The third of the constitutionally protected interests is that of a State within the federation. A State, it has been suggested, has an interest in encouraging childbirth rather than abortion.[57] Apart from this, the notion recurs in the American case law that a State has a vital interest in fostering such consultation as will assist the distressed minor in making her decision as wisely as possible.[58] Moreover, a State may also have an interest in the family itself, as the institution through which "we inculcate and pass down many of our most cherished values, moral and cultural."[59]

The complexity of American law is associated with the delicate balance which needs to be struck in the context of this trichotomy of interests. While each interest is central, none is absolute, since the abridgement of each interest is made necessary by the accommodation of elements connected with the others. Thus, a Massachusetts statute which required parental or judicial consent before an abortion could be performed on any unmarried minor has been struck down by the Supreme Court of the United States on the basis that its provisions entailed an unwarranted relegation of the first interest to the second and the third interests.[60] The unconstitutionality of the purported legislation was imputable to the inflexible requirement of parental consent, without provision of an opportunity for the minor to demonstrate that she is sufficiently mature to consent to an abortion.[61] A blanket, unreviewable power in parents to veto their minor daughter's abortion is, therefore, constitutionally impermissible. On the other hand, a legislative requirement of mere notice to the parents is not the functional equivalent of a requirement of parental concurrence, and the former is invulnerable, since a State may reasonably determine that parental consultation is often desirable, in that a girl of tender years, under emotional stress, may be ill-equipped to make a grave decision without mature advice and emotional support.[62]

Invasion of the child's privacy right, brought about by the interjection of additional parties into a confidential transaction, may be justified in these circumstances by having recourse to a compelling State interest. This is plainly so, since the notice requirement is specifically tailored to promote the objective of eliciting the fullest information relating to the case history, facilitating as it does the best medical judgment upon the matter.[63] At the same time the equilibrium produced by the American case law is hostile to recognition of the opinion of a single doctor as to the need or desirability of an abortion as outweighing all State and parental interests, and declines to elevate the decision of the minor and her doctor to an unimpeachable status in opposition to countervailing interests. An attractive *via media*, in the American context, is the device of an independent decision maker to whom a pregnant minor could resort if she believes that she is mature enough to make the abortion decision independently or that parental notification is in some way contrary to her best interests.[64]

A substantial commingling of approaches is precluded by the distinct conceptual patterns of the English and the American legal systems. In particular, the reconciliation of competing interests, which lies at the heart of American constitutional doctrines, is peripheral to the approach of English law. But an approximate convergence of result is suggested by recent American trends which look askance at the recognition of "reserved rights" in parents which seek unproductively to substitute for the spontaneous quality of emotional attachments within a family, coercive legal norms dependent for their effectiveness on direct State action.[65]

III. The Minor's Capacity to Consent

An integral facet of the controversy concerns the child's capacity to give a valid consent to contraceptive treatment which operates to forestall criminal or tortious liability on the part of the doctor.

(a) The age of consent

The effect of statute law is that a minor who has attained the age of sixteen years has full capacity in England to consent to any surgical or medical treatment.[66] The position in regard to a minor below this age was the subject of a lively conflict of judicial opinion in *Gillick's* case. It is clear that the quality of the minor's consent is crucial where the parents have not consented, and the conduct of the doctor would otherwise constitute a trespass.

A strand of authority in the common law, reflecting an obsolete code of values, attaches overriding importance to the legal norm identifying the age of discretion. In the middle of the last century Cockburn C.J., in a case where recovery of custody was sought by the father in habeas corpus proceedings, declared: "We repudiate . . . the notion that any intellectual precocity in an individual female child can hasten the period fixed by statute for the arrival of the age of discretion; for that very precocity . . . might . . . lead to her irreparable injury."[67] The explicit delimitation of specific ages of discretion—fourteen for boys and sixteen for girls—has been explained on the ground that "The court cannot inquire into every particular case."[68]

Surprisingly, this point of view found almost unreserved favour at the present day in the judgments of the Court of Appeal in *Gillick's* case. A vigorous appeal was made in these judgments to the need for certainty and stability in the law in an area where transgressions unprotected by consent are accompanied by sanctions of the greatest severity. Parker L.J. commented: "In relation to aspects of custody and control there must be a fixed age in order that parents, children and those dealing with children may know where they stand and what are their powers, rights, duties or obligations."[69] The absence of a fixed age of discretion, determined in the abstract, seemed wholly impractical to Fox L.J.: "It is inconvenient in practice, in that it may give rise to subsequent doubts and difficulties of proof, as to whether the child does have sufficient understanding."[70]

The unimaginative character of this view, which takes no account of other compelling factors pointing in a different direction, is all the more remarkable against the background of sustained developments in the common law which typify a refreshingly greater elasticity of approach. Foremost among these developments are the evolving principles governing the father's entitlement to restitution of custody of a minor possessing sound judgment, and largely parallel trends in the area of such a minor's capacity to consent to acts which, but for consent, would attract penal sanctions. In the former context, the common law, after initial vacillation, adopted the principle that, although a father is entitled to the custody of his children until they attain the age of majority, a court will not grant habeas corpus to hand over a child below that age to its father, "provided that it has attained an age of sufficient discretion to enable it to exercise a wise choice for its own interests."[71] In the latter area, the House of Lords has had no hesitation in rejecting the submission that a father, even if he had taken his child away by force or fraud, could in no circumstances be guilty of any criminal offence.[72] Their Lordships preferred the view that, in relation to the kidnapping of a child, it is in all cases the absence of the child's consent which is material and that it must be a question of fact for a jury whether the particular child had sufficient understanding and intelligence to give its consent.[73] In keeping with this view a girl under sixteen is capable of giving sufficiently effective consent to sexual intercourse to produce the result that the man involved does not commit the crime of rape.[74] This is consistent with ordinary experience, for "There are many girls under sixteen who know full well what it is all about and can properly consent."[75]

These developments, on any realistic view, erode drastically the foundation of any approach which regards fixity of the age of discretion as an immutable feature of the law. Yet the tenor of the judgments in the Court of Appeal displays firm resolve to circumscribe the liberal trends by regarding them as having no implications outside the specific contexts in which they have occurred.[76] This construction, apart from perpetuating modes of thought which can hardly enrich legal principles today, imparts to the law a scholastic and unreal quality. By far, the more convincing approach is to recognise, in preference to an arbitrary point of time at which a metamorphosis takes place from lack of capacity to full capacity, a natural process of continuous growth in the course of which, according to normal experience, parental authority diminishes in proportion to the physical and mental development of the child.[77] In a branch of the law intimately connected with problems touching the growth and maturity of the human personality, it is evident that straitjacket precision in regard to the age of discretion entails the unacceptable disadvantage of artificiality and remoteness from reality.[78] The view which carries conviction in the light of modern social ideas and values is that the parental right to determine whether or not their child below the age of sixteen will have medical treatment terminates when the child achieves adequate understanding to enable him or her to comprehend fully what is proposed.[79] The attitude of an American court, that the consent of a minor with sufficient intelligence to a nose straightening operation is legally valid, despite the opposition of her parents,[80] would seem to be dictated by good sense.

It is of interest to note that other legal systems sustained by different antecedents have acquiesced substantially in this development. South African courts, professing fidelity to Roman and Roman-Dutch legal principle in shaping the law of parent and child, have reached a result which is by no means dissimilar. A modern South African judge has found satisfying the view that "The mental and moral education of a child is clearly something which progressively decreases as the child grows more and more mature until, in the case of mentally normal and conforming children, it is reduced to the mere giving of advice."[81] This is almost an echo of Lord Denning's description of parental power as resting upon "a dwindling right which the courts will hesitate to enforce against the wishes of the child, and the more so the older he is."[82] Indeed, Teutonic customary law, in the aftermath of the reception of Roman law, was sensitive to a close relationship between the age of discretion and the ability to defend oneself, and acknowledged that enhanced physical prowess as a result of bodily development was a tentative precursor to legal recognition of adulthood.[83]

These nuances and gradations within the upper limits of legal minority represent a prominent characteristic of American judicial responses. The Supreme Court of the United States has declared: "Constitutional rights do not mature and come into being magically only when one attains the State-defined age of majority."[84] Minors, no less than adults, are held to possess constitutional rights, subject to the sole difference that the State has somewhat broader authority to regulate the activities of children than those of adults.[85] Several American States have resorted to statutory instruments to permit emancipation of minors for a specific purpose, such as obtaining medical care without parental consent. Thus, in Utah a minor may consent to medical treatment for venereal disease,[86] while it is lawful in Texas for a person who is more than thirteen years of age to consent to medical treatment for drug dependency.[87] A parallel development of a piecemeal character had been achieved almost two centuries ago within the framework of the English common law. At the beginning of the nineteenth century the common law permitted a boy of 12 to take the oath of allegiance, while at 14 he might consent to marriage or select his guardian and at 17 he could function as an executor.[88] These were juristic acts, some involving a fiduciary content, which a child was competent under the common law to perform long before attainment of the age of majority. The undeniable social reality has been explicitly identified and acknowledged in the United States: "Some minors, in some circumstances, have the capacity and the need to determine their health care needs without involving their parents."[89] The crucial criteria are those relating to the situation and degree of development of the individual minor.

It is hardly surprising that a variety of legal systems, adopting widely varying points of depature and following different lines of development, should eventually reach a large measure of confluence. The central challenge is that of revamping the common law which, a century ago, looked upon the father as having absolute and paramount authority, as against all the world, over any children of his who were under the age of majority, except for a married daughter, in such a manner as to enable adaptation of its principles to suit a radically changed social and cultural situation.[90] It is natural that a largely shared moral outlook should make it possible for Western legal systems, in responding to this challenge, to bring into being a body of law marked by a high degree of homogeneity of principle.

(b) Other requisites of consent

It may well be that the anti-Gillick school of thought won no more than a Pyrrhic victory. What detracts, in the main, from the strength of the ruling hostile to the contentions urged on Mrs. Gillick's behalf is the uniquely exacting test of consent formulated by Lord Scarman: "It has to be borne in mind that there is much that has to be understood by a girl under the age of sixteen if she is to have legal capacity to consent to (contraceptive) treatment. It is not enough that she should understand the nature of the advice which is being given: she must also have a sufficient maturity to understand what is involved. There are moral and family questions, especially her relationship with her parents; long-term problems associated with the emotional impact of pregnancy and its termination; and there are the risks to health of sexual intercourse at her age, risks which contraception may diminish but cannot eliminate. It follows that a doctor will have to satisfy himself that she is able to appraise these factors before he can safely proceed upon the basis that she has at law capacity to consent to contraceptive treatment."[91]

If these are strict prerequisites of legal validity of the consent given by the minor, it is apparent that the impact of the decision by the House of Lords is in practice marginal. The weighty moral and ethical issues involved in the minor's decision can hardly be expected to evoke clear-cut responses from many adults, let alone a child who had recently attained puberty[92]; and the doctor's task in exercising his clinical judgment in a situation of exceptional difficulty is certainly daunting if he must needs seek assurance in regard to the quality of the minor's understanding on each of these points before he could confidently embark upon contraceptive treatment.

It is submitted that the narrow parameters of consent demarcated by Lord Scarman are unsound in principle and policy, and are also hard to reconcile with lines of judicial authority in analogous situations. In an Australian trial for rape the trial judge, in his charge to the jury, indicated that understanding by the victim of the physical nature of the act was insufficient to sustain the defence of consent, and that some perception of "the social significance" of the act was essential.[93] This was held in appeal to be a misdirection which justified quashing of the conviction. In the opinion of the Supreme Court of Victoria, the sole understanding required related to the quality of the physical act of penetration.[94] The Court declared: "We are of opinion that capacity to consent does not involve, as a matter of law, knowledge or understanding of any of the ingredients referred to as 'rudimentary concepts' by the trial judge."[95] Insisting that understanding need not be complete or sophisticated, the court thought it sufficient that the child had knowledge of what the act comprised, and of its character, to enable her to decide whether to submit or not.[96] Similarly, the High Court of Australia has made clear its view that consent, as an exculpatory factor in relation to rape, calls for perception only as to the character of what is about to take place, and the identity of the perpetrator of the act.[97] The lightness of the burden which the law imposes on a defendant charged with rape contrasts sharply, and indeed jarringly, with the exacting burden of proof which, according to the House of Lords, a doctor discharging his professional duty is bound to undertake on pain of imposition of legal sanctions. But legal policy requires that the ingredients of consent should certainly be no more stringent in the latter situation than they are thought to be in respect of the crime of rape. Lord

Scarman's discussion of the requisites of consent takes the form of an unduly timorous concession which leads to the surrender of much that the speeches of the majority set out to salvage.

(c) "Informed" consent

Recent developments on both sides of the Atlantic in relation to informed consent to medical treatment, while giving a new impetus to recognition of the patient's right to make his own decision as a basic human right protected by the common law, cannot legitimately be called in aid to fortify the refinements in connection with a minor's capacity to consent, which Lord Scarman was inclined to support in *Gillick's* case. Contemporary judicial trends impart a new strictness to the duty of a doctor to give the patient sufficient information to enable him to decide whether he would accept the treatment proposed by the doctor. The striking development in English law is connected with the scope of obligatory disclosure or communication. The established view used to be that the question whether an omission to warn a patient of inherent risks of proposed treatment constitutes a breach of the doctor's care towards his patient falls to be determined by an application of the principle that no liability is imputable to the doctor if, in withholding any information regarding a potential risk or in omitting any warning, the doctor was following a practice accepted as proper by a responsible body of competent medical opinion.[98] But it has now been recognised, fortunately, that the focus on customary practice, to the exclusion of the vitally important relationship between the individual doctor and his patient which must play a large part in any discussion of proposed surgical treatment, in particular, with a patient, introduces into the law, in a fundamental respect, an element of incompleteness. Accordingly, English law accepts today that there might be circumstances where the proposed treatment involves a substantial risk of grave consequences in which a judge could conclude that, notwithstanding any practice to the contrary accepted as proper by a responsible body of medical opinion, a patient's right to decide whether to consent is so obvious that no prudent doctor could fail to warn of the risk save in exceptional cases.[99] This is in line with the contemporary American approach that protection of the parent's right demands "a standard set by law for a physician rather than one which physicians may or may not impose upon themselves."[1]

However, the function of the doctrine relating to "informed consent" to medical treatment is exhausted at the point where, subject to the "therapeutic privilege" which entitles the doctor to keep back particulars which are likely to cause psychological detriment to the patient and so impair the effectiveness of the treatment offered, the patient is in possession of the full range of information which equips him to make up his mind in regard to acceptance or rejection of the treatment recommended by the doctor. It is no part of the doctor's professional duty to go further and to satisfy himself that the patient has a clear conception of the moral and ethical dimensions of the decision which he is called upon to make. Indeed, if the position were otherwise, any surgical or medical treatment containing an appreciable element of risk would involve oppressive legal hazards for the doctor.

No special factor inconsistent with this basic reality applies to contraceptive treatment which a minor receives at the hands of her physician. In the typical case the doctor agrees to provide the treatment only because he is convinced that sexual intercourse, from the commencement or continuation of which the minor cannot be dissuaded, is likely to cause her serious physical or emotional damage in the event of a supervening pregnancy, or would probably expose her to a grave risk of sexually transmitted disease. Given these considerations which tilt the balance in favour of legality of the contraceptive treatment which the doctor decides to offer in the exercise of his clinical judgment, imposition of the fetters accompanying Lord Scarman's conception of the substance of consent given by the minor stultifies in large measure the gain which the views of the majority confers upon the law.

IV. Conclusion

The views expressed by Woolf J. in the Queen's Bench Division and by the majority in the House of Lords represent a courageous response to the challenge posed in recent times by social developments—in particular, the greatly facilitated access to means of contraception—to the stability of major assumptions which underpin the law of parent and child. An emerging life-style which makes possible teenage independence to an extent which was thought inconceivable a generation ago, has not brought in its wake the total eclipse of parental right. On the contrary, what basic changes in social circumstances and moral outlook require is a restructuring of concepts such as parental right, age of discretion and consensual capacity so as to ensure their continued relevance and vitality in the modern environment. Lord Denning's comment that "The child's views are never decisive"[2] remains as true today for English law as it was when he made this observation 20 years ago. American law, for all the solicitude it bestows on rights inherent in the distinct personality of the child, emphatically repudiates the suggestion that every minor, regardless of maturity, may give effective consent for termination of her pregnancy.[3] However, while parental preference remains in the generality of cases almost an infallible pointer to the child's welfare, estrangement of a child after puberty from parental affection and confidence is today an increasingly widespread phenomenon which the law needs to address. In these cases where evaporation of the security and re-assurance cementing the relationship between parent and child is a *fait accompli*, it is no more than a stark concession to reality for the law to recognise that the coercive implementation of a single, albeit important, parental decision at a time when the recalcitrant minor is approaching majority status, entails no worthwhile gain either in terms of the minor's own interests or from the point of view of a self-sustaining relationship with her parents. In this hinterland between infancy and adulthood the modern law has come into its own by developing a controlled principle of self-determination which underlines individual discrimination and experience as the key to wisdom.

Notes

* Professor of Law and Dean of the Faculty of Law in the University of Colombo, Sri Lanka; Distinguished Visiting Fellow of Christ's College, Cambridge, and Smuts Visiting Fellow in Commonwealth Studies in the University of Cambridge, 1985–6.

[1] *Gillick* v. *West Norfolk and Wisebech Area Health Authority* [1984] 1 Q.B. 581.

[2] [1985] 2 W.L.R. 413.

[3] [1985] 3 W.L.R. 830 [1986] A.C. 112.

[4] At p. 884.

[5] At p. 858.

[6] At p. 863.

[7] At p. 866.

[8] At p. 869.

[9] [1984] 1 Q.B. 581 at p. 585.

[10] At pp. 583–584.

[11] [1985] 2 W.L.R. 413 at p. 435, *per* Parker L.J.

[12] At p. 440.

[13] *Ibid*.

[14] At p. 442.

[15] At p. 443.

[16] *Ibid*.

[17] [1985] 3 W.L.R. 830 at p. 873.

[18] *Ibid*.

[19] See, for a striking illustration, the case cited at n. 32 *infra*.

[20] Livy 8.7.

[21] C. 8.51. 2.

[22] *Meyer* v. *Van Niekerk* 1976 (1) S.A. 252 (T.P.D.).

[23] At p. 255.
[24] See "Studiosus" in *Tydskrif vir Hedendaagse Romeins-Hollandse Reg* (1946), p. 34.
[25] See the case cited at n. 22 *supra*, at p. 257.
[26] *Ibid. per* Coetzee J.
[27] *Coetzee* v. *Meintjies* 1976 (1) S.A. 257 at p. 262, *per* Hiemstra J. (T.P.D.).
[28] See the *Gillick* case [1985] 3 W.L.R. 830 at p. 871.
[29] [1985] 2 W.L.R. 413 at p. 438.
[30] At p. 440.
[31] At p. 439.
[32] *Re Agar-Ellis* (1878) Ch.D. 49 at p. 56, *per* Malins V-C.
[33] *Re Agar-Ellis* (1883) 24 Ch.D. 317, p. 335–336. *per* Bowen L.J.
[34] Hargreave's note to Coke Co. Lit. 88b.
[35] *R.* v. *Howes* (1860) 3 E. & E. 332, *per* Cockburn C.J.
[36] See the case cited at n. 33, at p. 337; *cf. Re Carroll* [1931] 1. K.B. 317.
[37] Family Law Reform Act 1969, s.8(1).
[38] Mental Health Act 1959, s.5(2).
[39] Education Act 1944, s.48(4).
[40] Children Act 1975, s.85(2).
[41] *Id.* s.86.
[42] See *Gillick's* case [1985] 2 W.L.R. 413 at p. 422–423.
[43] At p. 431.
[44] *Ibid.*
[45] [1985] 3 W.L.R. 830 at p. 852.
[46] At p. 853.
[47] *Re Flynn* (1848) 2 De. G. Sym. 457 *per* Knight-Bruce V-C.
[48] *Re Plomley* (1882) 47 L.T. 284; *cf. de Manneville* v. *de Manneville* (1804) 10 Ves. 52.
[49] *Re Curtis* (1859) 28 L.J. Ch. 458.
[50] *Cf. Moore* v. *East Cleveland* 431 U.S. 494 (1977).
[51] *Cf. Planned Parenthood of Central Mo.* v. *Danforth* 428 U.S. 52 at p. 75 (1976).
[52] See *Gillick's* case [1985] 2 W.L.R. 413 at p. 427.
[53] *Brook* v. *Hoar* [1967] 1 W.L.R. 1336 at p. 1341, *per* Melford Stevenson J.
[54] *Duncan* v. *Lambeth L.B.C.* [1968] 1 Q.B. 747 at p. 763, *per* Donaldson J.
[55] For an example of the latter approach, see *Barnardo* v. *McHugh* [1891] A.C. 388.
[56] *R.* v. *Gyngall* [1893] 2 Q.B. 232 at p. 243, *per* Lord Esher M.R.
[57] *Thomasett* v. *Thomasett* [1894] P. 295.
[58] *Hope* v. *Hope* (1854) 4 De. G.M. & G. 328 at p. 344–345, *per* Lord Cranworth M.R.
[59] J.F. Fogarty, *Maintenance, Custody and Adoption Law* (1972) p. 232.
[60] For an extreme illustration, see the *Agar-Ellis* decisions, n. 32 and 33 *supra*, described as "horrendous" by Lord Scarman in *Gillick's* case [1985] 3 W.L.R. 830 at p. 853.
[61] See *Hewer* v. *Bryant* [1970] 1 Q.B. 357 at p. 369 *per* Lord Denning M.R. and at p. 372 *per* Sachs L.J.
[62] *Re O' Hara* (1900) 2 I.R. 232 at pp. 240–241.
[63] Supreme Court of Judicature Act 1875, 38 & 39 Vict. c.l.77.
[64] *Grinsberg* v. *New York* 390 U.S. 629 (1968).
[65] *Wisconsin* v. *Yoder* 406 U.S. 205 (1972).
[66] Guardianship of Minors Act 1971, s.1.
[67] Guardianship Act 1968, s.23(1) (N.Z.); Maintenance Act 1965. s.17(6) (Vict.)

68 *S.* v. *S.* [1972] A.C. 24 at p. 44, *per* Lord Reid.
69 Maintanance Act 1965, s.17(6) (Vict.)
70 *Cf.* for English law, *Re. L.* [1962] 3 All E.R. 1.
71 *P.* v. *P.* [1964] V.R. 430 at pp. 431–432, *per* Barry J. *cf. Cuartero* v. *Cuartero* [1968] V.R. 230.
72 *S.* v. *S. and P.* [1962] 2 All E.R. 1 at p. 3–4, *per* Wilmer L.J. But see, for a more cautious application of common law principle, *Hammond* v. *Hammond* (1962) 106 Sol. J. 610.
73 *Lister (Coleman)* v. *Lister* (1967) 11 F.L.R. 93 at p. 105; *cf. Innes* v. *Innes* [1970] A.L.R. 556.
74 *Dunscombe* v. *Willies* 1982 (3) S.A. 311. (Durban and Coast L.D.)
75 At p. 315.
76 At p. 317, *per* Milne D.J.P.
77 *Re Adoption Application* 41/61 [1963] Ch. 315 at p. 329, *per* Danckwerts L.J.
78 *Otter* v. *Otter* [1951] N.Z.L.R. 739 at p. 746 (C.A.).
79 Guardianship Act 1968, s.23(1) (N.Z.).
80 *Connett* v. *Connett* [1952] N.Z.L.R. 304 (S.C.).
81 *Re McGrath* [1893] 1 Ch. 143 at p. 148, *per* Lindley L.J.; *cf. Goldsmith* v. *Sands* (1907) 4 C.L.R. 1648 at p. 1652 *per* Griffith C.J.
82 *du Laurier* v. *Jackson* (1934) 1 D.L.R. 781.
83 *The State* v. *Markey* [1940] I.R. 421.
84 *Re A.B.* [1946] N.I. 1.
85 *McKee* v. *McKee* (1951) 2 D.L.R. 657 at p. 666 (P.C.).
86 *McKinley* v. *McKinley* [1947] V.L.R. 149 at p. 162, *per* Lowe J.
87 Talfourd's Act of 1839 (2 & 3 Vict. c.54) and the Custody of Infants Act 1873 (36 & 37 Vict. c.12) are striking illustrations.
88 *Re B.* [1962] 1 All E.R. 872; for the contrary view, see *Re S.* [1958] 1 All E.R. 783 at p. 786–787.
89 *Kades* v. *Kades* (1962) 35 A.L.J.R. 251 at p. 254 (H.C.A.).
90 *Mooney* v. *Mooney* [1965] V.R. 460 at p. 462; *Storie* v. *Storie* (1945) 80 C.L.R. 597 at p. 612, *per* Dixon J. (H.C.A.).
91 *Lovell* v. *Lovell* (1950) 81 C.L.R. 513 at p. 522–523 (H.C.A.).
92 *Travnicek* v. *Travnicek* [1966] V.R. 353.
93 *Re F. (An Infant)* [1969] 3 W.L.R. 165.
94 *Ward* v. *Laverty* [1925] A.C. 101.
95 See Voet 26.1.1.
96 *Shawzin* v. *Laufer* [1968] (4) S.A. 657 at p. 662, *per* Rumpff J.A. (A.D.).
97 *Clout* v. *Clout* (1861) 2 Sw. & Tr. 391; *Bent* v. *Bent* (1861) 2 Sw. & Tr. 392.
98 *B.* v. *B.* [1924] P. 176.
99 *Oliver* v. *Oliver* (1969) 13 F.L.R. 397; *Y.* v. *Y.* [1970] A.L.R. 503, *cf.* for New Zealand, *Wilks* v. *Asher* [1951] N.Z.L.R. 27 at p. 29, *per* Stanton J. (S.C.).
1 *Re O.* [1961] 2 All E.R. 10; *Official Solicitor* v. *K.* [1963] 3 All E.R. 191.
2 *P.* v. *P.* [1964] V.R. 430 at p. 432, *per* Barry J; *Miller* v. *Miller* (1968) 11 F.L.R. 226.
3 *Miller* v. *Low* [1952] N.Z.L.R. 575 at p. 589, *per* Adams J. (C.A.); *cf. Norton* v. *Norton* [1951] N.Z.L.R. 678 at p. 682, *per* Adams J. (S.C.).
4 *Palmer* v. *Palmer* [1961] N.Z.L.R. 702 at p. 723, *per* Cleary J. (C.A.).
5 *Downey* v. *Downey* [1965] A.L.R. 539.
6 *Cf. S.* v. *S.* [1962] 2 All E.R. 1 at p. 4.
7 *Zoneff* v. *Zoneff* (1968) 12 F.L.R. 415.
8 *Hepton* v. *Maat* [1957] S.C.R. 606 at p. 615, *per* Cartwright J.
9 See also *Re Baby Duffell* [1950] S.C.R. 737; *Re Agar* [1958] S.C.R. 52.
10 *Re Moores and Feldstein* (1973) 3 O.R. 921 (C.A.).

[11] *Re C. (an Infant)* (1968) 89 W.N. (N.S.W.) (Pt. 1) 235. (S.C.).
[12] *Re Thain* [1926] Ch. 676.
[13] J. M. Eekelaar, "What Are Parental Rights?" (1973) 89 L.Q.R. 210 at p. 217 citing *Re F.* [1969] 2 All E.R. 766.
[14] *J.* v. *C.* [1970] A.C. 668 at p. 724 *per* Lord Upjohn; at p. 727 *per* Lord Donovan.
[15] At p. 710–711, *per* Lord MacDermott.
[16] At p. 715, *per* Lord MacDermott.
[17] At p. 714, *per* Lord MacDermott.
[18] *Re Adoption Application 41/61 (No. 2)* [1964] Ch. 48 at p. 53, *per* Wilberforce J.
[19] See, for comment on these trends, C. Davies, "Custody and Adoption: Some Interrelated Problems" (1973) 23 U of T.L.J. 88; S. Fodden, *Canadian Family Law* (1977) p. 8–21.
[20] *Smith* v. *Goulet, sub nom. R.G.* (1973) 19 R.F.L. 45 (Ont. C.A.).
[21] *Wiltshire* v. *Wiltshire* (1975) 20 R.F.L. 50 (Ont. H.C.).
[22] *Re Thomas* [1911] 30 N.Z.L.R. 168.
[23] *R.* v. *Murdoch; Ex. p. Hoath* [1940] V.L.R. 61; *Barker* v. *Barker* [1967] V.R. 17. See also H.A. Finlay and A. Bissett-Johnson, *Family Law in Australia* (1972), p. 201.
[24] *Re Cuming* (1945) 72 C.C.R. 86 (H.C.A.).
[25] *Ward* v. *Laverty* [1925] A.C. 101 at p. 108, *per* Viscount Cave; *cf. Stourton* v. *Stourton* (1857) 8 De. G.M. & G. 760; *Re W.* (1907) 2 Ch. 557.
[26] *Mauger* v. *Mauger* [1967] Qd. R. 62 (S.C.).
[27] *Barker* v. *Barker* [1967] V.R. 17 at p. 20, *per* Barry J. (S.C.).
[28] *Beetham* v. *James* [1937] 1 All E.R. 58.
[29] *Peters* v. *Jones* [1914] 2 K.B. 781.
[30] *Ibid.*
[31] *Cf.* D. Stern, S. Smith and F. Doolittle, "How Children Used to Work" (1975) 39 (3) *Law and Contemp. Problems* 93.
[32] Law Reform (Miscellaneous Provisions Act) Act 1970. s.5 (U.K.).
[33] *Cameron* v. *Commissioner for Railways* [1964] Qd. R. 480 at p. 492 (S.C.).
[34] *Terry* v. *Hutchinson* (1868) L.R. 3 Q.B. 599.
[35] See Voet 47.10.6; *cf. Meyer* v. *Van Niekerk* 1976 (1) S.A. 252 at p. 256, *per* Coetzee J. (T.P.D.).
[36] See the deficiencies and contradictions pointed out in the 11th Report of the Law Reform Committee, Cmnd. 2017 (1963) and the Report of the Royal Commission on Civil Liability and Compensation for Personal Injury, Cmnd. 7054 (1978), para. 447.
[37] Administration of Justice Act 1982, s.2(*b*).
[38] Blackstone, *Commentaries* (17th ed., 1830), vol. 1, p. 452.
[39] See *Gillick*'s case [1985] 3 W.L.R. 830 at p. 841.
[40] At p. 843.
[41] At p. 853.
[42] *Ibid.*
[43] *H.L.* v. *Matheson* 67 L. Ed. 2d. 388 at p. 404, *per* Powell J. (1981).
[44] *Roe* v. *Wade* 410 U.S. 113 (1973).
[45] *Zoblocki* v. *Redhail* 434 U.S. 374 (1978).
[46] *Cleveland Board of Education* v. *La Fleur* 414 U.S. 632 (1974).
[47] *Eisenstadt* v. *Baird* 405 U.S. 458 (1972).
[48] *Ibid.*
[49] *Union Pacific Railway Co.* v. *Botsford* 141 U.S. 250 (1891).
[50] *T.H.* v. *Jones* 425 F. Supp. 873 at p. 881 (Utah D.C., 1975).

[51] *Ibid.*

[52] *Ginsberg* v. *New York* 390 U.S. at p. 639 (1968).

[53] *Stanley* v. *Illinios* 405 U.S. 645 (1972).

[54] *Wisconsin* v. *Yoder* 406 U.S. 205 (1972) at p. 255.

[55] *Belotti* v. *Baird* 443 U.S. 622 (1979) at pp. 633–639.

[56] *Cf. Parham* v. *J.R.* 442 U.S. 584 (1979) at p. 602.

[57] *Harris* v. *McRae* 448 U.S. 297 (1980).

[58] *Planned Parenthood of Central Mo.* v. *Danforth* 428 U.S. 52 (1976).

[59] *Moore* v. *East Cleveland* 431 U.S. 494 (1977).

[60] See the case cited at 154 *supra.*

[61] *Ibid.*

[62] *H.L.* v. *Matheson* 67 L. ed 2d 388 at p. 398, *per* Berger C.J. (1981).

[63] *Cf. Doe* v. *Bolton* 410 U.S. 179 (1973).

[64] *H.L.* v. *Matheson,* n. 161 supra, at p. 405 *per* Powell J.

[65] *Id.* at p. 417 *per* Marshall J.

[66] Family Law Reform Act 1969, s.8(1), giving effect to the Report of the Committee on the Age of Majority, Cmnd. 3342, (1967) para. 479.

[67] *R.* v. *Howes* (1860) 3 E. & E. 332 at pp. 336–337.

[68] *R.* v. *Gyngall* [1893] 2 Q.B. 232 at p. 250, *per* Kay L.J.

[69] See *Gillick's* case [1985] 2 W.L.R. 413 at p. 430.

[70] At p. 441.

[71] *R.* v. *Howes* (1860) 3 E. & E. 332 at pp. 336–337, *per* Cockburn C.J.

[72] *R.* v. *D* [1984] A.C. 778.

[73] At p. 806, *per* Lord Brandon of Oakbrook.

[74] *R.* v. *Howard* [1966] 1 W.L.R. 13.

[75] At p. 15, *per* Lord Parker C.J.

[76] See *Gillick's* case [1985] 2 W.L.R. 413 at p. 430, *per* Parker L.J.

[77] [1985] 3 W.L.R. 830 at pp. 841–842, *per* Lord Fraser of Tullybelton.

[78] At p. 855, *per* Lord Scarman.

[79] At p. 858; *cf.* P.M. Bromley, *Family Law* (6th ed., 1981), p. 317.

[80] *Lacey* v. *Laird* (1956) 139 N.E. 2d. 25 (S.C. of Ohio).

[81] *Meyer* v. *Van Niekerk* 1976 (1) S.A. 252 at p. 257, *per* Coetzee J. (T.P.D.).

[82] *Hewer* v. *Bryant* [1970] 1 Q.B. 357 at p. 369.

[83] *Cf.* Van de Linden *Inst.* 1.4.3.

[84] *Breed* v. *Jones* 421 U.S. 519 (1975).

[85] *Goss* v. *Lopez* 419 U.S. 565 (1975).

[86] Code An s.78–14–5(4)(*f*) (1977).

[87] Tex. Riv. Cir. Stat Ann Art. 4467 (Vernon 1976).

[88] Blackstone, *Commentaries* (17th ed., 1830), vol. 1, chap. 17, p. 463.

[89] *H.L.* v. *Matheson* 67 L. Ed. 2d. 388 (1981) at p. 426.

[90] *R.* v. *D* [1984] A.C. 778 at pp. 804–805, *per* Lord Brandon of Oakbrook.

[91] See *Gillick's* case [1985] 3 W.L.R. 830 at p. 858.

[92] *Cf.* G.L. Williams, "The Gillick Saga" (1985) 135 *New L.J.* at p. 1180.

[93] *R.* v. *Morgan* [1970] V.R. 337 (S.C.).

[94] At p. 341, *per* Winneke C.J.

[95] *Ibid.*

[96] *Ibid.*

[97] *Papadimitropoulos* v. *R.* (1957) 98 C.L.R. 249 at p. 261 (H.C.A.).

[98] *Bolam* v. *Friern Hospital Management Committee* [1957] 1 W.L.R. 582 followed by the House of Lords, in *Whitehouse* v. *Jordan* [1981] 1 W.L.R. 246 and in *Maynard* v. *West Midlands Regional Health Authority* [1984] 1 W.L.R. 634.

⁹⁹ *Sidaway* v. *Board of Governors of the Bethlem Royal Hospital* [1985] 2 W.L.R. 480.
¹ *Canterbury* v. *Spence* 464 F. 2d. 772 at p. 784 (D.C.Cir. 1972).
² *B. (B.R.)* v. *B. (J)* [1968] P. at p. 473.
³ *Planned Parenthood of Central Mo.* v. *Danforth* 428 U.S. 52 at p. 74 (1976).

Judicial Discretion

SIR ROGER ORMROD

A presidential address to the Bentham Club provides a unique opportunity for a judge, retired or not, to make a contribution to legal thinking which is otherwise denied to him, no matter how many judgments he has had to give. In a sense it enables him to escape from the two dimensional into the three dimensional world.

I decided to make judicial discretion my subject tonight for a variety of reasons. In the first place, I believe that it is playing and will continue to play an important part in our judicial administration which is more likely to expand than to contract: In the second, it provides an interesting, and perhaps unique, insight into what goes on just below the surface in judicial minds as they solve problems which are not fully amenable to the intellectual techniques in which they are trained and which they are conditioned to regard as pre-eminent.

I am uneasily aware that the shade of our illustrious progenitor which always hovers over meetings of his Club, particularly during presidential addresses, is looking over my shoulder with surprise mingled with disapproval, that so much attention should be devoted to judges in general and still more to such unruly and unpredictable activities as discretionary powers. His first reaction must be that they are interlopers into his scheme of things. But, perhaps on reflection, he may welcome some exploration of what has been happening, not only to judges but to his first love, the legislative process.

The first point to be made, because judges are uncomfortably aware that discretionary powers expose them to criticism, both academic and lay, is that such powers are all deliberately created by Parliament and bestowed upon, often unenthusiastic, recipients. It is important to recognise that Parliament adopts this method because its own legislative process cannot meet the demand which society to-day seems determined to make on it, that is, for justice and fairness to the individual, rather than for justice in the abstract. Certainly attempts to legislate in detail are discouraging. Successive Finance Acts and the legislation about Purchase Tax and V.A.T. are anything but a credit to this process.

123

Another way of putting it is to say that Parliament, and therefore, presumably society today, sets greater store by flexibility in the law, that is, its capacity to adapt to individual circumstances, than to certainty. The commercial world, however, still prefers certainty which it believes it can build into its calculations but even in this area flexibility is beginning to have its attractions. Discretion and flexibility go hand in hand.

The second point which I will develop in detail is the effect which these discretionary powers have on the judges who have to exercise them, manage and control them. I shall do this in two ways: First, by a brief historical study and second, by examining the attitudes of appellate courts to appeals from discretionary decisions which are surprisingly confused and, at the same time, indicative of unresolved conflicts of mind over this function of the judiciary.

The first example of a judicial discretion given by Parliament to English judges is to be found in the Matrimonial Causes Act 1857.

The circumstances are illuminating. This is the Act which is generally regarded as the origin of divorce in England but it was not the great piece of innovatory legislation which it is often supposed to be. So far as dissolution of marriage was concerned it was a codification of the Parliamentary practice which had been developed over a great many years to deal with the private Bills which were from time to time promoted by individuals to dissolve their marriages and to obtain the right to re-marry. (The remainder of the Act was a more or less direct transfer to the newly created Court for Divorce and Matrimonial Causes of the jurisdiction and powers exercised by the ecclesiastical courts in matrimonial matters.)

Since each private divorce Act was a separate piece of legislation, Parliament was free to treat each case individually on its merits. This meant that Parliament might reject a Bill and refuse a divorce to a petitioner who had himself committed adultery or otherwise behaved badly or conduced to the adultery on which he was relying. This is the origin of the "discretionary bars" so familiar to practitioners before the reforms of 1969–1970.

The Act converted a legislative act into a judicial decision, called a "decree." The problem was how to introduce into the judicial process the flexibility which was essential if justice was to be done in individual cases. The solution was found in section 31 which, while making it mandatory to pronounce a decree on proof of adultery, contained a proviso that "the Court shall not be bound to pronounce such decree if it shall find that the petitioner has during the marriage been guilty of 'adultery' (or unreasonable delay, cruelty, desertion or conduct conducive to the adultery relied on".

Those words "shall not be bound" introduced into English law the revolutionary concept of a discretion in the judge who was required to make a value judgment in the sphere of personal and moral values, far removed from property rights, and without the traditional protection afforded by the verdict of a jury.

The shock wave took some time to make itself felt because at first only one judge was exposed to this risk, the newly appointed Lord Ordinary, and there were very few cases. But 12 years later in 1869. Lord Penzance, then the Lord Ordinary, in the course of his judgment in *Morgan* v. *Morgan*[1] said:

> "A loose and unfettered discretion of this sort upon matter of such grave import, is a dangerous weapon to entrust to any court, still more to a single judge. Its exercise is likely to be the refuge of vagueness in decision, and the harbour of half-formed thought. Under cover of the word "discretion," a conclusion is apt to be formed on a general impression of facts too numerous and minute to be perfectly brought together and weighed, and sometimes not perfectly proved; while the result is apt to be coloured with the general prejudice, favourable or otherwise, to the person whose conduct is under review, which the course of the evidence has evoked. Upon such materials, so used, two minds will hardly ever form a judgment alike, and the same mind will often appear to others to form contradictory judgments on what seem similar facts. This invites public criticism and shakes confidence in the justice of the tribunal."

This passage epitomises the traditional attitude of judges and expresses the anguished conflict between Lord Penzance's perception of the judge's true role and the function thrust upon him by Parliament. The fantasy of the judge as a detached observer, reaching inevitably right conclusions by processes of impeccable logic, in perfect conformity with decisions of others, has its attraction for judges. It is not surprising that the realities of discretion were so alarming.

Different methods have been used to resolve or escape from the conflicts. The history of the discretion which so troubled Penzance is instructive. For many years the "discretion" was rarely exercised and the Court normally used its freedom to refuse a decree to a petitioner who had committed adultery or otherwise behaved badly. This was probably in accord with prevailing social views. But these gradually changed, particularly after the 1914–18 war. Petitioners had always been expected to be frank with the Court but eventually rules were made requiring the petitioner to file a "discretion statement," giving details of all acts of adultery committed during the marriage. Thereafter, the exercise of discretion became dominated by whether or not full disclosure had been made; the merits of the case and the difficult value judgments were generally avoided.

In 1943 these matters reached the House of Lords for the first time in *Blunt* v. *Blunt*.[2] Probably without fully foreseeing the consequences, Viscount Simon L.C. indicated that a primary consideration in exercising the discretion should be the interest of the community at large "to be judged by maintaining a true balance between respect for the binding sanctity of marriage and the social considerations which makes it contrary to public policy to insist on the maintenance of a union which has utterly broken down." The effect of this suggestion was to reduce the exercise of this discretion to a formality, only refused for incomplete disclosure and even this could be remedied by a last minute confession. It was finally abolished by the Divorce Reform Act 1969.

The 1857 Act created other discretionary powers, notably over the custody of children and financial matters after divorce. These did not provoke such an emphatic reaction but they were soon "fettered" and made relatively safe to operate, although they were quite unrestricted in the statute. This was achieved by use of the maxim "discretion must be exercised judicially." This meant in accordance with decided cases in which the limits were laid down. The result in practice was that the question, primarily considered, was which precedent to follow, while the underlying merits were not dealt with. For a long time in custody cases the predominance of the father persisted and then attention turned to "guilt." It is much easier to decide the question of guilt than the issue of the best interests of the child.

It took Parliament two Guardianship of Infants Acts, 1886 and 1925, to displace the dominance of the father and even then it was not until 1970 that the House of Lords in *J*. v. *C*.[3] finally asserted unequivocally that "paramount" in section 1 of the 1925 Act meant what it said.

The discretion in financial matters was limited to the question of periodical payments, (apart from variation of marriage settlements) up to the 1960/70 reforms but here too it was restricted by two factors. "Guilt" was almost always decisive, in spite of recurrent attempts by the Court of Appeal to get rid of this fetter and the "one-third rule," taken over gratefully from the ecclesiastical courts provided a useful rule of thumb. So the 1857 Act discretions were brought under control.

In the latter part of the nineteenth century, Parliament made other attempts to confer wide discretionary powers on the Courts with only limited success. Strict construction of the relevant statutory provision either eliminated or severely restricted these powers.

For example, the Judicature Act 1873, s.25, provided that the High Court might grant an injunction "in all cases in which it appears to the Court to be just or convenient to do so." Sir George Jessell M.R. took these words at their face value giving them their "natural and ordinary meaning" which enabled him to grant some innovatory but useful injunctions. But the Court of Appeal in *North London Railway Co.* v. *Great Northern Railway Co.*[4] put the narrowest construction upon them, holding that they did not enlarge the discretionary powers of the Court which could still only grant injunctions in support of a legal or equitable right.

Lord Denning M.R. frequently tried to emulate his great predecessor by giving similar words in later Acts their "natural and ordinary" meaning in order to extend the Courts, powers but usually unsuccessfully. He did, however, succeed in establishing two major extensions with the Anton Piller order and the Mareva injunction. Both however, have since been given statutory support.

Similarly, a series of Acts have given the Court the fullest discretion over costs which were to be "in the discretion of the Court or Judge" who was to have "full power to determine by whom and to what extent the costs are to be paid." The maxim "costs follow the event" has however effectively eliminated this discretionary power. (It is possible that this was a fortuitous effect of a relatively short-lived Act, the Supreme Court of Judicature Act Amendment Act 1875 which provided that where an action is tried by a jury, "costs shall follow the event," unless "for good cause shown" the judge shall order otherwise. This was repealed by the 1880 Judicature Act but the phrase has persisted.)[5]

Another attempt (if it was an attempt) to introduce some flexibility into the law regarding married women's property was made in the Married Women's Property Act 1882 s.17, which

provided that in any question between husband and wife as to
"the title to or possession of property" either party might apply
in a summary way to a judge who "may make such order . . . as
he thinks fit."

Lord Denning M.R. in a series of cases, used this statutory
discretion, as to property rights between spouses in an equitable
way but in *Pettit* v. *Pettit*[6] the House of Lords held that this provision too was purely procedural and did not give the Court any
power to interfere with property rights. (But, once again Parliament intervened to give this power to the Courts after divorce.)

Notwithstanding this chequered history Parliament has persisted with its policy of increasing the discretionary powers of
the Court. The reforms of the divorce law in 1969 and 1970
have converted this important sector almost wholly into a
discretionary jurisdiction, exercised by judges sitting virtually all
the time in chambers. On this occasion, prompted by the Law
Commission, Parliament included a section on guide-lines for
the exercise of the discretion which is now section 25 of the
Matrimonial Causes Act 1973. This has proved of the greatest
assistance to judges exercising the extensive powers created by
the Act, not so much because the guide-lines are original, most
of them are in fact culled from reported cases but because they
have the force of statute which obviates citation of precedent.
Perhaps for this reason there has been no sign of a latter-day
Lord Penzance, crying "Woe, Woe." Alternatively, modern
judges, particularly in the Family Division, are more pragmatic
and less philosophical and seem, at first instance, happy to exercise these powers.

This technique of a judicial discretion with statutory guide-lines
has been used also in the Limitation Act 1875 and the Unfair Contract Terms Act 1977 which, though modest in scope, represent
the extension of discretion into pure Common Law areas. The new
section 2D added to the Limitation Act 1939 by the 1975 Act, gives
the Court the unprecedented power to "disapply" various limitation periods "if it appears to the Court that it would be equitable
to allow the action to proceed." There is an analogous provision in
the Arbitration Act 1950, s.27, which empowers the Court to
extend the time limit for starting arbitration proceedings to avoid
"undue hardship." It cannot be said that these discretionary
powers have had an enthusiastic welcome from the older Common
Law judges, valuable though they are as a means of preventing
injustice in the occasional case. Lord Denning M.R. and Brandon
L.J., however, have breathed some life into s.27 which is now
being used more frequently.[7]

So, at the close of what I may call Act 1, the picture is of a reasonably contented judiciary, at first instance, administering without undue difficulty or fuss extensive discretionary powers, some of which go more or less unnoticed under other names such as sentencing, or assessment of damages, or determining what is reasonable, or even judicial review, operating, as far as their powers permit, a kind of new equity, aiming at fairness, not as comprehensive as Lord Denning would have liked, but tending to expand rather than contract.

For Act 2, the scene shifts to the Court of Appeal and the House of Lords and the picture is entirely different. It is one of bewildering confusion. An interminable discussion seems to have been going on about how appeals from discretionary orders ought to be handled and what limits the Court of Appeal should observe in dealing with them. It is tacitly assumed that orders made by judges in the exercise of the discretion are qualitatively different from all other orders which come to the Court of Appeal, and, therefore, ought to be treated differently. The question then is "how" and it has received a variety of answers. The law reports are studded with judgments in which judge after judge has tried to find words and phrases to express this difference but they cannot be reconciled and must reflect different perceptions.

No one, so far as I know, has been bold enough to challenge and ask "Is there really something so different about discretionary decisions?" The answer in these days is "probably not." Judges are required to make so many other value judgments that the difference, if any, is slight. In the past this was not so; juries made most of them. So the fact that there were two possible answers neither of which could be said to be necessarily wrong was disturbing. Lord Penzance was obviously very disturbed by it. However, Bowen L.J. seemed to take it quite calmly. In *Gardner* v. *Jay*[8] he said "that discretion must be exercised according to commonsense and according to justice, and if there is a miscarriage of justice in the exercise of it, it will be reviewed." The Court of Appeal would be a happier place if this were still the guide-line. As it is, the label "discretion" sets off immediately an argument, not about the justice of the order under appeal, but whether, and on what so-called principles, the Court of Appeal can properly intervene.

To demonstrate the confusion I propose to compare and contrast the views of three of the most distinguished Common Law judges of this century. Lords Atkin, Wright and Diplock.

The first two citations come from *Evans* v. *Bartlam*,[9] a case concerned with the discretion to set aside a judgment obtained in default of defence. Lord Atkin said:

"But while the judge has such a discretion as I have mentioned I conceive it to be a mistake to hold, as Greer L.J. seemed to do, that the jurisdiction of the Court of Appeal on appeal from such an order is limited so that, as the Lord Justice said, the Court of Appeal 'have no power to interfere with his exercise of discretion unless we think that he acted upon some wrong principle of law.'"

Lord Atkin continued:

"Appellate jurisdiction is always statutory; there is in the statute no restriction upon the jurisdiction of the Court of Appeal: and while the appellate Court in the exercise of its appellate power is no doubt entirely justified in saying that normally it will not interfere with the exercise of the judge's discretion except on grounds of law, yet if it sees that on other grounds this decision will result in injustice being done it has both the power and the duty to remedy."[10]

Lord Wright, agreeing, said:

"It is clear that the Court of Appeal should not interfere with the discretion of a judge acting within his jurisdiction unless the Court is clearly satisfied that he was wrong. But the Court is not entitled to say that if the judge had jurisdiction and had all the facts before him, the Court of Appeal cannot review his order unless he is shown to have applied a wrong principle."[11]

The third comes from *Hadmor Productions* v. *Hamilton*,[12] a case concerned with the discretion to grant an injunction. Lord Diplock said:

"Before adverting to the evidence . . . it is I think appropriate to remind your Lordships of the limited function of an appellate Court in an appeal of this kind. An interlocutory injunction is a discretionary relief and the discretion whether or not to grant it is vested in the High Court judge by whom the application for it is heard. Upon an appeal from the judge's grant or refusal of an interlocutory injunction the function of an appellate Court, whether it be the Court of Appeal or your Lordships' House is not to exercise an independent discretion of its own. It must defer to the judge's exercise of his discretion and must not interfere merely upon the ground that the members of the appellate Court would have exercised the discretion differently. The function of the appellate Court is initially one of review only. It may set aside the judge's exercise of his discretion on the ground that it was based upon a misunderstanding of the law or of the evidence before him or upon an inference that particular facts existed or did not exist which, although it was one that might legitimately have been drawn upon the evidence that was before the judge, can be demonstrated to be wrong by further evidence that has become available by the time of the appeal; or upon the ground that there has been a change of circumstances after the judge made his order that would have justified his acceding to an application to vary it. Since reasons given by judges for granting or refusing interlocutory injunctions may sometimes be sketchy, there may also be occasional cases where even though no erroneous assumption of law or fact can be identified the judge's decision to grant or refuse the injunction is so aberrant that it must be set aside upon the ground that no reasonable judge regardful of his duty to act judicially could have reached it. It is only if and after the appellate Court has reached the conclusion that the judge's exercise of his discretion must be set aside for one or other of these reasons, that it becomes entitled to exercise an original discretion of its own."[13]

It might have been Greer L.J. speaking! The contrast between this and the views of Lord Atkin and Lord Wright require no further comment at this stage.

Between these two cases in time and in opinion lie many others and I would like to refer to some of them. For brevity, I shall quote only the significant dicta.

"The question for consideration by this Court is whether his judgment is erroneous and not whether we would have exercised the discretion in the same manner as the judge below did. There is no appeal from his discretion to our discretion."

Per Sir Charles Swinfen Eady M.R. in *Holland* v. *Holland*.[14]

"The appellate tribunal is not at liberty merely to substitute its own exercise of discretion for the discretion already exercised by the judge. In other words, appellate authorities ought not to reverse the order merely because they would themselves have exercised the original discretion had it attached to them in a different way. But if the appellate tribunal reaches a clear conclusion that there has been a wrongful exercise of discretion in that no weight or no sufficient weight has been

given to relevant consideration . . . then the reversal of the
order on appeal may be justified."

Per Viscount Simon in *Charles Osenton & Co.* v. *Johnston.*"[15]

"It is of course not enough for the wife to establish that this
Court might or would have made a different order. We are
concerned with a judicial discretion and it is of the essence of
such a discretion that on the same evidence two different
minds might reach widely different decisions without either
being appealable. It is only where the decision exceeds the
generous ambit within which reasonable disagreement is
possible, and is, in fact, plainly wrong that an appellate body
is entitled to interfere."

Per Asquith L.J. *Bellenden (formerly Satterthwaite)* v.
Satterthwaite."[16]

"In my considered opinion the law now is that if an appellate
Court is satisfied that the decision of the Court below is
wrong, it is its duty to say so and act accordingly . . .
. . . Every Court has a duty to do its best to arrive at a proper
and just decision. If an appellate Court is satisfied that the
decision of the Court below is improper, unjust or wrong,
then the decision must be set aside. I am quite unable to subscribe to the view that a decision must be treated as sacrosanct
because it was in the exercise of 'discretion.' So to do might
perpetuate injustice."

Per Davies L.J. *Re O. (Infants).*[17]

"I am satisfied that the judge's decision was wrong. In my
judgment there is no reason in law why I should not give
effect to my conclusion and it is the right and the duty of this
Court to allow this appeal."

Per Browne L.J. in *Re. F.*[18]

"Can this conclusion [that the judge was wrong] prevail or is
there some rule of law which bars it? The judge was exercising
a discretion. He saw and heard the witnesses. It is impossible
to say that he considered any irrelevant matter, left out of
account any relevant matter, erred in law, or applied any
wrong principle. On the view I take his error was in the balancing exercise. He either gave too little weight to the factors
favourable or too much weight to the factors adverse to the
father's claim that he should retain care and control of the
child . . .

If in any discretion case concerning children the Court can clearly detect that a conclusion which is neither dependent on nor justified by the trial judge's advantage in seeing and hearing the witnesses, is vitiated by an error in the balancing exercise, I should be very reluctant to hold that it is powerless to interfere."

Per Bridge L.J. in *Re. F.*[19]

"In my judgment, in infant cases you cannot say that the decision of the judge was wrong, improper, or unjust unless he has erred in law, or has taken into account some matter which he ought not to have taken into account or failed to take into account a matter which he ought to have taken into account."

Per Stamp L.J. (dissenting) in *Re. F.*[20]

"There was not really a right solution; there were two alternative wrong solutions . . . I am sitting in the Court of Appeal deciding a quite different question: has it been shown that the judge to whom Parliament has confided the exercise of the discretion plainly got it wrong? I emphasise the word 'plainly.'"

Per Cumming-Bruce L.J. in *Clarke and Hunt* v. *Newcombe.*[21]

It was against this background that Lord Diplock's remarks in *Hadmor*'s case came as an unpleasantly reactionary surprise. The real issue seemed to have been thoroughly debated and settled in *Re F.* the only case in which there has been a direct confrontation between the opposing views. Browne L.J.'s judgment is still the most complete and balanced survey of the authorities and of the issues involved, and Bridge L.J.'s concept of the balancing exercise one of the most constructive and useful ideas. Yet Lord Diplock never referred to it in his speech in *Hadmor* or, indeed, to any of the other authorities like *Evans* v. *Bartlam.*

In fact, his remarks on discretion were little more than an addendum by way of rebuke to the Court of Appeal in a long and complex judgment on questions of Trade Union law.

Nevertheless, the consequences for the Court of Appeal have been very unfortunate, constraining the members of the Court from time to time to uphold discretionary decisions with which they do not agree because they cannot be faulted on Lord Diplock's criteria. (The situation in which, in effect, Bridge L.J. found himself in *Re F*, from which he escaped by using the "balancing exercise").

Fortunately, two years later, in 1985, the House of Lords had another opportunity in *G.* v. *G.* to consider this problem, this time in a custody dispute, without other distracting issues. Lord Fraser, a Scots lawyer, relatively detached from this controversy, who gave the leading speech was obviously concerned to steer a middle course.

He referred with approval to Bridge L.J.'s judgment in *Re F.*, citing at length the passage quoted above about the balancing exercise but also the well-known dictum of Asquith L.J. in *Bellenden* v. *Satterthwaite* about the generous ambit within which reasonable disagreement is possible. Ironically, Lord Diplock's remarks in *Hadmor*'s case were not referred to either in argument or in the speeches, a rather surprising state of affairs since Lord Bridge was a member of the Appellate Committee in both cases. The result seems to be that the authority of *Re F.* is restored but in a blunted form.

The officious bystander, listening to this recitation might be forgiven for asking "what are they all on about?" A more precisely framed question might be "why." This raises some interesting speculations. No other topic which is found in judgments has produced such a variety of responses and few have induced such emphatic expressions of opinion. This mixture of variety and emphasis suggests that the differences are deeper rooted than usual and involve personality factors and feelings.

My sample of dicta seems to bear this out. It can be divided into two groups with a little overlap: the anxious philosophers, beginning with Lord Penzance and ending with Lord Diplock, concerned with the seemingly anomalous character of discretion which is apt to give rise to two or more widely different decisions "without either being appealable," neither of which is really right, and the confident pragmatists beginning with Bowen L.J. and ending with Lord Bridge, who do not doubt their ability in a given case to say that the judge was "plainly wrong." The former, of course, belong to the school which believe that the real interests of justice are best served by certainty, consistency and logic while the latter think more in terms of justice in the individual case.

There is a middle group who would like to keep a foot in both camps. They would like to combine applying a wrong principle and being plainly wrong. This is really a tautology; to apply a wrong principle is to be plainly wrong; but one can be plainly wrong without it being possible to identify the violated principle. However, the word "principle" has an emollient effect on some anxious lawyers and has therefore, a certain value!

The anxious philosophers seem reluctant to exercise discretion, perhaps feeling in their heart of hearts that this is not really judges' work. In their judgments they certainly often sound defensive as if they were looking for reasons to avoid having to make a decision. Some of these defensive moves have been quoted in my sample.

A familiar one is the point that the judge saw and heard the witnesses, unlike the Court of Appeal. This can have considerable weight but it can become an incantation. Donovan L.J. once challenged it saying[22]:

> "In matters where credibility is in issue, of course that consideration is of great weight. I do not think it is of such weight when one is assessing a person's character and ability to look after a child. The encounter is too brief for any reliable conclusion."

Another one is to say that Parliament has conferred the discretion "on the judge." Very occasionally the statute does specifically give the discretion to the judge himself (*e.g.* as to costs) but mostly it refers to the court or judge. Since by statute there is an unfettered right of appeal (subject to leave) and the Court of Appeal has all the powers of the court below there is not much in this point.

Yet another is the formula which runs: "the discretion cannot be interfered with unless it is shown that the judge took into account irrelevant matters or failed to take into account relevant matters." This, with its echo of the Book of Common Prayer, is taken from Lord Green M.R.'s famous judgment in the *Wednesbury* case.[23] Unfortunately, he expressly said that it did not apply to judicial discretion and related solely to administrative discretion. He used it as a formula for testing whether a discretion had been *abused*, *i.e.* used for a purpose for which it was not given. It has now been expressly disapproved in *G.* v. *G.* so far as judicial discretion is concerned. The great disadvantage of this approach is as I have said earlier, that it diverts attention away from the merits of the case into relatively remote intellectual exercises.

The confident pragmatists run all the risks so graphically described by Lord Penzance but which in real life do not seem so threatening. They have the great advantage that they confront, at the outset, the consequences and the justice of the order of the judge; then they can analyse the reasoning. They insert the word "plainly" as a measure of the burden on the appellant which is to satisfy the appellate Court that the decision below should be set aside or varied. In practice, if I may interpose a personal reminiscence, I did not as a rule find it difficult to decide into which of three categories the order under appeal fell—right, plainly wrong or doubtful, in which case the appeal would be dismissed. Moreover, disagreements in the appeal Court were very infrequent. Successful appeals too were fairly infrequent. Perhaps, however, the strongest point in the pragmatists' favour is one which is rarely mentioned. Is it fair to the litigants that in matters of discretion they should not be able to obtain a second opinion? After all, two or even three minds may be better than one!

I would like to end with some of the simplest and wisest words I have discovered on this topic. They come from an unlikely but wholly uncommitted source, a judgment of the Dean of the Arches!

In the case of the *St Mary's Banbury*,[24] he said:

> "Sitting as I now do as the appellate judge, I may draw any inferences of fact which might have been drawn by the Chancellor. I may give any judgment or direction which the Chancellor ought to have given. I may remit the matter with a direction for re-hearing and determination by the Chancellor's Court or I may allow the appeal substituting my own discretion if the Chancellor's exercise of discretion was based on on erroneous evaluation of the facts taken as a whole."

Simple, compendious, and entirely reasonable!

Notes

[1] (1869) L.R.1 P & D 644.
[2] [1943] A.C. 517, 525.
[3] [1970] A.C. 668.
[4] (1883) 11 Q.B.D. 30.
[5] See Mustill L.J. in *Aden Refinery Co. Ltd.* v. *Ugland Managements Co.* [1986] 3 W.L.R. 949, 000.
[6] [1970] A.C. 777.
[7] See *Liberian Shipping Corporation* v. *A. King & Sons (Pegasus)* [1967] 2 Q.B. 86 and *Libra Shipping & Trading Corporation* v. *Northern Sales (The Aspen Trader)* [1981] 1 Lloyds Rep. 273.
[8] (1885) 29 Ch.D. 50, 59.
[9] [1937] A.C. 473.
[10] *Ibid.* at p. 480.
[11] *Ibid.* at p. 484.
[12] [1983] A.C. 191.
[13] *Ibid.* at p. 220.
[14] [1918] p. 273.
[15] [1942] A.C. 130.
[16] [1948] 1 All E.R. 343 at p. 345.
[17] [1971] Ch. 748.
[18] [1976] Fam. 238 at p. 263.

[19] *Ibid.* at p. 266.
[20] *Ibid.* at p. 253.
[21] (1982) 4 F.L.R. 482 at p. 488.
[22] *Re B (An Infant)* [1962] 1 W.L.R. 550 at p. 555.
[23] *Associated Picture Houses Ltd.* v. *Wednesbury Corporation* [1948] 1 K.B. 223.
[24] [1987] 1 All E.R. 247 at p. 254.

Minority Languages and the Law

MICHAEL BELOFF Q.C.

Almost six years ago, as a newly fledged Silk, I was, while on a seaside holiday in Brighton, telephoned by my Clerk. He told me that, as he had optimistically represented that I was competent in matters of constitutional law I had been briefed to appear in the High Court in Kuala Lumpur—a far away city of which at that time I knew little.

The case concerned the refusal by the Government of Malaysia to allow the establishment of a private university, and filial piety, if nothing else, made the cause dear to my heart.

The main reason for the Government's decision was the fact that the institution proposed to teach its students in Chinese. The Government asserted that this infringed those provisions of the federal constitution which guaranteed supremacy to Malay as the national language.

Section 152(1) of that Constitution states:

> "That the national language shall be the Malay language and shall be in such script as Parliament may by law provide:—provided that—
> (a) no person shall be prohibited or prevented from using (otherwise than for official purposes) or from teaching or learning any other language; and
> (b) nothing in this clause shall prejudice the right of the federal government or of any state government to preserve and sustain the use and study of the language of any other community in the federation."

The section has three notable features: firstly, it endows the country with a *national* language—as potent a symbol as a national anthem or national flag;

secondly, it permits, within limits, the use by minority communities within the state of their own languages;

thirdly, it permits governments both at state and local level to sustain such usage *and* the study of minority languages.

It illustrates, in a manner dictated, as such laws must be, by surrounding political and social conditions, that search for balance in the field of language rights that the law must always seek to achieve.

Those were, for me, heady days indeed. I was armoured with an advice drafted by four other Counsel, who included, among their number, a former Law Officer of the Crown, and one of the most eminent of English academic administrative lawyers,—an advice, whose only deficiency, from my point of view, was that it dismissed in one sentence and without discussion the point upon which the case was finally decided against my client.

I flew out to a reception headed by representatives of the ten juniors (almost all Chinese), whose names are to be found in the report of the case in the Malay Law Journal,[1] and the proper pronunciation of which proved to be by no means the least difficult part of my forensic efforts.

At first instance, my opponent, the Attorney-General, claimed that if my clients' application for judicial review of the government's decision succeeded, civil war would break out; and for once the submission, *fiat justitia, ruat coelum*, (Latin being the minority language of the common law) seemed the only appropriate retort.

When I returned for the appeal, I received a telephone call, menacing my life if I did not "get out of town"—more in the style of the western, than the eastern; and was then given not only the protection of the local chief of police, but also of two martial Sikh bodyguards, provided by my clients.

The Federal Court split four to one against our appeal. The four judges in the majority were all of Malay ethnic origin; the dissenter in our favour was a Chinese judge. Since Malaysia had by then abolished appeals on constitutional matters to the Privy Council my clients had reached the end of the legal road. I for my part was left not only with the memory of the most fascinating case in which I have yet appeared, but with the inspiration for this lecture which the faculty has with kindness, some might say courage, invited me to deliver. For I had learned, what with previous insular blindness I had ignored, that language, like race, like colour, like national origins, like religion, is one of the passions of our time—at once a powerful focus for the faith of minorities, and a potential source for fission in the community at large.

But is the relationship of minority languages and law a Current Legal Problem? Or is the theme of my lecture, like the Holy Roman Empire or the British Independent Deterrent, something which claims to be identified by three associated qualities, none of which it in fact enjoys?

If we lift our gaze above our national boundaries the question admits of only one answer. For language issues pervade the social and political life, and in consequence the fabric of the law, in many countries in every continent and corner of the globe—from Quebec to Sri Lanka, from the Aaland Islands to Singapore, from Austria to South Africa. Territorial expansion, the consequence of war or treaty, coupled with international migration, has meant that boundaries of states, and the limits of linguistic communities do not coincide: and a wholly monoglot nation must, if it exists at all, be an exception to the general rule.

May I illustrate my point by reference only to events which have occurred since I accepted the invitation and chose the title of my talk in the middle of 1986?

On November 5, 1986 the electorate in California voted heavily in favour of Proposition 63 which enjoined the local legislature not to take any linguistic action which "diminishes or ignores" the role of English—a reaction against the increase in Spanish speaking migrants in the southern part of the state.[2] In the early part of the same month, the dismissal of the mayor of Fourons, a French speaking enclave in a Dutch-speaking area of Belgium because he refused to speak the official language of local administration, all but brought down the national government. Three days before Christmas the Court of Appeal in Quebec ruled that a citizen had the right to display commercial signs in the English language, and that the relevant sections of Quebec's French language charter violated the constitutional freedom of expression. Vandalism followed the verdict.

On January 15 of this year it was reported that there were clashes in the Indian province of Goa, between those who wanted the sole official language of the territory to be Konkani, an unwritten dialect spoken by more than 90 per cent. of the population, and those who wanted it to enjoy no more than equal status with Marathi, the language of the adjacent state, Maharashtra.

But the United Kingdom enjoys no immunity from the linguistic issues. Within these shores it has two aspects. The first is the fight for survival of ancient tongues—Welsh and Gaelic. The second is the struggle for recognition of the tongues of the newer immigrants. These two aspects are manifestly distinct.

As regards the first the problem is confined to the outer regions. It is concerned with the languages of those who are elements of the indigenous population of these islands. It is concerned with languages which, if they do not survive here (or in the case of Gaelic in Ireland) will become, in effect, extinct. And it is concerned, in effect, with a handful of Celtic languages or dialects.

As regards the second the problem is confined to the inner cities. It is concerned with the language of those who are part of the recent immigrant population of these islands. It is concerned with languages which require no protection from the laws of the United Kingdom for their *survival* since they are spoken by millions of those in the countries of origin whence these immigrants come. And it is concerned with a babel of tongues—a 1981 census of ILEA pupils for whom English was not a first language identified a total of more than 131 different languages spoken by them, of whom more than 1000 spoke one out of 12 foreign languages as their first language.[3]

I want to examine in this lecture.

(i) The extent to which our national law recognises the rights of minority language speakers in the United Kingdom.

(ii) The impact, actual or potential, upon our national law of the accession of the United Kingdom to two European treaties

    (a) The Treaty of Rome
    (b) The European Convention on Human Rights.

(iii) Aspects of international law which bear upon the United Kingdom's obligations to linguistic minorities.

(iv) What lessons, if any, can be learnt from the way in which other countries, notably the United States of America have dealt *with* language *by* law.

English Law

In the absence of any written constitution, English is not enshrined by law as the national language of the United Kingdom. It is, of course, the language of Parliament, of legislation and of public administration; but this is the product of convention rather than of law. My researches have shown that while before 1483 Statutes were drafted in English *and* French, after 1483 they were—and are—drafted in English only—but not the reason why.

As far as the conduct of litigation is concerned it was a statute of the reign of Edward III; *anno domini 1362* which first provided that pleas should be pleaded in the English tongue, and not in French: although still enrolled in Latin. More recently Roxburgh J. held in *Re Trepca Mines Limited*[4] "proceedings before the Court must be conducted in English." A litigant has no right to open his case through an interpreter; but a Court can allow him so to address it in its discretion.[5] It is also a requirement for naturalisation as a British Citizen that the applicant "has a sufficient knowledge of the English, Welsh or Scottish Gaelic language."[6]

But only one language, apart from English, is accorded any other form of express legal recognition in the United Kingdom— that is Welsh. The Act of Union of 1536, enacted in an attempt to

bring about uniformity in Wales with England politically, culturally, *and* linguistically, provided by section 17 for the exclusive use
of English in all legal proceedings and by all office holders. (Welsh
was described as "a speeche nothing like ne consonanunt to the
naturall mother tonge used within this realm.") This section was
repealed by the Welsh Courts Act 1942, (although, in the language
of one commentator, "the habit of regarding English as the only
official language of the Courts and officials had, after four centuries, become too ingrained to be much modified by an obscure Act
of Parliament enacted in haste during a great world conflict, and so
matters remained largely unchanged."[7] The inadequacy of that
Act was exposed in the case of *Ex parte Jenkins*[8] where a school-
master versed in English, who was charged with having an
unlicensed vehicle on the road, was refused permission to cross
examine an officer in Welsh. He sought unsuccessfully to have his
conviction quashed on the basis of that refusal. Mr Justice
Widgery, (the future Lord Chief Justice) said:

> "Having spent the summer circuit in Wales where these prob-
> lems have arisen, I would like to have one word as to my con-
> clusions based on that experience of the Welsh Courts Act
> 1942. I think that it is quite clear that the proper language for
> Court proceedings in Wales is the English language. It is to
> my mind a complete misapprehension to believe that anybody
> at anytime has a right to require that the proceedings be con-
> ducted in Welsh. The right which the Act of 1942 gives is the
> right for the individual to use the Welsh language if he con-
> siders that he would be at a disadvantage in expression if he
> were required to use English. That is the only right which the
> Act of 1942 gives, and apart from that, the language difficul-
> ties which arise in Wales can be dealt with by discretionary
> arrangements for an interpreter, precisely in the same way
> that languages difficulties of the Central Criminal Court are
> dealt with when the accused is a Pole."

Subsequent to that decision—Parliament enacted the Welsh
Language Act 1967, whose limits are identified in its preamble:

> "whereas it is proper that the Welsh language should be freely
> used by those who so desire in the hearing of legal proceed-
> ings in Wales and Monmouthshire; that further provisions
> should be made for the use of that language with the like
> effect as English, in the conduct of other official or public
> business there";

Other relevant statutes are the Elections (Welsh Forms Act) 1964 which authorises the use of elections forms in Welsh throughout Wales and section 21 of the Education Act 1980 which empowers the Secretary of State to make grants for education in Welsh.[9] Government policy, expressed in a circular, is that "the bulk of grant payments, should be made to local education authorities in respect of projects related to the maintained education system. In recognition of this fact LEAs in Wales already show significant expenditure in Welsh language education."[10]

Although there is bi-lingual administration, bi-lingual education and bi-lingual justice in some areas of Wales, in this, the year of the 25th anniversary of the Welsh Language Society, there is bound to be a bid to build on the unsuccessful effort to enact a new Welsh Language Bill, introduced by Plaid Cymru M.P. Mr Daffyd Wigley in July 1986, with the object of assuring acceptance of both English and Welsh as official languages in the principality, on the basis of equality.

Race Relations Act 1976

I now turn to the Race Relations Act 1976. The Act prohibits within defined areas, racial discrimination both of a direct and of an indirect character. Language discrimination is not one of the grounds of discrimination covered by the 1976 Act. Nor does language by itself create a racial or ethnic group. In *Mandla* v. *Dowell Lee*[11] (in which a head teacher sought to refuse to admit a turban-wearing Sikh as a pupil of a private school on the basis of a "no headgear" rule) Lord Fraser said:

> "for a group to constitute an ethnic group in the sense of the Act of 1976, it must, in my opinion, regard itself, and be regarded by others, as a distinct community by virtue of certain characteristics. Some of these characteristics are essential; others are not essential but one or more of them will commonly be found and will help to distinguish the group from the surrounding community."

"A common language, not necessarily peculiar to the group" was identified as one, among five, relevant but not essential characteristics.

Accordingly, discrimination against someone on the ground that he does or does not speak a particular language is not unlawful. So Gwynedd County Council, were found *not* to be guilty of *direct* discrimination in barring jobs in old people's homes to persons who did not speak Welsh.[12]

But to make the ability to speak a particular language a precondition of obtaining employment or some other benefit *can* constitute indirect discrimination contrary to section 1(1)(*b*) of the Act. This section prohibits applying criteria for the obtaining of such benefits, which, while impartial on their face, have a disproportionate adverse impact on minority racial groups. In the Gwynned case the Industrial Tribunal held that the Welsh language requirement was not justifiable, since it was in their view, aimed more at preservation of the Welsh language, than the interests of the inhabitants of the homes. Gwynned only succeeded in their appeal on this issue because the Industrial Tribunal had determined that the victims of the language discrimination were ethnically Welsh. Had they been English, then indirect discrimination would have been proved.

Equally those who make the ability to speak *English* (as distinct from a minority language) a criterion of obtaining a benefit will usually be able to rely upon the defence that it is justifiable. It is unlikely that anyone would establish such a criterion merely to preserve or protect the *English* language! In *Raval* v. *DHSS*[13] the complainant's application for a clerical post with the DHSS was rejected because she did not have "O" Level English or its equivalent (the DHSS criterion for entry to its clerical grades) although it was undisputed that she had sufficient command of English to fill the jobs required. The Industrial Tribunal had, decided on balance that, "insistence upon an English language 'O' Level (or equivalent) as the sole and exclusive criterion of the ability to communicate in the English language required by the advertised posts had more to be said in its favour on the grounds of overall fairness than there was to be said against it on grounds of arbitrariness."[14]

The Race Relations Act does contain provisions which allow for positive discrimination in education and training for minority ethnic groups with special needs: sections 35, 37 and 38. But they are designed to ensure that special teaching in English be provided, not that mother tongue teaching be fostered.[15] The complexities of the law in this area are illustrated by the finding of the C.R.E. that teaching English to Asian children itself contravened the Act when it was carried out in separate teaching units in Calderdale in West Yorkshire.[16]

Section 71 imposes upon local authorities a general statutory duty "to make appropriate arrangements with a view to securing that their various functions are carried out with due regard to the need—(a) to eliminate unlawful racial discrimination; and (b) to promote equality of opportunity and good relations between persons of different racial groups." In *Wheeler and Others* v. *Leicester City Council*,[17] Lord Roskill said it conferred power upon local authorities in exercise of statutory functions "to have a regard to what they thought was in the best interests of race relations."[18] Arguably, at any rate, this would entitle local authorities to promote the use of minority tongues. Another material piece of legislation with the same potential effect, is the Local Government Act of 1966, s.11 which empowers the Home Secretary to pay grants in respect of the employment of staff to those local authorities which have to make special provision in the exercise of their functions in consequence of the presence within their areas of substantial numbers of Commonwealth Immigrants whose language and customs differ from those of the rest of the community.

By contrast it does not seem that the duty upon local education authorities under the Education Act 1944 to supply for their area schools "sufficient in number, character and equipment to afford for all pupils opportunities for education offering such variety of instruction and training as may be desirable in view of their different ages, abilities and aptitudes" could be stretched to extend to oblige them to provide schools teaching in mother tongues.[19]

So in short, national law provides little *positive* assistance for the speakers of minority languages. There is limited statutory provision for their encouragement. They cannot themselves discriminate to protect their language. They have no redress if they are discriminated against on the grounds of their language. And the protection given in the cases to *English* language requirements itself provides a powerful incentive for them to assimilate as quickly as possible.

I turn now to the European dimension.

Community Law

There is no section in the Treaty of Rome that refers directly to linguistic rights. However, by its Directive of July 25, 1977 (77/486/EEC) on the education of migrant workers the Council of the European Community pursued a twofold policy. Firstly that migrant workers' children should receive tuition, in the "official" language of the host state. This is reflected in Article 2. Secondly, that member states should take appropriate measures to promote the teaching of the mother tongue of the country of origin. This is reflected in Article 3 and is subject to the qualification that it "shall" be done "in accordance with their national circumstances and legal systems."

But what is the extent of the obligation? The DES Circular No. 5/81 (issued on July 31, 1981) stated "for the local education authorities in this country, this directive implies that they should explore ways in which mother tongue teaching might be provided, whether during or outside school hours, but not that they are required to give such tuition to all individuals as a right." This seems to be a civil service dilution of the text of the Article although the matter has not yet been tested in the Courts. It is, indeed, doubtful whether an individual could, upon the basis of this directive, bring any claim against a local education authority which has not provided for mother tongue teaching. In a somewhat opaque portion of its decision in the case of *Marshall* v. *Southampton Health Authority*[20] the European Court of Justice said that individuals could *only* sue in national Courts upon directives, if such directives were unconditional, sufficiently clear and precise to give rise to direct effect *and*, if the individuals' suit was against "the state" or "a state authority." What is meant by the state in this context has already been debated in a number of tribunals and courts; but in *Longdon* v. *Bedfordshire Education Authority* Mr Justice Peter Gibson held that a local education authority was not for this purpose the state.

The European Convention on Human Rights

The Convention contains several provisions bearing on minority language rights.

In the particular area of criminal process it provides that a person arrested should be informed of the reasons for his arrest, and a person charged of the nature and cause of the accusation in languages which he understands (Article 5(2) and 6(3)(*a*); and should have the assistance of an interpreter if he cannot understand or speak the language of the Court (Article 6(3)(*e*)).

In the general area Article 14 provides "the enjoyment of the rights and freedoms set forth in this convention shall be secured without discrimination on any grounds such as . . . language."

The limitation of this provision, in the critically important field of education, was illustrated in the Belgian Linguistic case,[22] where six groups of applicants, francophone residents in the Flemish part of Belgium and the Brussels periphery, claimed that the linguistic system for education in Belgium under the 1932 and 1963 Acts was incompatible with the Convention.

In relation to five out of the six complaints made, the Court held that relevant legal administrative measures maintained a proper balance between the requirements of the collective interest of the public, namely achieving linguistic unity within the two large regions of Belgium in which a majority proportion of the population spoke only one out of the two national languages, and the individual rights guaranteed by the convention.

A specific complaint of the applicants was that the authorities refused to recognise studies of secondary schools which did not comply with the language laws. The Court held that this refusal was not contrary to Article 2 of the First Protocol, (which provides that no person shall be denied the right to education) nor to Article 2 read in conjunction with Article 14, since those who had completed such studies could obtain recognition of them by passing an examination before a central board, a condition which did not, in all the circumstances, impose unreasonable requirements.

The applicants' *main* complaint was that the state refused to establish or subsidise in the Dutch speaking region concerned primary school education using French as a language of instruction. The Court held that there was no violation of Article 8 (which guarantees the right to respect for family life). If the parents sent their children to a Dutch language school, there was a "certain impact" upon family life; but Article 8 did not guarantee the right to be educated in the language of one's parents by the public authorities or with their aid. (Parents who sent their children to school in Brussels, or the French speaking region, or abroad, so that they should be taught in French, were themselves responsible for the consequent separation, which was not imposed by the Belgian legislation.) Moreover Article 2 of the Protocol did not impose an obligation on a contracting state to create a particular type of educational establishment. If it did do so, its only obligation was not to lay down discriminatory entrance requirements contrary to Article 14.

It would appear, accordingly, to have been conclusively decided by the Court that there is no right to mother tongue teaching guaranteed by the Convention. And it would also appear that Article 14 does not prevent a state from requiring or permitting an ability to speak the majority language as being a criterion, for example, for employment—as long as the test has a legitimate aim, and satisfies criteria of justifiability, not unlike those enshrined in the indirect discrimination provisions of the Race Relations Act. The right of an individual from the United Kingdom to obtain redress from the Convention organs, which the Government are by treaty bound to honour, is not of any great consequence in the field of minority language rights.

Other International Instruments

There are various references to the principle of non-discrimination on linguistic grounds in other international instruments to which the United Kingdom subscribes.

The United Nations Charter itself in a number of places emphasises the importance of human rights "without distinction as to race, sex, language or religion" (Articles 1(3) 13(16) and 55(*c*)); and there are similar provisions in ancillary or supplementary global treaties, the Universal Declaration of Human Rights (2), the International Covenant on Civil and Political Rights 2(1) and (26); and the International Covenant on Economic Social and Cultural Rights 2(2).

The Permanent Court of International Justice identified in the "Minority Schools in Albania case"[23] two elements as necessary for the "peaceful co-existence" of minority language groups, "the first is to ensure that nationals belonging to racial, religious or linguistic minorities shall be placed in every respect on a footing of peaceful co-existence with the other nationals of the state; the second is to ensure for the minority elements suitable measures for the preservation of their racial peculiarities, their traditions and their national characteristics" (*scilicet*: mother tongues). Post-war instruments have concentrated on the former as distinct from the latter; only Article 27 of the International Covenant on Social and Political Rights which provides (so far as is material) "In those states in which . . . linguistic minorities exist, persons belonging to such minorities shall not be denied the right in community with other members of their group . . . to use their own language" has the flavour of positive discrimination. (One author has indeed written "If Article 27 does not require positive measures it is not easy to see how it adds anything to the general equality and non-discrimination provision of Article 2(1). Article 27 must be interpreted as an additional provision to ensure for members of minorities the right to special assistance to practise their own culture, language and religion."[24] However, as is characteristic of such instruments, no method is prescribed whereby an individual (or indeed a group) can assert rights against a State before an international tribunal: and, in real terms, international human rights law in this area is an expression of good intentions rather than a guarantee of individual freedoms.

Let me now briefly examine the laws of some other countries.

United States

The United States of America does not by its constitution or federal laws expressly provide that English is to be the national language. English is, however, the language in which government documents are usually drafted (New Mexico supplying an exception at state level). It is the language of the Courts. Command of it is a bona fide occupational qualification for public employment, and the holding of elective office.[25]

For many years it was also the law that only those who knew English could vote. But by the Voting Rights Act 1965 Congress outlawed an English language requirement in the case of those with six years education in American flag schools, in which the predominant classroom language was other than English. The power of Congress to enact such legislation was endorsed by the Supreme Court in *Katzenbach* v. *Morgan*[26]; and the equal protection clause of the Constitution was also held to prohibit the language bar (*Cardona* v. *Power*[27]). In 1970 Congress suspended, and in 1975 prohibited literacy tests for the exercise of the franchise; and during the last decade the principle has been established that elections will be bilingual in districts where linguistic minorities are of substantial size.

But, typically, it has been education that has been the area of major conflict. In the nineteenth century, indulgence was shown towards the languages of Western Europe, and there were several instances of bi-lingual education or even education conducted primarily in a language other than English. The same tolerance was never shown historically to Latin or oriental languages, and by the turn of the century was in general retreat. By 1903, 14 states had enacted laws requiring English as the language of instruction in both public and private schools; by 1923 the number had climbed to 24; and while in that year the Supreme Court held in two pivotal decisions: *Mayer* v. *Nebraska*[28] and *Bartels* v. *Iowa*[29] that the imposition of criminal penalties for teaching in a language other than English was unconstitutional and in violation of due process, the power of the State to require tuition in English was accepted. The opinion of the Court delivered by Mr Justice McReynolds expressed the principle that:

> "the individual has certain fundamental rights which must be respected. The protection of the Constitution extends to all, to those who speak other languages as well as to those born with English on the tongue. Perhaps it would be highly advantageous if all had ready understanding of our ordinary speech, but this cannot be coerced by methods which conflict with the Constitution; a desirable end cannot be promoted by prohibited means."

But he added the proviso:

> "The power of the state to compel attendance at some school and to make reasonable regulations for all schools, including a

requirement that they shall give instruction in English, is not questioned . . . "

It is significant that Mr Justice Holmes, no illiberal figure, dissented and stated:

> "We all agree, I take it, that it is desirable that all the citizens of the United States should speak with a common tongue and therefore that the end aimed at by the statute is a lawful and proper one . . . Youth is the time when familiarity with a language is established, and if there are sections in the state where a child would hear only Polish or French or German spoken at home, I am not prepared to say that it is unreasonable that in his early years he shall hear and speak only English at school . . . "

In the post-war era the issue of bilingual teaching came again to the fore, prompted, in particular, by fresh immigration from the Orient and from Mexico. In *Lau* v. *Nichols*[30] non-English speaking Chinese students in New York alleged successfully before the Supreme Court that teaching classes only in English deprived them of a meaningful education although the Chief Justice commented:

> "Earlier generations of American ethnic groups have overcome the language barrier by earnest parental endeavours or by the hard fact of being pushed out of the family or community nest into the realities of broader experience."

The source of judicial inspiration was Title VI of the Civil Rights Act 1964 which, in broad terms, prevented racial discrimination, direct or indirect, in relation to programmes funded by Federal moneys. Other legislative enactments have given further foundation to mother tongue teaching programmes, especially the Equal Opportunities Education Act 1974.[31] But, even before the recent California Poll, there were signs that the new wave of the bilingual movement has crested. The American experience illustrates that such movements can ebb as they can flow, and that, in the last analysis, economic necessity will spur linguistic assimilation.[32]

Canada

In Canada the tension between the Anglophone and Francophone communities has permeated the nation's history. Recognition of the rights of the minority linguistic community has properly been reflected in the law. The British North America Act 1867 provided that either the English or French language might be used in the debates in Parliament or in the Quebec legislative houses.[33] It also prohibits the legislatures from prejudicially affecting any right or privilege with respect to denominational schools which existed by law at the time of the Union.[34] Whether this latter provision permitted Ontario to prohibit the French language as a means of instruction was considered by the Privy Council in *Ottawa Separate Schools Trustees* v. *Mackell*.[35] The restriction was held in the event to be *intra vires* since the class of persons to whom the right or privilege is reserved was a class of persons determined according to religious belief, and *not* according to race or language. In the course of their judgment the Board observed:

> "Their Lordships appreciate the affection which the French speaking residents in Ottawa feel for the French language; but it must not be forgotten that while the majority of the supporters of the English-French separate schools in Ottawa are of French origin, there are other supporters to whom French is not the natural language. This fact has no doubt caused great difficulty in adjusting fairly as between different inhabitants the natural rivalry as to the languages to be used in the education of their children."

The Board also expressly, and unusually, commended a report which stated:

> "The object of these schools is to make better scholars of the rising generation of French children, and to enable them to do better for themselves by teaching them English, while leaving them free to make such use of their own language as they pleased."[36]

The provisions of the Canadian Charter of Rights and Freedoms annexed to the Constitution Act 1982 now spell out the terms of a treaty between the two communities. French and English are both official languages of the Federation: 16(1). Both may be used in Parliament and in Court: 17(1) and 19(1). Members of the public have the right to communicate with federal institutions in either: 20(1). And minority language educational rights at primary and secondary school level are expressly guaranteed in sections 23(1), (2) and (3) including the right to public funding where numbers warrant it. The Canadian experience illustrates that if a minority linguistic community is of substantial size, equality of status is the necessary answer.

India

India, the most obvious example of a polyglot community, reflects in its Constitution (Article 343–4) the fact that Hindi is the language spoken by the largest section of the population—

although the 1971 census identified that section as embracing 28 per cent. of its citizens only—as well as acknowledging the imperial bequest of English as the lingua franca of law and public administration. Hindi is the official language of the Union; although the use of English for official purposes, originally envisaged to last for 15 years only, has now been extended indefinitely.[37] But the fact that there are more than 5,000 languages or dialects spoken throughout the state is reflected in Article 29(1) of the Constitution which provides that "Any section of citizens with a distinct language . . . has the right to conserve the same," a right that has been held by the Courts to be absolute and without restriction.[38] The Constitution also recognises the fact that no language can be preserved unless nurtured in educational institutions. Article 30 provides that "All minorities, whether based on religion or language shall have the right to establish and administer educational institutions of their own choice"; and this Article has been held to reinforce and not to qualify the prior right under Article 29(1).[39]

The law also requires that "it shall be the endeavour of every state and every local authority to provide instruction in the mother tongue at the primary state"[40]; but this is aspiration, not achievement. The Indian experience illustrates that human rights cost money; and that bilingual let alone multilingual education cannot survive on a diet of legal precept if the coffers are empty.[41]

Conclusion

There are, as this survey has demonstrated, many areas of sensitivity for the speakers of minority languages within a community. They may claim the bare right to use their mother tongue in ordinary social intercourse or the more expansive right to use it in the holding of meetings, and media of their own. They may demand to receive communications from officials, national, state, civic, in their own language; to have legal proceedings, especially criminal, conducted in that language; to establish schools or colleges, where students can study not only their tongue, but *in* their tongue, and ultimately to have the state sponsored education for their children in that tongue. These are claims which extend from the purely private to the wholly public sphere; from mere freedom from restraint to positive requirement for subvention.

In the United Kingdom many of these rights are enjoyed because they are not prohibited. It is unimaginable that any Government would seek to impede the use of minority tongues in private conversation: the use of minority tongues at public meetings or in the public press is subject to no special restraint: no law inhibits the provision of information on benefits by the DHSS in Urdu, Gujerati, Hindi, Punjabi, Bengali or Chinese[42]; the general powers of local authorities to incur expenditure "in the interests of their area or any part of it at all or some of its inhabitants"[43]; and to provide information about their services,[44] permit them, if they require them, to translate a variety of official communications into a variety of tongues—and many local authorities do so: there are street signs in Soho in Chinese, because the streets are largely flanked by Chinese restaurants. Pragmatism rather than legal precept rules: no passions are stirred.

But in the field of education, which all the evidence suggests is and always has been the major battle ground in whatever area or era, there is at most an uneasy truce. The Swann Committee: Education for All[45] favoured mother tongue teaching as part of the modern languages curriculum, but rejected both bi-lingual education and mother tongue maintenance as appropriate in maintained schools. This is rejected as conservation by the Commission for Racial Equality[46] who favour in due measure all three options; but endorsed by the present Government with the proviso that they cautiously accept the virtue of LEAs and schools supporting mother tongues at primary level.[47]

LEAs which favour mother tongue teaching do so for a variety of reasons: meeting children's educational needs, especially the young who enter schools with little or no English; adding to the range of educational opportunity, on the basis that our diversity of tongues is a valuable national resource: and promoting social and cultural development, especially a sense of ethnic identity and pride.[48] Ranged against them are those who argue that, as for example in South Africa blacks who are required to be taught in their mother tongue until level 5 are burdened with a disadvantage that, irrespective of apartheid, they will never overcome; so too immigrants or the children of immigrants taught in their mother tongues in the United Kingdom will culturally and economically become or remain alienated from the mainstream of society and that the urgent need is to strengthen and expand the teaching of English—and standard English too.[49] On occasion the truce has collapsed: and skirmishes broken out—witness the fate of schoolmasters Ray Honeyford[50] in Bradford and Jonathan Savery in Bristol,[51] who spoke out against multi-culturalism *within* the school; and the exploitation, arguably against the intention of the legislature, of section II powers, as in Brent,[52] not to provide additional teaching in English, but to foster mother tongue teaching.[53]

So what clues as to a solution do we gather from the experience of other countries? May I return, where I started, to Malaysia? The Federal Court had this to say:

"We think it reasonable to suppose that the framers of our constitution deliberately chose to use the expression 'national language' because they intended that [Malay] should be used not only for official purposes but also as an instrument for bringing together the diverse and polyglot races that live here and thus promote national unity. Before independence there were separate schools with Malays going to Malay language schools, Chinese to Chinese language schools and Indian to Indian language schools, thus keeping the three major communities apart. The only unifying factors were the comparatively few English language schools where children of various races were taught a common syllabus and a common tongue and mixed freely and later produced the leaders who were largely instrumental in developing the country economically and politically. We think it reasonable to suppose that the framers of our constitution came from this group of Malayans—later Malaysian—and concluded that just as before independence the English language could unify the small but highly influential group of leaders, so after independence the use [Malay] could and should be used as an instrument for unifying the whole nation. When considering [United States] authorities we could not help thinking that the most important factor in welding the Americans who originated from countries in Europe and elsewhere, each with a different language, into one nation, united and proud to be American, strong and prosperous, was the use in school and university there of the single language, namely the English language and no other and that while other languages are taught and learnt they are only so as foreign languages. Perhaps the framers of our independence too were aware of this and determined to profit from the American experience."

If there is some inner dynamic in the law, some common theme, underlying judicial pronouncements, that can be segregated from the particular legal instruments that they consider or construe, and from the particular features of the society in which they practise and pronounce, it is that a *single* language, like a *single* law, provides a necessary source of unity in any state. Differences of race, religion, colour, national origins, sex, can in many circumstances be ignored. Differences of language, if communication is to occur in speech or writing, cannot be. The search how best to recognise and cherish the vitality of other tongues within a community has to begin against the backcloth of that fundamental principle.

How each society should respond to minority claims is a matter for politicians. How each will answer it is a matter for prophets. As a mere lawyer, I would ask your indulgence only to conclude that English, an international language, spoken as a mother tongue by 350 million people, as a second language by 400 million others and in sum by over one billion people in the world, both is and should remain for that if for no other reason a national language too. Majorities, as well as minorities, have rights that the law should, if necessary, protect.

Notes

[1] [1982] M.L.J. 283.
[2] *New York Times*, November 25, 1980.
[3] Ethnic Minority Community Languages. A Statement. C.R.E. 1983.2.3.
[4] [1960] 1 W.L.R. 1273.
[5] *Re Estate of Fuld Deceased (No. 1)* [1965] 1 W.L.R. 1336 at p. 1339.
[6] British Nationality Act 1981, Sched. 1(1)(c).
[7] R. Ap Idris-Lewis, *The Welsh Language and the Law* at p. 209.
[8] [1967] 2 Q.B. 21.
[9] See also Grants for Welsh Language Education Regulations 1980, S.I. 1980 No. 1011 and Education (Grants for Teacher Training) (No. 2 Regulations) 1985 S.I. 1985 No. 1883 r. 7.2(ix).
[10] Welsh Office Circular 37/83.
[11] (1983) 2 A.C. 548.
[12] *Jones* v. *Gwynedd County Council, The Times*, July 25, 1986.
[13] [1985] I.R.L.R. 370.
[14] *Ibid.* at p. 375. See further MacDonald, *Race Relations—the New Law*, paras. 68–74.
[15] For the use made of these provisions see "Positive Action: Training for Black Ethnic Minority People" Equal Opportunities Review No. 10 1986.
[16] C.R.E. Report 2.12.78.
[17] [1985] 2 All E.R. 1106.
[18] *Ibid.* at p. 1110.
[19] Poulter, *English Law and Ethnic Minority Customs* (Butterworths, 1986).
[20-21] [1986] 1 Q.B.   401.
[22] Nos. 1474/62.
[23] PCI. Adv.Op. 6/4/35 Series A/B No. 64 pp. 4–88 at p. 17.
[24] McKean, *Equality and Discrimination Under International Law* at p. 145.
[25] Van Dyke, *Human Rights, Ethnicity and Discrimination*, (Greenwood Press, 1985).
[26] 384 U.S. 641: 16 L. Ed. 2d. (1966).
[27] 384 U.S. 672 (1966) 676.
[28] 262 U.S. 390.
[29] U.S. 409 (1923).
[30] 414 U.S. 563 (1974).

[31] "Bilingual Education and Desegregation" (1979) U.Penn.L.R. (127) (564 at p. 1600).

[32] Glazer (ed.), *Clamor at the Gates* (ICS Press, 1985) especially "Immigrants and Education," Chap. 10.

[33] S.133.

[34] S.93.

[35] [1971] A.C. 62.

[36] *Ibid.*

[37] Official Language Act 1963.

[38] *Jagdir Singh* v. *Pratap Singh* AIR 1965 S.C. 183.

[39] *Precost* v. *Bihar State* AIR 1969 S.C. 465 at pp. 468–469. Hingoram, *Human Rights in India*, 1985.

[40] Art. 350A.

[41] Seervan, *Constitutional Law of India* (3rd ed.), Vol. I: 937H, Vol. II 2141H.

[42] *Sunday Express*, December 21, 1986.

[43] Local Government Act 1972, s.137(1).

[44] *Ibid.* s.142(1).

[45] Cmnd. 9453 (1985).

[46] Swann "A Response from the Commission for Racial Equality" (1985) especially at pp. 8–9.

[47] "Mother Tongue Teaching in Schools." Speech given by the Secretary of State to the HMI/DES invitation conference at the University of Warwick, September 30, 1985. See also DES Mother Tongue Teaching in School and Community. H.M.S.O. 1984.

[48] *Ibid.*

[49] Honey, *The Language Trap* DCES 1983.

[50] Andrew Brown, *The Trials of Honeyford* C.P.S., 1985.

[51] *The Times*, May 21, 1986 and *The Times*, November 7, 1986.

[52] Butt, *The Times*, August 15, 1986.

[53] For the assimilationist origins of section II see Swann, para. 4.1.3.

Appendix

Mother tongue teaching:
See Multi-cultural Teaching. Summer 1983 (Hulton); Autumn 1984 (Geach); Spring 1985 (Ash).
ILEA Reports of Education Officer. June 25, 1982; December 18, 1985; March 5, 1986.

Co-ownership: What Could Be Simpler?

MALCOLM GRANT

Introduction

The idea of co-ownership of property is extremely simple. Theoretically, any right in property capable of ownership is capable of concurrent ownership; that is, ownership by two or more persons at the same time. But the translation of this simple concept into a workable legal form is highly complex. This has a certain inevitability, given that a system of co-ownership must always constitute a superstructure built on to the general rules of property ownership which have a tendency to complexity of their own.

There can be no doubt that co-ownership of property is a current legal problem of great importance. Take, for example, the simplest and commonest instance of direct co-ownership of real property, the family home. For the past 30 years there have been successive waves of litigation, proposals for reform and statutory intervention as the courts, academics, the Law Commission and Parliament have tried to adapt ancient property rules to the problems arising from the twentieth century phenomena of owner-occupation and matrimonial breakdown.

There are demands for new forms of co-ownership. There are currently proposals under consideration by the Law Commission for a new system of common tenure, tentatively labelled "commonhold,"[1] to deal with the legal problems of co-occupation of properties, such as blocks of flats and commercial buildings. The objective here is to establish a system which will allow individual ownership of units in a multi-occupied property, subject to a code of management obligations to secure common usage of shared parts and maintenance of the structure. Secondly, there is the phenomenon of timesharing, which in practice assumes a variety of different forms, but is based on the common objective of sub-dividing rights of occupation of property by time. And thirdly, there is currently considerable interest in the City in proposals for unitisation of property investment, which would allow investors to acquire, and to trade in, shares in individual properties. Proponents of this scheme see it as a means of widening the opportunities for direct property ownership into areas, such as

159

commercial and industrial property where single ownership is still
beyond the means of small investors, and, in the case of the largest
developments, beyond the means even of individual financial institutions. A report by a Committee of the Royal Institution of
Chartered Surveyors in 1985 foresaw other advantages as well[2]:

> "A particular objective would be to facilitate the deployment
> of the resources necessary to renew the country's infrastructure
> of commercial and industrial buildings. Increased liquidity in
> the market and the ability to spread risk could assist in the
> renewal of run-down inner-city areas which are not at present
> considered to be attractive for investment."

These are bold claims, and possibly overstated, but their implications are important. In all three cases some, if not all, of the
objectives can be attained through what I shall call "indirect co-
ownership," including most commonly the use of a limited company. There are also other devices available within conventional
property law, such as leasehold, which has provided a flexible
means in the past for regulating rights between co-occupiers of
land; and has additionally offered a means for financing property
development and, using rent review and rent gearing formulae, as
a means of participating in capital growth that is an alternative to
conventional debt secured by mortgage.

But in none of the three cases I have outlined is our present
system of direct co-ownership of land likely to satisfy the requirements of investors; nor has it yet, despite considerable judicial
ingenuity, provided a simple and clear structure to meet the needs
of ownership of the matrimonial home. Why not?

Before we turn to the legal structure of co-ownership, it is
necessary to attempt a basic classification of the phenomenon. To
this there must be two elements: concept and function. Under the
heading of concept, I shall look in turn at the modes of direct and
indirect co-ownership, including the extent to which concept has
been subordinated by statutory restrictions; and then at the statutory framework of co-ownership of property in land. Under the
heading of function I shall assess the requirements of acquisition,
management and disposal of co-ownership rights. In the final section, I shall assess proposals for reform.

The Concept of Direct Co-ownership of Property

The ownership of any property is in itself a complex legal concept.
The law deals in rights, not in absolutes; and it recognises different

rights subsisting concurrently in any property, whether realty or personalty. But these are not necessarily co-ownership rights. They may be rights of different qualities. A mortgagor and mortgagee are not regarded as co-owners; nor a lessor and lessee. The grant of a mortgage or lease creates new property rights. But although the relationship of the parties to them is not one of co-ownership, the rights created may themselves be co-owned.

Co-ownership therefore implies concurrent ownership of the same right in respect of property. Many legal systems, and all that have inherited the common law, however, recognise two basic concepts of concurrent ownership, though they vary in the rights they allocate to each. The first is joint ownership, in which co-owners have no individuality. Their rights are exercisable jointly and the benefits of ownership shared equally. French lawyers have an equivalent known as *avec clause d'accroisement*,[3] though it is rarely used. This is underpinned in our own version, the joint tenancy, by the concept of survivorship. Upon the death of a joint owner, his interest dies and is subsumed into the interests of the survivors. In the absence of any statutory restriction, the joint tenancy is usually severable by a co-owner, converting his entitlement into an undivided share outside the survivorship rule. An extreme version of non-severability is the tontine, well researched by Robert Louis Stevenson,[4] and named after Lorenzo Tonti, a Neapolitan banker who initiated it in France in the seventeenth century. It is a scheme by which subscribers to a common fund receive an annuity during their life which increases as their number is diminished by death, until the final survivor inherits the lot.

The second form of co-ownership, which in England is the tenancy in common, (in Franch law *en indivision*) recognises separate rights of individual owners in the common property. These rights are shares, though known to lawyers as "undivided shares" to indicate that they do not constitute entitlement to any particular part of the property. Subject to whatever limitations are imposed by contract, statute or otherwise, co-owners may deal in their shares independently of other owners, and may dispose of them or charge them.

This structure of co-ownership extends to personalty as well as real property, although it is anomolous to speak in this context in terms of tenure. But Blackstone[5] was clear:

> "Things personal may belong to their owners, not only in severalty, but also in joint tenancy, and in common, as well as real estates . . . if a horse, or other personal chattel be given

to two or more, absolutely, they are joint tenants thereof; and, unless the jointure be severed, the same doctrine of survivorship shall take place as in estates of land and tenements.''

But that broad statement requires some qualification. Certainly both forms of co-ownership are recognised in the case of a chose in possession, such as a chattel; but it has been suggested that the common law could not recognise the concept of a legal tenancy in common in a chose in action,[6] because, it was said,[7] the law looked on a chose in action merely as a right of action, and was concerned only with the proper persons to bring an action. Since they were regarded as one person at law, ownership was recognised only through joint tenancy. That assertion is too broadly stated for today. Although there is little consistency in treatment, co-owner-ship of choses in action has been handled flexibly by the legisla-ture, and the courts too have been willing to adapt the rules. They had no difficulty, for example, in recognising a legal tenancy in common of copyright,[8] even to the point of suggesting that copy-right in several might always be a tenancy in common rather than a joint tenancy[9] and in acknowledging the right of a co-owner to sue for infringement in his own right.[10] But they have insisted that, both at common law and under statute, the right to reproduce copyright material, though divisible as to title, must be indivisible as to exercise.[11]

Evidence of legislative pragmatism in relation to personal prop-erty also exists. In the case of a joint bank account, for example, the bank owes a single obligation to the account holders jointly,[12] but for the purposes of the Deposit Protection Fund each of them is treated as having a separate deposit of an equal share.[13] But where a patent is granted to two or more persons, the effect is to confer on each an equal undivided share in it subject to any agree-ment to the contrary.[14] Although none of the patent owners may grant a licence under it or assign or mortgage a share in it without the consent of the other co-owners,[15] the legislation preserves a right for each of them to exploit it for his own benefit and without the consent of the others without it constituting an infringement.[16]

Restrictions on the degrees of direct co-ownership

At this point, we need to stretch into a further stratosphere of abstraction. Given that an undivided share in property is itself a separate property right, it must theoretically be capable in turn of being co-owned, and so on to infinity. But whilst there is no necessary conceptual difficulty in this, there are obvious practical difficulties when property rights become increasingly divorced from their ultimate subject matter, and so widely dispersed as to have no real value, or as to fetter the alienability of the property. In many areas, therefore, concept yields to statutory intervention, often quite arbitrary. There are several examples of legislative determination to restrain any natural tendency to infinite co-ownership. A ship, for example, is divided by statute[17] into 64 shares; and not more than 64 individuals are entitled to be registered at the same time as owners of any one ship. Further, no person is permitted to be registered as owner of a fractional part of a share in a ship, though up to five persons may be registered as joint owners of a ship or of any share therein.[18] None of them may dispose in severalty of any interest in the ship or the share.[19] But a quite different regime extends to Scottish fishing boats, which are limited to 16 shares, with up to five persons registrable as joint owners.[20]

Mention must also be made of the co-ownership restriction indirectly imposed by the long standing prohibition, now reproduced in the Companies Act 1985,[21] on the formation of any company, association or partnership consisting of more than 20 persons for the purpose of carrying on any business that has for its object the acquisition of gain by the company, association or partnership, or by its individual members, unless it is registered as a company under that Act.

In company law itself there is no statutory limit on the number of persons who may be registered as owners of an individual share, though the provisions of Table A assume that their ownership will always be joint and not in common,[22] and a company may, for reasons of administrative necessity, impose its own restrictions through the memorandum and articles of association.

Modes of Indirect Co-ownership

So far, we have considered the structure of direct co-ownership of property. But to complete our conceptual overview we need also to consider the machinery of indirect co-ownership, in which some further level of ownership is inserted between co-owners and the property right concerned. Companies and trusts, for example, provide an alternative abstraction behind which co-ownership may subsist.

The company, a legal fiction, is the owner of its property, and the rights of its shareholders in relation to it are limited to their entitlement to share in the profits of the company and to influence, through their voting power and to the extent prescribed by the company's articles of association, management decisions in respect of the property. They are not therefore co-owners of the individual assets of the company, but co-owners of the company itself by dint of owning shares in the share capital of the company[23]; and individual owners of their individual shares, which, whatever the assets of the company, are deemed to be personal estate.[24] But it need not stop there. Any share may in turn be directly co-owned on joint tenancy (subject to any limits imposed by the company's memorandum and articles of association) or indirectly co-owned through another company or behind a trust.

By subordinating property interests to management, the company structure provides a flexible instrument for investment based co-ownership. It is the principal mechanism through which shared investment in all forms of property is undertaken. But the denial to shareholders of any direct property interest means that it is unsuited to cases where the purposes of the co-ownership is to secure not merely investment ends, but distinct property benefits, such as rights of user, occupation or possession of the property itself, or its use directly as security.

The trust, by comparison, provides a property-based means of splitting beneficial ownership from management, which it achieves by severing title to the property. Trustees hold as legal owners (at least, where the right is itself a legal right), with power to manage the property, duties in relation to beneficiaries and, subject to certain conditions, the ability to pass on good title to purchasers; and the beneficiaries hold as equitable owners. In theory, any property right is capable of being held on trust; so that co-ownership may exist behind the trust, even in the case of shares in a ship where direct co-ownership is statutorily limited.[25] A potential advantage of such indirect ownership is its anonymity. So in the case of company shares, where in addition to joint ownership on the register, there may be trust ownership off the register; but it is nonetheless expressly subject to the requirements under Part VI of the Companies Act 1985 requiring disclosure of beneficial ownership in certain cases.

Partnership is a hybrid form of co-ownership. The mere fact of co-ownership of property is not in itself to be taken as evidence of partnership.[26] Land owned by the partnership is required to be treated as between the partners as personal and not real estate,[27] and there is no doctrine of survivorship.[28] A partner cannot force a sale of the property during the subsistence of the partnership,[29] and hence has no share as such until the dissolution of the partnership.

The Special Case of Land

Thus far, I have deliberately avoided drawing any clear cut distinctions between real and personal property. There are of course practical, statutory and conceptual differences between the two. Property rights in land, for example, relate to a fixed and immovable segment of the real world; whilst, at the other extreme, chattels are destructible. Different rules apply to the formalities for disposal of interests in, and the declaration of trusts respecting real and personal property. Property rights may be converted from one classification to the other, either by the interposition of a separate mode of ownership or by operation of some rule of law, such as the equitable doctrine of conversion or the statutory doctrine of overreaching.

But land is always different. The principles of land law generally, and those of co-ownership in particular, are the product of an awkward marriage of historical concept and technical legislative intervention.

Holdsworth observed in 1926[30]:

> "Throughout the history of land law, contrary to the usually received wisdom, the legislature has had a larger share in shaping the land law than it has had in shaping any other branch of private law. At all periods in the history of land law, statutes have been the parents of a great many of its fundamental principles, and the starting points of new epochs in its development."

In 1925, the overriding objective of the legislature was to achieve greater simplicity in conveyancing.[31] Even in concept, co-ownership of land had never been straightforward. For some 500 years there were four modes of co-ownership of land recognised by the common law.[32] The first of these was coparceny, a form of co-ownership through succession, which provided for the devolution of real property upon intestacy. If the deceased left no son, who would normally otherwise be the heir, then his daughters would take together as coparceners. It was neither a joint tenancy, nor tenancy in common, but a hybrid. Coparceny was effectively abolished by the 1925 legislation. The second was a status-based co-ownership, the tenancy by entireties, which was a form of joint tenancy by married couples. Although land in theory was owned by both spouses, the husband had sole management power and the right to possession and all profits from the land; and the wife retained only the right to possession of the land if she outlived her husband. The Married Women's Property Act 1882 prevented the creation of any further tenancies by entireties thereafter, and this form of tenure was finally abolished in 1925 by the Law of Property Act 1925, s.37 which pronounced that henceforth a husband and wife should, for all purposes of acquisition of any interest in property, be treated as two persons.[33]

Joint tenancy and tenancy in common of land, though retained in concept by the 1925 legislation, were fundamentally recast. Simplicity was sought by limiting direct co-ownership of legal estates in land to no more than four co-owners holding as joint tenants, and interposing a trust between legal and beneficial co-ownership. Three principal provisions were designed to bring about this end:

(1) where land is conveyed to persons in undivided shares (*i.e.* as tenants in common) it is to be held by the first four of them named in the conveyance as joint tenants upon the so-called "statutory trusts," which is a trust for sale (Law of Property Act 1925, s.34(2)).

(2) if the land has passed by devise, bequest or testamentary appointment, then it is to be so held by the trustees (if any) of the will for the purposes of the Settled Land Act 1925, and otherwise by the personal representatives of the testator (s.34(3)).

(3) if a legal estate is beneficially limited to or held in trust for any persons as joint tenants, it is to be held on trust for sale in the same manner, but not so as to sever their joint tenancy in equity (s.36(1)).

The formulae are clumsily expressed, and significant gaps have appeared over the years. They do not deal comprehensively with all co-ownership, in particular the case where rights of co-ownership have arisen behind a resulting or constructive trust, are rights in common rather than joint, and there is no conveyance or other instrument. But the background to the legislation, and its design, suggest that the formulae were intended to provide an exhaustive code of co-ownership, particularly in their simplification of dealings with the legal estate. It was part of the simplification package built around the reduction in the number of legal estates in land and the removal of fetters on their alienability.

Sir Arthur Underhill, Senior Conveyancing Counsel to the Court had prepared in 1919 a pamphlet entitled "The Line of Least Resistance: An Easy but Effective Method of Simplifying the Law of Real Property," and his proposals were adopted with only minor modifications by the Scott Committee.[34] Underhill argued that tenancy in common was "a far greater detriment to the proper management of land than settlements (which are popularly debited with this sin) and introduces infinitely greater difficulty with regard to its sale, as, not only must the parties be unanimous, but the title of each of them has to be deduced."[35] Moreover, a tenant in common of a legal estate could require the physical partitioning of the land, in an action so complex that it was liable to exhaust any value left in the land.[36]

He urged that trust ownership, at least in the case of an express trust, should be made to carry full rights of transfer upon which a purchaser could rely, unless he had actual notice of lack of authority; and that the remedy of any beneficiary should be against the trustee only. The Scott Committee[37] accepted this in principle, but in the form adopted by Cherry's draft Law of Property Bill which proposed that all land held under an existing tenancy in common, and for the future, should be vested in trustees for sale, "leaving the beneficial interests (including charges on undivided shares) to take effect as trusts affecting the proceeds of sale and the rents until sale, so that a purchaser will not be concerned therewith,"[38] providing the purchase money was paid to two trustees, except where the trustee was a corporation. In this way, the Committee concluded, the equitable interests would be properly protected without the registration of cautions or inhibitions.

That decision was, in retrospect, unfortunate. Resort to the doctrine of the trust for sale introduced an unnecessary fiction; and the draftsman compounded the problem by omitting to extend the doctrine to all cases of beneficial co-ownership. Moreover, it was a conveyancer's package: it failed to consider other rights flowing from co-ownership of land, not least the rights of occupation of co-owners.

But so far as it went, both the legislation and its purpose were clear enough. Notwithstanding its clumsiness, the trust for sale was a device familiar to conveyancers at the time. As defined by the Act, it was to be an immediate binding trust for sale, though subject to a discretion to postpone sale[39]; and in accordance with general equitable principles its intended effect was that the rights of beneficiaries should be translated into interests in the proceeds of sale, and the income and profits from the land pending sale. But there was in truth no consistent line of authority on the doctrine of conversion. Anderson has recently argued persuasively that the notion that he describes as "conversion-absolutism," which portrays the doctrine as somehow logical and timeless, is nothing more than an invention of the textbook writers, without reference to logic or commonsense.[40] Nineteenth century judges had shown considerable pragmatism in considering whether or not to employ it in different situations, and the approach of the House of Lords in the celebrated case of *Williams and Glyn's Bank Ltd.* v. *Boland*[41] in 1981 was in the middle of that tradition. In that case, the idea that a co-owner's rights in the matrimonial home were no more than rights to income and profits pending sale simply proved too gross a fiction for the judges to stomach. In Lord Denning's view, for example, reinforced on appeal by Lord Wilberforce, "to describe the interests of spouses in a house jointly bought to be used as a matrimonial home as merely an interest in the proceeds of sale, or rents and profits until sale, is just a little unreal."[42]

But it seems, so far as he analysed it in detail, that Underhill believed in the magic of the doctrine and believed also that Cherry's Bill, which the Scott Committee had prepared on the basis of Underhill's proposals, had achieved it. Underhill[43] wrote in 1922 that, as a result of the trust for sale:

> "a *bona fide* purchaser or lessee may, in the words of Shakespeare, 'Close up his eyes and draw the curtains close'—in other words, deal with the owner of the legal estate without troubling himself with the equities of third parties, even if he had notice of them."

But although the doctrine provided a clear management device for cases of investment co-ownership, it was to prove an awkward solution in the case of the growing phenomenon of co-owned housing, particularly the matrimonial home, where co-ownership was accompanied by co-occupation. Instead of simplifying dealings with the legal title, it succeeded in confusing the rights of co-owners during the subsistence of the co-ownership: were their shares still to be regarded as interests in land, or did they subsist only in personalty? If the latter, then how was that to be reconciled with the definition of "minor interest" under the Land Registration Act 1925 which includes an undivided share in land? Fundamental conceptual issues were suddenly at stake: whether, for example, an undivided share passed on death as personalty or realty; whether dealings by a co-owner with his interest were dealings in land and thus created rights protectable by registration, or chargeable by a judgment creditor, or requiring a written memorandum for their enforceability. Different answers had to be devised for different situations, balancing the demands for security in conveyancing against the risk of loss to innocent co-owners.[44]

In case the doctrine of conversion were to prove faulty however, the Act provided a second line of defence: provided the purchase price was paid to two trustees, then the beneficial interests would be statutorily overreached at that time and converted into interests in the proceeds of sale.[45] In *Boland*, that possibility did not arise, because the mortgage money had been paid to the husband alone; and many commentators, including the Law Commission,[46] assumed that overreaching would have operated had the capital been paid to two trustees.

But even that line has now been overturned by the Court of Appeal, in *City of London Building Society* v. *Flegg*[47] (currently on appeal to the House of Lords). A married couple were legal joint tenants of a dwelling which they occupied with the woman's parents, who had provided at least half the purchase price. The couple later moved out and left the parents in occupation, but mortgaged the property to a building society without the parents' knowledge or consent. They defaulted on the repayments, and the mortgagees sought to repossess. They had no knowledge of the parents' rights, but they had made no inquiries as to the occupation of the house before lending the money. The Court held that as persons in actual occupation, the parents' rights bound the building society; and that they had not been overreached. Their occupation provided protection, both under section 14 of the Law of Property Act 1925, which (ambiguously) protects interests to which occupiers may be entitled in right of occupation, and as rights of persons in actual occupation under the Land Registration Act 1925.

That was an outcome reached entirely on legal analysis, but there is a clear antipathy that runs through that case, and through *Boland*, towards the claims of financial institutions who have advanced capital without making adequate inquiries. Conflicts like this tend to arise in the second mortgage market because the transaction is not accompanied, as it usually is on sale, by a grant of vacant possession. Careless lenders must look after themselves, whether through inquiries or by spreading the risk through insurance, and the courts will be anxious to secure that complex technicalities are not used to defeat innocent third parties. But the point of the overreaching machinery was precisely that it should protect purchasers and lenders, and provide continuing proprietary rights against the proceeds of sale for co-owners whose interests have been, albeit involuntarily, overreached.

The Functional Requirements of Co-ownership

The law of property is the law of relationships between people in respect of property, and the operational requirements that the rules regulating co-ownership are required to satisfy are potentially as wide ranging as all human needs in relation to property.

The needs of a husband and wife in relation to the matrimonial home are quite different from those of commercial property investors. Security of occupation for them and their children is likely to be higher in their list of priorities than the need for liquidity, risk sharing or tax efficiency. No single system is likely to meet every need, nor should it necessarily be distorted to satisfy competing demands if other forms of property ownership which can provide suitable alternatives are readily available. In many cases, potential co-owners have other choices, and the advantages to them of direct co-ownership, however flexible the legal framework, may be outweighed by other factors, not least taxation advantages.

But some co-owners, particularly residential co-owners, are locked into the 1925 scheme of co-ownership, and its artificiality and inflexibility is in their case a particular cause for serious concern. It is an unnecessary absurdity that a couple who buy a dwelling should have, for the sake of property law, to hold it upon trust for themselves with an immediate binding duty to sell it again, however reassuring it may be to know that they have the right to postpone the sale.

It is a basic requirement of any system of co-ownership that it should provide the basic machinery, first, for regulating the acquisition of co-ownership rights and for providing security of ownership and investment; secondly, for dealing with decision-making by co-owners (or by others on their behalf) as to the use, enjoyment and disposition of the property; and thirdly, for enabling, in accordance with the decision-making structure, the ready alienability of the property, by allowing good title to be passed to purchasers free from the claims of dissenting co-owners. These inter-related, and often competing, requirements need to be further examined.

Acquisition

Rights of co-ownership may in theory be created through the same modes as any other property rights, including express transfer, whether for consideration or by gift or by declaration of trust. Or rights may arise by implication, or by status or under statute.

Implied rights have proved the most difficult, from the point of view both of creation and of protection. Take the common case where property has been purchased out of funds provided unequally by more than one party, but is transferred into the sole name of one of them. It is now clear that, although there is no co-ownership of the legal estate, a relationship of beneficial co-ownership arises. In the context of personal property no necessary difficulty arises. But in the case of land, the resulting trust upon which the contributing party's rights are said to be based is not a conveyance, nor is it a beneficial limitation or trust of the legal estate for any persons as joint tenants. For the purposes of the Law of Property Act 1925 a beneficial tenancy in common can arise in no other way. And so, in the interests of common sense and justice the machinery of the Act has had to be stretched quite artificially to encompass an arrangement which appears not to have been contemplated by its draftsmen.[49] And that is not the end of the difficulties arising in contribution cases. The courts have had to wrestle with the difficulties of indirect contributions, that is, contributions referable not to the initial purchase price, but to the subsequent living arrangements of the parties. An initial, though ambiguous, reluctance displayed by the House of Lords in *Pettitt* v. *Pettitt*[50] and *Gissing* v. *Gissing*[51] has given way over time to a pragmatic readiness to imply co-ownership through constructive trusts, on the basis that it would be inequitable for the legal owner to claim sole beneficial ownership where there was a common intention that it should be shared and that the claimant has acted to his or her detriment on the basis of that common intention.[52]

In relation to the matrimonial home, property law cannot be expected to provide sensible answers to issues of quantum of co-ownership shares, because the relationship of the parties is based on more personal considerations than property, and also because of the socially overriding need to ensure provision for any children of the marriage. Discretionary power for the courts to adjust property rights upon divorce or death has therefore had to be introduced to supplant the need to indulge in artificial inquiries into intention. The problem remains, however, with non-matrimonial relationships; and the question whether co-ownership rights exist (quite apart from quantum) creates, in all cases, potential difficulties upon sale where the issue comes to be asserted against a purchaser or mortgagee of the property.

Management

Management in the case of personalty is undertaken chiefly through modes of indirect ownership, and direct co-ownership has given rise to little litigation. Despite the potential breadth of co-ownership rights, whether direct or behind a trust, the ready liquidity of most personalty and the absence of related occupation rights makes for an easier resolution of disputes. Sale is the easiest method, though in the case of chattels, there is also an express right for a co-owner to the extent of a moiety or more, to apply to the court for an order for partition.[53]

But management in the case of realty is considerably more complex, since it encompasses not only the decision to sell or retain the property, but also the respective rights of co-occupation of it. Commercial co-owners may settle these issues in an express declaration of trust, and introduce a management system which takes advantage of the 1925 Act by, for example, imposing a requirement of consent to sale (under section 26), expanding upon the requirement in section 27(2) of consultation with beneficial owners and arranging for delegation of powers of management by the trustees for sale. But the statutory formulae are mandatory and relatively inflexible, and section 30, which confers a right of application to the court on the part of any person interested, appears not to be excludable. There is thus always the prospect, no matter what internal management system the parties may have settled, of an overriding order of the court directing the trustees to sell or to exercise any of the other functions conferred by the Act.

Co-owners who have made no other arrangements are left with the bare management structure that the Act provides, at the heart of which is the section 30 order. It has come to be used pragmatically as a means of providing indirectly entitlements which do not arise directly. Take rent, for example. Whilst there is in general no right by virtue of co-ownership to claim rent from a fellow co-owner who is in occupation, even where the other has been excluded from occupation by order of the court, it is now established that the court will in appropriate cases exercise its discretion under section 30 against granting an order for sale, provided arrangements are made for an occupation rent to be paid.[54]

Marketability

Marketability of land provides no particular difficulties in the overwhelmingly usual situation where the decision to sell has the consent of all co-owners, and a purchaser can be satisfied that that is so. But, as we have seen, there remain major doubts as to the enforceability of co-owners' rights against a purchaser. The market for an undivided share on its own is limited in any event by the practical shortcomings of the co-ownership mechanism itself, and particularly where another co-owner is already in occupation.

Reforming Co-ownership

There appears to be some measure of agreement that co-ownership systems have failed to meet the property requirements of contemporary society. Should they be reformed? At this point, it is interesting to note a certain difference between private lawyers and public lawyers. The latter, when they perceive a defect in the law, proclaim it noisily abroad and campaign for immediate legislative reform. Private lawyers tend to assume that if there were a possible and desirable solution, it would have happened by now. In the area of private property relations there are always good practical and political reasons for restraint. Changes affecting the management and marketability of property, if they are to have retrospective effect, may damage existing rights (or vested interests); but if they are to have only prospective effect, then they merely add a further level of complexity. Too often these considerations stifle beneficial reform, until sufficient political momentum is built up to carry it through. It has ever been so. Dicey, writing in the *Law Quarterly Review* in 1905, maintained that the history of land law was fully explainable by the history of public opinion[55]:

> "The fundamentals of the land law stand unchanged though not unshaken, first, because their amendment is a task of great technical difficulty; secondly because there has never as yet existed an effective demand for root and branch reform; and lastly, because the conflict between radicalism and socialism has for a time arrested every attempt to modify our system of land tenure."

The political debates of 1905 may be different from those of a privatised property owning democracy of 1987, but the paradox remains. The unsuccessful efforts of the Law Commission to rationalise co-ownership rules relating to the matrimonial home and to review the *Boland* decision,[56] have demonstrated the barriers that remain to law reform in Britain. But there is a need nonetheless to take a fresh look at co-ownership, not just in terms of the obvious need for rationalisation and simplification but also in terms of the differing functions required of it.

Two lines of reform are open. The first, which is aimed at simplification, involves a recasting of the statutory machinery of land co-ownership. The lead has been taken in a Working Paper from the Law Commission, *Trusts of Land*,[57] which sets out five separate proposals for discussion. They realistically accept that the doctrine of conversion today serves little purpose, and should be abolished[58] and that the automatic imposition of a trust for sale is artificial in many contexts of co-ownership. In one of their proposed models, the Commission would replace settlements and trusts for sale entirely by a new simple trust of land; in another (Proposal IV), and more radically, the Commission advances the idea of co-ownership without a trust at all. Co-owners would be treated in the same way as a sole owner. But since it is proposed to retain a right of severance, trustless co-ownership could subsist only until the right was exercised; that is, for so long as there were no undivided shares and thus no need for the management device of a trust. But the idea is conceptually attractive, and offers a much simplified approach. With no trust for sale there would be no presumption in favour of sale, and there would need therefore to be an extended version of section 30 which would give the court wider power to regulate relationships between co-owners, including occupation rights, in accordance with new prescribed criteria. But disposal, except in the case of the trustless joint tenancy, would depend upon the doctrine of overreaching, to which the *Flegg* decision in the Court of Appeal dealt a serious blow. The House of Lords ruling (noted in footnote 47) now renders the proposal viable again, by reasserting the overreaching doctrine.

The second line of reform would be to stop stretching the existing structure to accommodate competing demands, and instead, as has happened with new forms of personalty, to create separate co-ownership modes designed to meet specific needs, and to design acquisition, management and disposal systems for each. In addition to retaining a simplified version of existing co-ownership along the lines proposed by the Law Commission, three new co-ownership tenures may be considered.

First, a matrimonial home co-ownership. This is by no means a new idea, and has been pursued with varying degrees of enthusiasm by the Law Commission in various forms for over 15 years.[59] The potential complexity of such a system is daunting. Should there be automatic equality of ownership for example? If so, then many of the acquisition problems discussed earlier fall to one side. Should one party be able to sell the home, or his/her share, without the consent of the other? How can purchasers be protected? What role should remain with the courts in adjusting property rights? Should there be, as with "homesteading" legislation, some protection against creditors? Should it be limited to spouses?

Yet other states have already implemented such a change. The New Zealand Matrimonial Property Act 1976, for example, creates a form of community of matrimonial property through which spouses automatically share equally in the matrimonial home and the family chattels, except where the marriage has been of short duration or there are other exceptional circumstances that would, in the opinion of the court, render equal sharing "repugnant to justice"; and specific inroads are made against the Torrens indefeasibility of title for purchasers who are protected only if they received the property in good faith and for valuable and adequate consideration.[60] Ontario legislation[61] offers an alternative model. It simply prohibits one spouse from disposing of or encumbering any interest in the matrimonial home, unless the other spouse joins in the instrument or consents to the transaction. If the requirement is breached, the transaction can be set aside, unless the person holding the interest at the time of the application acquired it for value, in good faith and without notice that the property was, at the relevant time, a matrimonial home.[62]

The English Law Commission in their 1973 *Report on Family Property*[63] urged that husband and wife should by statute become equal co-owners as joint tenants of any ownership interest in the matrimonial home. They favoured the joint tenancy model, because people seemed to favour it in practice, and survivorship was "a natural and desirable course of events." A further Report in 1978[64] spelt out the idea in more detail, and was accompanied by a draft Bill. A joint tenant under these arrangements who was not also a joint tenant of the legal estate would be at risk, but instead of putting purchasers on notice by reason of their dealing with a matrimonial home, the proposals suggested protection for the co-owner by registering a special charge. Such mechanical protection raises obvious difficulties,[65] particularly the prospect of it operating as a hostile step and thus precipitating conflict, and also the likelihood of it operating largely as an exclusionary device, denying protection if there has been a failure—for however good a reason—to register. The important consequence for conveyancing of a status tenure of the matrimonial home should be that it provides automatic notice to every purchaser of the existence of joint rights.

Secondly, there is a need for condominium-type statutory machinery to handle multiple occupation of residential and commercial buildings, and to satisfy the desire of purchasers to own their individual units and to exercise rights over common parts. There are various methods of achieving this end at the moment, such as leasehold ownership of individual units, supported by the necessary easements of access and support, and enforceable covenants in individual leases to establish funds for maintenance and services. But there are shortfalls, both where fee simple ownership and management responsibility is outside the leaseholders' control, and also in the complexity of handling transfers of property when the fee simple is owned separately by tenants jointly through a company or trust structure. Leasehold conveyancing can be expensive and time consuming, and tenants' difficulties with management companies are widespread and look likely to be exacerbated as existing buildings deteriorate over time.[66] The commonhold tenure currently under consideration by the Law Commission may be able to offer developers and purchasers a workable system based on freehold ownership tied to mutual rights, obligations and voting power in management. An adaptation of commonhold tenure might also be appropriate to timesharing, for which the normal co-ownership rules have apparently been seen as disadvantageous because of the prospect of a charging order being made against the interest of an owner.[67] Timesharing presently in Britain is usually based either upon discontinuous leasehold,[68] which has in the past been the most popular method; or through membership of a club, either proprietary (where the freehold remains with the developer) or members', where the freehold vests in trustees. Occupancy rights in either case are conferred by contract, and the purchaser acquires no beneficial interest in the property.

Thirdly, consideration needs to be given to a different co-ownership structure which would allow direct investment in individual properties, though carrying no occupation rights. Because of the relative inflexibility of direct co-ownership, particularly behind the inappropriate machinery of the trust for sale,[69] the current proposals for unitisation of property investment which I mentioned at the beginning of this paper have followed a variety of different paths, and no clear single version has yet emerged. There have long been doubts as to whether a unit trust designed as a vehicle for real property investment could be authorised under the Prevention of Fraud (Investments) Act 1958, but the Financial Services Act 1986 has deliberately opened the door to unitised real property investment, and taxation amendments look likely to extend to these trusts the exemption from double taxation that other unit trusts enjoy, but which are inherent in an ordinary company structure.

But the unit trust is a comparatively complex mechanism suited only to relatively large scale development. Under the 1986 Act, single property schemes will only be exempt from restrictions on promotion if the units can be dealt with by a recognised investment exchange. It is possible that a specific model of direct co-ownership of land for investment purposes could readily open up a further market for longer term investment in more modest properties. There are different models upon which it could be based which could draw together existing models of real and personal property co-ownership: for example, by a notional division of the fee simple into a pre-determined quantity of shares, as with a ship, which could give a manageable quantity for land registration purposes; or it could merely establish the necessary basic machinery for management between co-owners, laying a basis for distribution and reinvestment of profits and allowing ready marketability of shares.

There is a need to strike a balance between tenure and contract and provide a mechanism which parties will find attractive for securing investment whilst providing a flexible internal management structure, adaptable to their own requirements but with a right of application to the courts and clear protection for purchasers and secured debtors. This implies a move from traditional conveyancing devices towards new tenurial forms. Making new tenurial choices available will not solve all the complexities of co-ownership, least of all those of informally created rights. But it could be an important step in the process of clarification and simplification of the law of co-ownership, for which there is an even more pressing need today than in 1925.

Notes

[1] Noted at [1986] Conv. 361.

[2] *The Unitisation of Real Property.* A Report by the RICS. December 1985, para. 1.3.

[3] Co-ownership in German and Italian law is expressly regulated by the civil code: see the *German Civil Code*, arts. 1008–1011 (as to co-ownership in fractions); *Italian Civil Code*, Arts. 1100–1116 (common ownership).

[4] *The Wrong Box* (1889).

[5] *Commentaries on the Laws of England*, Vol. 18, p. 399.

[6] See, *e.g. Halsbury's Laws of England* (4th ed.), vol. 18, para. 1145; though citing as the principal authority for this suggestion (as does *Crossley Vaines*, n. 7 below) the unsupported proposition of Joyce J. in *Re McKerrell* [1912] 2 Ch. 648 at 653, and accepting on the basis of *Re Butler's Trusts* (1888) 38 Ch.D. 286 and *Re Hewett* [1894] 1 Ch. 362 that co-owners could sever in equity.

[7] Tyler and Palmer (Eds.), *Crossley Vaines' Personal Property* (5th ed. 1973), 57.

[8] *Powell* v. *Head* (1879) 12 Ch.D. 636.

[9] *Lauri* v. *Renad* [1892] 3 Ch. 402, *per* Kekewich J., citing *Powell* v. *Head (supra)* for too broad a proposition; upheld in the Court of Appeal on different grounds (*ibid*. 417).

[10] *Prior* v. *Lansdowne Press Pty. Ltd.* [1977] V.R. 65.

[11] *Cescinsky* v. *George Routledge & Sons Ltd.* [1916] 2 K.B. 325.

[12] *Brewer* v. *Westminster Bank Ltd.* [1952] 2 All E.R. 650.

[13] Banking Act 1979, s.30(5); and see also Bills of Exchange Act 1892, s.32(3) as to the requirement of joint endorsement by joint payees of a Bill, thus codifying the rule in *Carvick* v. *Vickery* (1783) 2 Doug. 653n.

[14] Patent Act 1977, s.36(1).

[15] *Ibid*. s.36(3).

[16] *Ibid*. s.36(2).

[17] Merchant Shipping Act 1894, s.5.

[18] *Ibid*. s.5(iii).

[19] *Idem.*

[20] Sea Fishing Boat (Scotland) Act 1886, s.314.

[21] S.716. Certain professional partnerships are excluded from the prohibition.

[22] The Companies (Tables A to F) Regulations 1985 (S.I. 1985 No. 805), especially Table A, reg. 14 (which imposes joint and several liability on joint share holders to pay all calls), and reg. 55 (which confers voting power only on the senior joint holder who tenders a vote, seniority being determined by the order in which the names of the holders appear in the register). By the Companies Act 1985, s.208(3), the owners of a joint interest are taken each of them to have that interest for the purpose of the ownership disclosure requirements under Part VI of the Act.

[23] Companies Act 1985, s.744.

[24] Companies Act 1985, s.182.

[25] Thus although no notice of any trust is permitted to be entered in the register, the Merchant Shipping Act 1894 expressly preserves the right for equitable interests to be enforced against owners and mortgagees "in the same manner as in respect of any other personal property" (ss.56 and 57; and see, *e.g. The Venture* [1908] P. 218).

[26] Partnership Act 1890, s.2.

[27] *Ibid*. s.22.

[28] See further Potter; "Undivided Shares in Land" (1930) 46 L.Q.R. 71.

[29] *Re Buchanan-Wollaston's Conveyance* [1939] Ch. 738.

[30] "The Reform of the Land Law: an Historical Retrospect" (1926) 42 L.Q.R. 158.

[31] Although as Offer has compellingly demonstrated, this was a compromise objective to stave off the pressure for more fundamental social reforms in relation to property: the law of property had itself become a species of corporate property, and a vested interest of the legal profession (Avner Offer, *Property and Politics 1879–1914*, p. 82).

[32] For a detailed account, see W. S. Holdsworth, *A History on English Law*, Vol. III, pp. 126–128.

[33] Unfortunately, that good news came too late for those former colonies who had inherited English property law in the eighteenth and nineteenth centuries. A recent survey of American states shows that tenancies by entireties are still very much alive there: 25 states and Columbia D.C. affirmatively recognise it and another five mention it in their codes while neither governing nor restricting its use. Only 13 states have either expressly or by strong inference abolished it, four have conflicting statutory or judicial pronouncements and three have no known position; which means that it remains valid in no less than 25, and possibly as many as 37 states. In those states where there has been reform it has in some cases been by judicial declaration and in others by state legislation, prompted not only by disgust at the subordination of women inherent in the doctrine, but also the determination of creditors to be able to get at married women's assets: see further, *Powell on Real Property*, Vol. 4A, para. 620[4].

[34] *Fourth Report on the Acquisition and Valuation of Land Committee on the Transfer of Land in England and Wales*, Cmd. 424 (1919). The Committee, whilst finding the law of property archaic and unnecessarily complicated, thought that it was "obviously impossible to repeal the whole of the existing law of real property and to impose a new model" and therefore resolved to adopt the proposals put forward by Underhill, which they thought offered "the best and simplest remedy to effect the required simplification with as little disturbance as possible."

[35] *Ibid*. Appendix I, p. 30.

[36] And see also Box, "Division of Property into Real and Personal Estate" (1887) 3 L.Q.R. 406, 407.

[37] *Op. cit.* para. 24(e).

[38] *Memorandum by Mr B. L. Cherry on the Principles and Objects of the Law of Property Bill*, Scott Committee Report, Appendix IV, p. 43.

[39] Law of Property Act 1925, s.205.

[40] "The Proper, Narrow Scope of Equitable Conversion" (1984) 100 L.Q.R. 86.

[41] [1979] Ch. 312, 329–330; [1981] A.C. 487, 507. Note, though, the difference in approach between the two, and particularly Lord Denning's insistence that there was no trust for sale at all, but merely a simple trust arrangement.

[42] And see also the insistence of Ormrod L.J. ([1979] Ch. 312 at 333) that the legal fiction should not be pressed to its logical conclusion and beyond the point necessary to achieve the primary objective of simplification, particularly when it involves the sacrifice of the interests of a class or classes of persons.

[43] *A Concise Explanation of Lord Birkenhead's Act in Plain English*, p. 91.

[44] For a useful discussion, see Warburton, "The Doctrine of Conversion: fact or fiction?" [1986] Conv. 415.

[45] Law of Property Act 1925, s.2.

[46] *The Implications of Williams & Glyn's Bank Ltd.* v. *Boland* (Law Com. No. 115).

[47] [1986] 1 All E.R. 989. The Court of Appeal decision was overturned by the House of Lords on May 14, 1987. The House held that the parents' beneficial interests were overreached by the legal charge and were transferred to the equity of redemption; they could not thereafter subsist as overriding interests under s.70(1)(g). The House reasserted the "whole philosophy of the Act in relation to individed shares in land", that a purchaser of a legal estate should not be concerned with the beneficial interests of tenants in common.

[48] See, *e.g. Bull* v. *Bull* [1955] 1 Q.B. 234; *Williams & Glyn's Bank Ltd.* v. *Boland* (*supra*).

[49] See further Swadling, "Beneficial co-ownership behind a resulting trust and the problems of a trust for sale" [1986] Conv. 379.

[50] [1970] A.C. 777.

[51] [1971] A.C. 866.

[52] See, *e.g. Eves* v. *Eves* [1975] 1 W.L.R. 1338; *Burns* v. *Burns* [1984] Ch. 317; *Grant* v. *Edwards* [1986] 2 All E.R. 426.

[53] Law of Property Act 1925, s.188.

[54] See, *e.g. Dennis* v. *McDonald* [1981] 2 All E.R. 632 (affd. [1982] 3 All E.R. 176); *Bernard* v. *Josephs* [1982] 3 All E.R. 162.

[55] "The Paradox of the Land Law" [1905] L.Q.R. 221, 232.

[56] *The Implications of Williams & Glyn's Bank Ltd.* v. *Boland* Cmnd. 8636 (1982).

[57] Working Paper No. 94 (1985).

[58] *Ibid.* para. 16.4.

[59] See, *e.g.* Law Com. 52 (1973); Law Com. 58 (1978).

[60] Matrimonial Property Act 1976 (N.Z.), s.44(2).

[61] Family Law Reform Act R.S.O. 1980, s.42.

[62] *Ibid.* s.42(2); and see *Kozub* v. *Timko* (1984) 31 Real Property Reports 254.

[63] Law Com. No. 52.

[64] *Third Report on Family Property*, Law Com. No. 86.

[65] See the further discussion by the Commission in Cmnd. 8636, paras. 73–84.

[66] See further the *Report of the Committee of Inquiry on the Management of Privately Owned Blocks of Flats* (the Nugee Committee). Department of the Environment, 1985.

[67] Edmonds, *International Timesharing* (2nd ed., 1986), p. 20.

[68] See, *e.g. Cottage Holiday Associates Ltd.* v. *Customs and Excise Commissioners* [1983] 2 W.L.R. 861.

[69] For a discussion, see Bailey, "Unitisation and Multiple Ownership" in *Current Problems in Property Law*. Blundell Memorial Lectures, 1986, p. 53.

A View from The Lord Chancellor's Office

ROBERT STEVENS

(a) The Lord Chancellor's Office and Department

This paper deals with the Lord Chancellor's Office or, as it has been known since 1972, the Lord Chancellor's Department. In particular, I am interested in what the largely untapped papers of the Office—now available until 1955 under the Thirty Year Rule—tell us of the operation of the Department as a whole, and in particular about law reform.[1]

The Lord Chancellor's Department appoints the judges (including the Magistrates) and the Q.C.s. It runs the High Courts and the Circuit Courts; it is the ultimate administrator of the legal aid scheme and thus, as we know from the recent litigation,[2] is highly significant in determining the payment of the profession. It commissions reports[3] and staffs most of the major Commissions and Committees that touch on the law[4]; it is responsible for the Law Commission, the Council on Tribunals, and various other bodies; it comes close to being, if in fact it is not already, depending on how you define the term, a Ministry of Justice for England and Wales. It is, however, more than that, for, in a very English way, it continues to present Crown livings, as well as being responsible for the Queen's Speech at the opening of Parliament, and the Lord Chancellor's political and judicial work.[5]

We all run the danger of overrating the importance of our own research. The Office papers partly do no more than confirm what we already knew or suspected about changes in the English legal system. Among other things they remind us that some constitutional skirmishes, like the issue of a Ministry of Justice, are inevitably resurrected each couple of decades. They remind us of the simplicities that exist in so many of our discussions of basic concepts like the separation of powers. It is not a question of the judicial, executive, and legislative; it is a question of how far, and with what political guidance, the civil servant should be choosing members of the judiciary, or what role the judges themselves should play in deciding appointments, terms of service, and in running the courts. As we become more sophisticated in our analysis of the nature of the law-making process, however, delving into these records reminds one that the process may need to become still more sophisticated. What is interesting is not merely who set up the Committee, but how and with whom the Office talked in deciding its composition, who staffed the Committee, who drafted the Report and negotiated away the rough edges. If legislation was needed for implementation, the Department's or the profession's lobbying could be important; if the report might be implemented administratively, the views of senior members of the Department may have been crucial. If the thirty year rule keeps us from looking in this way at the immediate past, I trust the messages are important for those considering current legal problems. Certainly for those writing about the English Legal System, the Lord Chancellor's Office papers are a "must."

One of the difficulties in assessing the role of the Lord Chancellor's Department is that the Department can claim not only the political anonymity of the Civil Service, but the political asexuality of the lawyers, since the Department was, until the 1972 reorganisation, staffed exclusively by lawyers rather than regular civil servants. It is indeed a remarkable example of professional self-regulation. A body that is responsible not only for reform but also, more importantly, for running the legal system, had until the 1970s no regular civil servants, by which I mean persons who formerly fell in the category we used to dignify by the title "the Administrative Grade." Even today the most important of the senior civil servants are either lawyers or have had a legal training. The idea that the Ministry of Defence would be solely run by regular officers or the Ministry of Health solely by health professionals, would be regarded as risible. If it is the civil servants in the Chancellor's office who have refused to increase the earnings of the Criminal Bar—or have set a salary scale for the new Prosecuting Service which is excessive—it is not solely some Machiavellian act of the regular Civil Service. Whatever the overriding political considerations, in the mechanics lawyers have been heavily involved.

The actual founding of the Office goes back to the two old warhorse Chancellors of the 1860s, 1870s and 1880s—Selborne for the Liberals and Cairns for the Conservatives—who had, between them, dominated the dramatic restructuring of the English legal system in that period. In 1880, when Selborne returned to the Woolsack, he brought in Sir Kenneth Muir Mackenzie as Clerk of the Crown in Chancery, and as such Mackenzie was also referred to as Principal Secretary. The appointment, however, was unlike the Permanent Secretaries in the reformed Civil Service; the appointment had been made by Selborne, and it was far from clear that Mackenzie would stay when Selborne disappeared. Already in 1882, however, Mackenzie was suggesting that the two offices might be merged[6]; and Selborne was pushing the idea of a permanent staff for the Lord Chancellors. The crucial move came in an 1882 letter from Cairns to Selborne, in which the former— although out of office—announced, "I have come to the conclusion that the new Judicature System has thrown around the Chancellor such a network of departmental business . . . that . . . it will not be possible to prevent serious inconvenience to the public business on a change in the Great Seal . . . without a really efficient Permanent Secretary."[7] The following year, 1883, Selborne sought Cairns' support in approaching the Treasury for a permanent establishment, "in fact, a permanent secretary of the Ministry of Justice."[8]

The Treasury put up little resistance and by 1884 agreed that the work in the Office since 1874 had changed dramatically. The memorandum saw it as one of two types: first, the confidential and political variety for which the Lord Chancellor should have a political Private Secretary, and second, that "belonging to a permanent Ministry of Justice" which "will be best performed by a permanent staff . . . on whose experience each successive Lord Chancellor may rely." This role was to be fulfilled by the new Permanent Secretary, who was to be a barrister of seven years standing, exempt from the Civil Service entry regulations. The Treasury also assumed that this person would serve, among other things, as secretary to the Council of Judges (that is the parliament of the judges of the Supreme Court of Judicature called for in the 1873 legislation) and, by vetting all Bills presented to Parliament, would act as parliamentary draftsman; two revenue saving dreams that were not to be fulfilled.[9] The basic scheme, however, went through, and on May 28, 1884 Mackenzie became the Permanent Secretary to the Lord Chancellor and Viscount Wolmer the "political" Private Secretary.

The significance of the concessions the Treasury made in establishing the Lord Chancellor's Office has undoubtedly affected the course of law reform. First, as I suggested, the Office for much of its life has been lawyer-run. Moreover, the Department has also been top heavy for much of its history. Compared with other departments there has been a predominance of senior appointments and, at least until the 1970s, the Office managed to beat off attempts to change that situation.[10] The fact that the Office operated largely outside the regular Civil Service also gave great power to the Permanent Secretary. He (and they have all been "he's" thus far) is likely to have spent his whole career in the Department; historically they have stayed as Permanent Secretary far longer than persons in similar positions in other departments, since retirement in the Department is not until 72 or, with permission, 75; and, in the past, they have effectively chosen their own successors. The deputy, since the first one was created in 1915,[11] has invariably succeeded as Permanent Secretary; and the files make it clear that the outgoing Permanent Secretaries, rather than the nominal Head of the Civil Service, *de facto* chose the new Permanent Secretary.[12]

The Department's history falls into three clear parts. For the first 30 years (1884–1915), the Office was Muir Mackenzie. The next 57 years (1915–1972) were the golden years of the Office. While it was still more a private office than a genuine Department, its power—and its control of reform—was awesome. This period of the Office's history was dominated by Lord Schuster and Sir George Coldstream. Since 1972 the Office has become more of a Department; and one suspects with the recent renewed interest in a Ministry of Justice, coupled with the unfavourable publicity associated with the recent litigation by the Bar Council and the Law Society, there will be increased pressure to assimilate the Department to a regular department. The legal profession may well have won a Pyrrhic victory.

(b) The Mackenzie Era

Muir Mackenzie[13] was only 35 when he became Clerk of the Crown in Chancery; he was to retire forty years later, in 1915. He then served (by then Lord Muir-Mackenzie) as a Lord-in-Waiting and ultimately a Minister during the two minority Labour administrations of 1924 and 1929. (He was incidentally the oldest person to hold government office in this century.) Mackenzie created the office of Permanent Secretary to the Lord Chancellor; and he was the Lord Chancellor's Office. It is unclear from the Lord Chancellor's papers who ensured that this would happen; but it is quite clear that after the Judicature Acts and certainly after Mackenzie's arrival, all communications to the Lord Chancellor passed through his Permanent Secretary. Any other member of the Cabinet who had views on the legal system, or more importantly wished to express views about the Judiciary, wrote to Mackenzie. Thus the Home Secretary who, prior to the Judicature Acts had felt free to deal directly with the Judges, thereafter dealt through Mackenzie. While Mackenzie insisted he was but "the Lord Chancellor's postman,"[14] a reading of the files of that period show a man increasingly the *eminence grise* in dealing with the High Court judges and more obviously a power in dealing with other judges and the profession.

When one looks at the changes which Mackenzie orchestrated, it is difficult to know where to begin describing them. For instance, Mackenzie was heavily involved in working out a reformed Judicial Committee of the Privy Council as the implications of Commonwealth status became clear; although the Imperial Court of Appeal was dead.[15] He was in office when the Criminal Appeal Act of 1907—setting up the Court of Criminal Appeal, first suggested by the Council of Judges in 1892, was passed.[16] It was he who acted as shop steward for the judges as the Council Courts Bill of 1903 was going through its various stages.[17] It is true that in his later years Mackenzie did not exploit the Permanent Secretaryship, having apparently lost his early energy for reform. His successor Sir Claude Schuster later wrote confidentially:

" . . . Mackenzie . . . was a man of subtle brain and keen wit. He hated waste or disorder, and he was industrious to an almost incredible extent. He was also extremely ingenious. He learned his business under Lord Selborne, and had imbibed many of Lord Selborne's views . . . to it [the Permanent Secretaryship] he devoted his very considerable mental and physical powers. But he was a man naturally secretive, unwilling to trust to his subordinates either his plans or their execution, and though an advanced Radical in politics, he was in many matters exceedingly conservative. He, for example, detested the use either of shorthand or of typewriting. So far as he allowed any record to be kept of what took place in the office or of what letters issued from it, he noted these matters in very summary fashion in his own handwriting. He wrote his letters himself and kept no copies, and he directed the envelopes and stuck them up. He kept no record of the understandings or pledges to which he became a party. By reason of his unwillingness or inability to delegate, he took care to be served only by those who were unlikely to oppose his will. Furthermore, during the long reign of Lord Halsbury he gradually lost heart in the reforms which he had either planned himself or the idea of which he had inherited from Lord Selborne. Hence during the last years of his office, though he remained skilful and laborious, he ceased to make any attempt to accomplish reforms which he knew to be necessary . . . "[18]

In fact, the work of the office was done by Mackenzie as Permanent Secretary and Adolphus Liddell, his Private Secretary seconded from the Parliament Office, who was allowed to decide nothing.[19] The Assistant Serjeant-at-Arms of the House of Lords acted as Mackenzie's secretary. In addition to these two, there were two clerks and an odd job man. That was the Office.

In some ways it is not easy to reconcile the two visions of Mackenzie—the spare administrator and the *eminence grise*. Despite the secretiveness, and the paucity of staffing, Mackenzie established the reputation of the Office as guardian of the legal profession and "administrator" of the judiciary. These were not easy times and perhaps the best example of the way he operated was his dealings in the first few years in implementing the Judicature Acts. Those Acts established the Court of Appeal, retained the judicial functions of the House of Lords, merged the common law divisions and established a High Court. The actual implementation was highly complex; while we tend to think about the legislation, it was the Statutory Instruments and the informal decisions that actually shaped the way the English legal system would develop. Obviously the most important actors were the two branches of the profession and the Judges themselves but the Cabinets—particularly Liberal Cabinets—had strong views; and Muir Mackenzie was no mere cipher.

It is easy enough to suggest that the decisions were made solely in the interests of the profession. That would be unfair; the mono-causal interpretation of history is almost invariably wrong. The profession and the judiciary were both interested in providing an efficient service. Yet two things do become clear.

First, Mackenzie was operating in an atmosphere which underlines Dangerfield's argument in the *Strange Death of Liberal England*. The Irish issue did change the face of English politics, and strangled the liberal reform movement. While Cairns, who had been Disraeli's Lord Chancellor until 1880, was certainly a reformer, he was not a Liberal reformer in the way that Selborne was; and Halsbury, Cairns' successor as Conservative Lord Chancellor, was more interested in protecting the prerogatives of the judiciary and the profession. Similarly, the Liberal Home Secretaries were far more convinced of the need for reform than were their Tory opposite numbers; and the frequency of Conservative Cabinets, at least until 1905, as a result of the Irish question, meant that decisions were made primarily by Conservative politicians who generally had less concern for the litigant than for the professionals.

Since the decline of Liberal England is significant in understanding how the spate of reform that began with Brougham petered out in the 1880s and 1890s, a weakening that Mackenzie obviously felt, one should remember that Selborne, categorically, and Cairns, significantly, spent their time chivvying and bullying the judges and the profession into accepting reforms and putting their own houses in order. The judges feared Commissions. Imagine, then, what a Selborne or Cairns would have done if they had received a printed memorandum from the Lord Chief Justice calling for a Royal Commission on the Judicature, to examine, among other things, the cost of appeals, the backlog of cases in Chancery, the expense of litigation as a whole, the weakness of the appeal system in criminal cases and the collapse of commercial work. Yet this is precisely what Halsbury received from the Lord Chief Justice, Coleridge, in 1891.[20] Halsbury, to the horror of Mackenzie, wrote back to say the time was not ripe and the Council of Judges should address the issues.[21] An opportunity to complete the work of the Judicature Commission of the 'sixties and 'seventies was lost. The bipolarisation of politics resulting from the Irish issue made it possible to stifle reform.

The second thing that becomes clear about the decisions shaping the English legal system in the 1880s was that many of them were taken for the convenience of the profession and, even more so, for the convenience of the judges.

It was the Conservative Home Secretary, Asherton Cross, who in 1876 attempted to rationalise the circuit system by grouping county towns for criminal business and having the judges on circuit only visit them in rotation; more importantly, he increased from three to four the number of Assizes each year in order to provide regular criminal proceedings around the country and more general civil assizes. The judges fought the changes vigorously. While there was much talk about the needs of litigants, at bottom it was a battle about the nature of the English judiciary. In 10 years, between the Cross changes in 1877 and the year 1886, the judges had their way. The Lord Chancellor's Office papers both record these changes as well as illustrating Mackenzie's role.

The Liberals were anxious to go further than the Conservatives, indeed further than the 1873 legislation, and have permanent courts in the major cities of the country. The Liberal Home Secretary, Sir Vernon Harcourt, put it this way in 1884:

> "To break up the whole judicial staff of London four times a year utterly disorganises the administration of the law in the metropolis and produces vast delay, cost and inconvenience to everyone. Much fewer judges would do the London work a great deal better if it was done continuously and without interruption."

He went on:

> "You might dispose with circuits altogether and their para-
> phernalia of grand juries, sheriffs, javelin men and the rest of
> them. Civil business of the district would be continuously and
> satisfactorily disposed of as regards proceedings of the first
> instance by younger and more vigorous men fresh from their
> practice at the Bar. The older and less locomotive sages of the
> law would remain in London. Instead of the outcry against the
> general gaol delivery with which you are now pestered, there
> would be a monthly trial of assize prisoners to which the
> accused are as much entitled in the provinces as in London.
> This simple division of labour would save time, money and
> injustice but I know that the judges and leading lawyers fight
> 'in their courses' against it."

To get some sense of the opposition, one should perhaps look at
Lord Justice Fry, a Quaker and one of the more liberal judges. "I
think any attempt to require the residence in Lancashire of the
judges of the High Court whether by means of an obligation cast
on the junior judges for the time being or by a rota of all the
number, would have a disastrous effect on the judicial office. If I
judge others by myself I believe it would form a grave obstacle to
the acceptance of a judgeship and so seriously affect the character
of the Bench." It was not until the Courts Act of 1971 that the
Liberal goal was achieved.[22]

The story was, of course, complicated and complex. From 1878
onwards the Council of Judges was strongly against the Winter
Assize as the fourth assize was called. Baron Huddlestone noted in
a letter to the Lord Chancellor that "it was almost unreasonable to
call upon the judges many of whom are of advanced years . . . to
be exposed at Assize towns to the usual inclemency of the weather
at that period of the year." On the other hand, the Council of
Judges resolved collectively that:

> "we say nothing about the inconvenience to the judges. They
> must discharge such duties as the general good of the country
> imposes upon them and they will always discharge them in a
> cheerful and ungrudging spirit but the office of the judge is
> becoming less and less desirable and it would be a result to the
> country really disastrous if that office ceased to be an object of
> desire to the best men of the profession. It is not only the
> profession that would suffer by its best men declining judge-
> ships, the whole country would suffer grievously, far more
> grievously than it suffers because in a small minority of cases
> prisoners are kept too long in gaol."[23]

The Conservative Home Secretary Cross wrote to the Conservative Chancellor Cairns agreeing that sometimes the system was inconvenient but that it would be "retrograde" to go back on the Fourth Assize. When the Liberals returned in 1880 it was suggested one way of adding judicial time would be to cut the long vacations by 10 days, a suggestion opposed by the Council of Judges by a vote of 20 to four.[24]

Even after the government made various concessions, Mr. Justice Manisty went to the Newcastle Assizes and lectured the populace on the awfulness of the new system. Selborne's reaction, drafted by Mackenzie, was chilly: "After the general concurrence of the Judges in the most recent Assize arrangements and after all that had taken place with respect to the allowance of circuit expenses, on the faith of these arrangements by the Treasury I must own I was not prepared for a denunciation of them in an address by the Judge to a Grand Jury at the Commencement of an Assize in an important town upon the first occasion of their being put into practice, least of all from a Judge whose disapproval of them I had received no notice."[25] After the Chancery and Court of Appeal judges were excused from going on circuit, the only other group thereafter who were supposed to go on circuit were the judges of the Probate and Divorce Division. Selborne was displeased when, in 1882, they had point blank refused to go. As he wrote to the Master of the Rolls, "the disposition recently shown in the Probate Division to refuse circuit duty will, I fear, increase these difficulties and perhaps make it necessary to think of remedies for them of a different kind which have hitherto not found favour with the judges or the Bar but for which (unless I deceive myself) a demand is growing both in the House of Commons and in the country."[26]

So at least the Queen's Bench judges went on circuit and the Divorce Judges were put under pressure to go, but the judges still wanted that fourth assize killed and they did not want any grouping of circuit towns. Having failed under the Liberal administration to get rid of the fourth assize or the grouping of assize towns, the judges tried again when Lord Halsbury returned to the Woolsack in 1885, keeping Muir Mackenzie as his Permanent Secretary. The judges voted at their first meeting in 1886 formally to get rid of the fourth assize and to end grouping for criminal cases. What they were prepared to do, they said, was to have grouping for civil cases; indeed they were prepared to have all the litigation in the Home Counties heard in London.[27]

Halsbury had a good deal more sympathy for the personal preferences of the judges than had Selborne. Selborne thought they were pampered. Halsbury accepted the report of the Committee established by the Council of Judges and drafted an Order in Council to give effect to it. While some old time judges like Mr. Justice Day were anxious to return to the system when circuit riding and London sittings did not overlap, and some of the younger judges like Mr. Justice Cave would have been happy to see more grouping and more work given to the County Courts, the basic judicial position seemed reasonable to Halsbury, who tried to implement it. Halsbury, however, had less experience with the judiciary than had Selborne; and had not the scepticism of Mackenzie. No sooner had Halsbury published a draft Order in Council attempting to implement the advice of the judges than Mr. Justice Grantham, famous later as the last of the judges to be threatened with impeachment, announced it as "unconstitutional, ill-considered and most injurious to the interests of all those concerned." Perhaps the most bizarre outburst, however, came from the Chief Justice, Lord Coleridge, the advocate of reform.[28] The new arrangement for civil work was "revolutionary" and it would "virtually destroy the circuit system," he said. Halsbury was unable to understand Coleridge's letter but agreed to do nothing because of his opposition. Meanwhile Mackenzie's minutes on the letters from the judges became more acerbic. Of the Chief Justice he said, "He seems to have forgotten that the principle of the scheme was settled by a unanimous vote of all the judges present at the first Council and the scheme confirmed by a large majority afterwards."[29]

The matter was, of course, tabled, and a new committee of judges was set up, this time with Coleridge as a member. The judges had their way on the fourth assize. They had their way on the grouping of the criminal Assizes and Lord Chief Justice Coleridge had his way—supported by lobbies from County towns: there would be civil assizes in the Home Counties. In other words, with the support of Halsbury, all the changes since 1877 were abandoned within a decade.[30] If this made Mackenzie's role as handmaiden of the judges more tolerable, it certainly did not help what he saw as the Office's responsibility for reform.

(c) The Golden Era of the Office

While certainly Mackenzie was far more than the "postman" he claimed to be, there is little doubt that his was something of a passive role—especially in his later years. He humoured the judges; he soothed the bar; he even began to pamper solicitors. His original hope of moving to completion the reforms of the Judicature

Acts of the 1870s lapsed. This style was not to the liking of Lord Haldane, a Liberal reformer, when he took office as Lord Chancellor in 1912. Mackenzie was replaced in 1915 by the most powerful of the Permanent Secretaries—Sir Claude (later Lord) Schuster. Schuster's family had come to England from Frankfurt in the early nineteenth century and became successful Manchester merchants. Educated at Winchester and New College, Oxford, Schuster began practice on the Northern Circuit, only to give up practice when his father suffered financial reverses. Schuster then joined the Civil Service, working first in the Ministry of Education under Sir Robert Morant and then with Lloyd George on the National Insurance Bill. In 1915, Haldane, anxious formally to establish a Ministry of Justice,[31] appointed Schuster as his Permanent Secretary; and Schuster rapidly established himself as the dominant force in the Office and a power in the wider professional and political arena.

Schuster was a doer; and a considerable contrast with the later years of Mackenzie's reign. When Schuster was faced with a vacancy for the High Court his briefing paper to the Lord Chancellor seemed to leave the latter little discretion. In 1917, for instance, he offered the Chancellor a list of senior silks but added, "All these were in their time *papabili*, but they are now so old that the appointment of any one of them would be an infraction of the recommendations of innumerable Royal Commissions . . ." Of a list of Q.C., M.P.s he noted: " . . . Salter seems the most considerable both in the eyes of the party and professionally. It seems to me . . . that if you wish to make an appointment from the House of Commons it is difficult to look beyond him . . . Of those who are not M.P.s you will have no difficulty passing over Marshall Hall, Powell, Langdon, Ashton, Gregory, Compton, Schiller and Charles[32] and it is not necessary for me to give the reasons . . . There remain Gore-Brown, Talbot, Greer, Disturnal and Hawke." Of these, Hawke was too young; Gore-Brown "too much of a Chancery man"; Disturnal was "very undistinguished"; Greer at least "could be safely trusted with the Commercial List"; Talbot's appointment "would be in every way distinguished." Finally he noted that Roche was the one regarded as best by the Bar but he probably could not be induced to take a judgeship.[33] Schuster, however, put out feelers and later reported that "if an offer were made now to [Roche] his decision would be different . . . "[34] Thus Lord Findlay prevailed where Buckmaster, Haldane's immediate successor, had failed and Roche accepted. The next appointment went to one of the other favourites—Greer, and shortly thereafter Talbot was promoted. In the Chancery Division,

Schuster told Findlay: "I think our list should be very short indeed." It consisted of only P. O. Lawrence and Mark Romer. The next appointment to the Chancery Division was P. O. Lawrence. Mark Romer ("He has always seemed to me to have the most distinguished mind of any leading practitioner of the Chancery side") had to wait a few years but was almost at once promoted to the Court of Appeal.[35] In baseball terminology, Schuster was batting five for five.[36]

I shall have to limit myself to this single example of Schuster's decisive and directive style. It was not a style which was popular with all the judges. Schuster undoubtedly achieved much. The Law of Property Acts of 1922 and 1925, his work on the County Courts, the more relaxed approach to judicial manpower which led to the gradual increase in the numbers of High Court judges and his support of the Law Revision Committee established in 1934 were all important. His successor Napier was undoubtedly right in describing Schuster as a "quick reader, fluent on paper and lucid in stating a case . . . always alert, his reaction to the news immediate, his course of action soundly planned and quickly put in train." It was also true that he "gave pungent expression to his dislikes."[37] It was not true, as Napier also alleged, that all the judges, excepting Hewart, liked him.[38]

In 1931 there had been a judicial outburst of considerable proportions when the Government attempted to reduce judicial salaries during the economic crisis.[39] Mr. Justice MacNaughton complained that "whereas the power and remuneration of the Civil Servants has been increased in the last twenty years, the power and prestige of the judges has been reduced . . . "[40] Mr. Justice McCardie, who proved the most embarrassing of the judges[41] and whose attitude to judicial remuneration would have made the TUC blush, announced that far from being cut, "in view of the special duties of the judges," the salaries should be paid tax free. This was especially important because "the salary of the Permanent Secretary of the Lord Chancellor has *almost doubled* in the last twelve years."[42] (In fairness to McCardie, in the 1880s the Permanent Secretary's salary was one-quarter that of High Court judges and two-thirds that of County Court judges. Today it is the same as High Court judges, while County Court judges earn two-thirds of the salary of the Permanent Secretary.) To return to the story, however, the real threat to Schuster was the Lord Chief Justice, Gordon Hewart, whose view of Schuster was similar to that of Salisbury towards McLeod: "too clever by half."

Hewart had come by the Lord Chief Justiceship in a devious political way—perhaps Lloyd George knew of no other. Hewart's predecessor, Lord Trevethin, read of his resignation in *The Times*, as the Coalition collapsed in 1922. Although Hewart began his career on the radical wing of the Liberal Party and, as Attorney-General, was sympathetic to civil servants, he moved to a more libertarian position. He turned out to be a difficult (and poor) judge, and rapidly began feuding with the Lord Chancellor's Office, accusing it of "petty larceny."[43] The "big bang" came with publication of his *New Despotism* in 1929, a rather excitable volume whose main theme was the decline of the power of the judges, with that of the civil servants growing ever stronger.[44] Among many charges was the allegation that the talk of a Ministry of Justice would mean the Permanent Secretary, reporting to a politician rather than to the senior judge, would appoint the judges.[45] The book led to the establishment of the Committee on Minister's Powers (Scott-Donoughmore Committee) on which Lord Chancellor Sankey placed Schuster—or "Shyster" as Hewart called him. The Chief Justice refused to appear before the Committee. "They've got my book, why should I appear—especially with Schuster on the Committee."[46] The Committee produced an undistinguished report, but the feud continued. Hewart was certain that the appointment of the Committee on the State of Work in the King's Bench Division in 1934 was an effort by Schuster to humiliate him. Sankey tried to bring Hewart and Schuster together; but Hewart refused to meet.[47]

In October 1934 things began to get worse. Schuster wrote to Hewart saying that the Cabinet had decided to add two King's Bench judges, but while authorised, they would only be added after a resolution by Parliament. Hewart claimed he had not been consulted although there is some evidence that he threw the letter marked "Secret" into the fire. At the same time, the Lord Chancellor's Office was flying the idea of a Vice-President of the Court of Appeal—in Hewart's view an effort to deprive Lord Justice Slesser of his seniority because of his politics, which, at least while at the Bar, had been sympathetic to Labour.[48] Hewart called a meeting of the judges and then went down to the House of Lords and made an intemperate speech. He emotionally described receiving letters written by a "secretary" (Schuster), rather than the Lord Chancellor, about a Royal Commission (actually a Committee) on the Courts. He was not told about the Supreme Court Bill which was drafted without consultation. The "intended inquiry" was "wholly unnecessary"; the High Court judges were underpaid; and since Hanworth—the Master of the Rolls—had told Slesser he should not preside in Appeal Court 2, the Chief Justice had advised him to refuse to sit. It was all a case of "rigging the judicial bench"; and it was part of a scheme to facilitate a Ministry of Justice run by the permanent officials.[49] It was left to Lord Hailsham, the new Chancellor, to claim in a later legislative debate that Sir Claude Schuster was "incapable of such conduct as is imputed to him," particularly "the plot" to have a Ministry of Justice. Indeed, said Hailsham, Schuster "has been fighting against it all of his life."[50]

That may not have been true. In 1943, the year before he retired, Schuster put a memo on the Ministry of Justice in the Office files. It was Haldane who wanted the judicial functions removed from the Chancellor and to substitute an Imperial Court of Appeal in place of the House of Lords. While the Chancellor would remain in the Cabinet, he would not sit regularly as a judge. The Chancellor would make all judicial appointments; the Home Secretary—shorn of other functions—would be Minister of Justice. As Schuster realised, many of the things which the 1918 Report of the (Haldane) Commission on the Machinery of Government said could not be done by the Lord Chancellor's Office, had in fact been done.[51]

Schuster retired in 1944, to be replaced by Sir Albert Napier,[52] Permanent Secretary 1944–54, followed by Sir George Coldstream[53] (1954–68). Sir Albert Napier, son of one of Victoria's most honoured Indian generals, came to the Lord Chancellor's Office in the restructuring of 1915 and, after a painfully slow progress up the *cursus honorum*, became Permanent Secretary in 1944. Already, however, the power in the Department was shared with Napier's deputy, Sir George Coldstream, who had come into the Office in 1939 after serving in the Parliamentary Counsel's Office.

One can get some sense of the Department's effective control of the process of legal reform from looking at the work of its representatives on Committees.[54] (It generally had a member on legal committees as well as staffing them.) As secretary of the Rushcliffe Committee, which led to the Legal Aid and Advice Scheme, the minutes make it clear that Napier's interjections were significant in guiding the scheme in the directions which still shape it today. Napier opposed the idea of a body interposed between the Law Society as administrator of the Scheme and the Government—a kind of Legal Services Corporation—although he had to agree to an Advisory Committee. Meanwhile Schuster (by now Lord Schuster), as a member of the Rushcliffe Committee, managed to persuade his colleagues that there was no need for a new system of criminal legal aid (while he and Napier said they had not heard any criticism of the Poor Person's Procedure); and neither thought it necessary to inform the accused of their right to such aid. The Office opposed the right of appeal from the denial of a legal aid certificate; and was adamant the Office should not review denials of aid. At the same time they saw no reason why the office should not run the scheme, providing the Lord Chancellor could not be asked detailed questions. The Office was also responsible for the compromise that provided the State's recovering costs from the other party when an assisted litigant won, but not vice versa.[55]

A sense of the relative power within the Department may be gained by looking at the Cabinet Committee on the Reform of Legal Procedure established by Clement Attlee when Labour was returned to power in 1945. Jowett, the Lord Chancellor, was not trusted by many members of the Labour Administration of 1945[56]; and he wrote a secret memorandum setting out his views on the reform of the legal system in November of that year. His three main thoughts were that divorce—even uncontested petitions—should be kept out of the hands of County Court judges lest their diversity in decisions would produce the confusion he saw in the United States; he was concerned about the implementation of Rushcliffe; and while he thought there ought to be a Royal Commission on the cost of litigation, it would not be fair to the profession which was just recovering from the war.[57] Some of the members of the Cabinet Committee were, in Jowett's eyes, "safe," but sceptics like Nye Bevan were not likely to be sympathetic to the judiciary or the profession. The Committee was staffed by Coldstream from the Lord Chancellor's Office and Topham from the Cabinet Office. The Prime Minister said the priority was to deal with the huge divorce problem. Bevan argued for the simple solution: just transfer it to the County Courts—a view shared, generally, by the Labour Party; while most other reformers—including Goddard, the Lord Chief Justice, thought that at least undefended divorces should go there. Lord Merriman, President of the Probate, Divorce and Admiralty Division, however, was strongly opposed. He wanted a Commission of Conciliation and Enquiry, consisting of barristers and social workers, which would sit *in camera*, supervised by High Court Judges. Merriman had half convinced Jowett and fully convinced both Archbishops this was the way to go. There was no way but to establish a committee; and the Cabinet Committee agreed.[58]

There were delays. The Lord Chancellor's Office wanted Lord Lindsay as Chairman, and a legally oriented Committee. The haggling over names, and the evaluation of members of the Bar, make fascinating reading. Coldstream managed to veto no more than one Labour M.P. and had his way on most issues, but Shawcross, the Attorney-General, had his way on the Chairmanship, which went to Denning.[59] Denning was superb and worked his committee ferociously. Its Interim Report, calling for County Court judges to be used as Special Commissioners for hearing undefended cases, was ready by October—a five month sprint.[60] Merriman was beside himself. He told Coldstream that County Court judges undermined "the safety of the marriage tie." As Coldstream noted: "The President thereupon sent for Denning J., and told him that he considered that his proposals amounted to selling the fort, and that he wished to make it plain he opposed them root and branch." By November, however, Goddard had come out in favour of using the County Court judges and the Cabinet decided to go with Denning.[61]

The final Denning Report, recommending changes in many of the Divorce procedures, which the Chairman found "archaic," was no more attractive to Merriman. Denning had failed to invite Merriman to appear before the Committee a second time. "I take serious exception to this method of proceeding," said Merriman. According to a memo from Coldstream, Merriman was only prepared to accept 12 of the 40 recommendations. Merriman wrote that although Denning had spent two years in the Probate, Divorce and Admiralty Division, he "seemed to have learned very little." While the Government accepted the Report, the President stalled. In December, the Chancellor set up the Hodson Committee, comprised of two High Court judges and Coldstream, to implement the Report. The Division used it as a blocking device. Coldstream urged Jowett to warn Merriman that political pressure was mounting; and to tell Hodson that his Committee was there to implement the Denning recommendations, not judge their merits.[62] To cut a long story short, Merriman was ultimately overruled by Jowett and all but one of the Denning Committee's recommendations were implemented. Denning—and Coldstream—had won.[63]

With the divorce issue out of the way the Cabinet Committee turned its attention to litigation in general.[64] While some Cabinet members clearly hankered for a radical approach, Jowett and the Lord Chancellor's Office played the cautious role and persuaded the Cabinet committee that what was needed was two Committees—one on the High Court and one on the County Court—thereby ensuring that the existing structure would not be threatened. Indeed, the Lord Chief Justice (Goddard) and the Master of the Rolls (Greene) saw little point in having a Committee on the High Court at all; and certainly did not want any non-lawyers on it. Jowett put his conscience at rest by appointing a Committee with non-lawyers, but making Raymond Evershed chair, since "I know from previous correspondence that he does not want to do anything so drastic as to substitute for our procedure something analogous to French procedure." In fact Evershed was, in many respects, radical; and he was aided by Gerald Gardiner Q.C.[65] and Mr. Justice Upjohn,[66] but much of the power lay in the hands of Coldstream.[67] He was able to cool the urge of Professor T. H. Marshall—one of the unwanted laymen—to investigate the French system so that courts might consider cutting down on oral evidence and have the Committee review the rules of evidence with a view to lowering the cost of litigation. Geoffrey Crowther, the economist, favoured the formal abolition of the distinction between barristers and solicitors.[68] Even Evershed, as he originally drafted the Report, had the recommendation that the Bar Council be made the controlling force at the Bar, with barristers, like solicitors, taking out practising certificates. Upjohn and Gardiner[69] saw this as an implied criticism of the Inns of Court and the ideas were dropped.[70] Had they not been, the current recommendations of the Rawlinson Committee would have been unnecessary.[71]

It would be wrong, of course, to assume that the Lord Chancellor's Office always managed to control Committees and Commissions. The Beeching Committee, which led to the Courts Act of 1971, in some ways got away from the Lord Chancellor's Department. Over the opposition of the Bar the court structure was rationalised and the objections of the judges to permanent or semi-permanent courts of general jurisdiction outside London became possible. The idea that "more means worse"—a notion that had kept the High Court bench artificially small—was finally abandoned. Beeching, however, was almost unique among laymen; he was not intimidated by lawyers or judges. Of the Bar's evidence he said the Bar really wanted nothing to change, but things simply to improve.[72] Coldstream (a member of the Committee) would ask hard questions; but he could not control Beeching. Judges were not able to get away with their usual platitudes.[73] Denning appeared and was much in favour of reforming the Chancery Division, but was somewhat defensive about the Queen's Bench Division.[74] Indeed as Beeching pressed on, Denning increasingly mouthed traditional judicial views. While he was in favour of permanent courts in the provinces,[75] and while he thought blurring the distinction between the High Court and County Court acceptable, he also thought it important that the High Court be kept small ("I am sorry we have got so many (judges) as we have at the moment") and that its judges go on circuit. ("The impact on a community is very great if you go into these outlying districts . . . ")[76] To this latter remark, made in oral evidence, Beeching replied: "Except that you are discouraging crime where it does not happen . . . "[77] When asked about lay magistrates Denning said he enjoyed sitting with them in Quarter Sessions and thought "their views were worth just as much as mine." This led to the obvious Beeching response: "Do you think High Court judges ought to have them in that case?" His Lordship was not amused.

Perhaps I have already deviated, however, too far into the memoranda and hearings of the Beeching Committee, for I have one last area of the Lord Chancellor's work to discuss. Over the last 100 years, it becomes clear from reading the archives that the Office has gradually come to treat solicitors as almost the social and intellectual equals of barristers. Yet County Court and Circuit Court judges are still treated with rather less deference than High Court judges. Before the Top Salaries Committee, High Court judges were more humoured about their salaries than County Court judges.[78] Egos of High Court judges also received greater massage than those of the County Court. When *New Times*, a Soviet magazine published by Truth, criticised Mr. Justice Birkett as "the favourite judge of Lord Haw Haw,"[79] there was talk of libel and contempt proceedings against Colletts, the bookstore which stocked the newspaper. Napier wrote to the Foreign Office, which consulted the British Ambassador to Moscow, and (via Sir Alexander Cadogan) replied, "Her Majesty's Ambassador does not think a protest to the Soviet Government would be effective." Napier, however, insisted the protest be made.[80] When, however, in 1950, Truth opined that "those appointed to the County Court bench seldom have very much, and not infrequently very little, work at the bar," a remark which led to a formal protest to the Office from the County Court Judges Association, Coldstream was cool. "I showed the 'Truth' paragraph to the Lord Chancellor, but he does not seem to have been so violently affected as the Judges at your meeting, and, as a matter of fact, it did not appear to me quite as violent as I had expected." The County Court judges were not pleased with the response.[81]

A similar dichotomy applied when resignations or reprimands were at issue. High Court judges on the Consolidated Fund were sacrosanct. Jowett wrote wearily to Goddard in 1950: "I do feel the time has come when old Humphreys ought to go . . . But there is nothing I can do about it, and I do not suppose there is anything you can do about it."[82] Judge Pickles, however, who has his problems today, no doubt aggravated by his views on page three nudes, should take note of what happened to Judge Gaman. The good

County Court judge, hearing undefended divorces in 1952, was particularly shocked by a case in which a woman had left her husband and committed adultery at her mother's house. Indeed the judge was so outraged, that he opined, in a quote picked up by the press, "the morals of West Hartlepool seem to be lower than any other place in the country." The Mayor and Town Council were outraged and the matter was not helped when Gaman explained that he was referring only to the "bottom section" of inhabitants. Gaman, a product of Harrow and Oxford, apparently meant the lower classes[83] (although he later said he really meant the least moral) but unfortunately there was an area of West Hartlepool known as the "bottom" and its inhabitants—and the Town Clerk, the Boys Brigade and the Salvation Army—were outraged. The Mayor and Town Clerk wrote to the Lord Chancellor. Rieu, head of the County Court Division, asked for an explanation. Gaman explained that he was concerned about the "moral laxity" and "the attitude of women as well as men toward the marriage bonds. The restraining influence which such public opinion commonly exerts elsewhere seems to be largely lacking in West Hartlepool." At the same time the Judge complained it was "not fair of the paper to fasten on the quoted word."[84] The Lord Chancellor's Office was not amused. "No record of any previous complaint" minuted Coldstream. The judge wrote a letter of apology to the Mayor. Both Coldstream and Lord Simonds said it would not do[85]; and Gaman apologised in open court.[86] Similar reprimands were meted out to other County Court judges who found unwelcome publicity,[87] and finally, in 1962, Coldstream sat down with them and told them exactly what they were entitled to say publicly. Unfortunately for us—and Judge Pickles—that file is sealed until 1995.

(d) The Lord Chancellor's Department: Conclusion

Since I have been working largely from the papers of the Lord Chancellor's Office, I am not in a position to comment on the three most recent Permanent Secretaries: Sir Denis Dobson (1968–1977),[88] Sir Wilfred Bourne (1977–1982)[89] and Sir Derek Oulton (1982–date)[90]; they shall be largely left in peace. It is clear that the work of the Office has grown to that of a Department. The staff now includes more persons at the policy-making level who are either not lawyers or whose legal qualifications are perhaps not their most significant attributes as administrators. Individuals, however, continue to influence the thinking of the whole Department.

The Courts Act brought the fiscal side of the Courts within the ambit of the Department, and in so doing, emphasised that in the English system the judges neither control the administration of the courts nor their finances. At the same time, the increasing sense of fiscal stringency in the seventies and eighties has underlined the importance of the ultimate control of the Legal Aid Scheme by the Department. As the "fairness" concept of criminal fees was extended in the late sixties, at the very time Beeching left vague how to handle Class Four crimes, the Department became the paymaster of a scheme which led to a doubling of the size of the bar, as well as becoming a source of some profit for solicitors. When the Thatcher administration ultimately decided that the apparently open ended had to have limits, the bar, a long time bastion of free enterprise, became the advocate of socialised law. The current litigation by the Bar Council and Law Society is underlining the change from Office to Department. No longer is the Lord Chancellor's Department a sole preserve of the legal (and judicial) profession (and the judges) at a special advantage. The irony of the current litigation is that the Department may be opened to further political scrutiny which will lead to administrative restructuring, a result which is unlikely to be in the long-term professional interests of judges or lawyers.

As to whether there will be a Ministry of Justice, I would argue that one can look at that as much ado about nothing. In the past, many have viewed even the lean Mackenzie-esque Office as a Ministry of Justice. Haldane would have made the Home Office the Ministry of Justice—the Irish model. The SDP would have a version of the US Department of Justice, by incorporating the Law Officers, the DPP and the Treasury Solicitor. This would in some ways push the Office back to being the sole preserve of lawyers, and would have all its ministers be lawyers. Silkin, on behalf of Labour has argued that, if the Law Officers were kept independent, there would be no reason why the Ministers should be lawyers.[91] Perhaps Hewart did put his finger on the most sensitive nerve. Why do judges need to be chosen only by judges? If a Bill of Rights were to work, there is a strong case to be made that they should not be.

Whatever the future holds—whether it is a more formalised Ministry of Justice or a less professional department—the likelihood is that the Department will be further integrated into the Civil Service and will increasingly treat the courts as part of the welfare state and judges and lawyers as providers of services within such a social service. That in itself is scarcely a radical vision; yet it may well underline still further the need for fiscal constraint. The role of the Lord Chancellor's Office and Department has been consistently underrated. It may not be the lynchpin of the Constitution, but it is certainly a bellwether of the separation of powers. If one is serious about looking at how law is made in England, the Department's operation cannot be ignored. Its control will not only tell us much about the future directions of the English legal system, but will raise issues of more than passing constitutional significance.

Notes

[1] A distinguished "crit," who unwisely takes my hyperbole seriously, has recently either accused or complimented me on writing my books in airports. David Sugarman, "Is the Reform of Legal Education Hopeless? or, Seeing the Hole Instead of the Doughnut," (1985) 48 M.L.R. 728, 736. I therefore have to confess that, owing to the insistence of the Public Record Office, I have been reading the Lord Chancellor's Office papers in Kew rather than at Heathrow.

[2] See, *e.g. The Times*, March 10, 11, 19, 21, 22, 28, 1986.

[3] What is perhaps less well known is that the Office also commissions its own reports, some of which are not published. For example, Committee on Charitable Trusts (1956) L.C.O. 29/94; Committee on Common Market Law (1961) L.C.O. 29/108.

[4] For some of these files see Compensation for Taking Land 1917–1919, L.C.O./3; Beeching Committee L.C.O./7; Committee on Defamation 1971, L.C.O./13; Extension of Legal Aid to Tribunals, L.C.O./14; (Franks) Committee on Administrative Tribunals (1957), L.C.O./15; (Winn) Committee on Personal Injuries (1968), L.C.O./16; (Lakey) Committee on Age of Majority (1965), L.C.O./17; (Benson) Royal Commission on Legal Services (1979), L.C.O./19; (Pearson) Royal Commission on Compensation (1978), L.C.O./20; War Time Adjustment Acts, L.C.O./26; (Payne) Committee on Enforcement of Debts (1969) L.C.O./31; (Lawrence) Committee to Enquire into Poor Persons Rules (1925), L.C.O./32.

[5] See, for instance, Returns from Crown Livings L.C.O./5; Crown Office, L.C.O./6; Lord Chancellor's Visitors, L.C.O./9; /10; /11; Sovereign's Speeches, L.C.O./21; (Wilson) Committee on Public Records (1982) L.C.O./27.

[6] Letter, Muir Mackenzie to Selborne, September 24, 1882, L.C.O. 2/262.

[7] Letter, Cairns to Selborne, March 29, 1882, *ibid.*

[8] Letter, Selborne to Cairns, August 16, 1883, *ibid.* Letter, Cairns to Selborne, August 28, 1883, *ibid.* Selborne was suggesting £1,200, a figure he knew Mackenzie would accept. Actually he had in mind £1,500, but not until one of the existing clerks resigned. Letter, Selborne to Cairns, March 24, 1884, *ibid.*

[9] Treasury to Selborne, May 3, 1884.

[10] During the 1960s the Treasury, responsible for Civil Service staffing, grumbled regularly about this. L.C.O. 4/23.

[11] Since 1972 there have been two Deputy Secretaries (Grade 2).

[12] In 1953, Napier effectively told Bridges (Head of the Civil Service) that Coldstream would be replacing him. Formally the Prime Minister has to approve the choice as Permanent Secretary to the Lord Chancellor. The Queen still has to approve the joint appointment as Clerk of the Crown in Chancery, L.C.O. 4/23.

[13] Lord Muir-Mackenzie, born 1845, educated at Charterhouse and Balliol Col-

lege, Oxford; barrister, 1873 (pupil of Lords Bowen and Davey); 1880 Lord Chancellor's Office.

[14] R. F. V. Heuston, *Lives of the Lord Chancellors* (1964), p. 502.
[15] Robert Stevens, *Law and Politics* (1978), pp. 72–76.
[16] L.C.O. 2/232.
[17] See generally L.C.O. 2/153. Mackenzie's soliciting of judicial views appears in L.C.O. 2/154 and 2/155. After the first Bill in 1903 Halsbury introduced a further Bill, which was not passed, calling for selective jurisdictional increases, L.C.O. 2/157, 158, 160. The County Court judges seemed mainly interested in an increase of salary to £2,000 p.a. (L.C.O. 2/159, 209, 210), a goal not achieved until the 1930s (L.C.O. 12/40). For the County Court legislation of 1907–1911 see L.C.O. 2/206, 207, 208, 209.
[18] Memorandum by Lord Schuster, January 31, 1943, pp. 4–5, L.C.O. 2/3630. Schuster later wrote: "You will bear in mind that Mackenzie was completely unscrupulous in interpreting a statute and disregarded its provisions if they did not suit him." Schuster to Coldstream, July 12, 1955. L.C.O. 2/5233.
[19] "Liddell was the most charming of men. He had passed many years in the office, but had never been allowed to decide anything and was not of a temper to oppose, or even to criticize, such of Mackenzie's designs as were made known to him," *ibid.* p. 5.
[20] Coleridge was also interested in codification of English law. As Attorney-General, in 1872, he had argued for this, as well as for merging the two branches of the profession. He had also favoured a Ministry of Justice, E. Coleridge, *Life and Correspondence of John Duke, Lord Coleridge, Lord Chief Justice of England* (1904), Vol. 2, pp. 89–92.
[21] Letter, Halsbury to Coleridge, January 2, 1892, L.C.O. 2/242.
[22] The most dramatic of these moves was when a large deputation from Manchester and Liverpool called on Lord Loreburn in 1909: Report of May 5, 1909. In fairness, Loreburn endeavoured to rearrange the circuits to help Lancashire.
[23] L.C.O. 1/4.
[24] Report of the Committee of Judges to the Council of Judges, April 1878, *ibid.*
[25] July 16, 1884, L.C.O. 1/7.
[26] April 15, 1889, L.C.O. 1/11.
[27] L.C.O. 1/8, 1/9.
[28] He had, after all, been Liberal Solicitor-General 1868–1871 and Attorney-General 1871–73. When he was appointed Chief Justice of Common Pleas in 1873 he wrote to his constituents: "my political principles are as strong as ever, and my political sympathies as keen as ever; though henceforth I can allow them, as a judge, neither influence or expression," Coleridge, Vol. 2, p. 231.
[29] L.C.O. 1/9.
[30] Although, not unnaturally, the Assizes continued to cause trouble. There was a suggestion in 1892 that the number of Assize towns be dramatically reduced; and again in 1896. Brian Abel Smith and Robert Stevens, *Lawyers and the Courts* (1965) p. 89. The judges tinkered with the circuit and assize system throughout the Edwardian period: L.C.O. 2/242.
[31] See, for instance, a memorandum, apparently written in September 1917, L.C.O. 2/601.
[32] Many years later Charles was in fact appointed.
[33] L.C.O. 2/601.
[34] Memo, September 20, 1917, L.C.O. 2/601.
[35] Memo, January 18, 1918, L.C.O. 2/601.
[36] Even in his first year in office, he was capable of killing appointments. When the Irish Solicitor-General, Campbell, was lobbying for an English judgeship,

Schuster warned Buckmaster of the mood of the bar that such an appointment would be "outrageous." Heuston, *Lives of the Lord Chancellors*, p. 272.

[37] See, for instance, his testy reaction when the Treasury failed to live up to its promise that the Lord Chancellor's Office should have one "free floating" Knighthood in every Honours List: Memo, Schuster to Lord Simon, March 18, 1942, L.C.O. 4/7.

[38] Albert Napier, "Schuster," *Dictionary of National Biography, 1951–1960*.

[39] See, generally, *Lawyers and the Courts*, pp. 127–129.

[40] Heuston, *Lives of the Lord Chancellors*, p. 517.

[41] McCardie sent a note to all King's Bench judges warning that "if *a government of a Certain Type should obtain a majority in the House of Commons* it could practically *destroy* the High Court judges by a *mere Order-in-Council* reducing their salaries to a *nominal* figure. We have been placed in a position *inferior* to that of an Ordinary Civil Servant," October 7, 1931, Hanworth Papers (Bodleian, Oxford), C. 948.

[42] McCardie to Hanworth, October 12, 1931, *id.*

[43] Robert Jackson, *The Chief: Biography of Gordon Hewart, Lord Chief Justice of England 1922–1940* (1959), pp. 65–66, 126–144, 157–161, 214. Ironically, Hewart in 1940 was told by the Prime Minister that his resignation was to be announced the next day, *ibid.* p. 335.

[44] *The New Despotism*, pp. 104–108.

[45] *Ibid.* p. 258.

[46] *The Chief*, p. 215.

[47] *Ibid.* p. 259–260.

[48] *Ibid.* p. 261–262. For Slesser L.J.'s view of all this, see Sir Henry Slesser, *Judgment Reserved* (1940), pp. 257–264.

[49] Parliamentary Debates (5th Ser. H.L.) vol. 195, cols. 219–37 (December 11, 1934).

[50] *Ibid.* cols. 379–402 (Dec. 14, 1934). Sankey also defended Schuster, saying that Hewart's speech "amazed me." As a judge, he knew Hewart did not like Schuster; Schuster had asked him to act as "peacemaker." "I greatly deprecate . . . attacks on permanent officials. Their lips are sealed. They cannot defend themselves." *Ibid.* Cols. 402–15.

[51] Memorandum, January 31, 1943, L.C.O. 2/3630.

[52] Born 1881; educated at Eton and New College, Oxford; Barrister, 1909; Private Secretary to Lord Chancellor, 1915–19; Deputy Serjeant-at-Arms, House of Lords, 1916–19; Deputy Secretary, Lord Chancellor's Office 1919–44; Permanent Secretary 1944–59.

[53] Born 1907; educated at Rugby and Oriel College, Oxford; Parliamentary Counsel's Office, 1934–9; Lord Chancellor's Office, 1939; Deputy Secretary, 1944–54; Permanent Secretary, 1954–68.

[54] L.C.O. 2/3900.

[55] Schuster agreed it was unfair but he could see no way out of the difficulty. He was strongly opposed to leaving the judge to decide about recovery. Major W. T. C. Skyrme, secretary, minuted that the issue of the recovery of costs gave rise to heated debate throughout "the whole of our deliberations," November 21, 1945, *ibid.*

[56] Stevens, *Law and Politics*, pp. 335–341.

[57] The other members were Shawcross (Attorney-General), Soskice (Solicitor-General), Thompson (Lord Advocate), Ede (Home Secretary), Bevan (Health), Wilkinson (Education), and Silkin (Town and Country Planning). CAB 134/657. Jowett, in a memorandum to the Cabinet (November 24, 1945) also argued there was "real urgency" about Codification.

[58] L.C.O. 2/3946.

[59] The creation of the Committee was revealing. Coldstream wrote (May 2, 1946) to Sir Thomas Lund, Secretary of the Law Society, asking if Littlewood (later President of the Law Society) was "too conservative." He was vetoed. Ellen Wilkinson, the Minister of Education, wanted a woman. Coldstream suggested Mrs. Lane. Judge Engelbach (May 12, 1946) thought Mrs. Lane did her cases "pleasantly" but "certainly not with outstanding ability." Coldstream vetoed any Matrimonial Registrars.

[60] L.C.O. 2/3951.

[61] November 7, 1946, *ibid.* Merriman was "bitterly hostile."

[62] L.C.O. 2/3957.

[63] The Bar and Solicitors suggested the recommendations. There were two parliamentary questions and Gerald Gardiner was pushing on behalf of the Haldane Society, *ibid.* The mechanics of having County Court judges sit as Divorce judges are collected in 2/3953. It led to the appointment of two more County Court judges in London. Coldstream told the judges to wear black robes and, ideally, morning coats. They were to be given clothing coupons, but had to buy them themselves. In July 1947, the office relented, and paid half the cost of the robes.

[64] L.C.O. 2/4012.

[65] The "robust" Summons for Direction was largely his work.

[66] He sold the idea of shorter vacations for the judges.

[67] See, for instance, his letter to Evershed, February 15, 1952.

[68] See dissents of these members. Final Report of the Committee on Supreme Court Practice and Procedure, 1953, HMSO, Cmd. 8878, p. 317.

[69] See their letters of April 1, 1953.

[70] Evershed still urged the Chancellor to do something about Counsel's fees. Letter, May 20, 1953.

[71] *The Times*, April 25, 1986.

[72] Hearing, July 18, 1967, L.C.O. 7/1.

[73] In fairness, he did pressure the Bar Council on the shortage of counsel; the implications for increase in provincial chambers, *id.* Derek Oulton was the secretary. Under Beeching's guidance he put hard questions to the Bar, *ibid.*

[74] The memorandum of the Lord Chief Justice, Parker, was relatively open minded (L.C.O. 7/55); that of the High Court Judges less so (L.C.O. 7/66).

[75] L.C.O. 7/56/A: "There is a strong case for merging the Divisions of the High Court."

[76] He was then asked by Mr. L. Cannon: "In view of the fact that we have so few judges, is this not extremely wasteful just for the sake of whatever marginal effect it has in impressing people of the sanctity of the Law?" To this Denning replied: "I can see the force of that from the point of view of administration and efficiency . . . (B)ut there are intangibles beyond." *Ibid.*

[77] Beeching noted: "I think you are trying to have it both ways. If you had a very few judges in order to preserve the respect for and the quality of the High Court judges, I do not think you can afford to have them spending their time relatively unproductively in very small centres." Denning's view was that if the number of High Court judges were increased very much, not only would quality decline, but it would be impossible "to get a common uniformity of approach on matters of principle on problems that arise," *ibid.* The traditional view appears neatly in an earlier file. Goddard had written to Jowett (October 5, 1950) opposing an increase in numbers of High Court judges: "A team of 24 is quite as much as I can manage to drive satisfactorily." L.C.O. 2/3889.

[78] For the County Court position, see, *e.g.* L.C.O. 12/54; for contrast, *e.g.* L.C.O. 2/3881. Both deal with the post-1945 period.

[79] August 5, 1945, L.C.O. 2/2967.

[80] September 27, 1945, *ibid*.

[81] L.C.O. 12/57.

[82] October 5, 1950, L.C.O. 2/3889.

[83] What the Judge appears to have said was that "Moral standards at the bottom end of the scale are a good deal higher on the average in Darlington, Stockton, Middlesbrough and the Durham mining areas than they are in West Hartlepool," Gaman to Rieu, February 1, 1952, L.C.O. 12/76.

[84] Gaman to Rieu, January 31, 1952, *ibid*.

[85] Lord Simonds said: "Judge Gaman should apologize publicly. Nothing else will meet the case," *ibid*. He then signed a letter, drafted by Coldstream dated February 4, 1952.

[86] See *Northern Echo*, February 14, 1952, *ibid*.

[87] See, for instance, the case of Judge Ingram Bell who wrote to *The Times* signing the letter "A County Court Judge," arguing that part of the judge's salary should be tax free, L.C.O. 12/78.

[88] Born 1908: educated at Charterhouse and Trinity College, Cambridge; Solicitor, 1933; barrister, 1951; Deputy Secretary 1954–1968.

[89] Born 1927; educated at St. Edward's, Oxford and King's College, Cambridge; Ph.D; private practice, Kenya 1952–60; Lord Chancellor's Office, 1961; Deputy Secretary 1968–1977.

[90] Born 1922; educated at Eton and New College, Oxford; Bar 1949–56; Lord Chancellor's Office, 1956; Deputy Secretary, 1972–1982.

[91] S. C. Silkin, "The Legal Machinery of Government" [1984] *Public Law* 179.

The author would like to thank the following for comments: Cyril Glasser, Christopher McCrudden, Katherine Stevens and William Twining. He would also like to thank Noel Blatchford and the staff of the Socio-Legal Centre for secretarial support.

The Use of "Contracts" as a Social Work Technique

DAVID NELKEN

Introduction: What are Social Work Contracts?[1]

The use of contracts as a tool of social work intervention is now widespread.[2] The various factors that help to account for the spread of this way of working look likely to lead to greater use of this technique. Yet there has still hardly been any research into the reasons for the use of this method, the kinds of contracts used in different situations and the success which has attended their use. Indeed, the problem of deciding what "success" would mean in any project set up to evaluate contracts has hardly been confronted. The promise of effective use of contracts for the benefit of clients, field social workers, social work management and policy makers is so great that the topic is one which cries out for careful investigation and appraisal. But beyond these policy issues the use of social work contracts provides an ideal setting for observing the difficulties of securing "agreement" in a structured situation of unequal power and, by the same token, a rare insight into the modalities of a new form of social control.[3]

There is also an important, if sometimes elusive, legal side to these developments. Because the use of social work contracts involves the fusion of "juridical" and "disciplinary" forms of power,[4] probably the least helpful question to ask is—are these really "legal" contracts? Social work contracts are unlikely to be legally binding because there is no "intention to create legal relations" in addition to other legal defects; in any case they normally only reinforce already existing legal obligations. Nevertheless some discussions in the social work literature do look to the rules of contract law to provide principled guidance to social workers in relation to problems of inequality, duress or undue influence. They seek to establish if "consideration" is required and whether the inclusion of standard non-negotiable terms is acceptable.[5] Rather than these questionable analogies, however, it may be that social workers have more to learn from sociological studies of the way legal contracts *are actually used*, especially as these investigations demonstrate the extent to which the success of contractual agreements depends on the existence of further reasons for the parties to wish to continue their relationship.[6] Other valuable enquiries would include the public law status of these ostensibly private legal forms, as well as the question of how far the social work profession may have adopted and adapted the language of contract as a form of *self-protection* against legal review. However, as this is an introductory paper, these matters will not be enforced here. I propose instead to try to show some of the interest and perhaps also the significance of the topic of social work contracts by describing the background and context of their use and reporting on a pilot study which I carried out into the attitudes of social workers and others to the use of this technique.

What are social work contracts? As will be seen, the term covers a promiscuous variety of techniques for achieving agreement, setting conditions, co-ordinating arrangements, identifying tasks and so on. Moreover, contracts range from complex written forms to mere oral agreements. The only common denominator—if there is one—is that social work contracts identify an agreement (on its face voluntary) between social workers and others concerning the content of social work. Even this definition fits some types of social work contracts better than others. One of the first necessities of research in this area is the formulation of a satisfactory typology of social work contracts.

Contracts similar to those used in social work are increasingly becoming the stock-in-trade of others involved in welfare and educational interventions. Thus marriage counsellors arrange for unhappy spouses to enter into contracts to encourage mutual satisfaction, divorce mediators use contracts to establish the outcome of their conciliation work and children excluded from school are issued with contract forms which they must use to write acknowledgement of past misdeeds and warrants of future good behaviour before they gain re-entry to school. Contracts are also utilized as part of the increasing vogue for mediation and conciliation, as well as by professions drawing on psychology and pyschiatry. Welfare contracts are therefore not unique to social work. Nor are they necessarily borrowed directly from the lawyer's use of contract. Putting the responsibility on people to comply with their own volunteered agreements is a widespread feature of institutional, business and, of course, family life. Nonetheless there seems to be enough in common in this special area of the use of contracts for a study of social work contracts in their own right.

I The Rise of Social Work Contracts

A number of factors are associated with the increasing popularity of contract work since its early development in the 1960s in the United States. I shall discuss six of the most important ones, all of which, as will be seen, continue to shape theoretical discussions and practical uses of contracts.

The move to task-work

The use of contracts is closely associated with the increased stress on *task-oriented* social work, in which intervention is geared to improving specific problems within short, time-limited periods. Contracts provide the ideal tool for constructing a framework of such intervention and for identifying an agenda of agreed tasks which fall on the parties concerned.[7] A further source of this development (in addition to the declining faith in the success of extended casework) was the approach of behaviour modification. Those writers who emphasize behaviour modification as a catalyst for change in attitudes and feelings rather than vice-versa argue that contracts help to ensure that social workers do not lose sight of this fact.[8]

Table I sets out some of the relevant/ideal/typical/disperates between task work and traditional social work. In fact, any given example of social work intervention will probably incorporate elements which are found in both lists. Indeed, it will be seen later that the continuing relevance of matters and approaches listed under the heading of traditional social work sets limits to the successful use of contracts. Other qualifications need to be noted. This characterization of traditional social work undoubtedly exaggerates the extent to which local authority social workers, under the stress of case-loads and crisis work, ever found it practicable to offer such sustained and demanding intervention. It should also be remembered that taskwork was originally put forward as a more effective form of client-centred psycho-dynamic casework although contract work tends to embrace a wide variety of tasks of which work on relationship problems is only one. For the sake of completeness it should also be added that there are variety of social work activities such as welfare rights advocacy or community work which do not fit at all easily into either mould. There are also some uses of contracts, as in behaviour modification programmes in residential homes or in groupwork with self-help groups of alcoholics, addicts or offenders, which are not so directly tied to the growth of taskwork. Nonetheless, it would be hard to over-emphasize the importance of taskwork for the rise in the use of contracts, both in its own right and in relation to the other factors to be considered.

TABLE I Differences between Task Work and Traditional Social Work

The Use of "Contracts" as a Social Work Technique

		Task Work	"Traditional" Social Work
Characteristics of Work Styles	1.	Short-term Intervention(s)	Long-term involvement
	2.	Written agreement	Oral (mis)understanding
	3.	Mutually-binding promises	Ongoing commitment
	4.	Specific focus	Diffuse unrestricted focus
	5.	Assistance	Engagement
Nature of Work	6.	Problem-centred	Client-centred
	7.	Target-setting	Developing a relationship
	8.	Help to self-help	Friendship and support
	9.	Working on agreed tasks	Building up trust
	10.	Working to implement solutions (shared definition of problem is the starting point)	Working to understand causes of the problem (shared definition of the problem is end point)
Goal of Work	11.	Apportioning and Monitoring performance of tasks	Identification of problems and remedies
	12.	Problem amelioration	Progress towards goal of mental health, normal functioning etc.
	13.	What client wants	What client needs
	14.	Stress on presenting problem	Stress on underlying problem
	15.	Action by client	Insight by client

The return to responsibility

There is another important factor which explains the rising use of contracts, particularly in work with offenders. Probation work with offenders and social work supervision have long embodied or lent themselves to contract work, and the growth of "diversion," community service and other schemes will increase the scope of such work. But contract work is particularly reinforced by what has been called the "decline of the rehabilitative ideal." Disillusion with the "treatment philosophy," under which offenders were seen as having needs which required expert diagnosis, has led to calls for a "justice model" of limited intervention in people's lives. Stress is put on asking social workers and probation officers to separate their caring and controlling roles and ensure that the former is restricted to concrete practical assistance rather than intrusive case-work. The search is for a "non-treatment paradigm" for probation officers in which specified areas of help replace an open-ended casework relationship.[9] Much of this remains controversial and out of touch with practice, yet there is no denying the relevance of these debates to the move towards "agreements" as the (only) legitimate basis for social work intervention.

All clients, and not merely offenders, are now to be seen as free agents capable of determining like other consumers what they wish to take from social workers and what they will choose to do about their own problems (however inconsistent this is with the Freudian or any other psychodynamic approach). This is manifest in Collins' plea for greater use of contracts:

> "What goals do we seek, and what are the limits we should set, or must set? The terms of agreement—essentially a contract—should be spelt out. The basis of the contract between worker and client is not so much the meeting of minds as the concept of bargain, the market place and horse trading, the quid pro quo. The client is a consumer and a participant entering into a transactional relationship. If it is to have a basis of trust then the nature of the transaction should be specified as explicitly as possible, as soon as possible."[10]

This rationale for contract shows the continued political and moral resonance of assuming that respect for individuals requires that they be viewed as possessing rights and freedom of choice.

Deinstitutionalization

The third factor which appears relevant is the decline in the use of institutional and residential facilities for social work. Largely for financial reasons and partly because of a loss of confidence in residential care and a positive attraction to "community" and "family" care as the best preparation for life in the community, there has been a considerable upsurge in schemes to empty institutions of all but the most difficult residents. The impact of "decarceration"[11] for offenders leads to control in the community.[12] But it also has momentous significance for child care. Adoption, foster care, day care and community care placements all lend themselves to the use of contracts. Nancy Hazel's pioneering community care project, for example, which served as a model for others, laid great stress on contracts.[13] Care in the "community" requires careful coordination of all those dealing with a case and often requires that foster parents, community carers, day carers, etc. be treated as "para-social workers" delegated to carry out specified social work tasks and paid accordingly. Contracts provide the requisite method of co-ordinating this process and offering the right degree of "job description," without expecting or intending these workers to operate as properly trained social workers.

Private and voluntary social work

A further reason for the rise of contracts in social work practice is the encouragement being given to voluntary effort accompanied by increasing pressure on local authorities to ascertain that this effort does not duplicate statutory services and that it offers good value for the grants-in-aid received. Contract work offers a clear method of demonstrating the nature of the tasks being tackled and the commitment to monitor progress being achieved. Thus a threat to its funding helped to explain a shift to contract work in one Family Service Unit.[14] Organizations like the N.S.P.C.C. and Barnardo's have a long history of using contracts. The more that local authorities and statutory social workers are made to depend on inputs of social work by voluntary agencies and by volunteers, the more contracts are likely to be used to formalize these arrangements.

Measurable achievements

Pressure to demonstrate results is not restricted to private and voluntary agencies. Social work in general has come under severe, if often ill-informed, criticism, and it must be tempting to move towards a form of social work which appears to promise measurable achievements and even a possible yardstick of cost-benefit "productivity." However, despite the attractions to management or to politicians of requiring a style of work which could so easily be monitored, there is yet little evidence of erosion of social work autonomy in choosing how to work.

Accountability

Last, but not least, contracts provide something of a solution to the problem of making social workers "accountable" for the exercise of their discretion.[15] Contracts specify the conditions under which a child will be returned home to its natural parents, a probation order will be breached, parental rights will be sought, etc. This is important both for the people affected and for those in courts and local authorities who have to take decisions on the basis of social work recommendations. For social workers themselves, contracts allow them to justify and document their decisions and avoid charges of poor communication and liaison. Responsibilities are clearly defined, not least those of the clients who are being encouraged to exercise self-help and avoid dependence on the Social Work Department.

Types of Social Work Contracts

Whatever the reasons for the growth of contracts a diverse and confusing range of agreements currently go under the name of contracts. Some attempts have been made to clarify their different uses. For example Sheldon distinguishes between *contingency contracts* which he sees as geared to operant conditioning methods of reinforcing desirable behaviour and *service contracts* which are more concerned with defining the service on offer.[16] Examination of a sample of contracts obtained in my pilot study (see p. 217) produced the following variety of agreements.

1. Working agreements

Many social workers prefer this term to "contract" and it is often used in place of it on the relevant documents. Such contracts or sets of contracts provide a framework for the organization of social work intervention for example with "community care" placements of adolescents.[17]

2. Task agendas

Check lists of tasks are found to a greater or lesser extent in all social work contracts but are the central feature of contracts made with alcoholics, drug addicts, etc., or those used to bring about family harmony, as with contracts devised by Family Service Units.[18]

3. Programmes of behaviour modification

These contracts incorporate graduated rewards and sanctions adjusted to the progress of the individual. They are widely used in children's homes and other residential institutions.[19]

4. Contracts of delegated responsibilities

These lay down the responsibilities of para-social workers, private and voluntary workers and others in relation to the overall goal of social work intervention.

5. Contracts of conditions or requirements

Many contracts spell out or add to the legal conditions for the satisfactory discharge of a probation order or supervision orders of various kinds. Others set out the requirements (whether legal or organizational in origin) for the use of social work department care facilities or the steps necessary before the department will support an application for the return of a child to its natural parents.

6. *Agreed rules of procedure*

Some contracts are concerned exclusively with the "agreed" rules of procedure for those taking part in group work, for example in a group of sex offenders[20] or family therapy group.[21]

7. *Mutual undertakings*

These contracts lay down a set of mutually interlocking acts or forbearances which are required of the relevant parties. Again this feature is common to most contracts but is particularly characteristic of situations in which the social worker is playing the role of mediator between disputing spouses or parents and children.[22]

Clearly what is presented here resembles a list rather than a typology. But it could provide at least a starting point for further research and for a comparison of the nature and success of the contracts used in different situations. Four analytic distinctions which cut across these types would also seem heuristically important for research.

It will often be relevant whether the contract forms part of a voluntary arrangement between worker and client or whether it rests upon a statutory basis, as with probation and supervision orders. This will affect, for example, the real meaning of "consent" and the scope for negotiation over the terms of the contract. On the other hand, even some "voluntary" agreements such as community care contracts, incorporate standard conditions to which individually-bargained details are then added.

A related but not identical distinction can be drawn between conditions in contracts which are derived from requirements laid down by law or by the social work department and conditions which are technical necessities built into the performance of a given task. The difference, which is important just because it is a subtle one, is illustrated by the contrast between the Social Work Department requiring improved marital harmony before a child is returned home and a social worker requiring a gradual reduction in drug-taking as part of a rehabilitation programme for drug addicts.

It will also usually be valuable to identify how far contracts are concerned with the *means* or *goals* of intervention and whether the social worker and client are agreeing on means, goals or both. In community care contracts, for example, social workers and young people heartily agree on the means—going to live with a family, but are less united over the goal—to work on the child's problems and become independent.[23] By contrast, in contracts concerning what a family must do in order to receive its child back from care, the family and the social worker agree on the goal—the return of the child—but are less at one over the means, the tasks which the family must first perform. This situation may be still more complicated by the possibility that the social work department may not be totally committed to the goal of returning the child to the family and that the means is partly intended as a hurdle or at least a test for the family's suitability for the goal itself.

The Functions of Contracts

As a preliminary to investigating the actual use of contracts I reviewed the social work literature so as to see the advantages they are supposed to offer. My survey suggests that there are five major functions which contracts are said to fulfil.[24] The most frequently mentioned advantage was the contribution which contracts made to *clarifying social work interventions* (a topic much exercising social workers in the light of considerable research evidence that clients was frequently uncertain about what were expected of them, why the social worker was involved and even what social workers were!). Contracts, it was said, could do much to clear up confusions about the social workers role and the tasks she would be able and willing to fulfil in the particular case. They could make manifest the responsibilities of the client and others involved stating where these expectations were interdependent and mutual. In other cases contracts could be used to specify the job descriptions of those carrying out delegated or collaborative social work tasks. Actually working with clients contracts could help social workers and clients to agree on the definition of the problem. They could provide a precise target for intervention as well as be used to monitor those aspects of the problem where limited or no progress was being achieved.

The second most emphasised benefit of contracts involved their *coordination* function. Contracts could help social workers, social work departments and other agencies make better use of their resources. They facilitated forward planning in setting time limits for clients, and in preparing them for a change of status. They made it easier for social workers to mediate when things went wrong. Above all, they helped local authority departments liaise with other professions, voluntary and private social work agencies, quasi-social workers and others.

A Social Work contract was taken to have particular advantages for the *relationship* between the social worker and client. The first of these was that it treated clients with *respect* and helped them become more *responsible* for their choices. It avoided "the stereo-typing of the client by focusing on the problem and not the client." It treated the client (and others involved in social work interven-tions) as capable of independent and rational decisions and pos-sessing the capacity to enter into and abide by undertakings. In social work terms "it mobilized the adult, coping, side of the client." Contract work put responsibility clearly onto clients thereby helping to avoid their tendency to become dependent on the social work department. It gave clients experience in negotiat-ing and provided evidence of obligation and consent on the clients' part and commitment on the side of the social work department. This emphasis on the responsibility of the clients in a welfare state was sometimes expressed, in unusually strong terms for the social work literature, to include "a duty not to become destitute if he can help it."

A further benefit was that contracts were thought to supply a definite spur to *motivation* and *achievement*. Because contracts provided a clear specification of the goals of social work interven-tion they made it possible (sometimes all too possible) to see what progress had been achieved. Clients would be motivated by their involvement in drawing up the contract, by their consent to what it contained, by the incentive of the reciprocal promises of the social work department and, where applicable, by fear of sanctions if it broke down.

A final set of functions related to control by the social worker and her *accountability*. Contracts were capable of helping both social workers and clients gain more control of their interaction so as to better achieve their aims. For the social worker they could be used to help keep the clients to their agreements, making it more difficult for them to "manipulate social workers or dodge the real issues." They prevented social workers from being at the beck and call of clients and placed limits on the extent to which social workers had to persevere with unpromising cases (thus reducing worker anxieties). They allowed the social worker to be "pro-fessional" in saying that there were some cases where she was unable to assist and made it easier for social workers (and clients) to disengage if undertakings were not kept. Contracts were invalu-able in presenting evidence of efforts made once cases came to legal proceedings. On the other hand, contracts were also a potential tool for clients to hold social workers accountable. They provided a basis for complaint if social workers did not keep to their part of the agreement. They would be open to scrutiny by outsiders, including courts, and could help the emergence of "discretionary rights." They could be used by local authorities seeking to exercise control over social workers or private social work agencies and might even begin to provide a measure of "productivity" of social work.

This overview of the literature has been deliberately broad-based and open-ended. Different of these advantages would no doubt tend to be associated with distinctive types of social work intervention although this is not always apparent from the literature itself. More to the point, since most of these alleged virtues of contract are hardly novel aspirations of social work, it would be interesting to know how they were thought to be achieved in the past. With the tendency in social work to seize on new ideas with a certain lack of critical appraisal the potential disadvantages of using contracts are not much debated. But in any case, there is no substitute for empirical research here.

II A Pilot Study of Attitudes to Contracts

Claims in the social work literature are likely to be more of a guide to the ideals which contracts are intended to achieve than to the practicalities and difficulties of using them. The following pilot study in the Lothian Region of Scotland was set up in order to find out more about the extent of use of social work contracts "on the ground," to discover the situations in which they were used and, above all, to ascertain the range of opinions of social workers (and others) on the value of developing this style of work.[25] The main interviews were with members of three generic social work area teams, in two different towns.[26] In addition to this two hospital social workers, a day care organiser and community carers scheme organiser were interviewed. Other interested parties consulted including sheriffs, Childrens Panel Members and others who came across contracts in the course of their work. I was also fortunate to be given access to the results of unpublished research interviews with a range of adolescents who had been asked to agree to contracts as part of a community care scheme. As part of the research I was able to obtain and examine examples of the different types of contracts which were being used. Although the findings of this study are necessarily tentative and exploratory it will be seen that there are interesting contrasts amongst social workers in their attitudes to contracts. While some endorsed their use for all their interventions, others welcomed them for limited purposes only and yet others objected to their use more or less entirely.

In general all those approached had heard of contracts even if they did not make use of them in their work. The prevalent view was that resort to contracts was increasing and that they were particularly likely to be used by young "go-ahead" social workers. All the social workers interviewed, *whether or not they used contracts*, repeated some at least of the virtues of contracts as described in the social work literature. As might be expected, however, they tended to lay most stress on the practical advantages of contracts in keeping clients to their promises and ensuring that arrangements ran smoothly. There was less mention of the importance of client respect or increasing social work accountability. Instead they claimed that contracts could also make a difference to *their* responsibilities (in a way not stressed in the literature) by obliging them to arrange and keep to definite appointments with those clients with whom contracts had been agreed. Some social workers thought that contracts were particularly useful as a reminder to clients, especially young people, who tried to deny having entered into agreements and as "documentation" when this was needed to justify adverse decisions in probation, supervision, child care or parental rights cases. Others considered that the advantage of contracts for social work practice was that they made social workers be more specific to themselves about what they were trying to achieve and made them more aware of their use of language in discussing problems. They set limits to what social workers could expect from clients since they tended to set out minimal requirements rather than unrealistic expectations. They therefore made it clearer which matters were optional (for both social worker and client) and allowed the client to say which "problems" they would and would not work on. Nonethless, beyond any points of agreement, there were also considerable differences between those who did and did not favour their use. I shall begin with those who were most positive.

The enthusiasts

Keen supporters of contract work used them for *every case* of social work intervention; this included work with offenders on probation; children on supervision orders, day care arrangements and arrangements for the return of children from care to their natural parents. These social workers argued that contracts were especially useful for young people who did not remember things too well. Children would now remember crucial contract terms such as the need for four weeks notice before changing arrangements. A contract was even (or especially) useful in the case of an illiterate, scatty, simple parent who required help with child arrangements. ("The contract

was kept by her landlady who read it out to her when necessary"!)
Contracts were useful because they provided information to the
client, often this was the only information other than appointment
letters which the client received. Contracts set out the aims to be
worked on, and showed progress that had been achieved. They
highlighted, for the attention of all concerned, which of a number
of problems were not yielding to intervention. Contracts helped to
develop motivation even where clients were not really very motivated. Clients could feel involved in the drawing up of contracts
which were written down from notes taken after a meeting where
all could discuss the problem and these notes were read back to the
client who could disagree with any point made. Finally, contracts
could help in the management and planning of social work, for
example by making it easier to allocate training time and supervision and space.

Examination of the contracts used by these social workers
illustrated something of how these ideas turned out in practice.
Some contracts involved conditions added to an otherwise standard form agreement (*e.g.* probation order) and included rather
nebulous phrases such as an agreement "to be of good behaviour." Other contracts also include aims which were general and
imprecise, *e.g.* "the aim is to *ultimately enable* Karen to reach a
degree of *independence* in her own life." This was followed by
the conditional requirement that therefore she should keep her
appointments at the Social Work office. Contracts mixed aspirations and precise tasks. They also often left it unclear who were
actively the parties to the contract. Perhaps inevitably, the
Social Work Department retained explicit discretion in judging
how the contracts were succeeding. On the other hand, these
contracts were a determined attempt to set out the purpose of
social work intervention and some of the expectations of the
Social Work Department. The time-limits of intervention were
particularly clearly set out.

Some social workers made use of contracts only for specific purposes. For example, work with offenders on probation and work
with parents awaiting the return of their children from local authority care or wishing to make use of care. For probation work,
contracts were used as part of a scheme which examined the
progress made by (cooperative) offenders at regular intervals. An
interesting feature of these contracts was their attempt to incorporate the rationale for the required tasks by setting out as a
preamble a summary of the relevant discussions of progress and
problems. In child care cases contracts were thought to be useful
as a way of specifying requirements which parents had to meet

before being entitled to social work support. Contracts were said to be useful where parents in fact failed to meet their obligations because it then helped to justify an application for parental rights. In some cases parents' failure to meet requirements convinced the parents themselves that the best place for the child was not at home (the example given was of a single father who failed to beat a severe drink problem).

The interesting question of the exact role contracts were expected to play came up in connection with the use of contracts in community care schemes. These schemes place children between the ages of 12–16, with long histories of residential care, into families in the community for renewable periods of two years. The families are paid a professional fee. As with Nancy Hazel's Kent scheme, on which this type of programme is based, contracts were considered to be a crucial feature of the organization. According to the organizer of the scheme the contracts were intended to serve three main purposes. Firstly, they represented a *statement of commitment* by all those involved in the placement, which acted as a testimony to the agreement reached in the meetings during which the placement was arranged. Secondly, contracts provided a *statement of objectives*. This always included the general goal for all carers of helping the child to independence. In addition, more specific matters would be added depending upon the particular problems of the child concerned such as trouble in school, offences or relationship problems. Some, but not all, contracts also included more detailed expectations of the child such as the time she was required to be in at night or the need to "attend to hygiene." Thus contracts made it clear for carers "what the job was about"; for children, what was expected of them, and, for social work staff, what their role was to be in facilitating the success of the placement. The Organizer insisted that only those problems which a child recognised and accepted as being his or her problems would be included in the contract. He felt that this age-group of children was particularly adept at "negotiating" with adults so that their views would be heard. Thirdly, contracts provided a *sign of achievement* because it was almost certain that progress would be achieved on at least some of the assigned tasks. Such a visible indicator (since problems could be ticked off once solved) was thought to be a great boost to confidence and morale.

However, in discussion the organiser revealed that he did not place quite as much emphasis on contracts as might appear from the attention devoted to drawing them up. Contracts were not, he thought, "the be all or end all"; they were merely a helpful tool.

Trust and commitment were more important ingredients for success than contracts. He would not be concerned if it turned out that contracts were not actually referred to during the placement itself. If things were going well, then this showed that contracts were not needed. On the other hand (perhaps inconsistently) he argued that contracts should not be identified with the original documents. Contracts should be seen as a live and growing agreement which had to be both flexible and changing during the course of the placement.

There were, he thought, dangers in taking the analogy with legal contracts too seriously. Social work contracts were usually rather one-sided and the children entering into them were too young to enter legal obligations. Because their prior experience had been in residential settings, they were not in a position to anticipate what life will be like in a "normal family." If a placement ran into difficulty it would be a mistake to refer too closely to the contract. Contract was not a recipe for success; rather, some troubles were best left to sort themselves out. It was also unwise for the family to take contracts too seriously. The example was given of one family who tried too hard to resolve the problems itemised in the contract. The new carers who replaced them were told to go easy and not pick on all the child's problems, but focus instead on one important but manageable area of concern. This ambiguousness about the significance of contract terms also applied to the role of social workers once the placements were effected. The social workers' view was that carers had complete responsibility for the children. When things were going well contracts were not needed and even where the placement ran into difficulties, it was best to leave it to the parents and children to sort the problem out by negotiation. Otherwise there was a risk that the trust between the family and the child would be broken and families would be encouraged in the belief that social workers were always able to provide solutions.

Some of this ambivalence as to the significance of contracts for community care placements was evident in the contracts themselves. These varied widely in the amount of detail they included, some confining themselves to the most general of aspirations for the placement, whereas others provided an exhaustive list of the tasks to be tackled. Some contracts made much of the social work role, others made passing reference to it. Some contracts carefully listed the mutual responsibilities of the child and other parties (carefully re-stating as duties on one party what were elsewhere listed as rights for another). Generally, however, the main purpose of contracts, or rather the set of contracts, in this area of social work seemed to be that of co-ordinating and demonstrating the various responsibilities of the various parties concerned with these placements. The scope for misunderstanding where so many people are involved is obviously considerable; the care taken to append a long list of the relevant signatures suggests the attempt being made to ensure that all parties acknowledge their awareness of the various agreements. By contrast to some other uses of contracts, much of the contract seems to deal with how the parties should be kept in touch. The stress was on *who* was responsible for different tasks; *how* those different tasks were to be achieved was, in most cases, left to the parties concerned.

Fortunately it was possible to supplement the account offered by the organiser of the scheme with the results of a research study into the attitudes of the children involved.[27] Most children remembered being involved in making the agreement, although four (out of 23 children interviewed) said they had been involved only to the extent of signing the contract. But there was patchy knowledge of the contents of the contracts; six children were not even aware of the time-limit on the placement. Both carers and children saw the object of the placement as allowing the child to feel part of a normal family. On the other hand, the organizer had told me that he warned the children that they would not be fully part of that family, which is why they remained attached to a supervising social worker. Carers saw the contract as relatively unimportant for day-to-day living and said "You don't really go by the contract—it's just to keep the Social Work Department happy." It appeared then that the families made little reference to the contract after the initial meetings and carers did not use the contract as a. mode of discipline. All in all, some of the aims and tasks laid down in the contracts were undoubtedly being achieved but with little explicit use of the contracts themselves. It might even be concluded that contracts were a dispensible part of the scheme, except that it seemed that the organiser had anticipated most of these findings and still thought contracts were valuable.[28]

The doubtful

Some social workers explicitly distinguished carefully between what they considered to be effective and ineffective use of contracts. One of the hospital social workers interviewed had experience of using contracts in four settings. Firstly, he used contracts in a List "D" school in the early 1970s, then, more recently, as a social worker involved in community care placements and in child care interventions. Currently he worked in a hospital using contracts as a method of organizing therapeutic intervention in the lives of those with alcohol and drug-related problems. Although contracts formed a central part of his present hospital-based social work practice, he had the gravest doubts about the value of contracts within institutions or in community care schemes. The key distinctions which emerged from his reflection on his experience was that contracts were ineffective if they became a fixed feature of an institution's or organization's practice, if they served the needs of the organisation rather than the client and if they became standardized or formalistic. Above all, contracts could only be effective if they truly represented problems which the clients concerned wished to solve. None of these conditions for effective contract work were satisfied, in his view, in the way contracts were used in residential settings or, for that matter, in community care placements. In the residential List "D" school in which he had worked, great stress was laid on contracts both as a way of organizing work with each child admitted and as a form of behaviour modification. But the use of contracts soon became a meaningless ritual. A "key worker" was responsible for producing a contract by the end of the initial meeting after a child's reception into the school. But at this stage "there weren't a lot of issues available to be put into a contract because the child hadn't been sufficiently well assessed to be able to see them." As a result the key worker (who was often keen to get away to other appointments) "would sit down" with an inarticulate kid and invent things which would be put into the kid's record and stay with him throughout his stay and rarely be modified."

Within the school, contracts were seen as an idea imposed by "trendies from college" and the "ordinary workers" did not feel committed to them. At reviews of a child's progress contracts were usually not referred to; alternatively, "hard-line staff would wave the contract at a kid" in order to justify sanctions for some breach of the contract. Anything put into the initial contract was soon out of date but staff were reluctant to change it because of the paperwork that this generated. It required a time-consuming effort to re-negotiate a contract with the child and then have it all re-typed especially as the kid was quite likely "to break it again next week" so that the whole process would have to be repeated endlessly. Contract terms which *were* meaningful and did reflect a careful assessment of the child's problems were just for that reason most likely to be broken. But it was then a problem what do do next and how to decide whether to renegotiate or impose sanctions. Therefore, contracts were related more to the needs of the staff than those of the children. They came to be nothing more than part of the institutional furniture, one of the procedures which those admitted to the school had to undergo, but which had little relation to what they wanted or thought they needed.[29]

On the other hand, he felt that contracts were an important and valuable element of his current work with alcoholic clients referred to him because of associated problems which were thought to require social intervention. To do this kind of work it was necessary to have some kind of agreement, in writing, between worker and client. This agreement, which did not necessarily have to be a contract, could take a number of different forms depending on the particular case. He chose to refer to the agreements he negotiated with most clients as "work programmes." Clients were expected to bring them with them to interviews and they helped to make them self-aware and clear about which goals they were expected to work at. Such agreements were arrived at at an early stage by breaking down the client's life into a number of areas where problems might be occurring, *e.g.* finances; accommodation; occupation (*i.e.* job or how else time spent); health and relationships with other people. The client was asked whether or not he was satisfied with each of these areas of life and then requested to place his problems in order of priority. The social worker was not entirely passive during this recital. If he thought that the client was "missing the point" [*sic*] he would interject his views and elicit the client's response. For example, if the client stated that he thought his main problem was to do with health, the social worker might comment that he thought the problem was more to do with his relationship with his wife. The client and worker would then "negotiate" about how the client's problems should be defined. The social worker admitted that this process could become a "cop out mechanism" which preserved the appearance but not the reality of client self-determination.

Nonetheless, the effective use of contracts was seen to be bound up with the degree to which the client did succeed in articulating for the social worker what he took his problems to be. The role of the social worker was not to advise the client that he can offer him the "treatment which he needs" but to decide with the client "the quickest way (to) get what you say you want." For this reason he was suspicious of contract work with children. Unlike the organizer of the community care scheme, he felt that contract work with children was *more* difficult than using contracts with adults. Adolescents might enjoy negotiating, but the important point was whether they could or should exercise self-determination. Children often wanted to do things which were self-damaging but they could not be allowed to do so. In child care you sometimes did harm to give the client what he wanted, not what he needed.

The details of his use of contracts in a hospital setting bear out the strong connection between task-oriented work and contracts. The cause of the problematic behaviour was felt to be a less important matter than the means which should be used to ameliorate it. It was not, at first anyway, helpful to ask why the patient regularly got drunk on Carlsberg Specials; the issue was "what to do about it." Often nothing could be done about the "cause" of a problem. In any case with this method you would "eventually get down to what makes people (the) way they are . . . (to the) long-standing and painful areas. In the long run this way of working was also that best way of getting to know the person." But work with patients usually began when they were at a rock-bottom stage. It was important for the worker to capitalize on offering "quick-money-back guarantees" on helping with a client's major problem. These patients were often concerned with "instant gratification" anyway so that the promise of an improvement, "in six weeks, if you follow this programme, you'll have reached this stage" were welcome. A typical contract for a client with a serious drinking problem would involve seeing him twice a week for the first six weeks, giving a programme for reduced drinking, advising him that withdrawal pains would only last ten days and assuring him that the programme would eventually allow him to return to moderate drinking. Agreement on the programme was then committed to paper. This was done for the sake of the client. The social worker did not usually keep a copy of the contract but expected the client to bring it with him to appointments or at least they could both refer to the agreements it contained. The agreement would often have to be changed, for example as the client progressed (or regressed), and a new agreement could be drawn up without fuss if the original agreement was wrong or if new problems had intervened. If part of the agreement was not kept, it became the subject of the next interview and a new contract/programme was often devised to deal with that particular item. Part of the role of the worker was to show how one problem (*e.g.* drink) was linked with a series of other problems (*e.g.* finances, sex life, marriage relationship, etc.)

Unlike contracts used in institutions, these agreements were in his view solely concerned with the client's stated problems. Instead

of the difficulty of "thinking up something to put into each contract" the contents of the contract could and did reflect only what
the client agreed was a problem with which he required assistance.
If the client said his problem was to do with housing, then the issue
became what to do about that and what steps should be taken to
deal with the problem. If the client then showed himself unable to
take the step of getting his housing application processed, this
raised the question of what problem prevented him from doing so
and this became the subject of the next meeting.

There were two practical requirements for the effective use of
contracts. Firstly, the client had to have a "bunch of problems"
which could respond to action *"on the client's part"* (albeit with
social work assistance). If the problem was located outside the
client (for example, a parent's concern that his child was sniffing
glue) then contract work could not be restricted to the parents.
They might need to work on their parenting skills but the child
concerned would also have to want to work on his problems. Similarly, contracts had only a limited role in helping someone over an
"excessive" grief reaction. If they wanted this form of help it
would have to take the form of a programme designed to reduce
the manifestations of such grief, for example no longer setting a
meal place for the loved one now dead.

Contracts also had little application to the side of social work
devoted to the assessment of needs and provision of welfare services. It worked best for therapeutic interventions by ensuring that
the problems were put in writing, that a strategy for dealing with
them was established, that (symbolically at least) there existed a
commitment to action and a prescription of what should be done
and providing a record to which the client could refer for the vast
majority of his time when he was not with the social worker.

In the second place, contracts must represent what the client
wants. They must be phrased in a "common language" shared by
the worker and client (some bowdlerization is allowed by which
"it's my fucking wife" becomes the problem of "sexual rejection").
They should not be concerned with dictating a style of life but with
realizing a strategy for helping the client achieve his own goals. If
the problem is to reduce drink intake, and the client's regular bus
stop is outside his local, then the suggestion might be to get off a
stop before! Where traditional social work would be imposing solutions as a "prescription for salvation" from the outside and seeing
the client as a victim, with the contract method the problem is
looked at from the inside and all change is a result of adult choice
and the provision of "information" which will make an informed
choice. Unlike contracts in List "D" schools, these contracts are

not "directive" and were never used as a justification for sanctions. All rewards and sanctions were *inbuilt*. If the client complies, he will look and feel better: by reducing drinking he will avoid being taken to the nick; save money to spend on something he wants, be able to use his Giro on accommodation rather than drink. The client's agreement was an essential part of the programme because it permitted leverage to remind the client that it was his problem and that he wanted to work on it. But this sometimes rebounded because the client felt ashamed to come back to see the social worker if he had not managed to keep the agreement, aware that he had let himself and the social worker down. Yet this was a small price to pay for an approach which had so many other benefits. Incidentally it also provided an excellent way of *managing* a case-load of up to 150 therapeutic involvements in a total case-load of up to 450 hospital patients a year who were referred for social work assistance.

In view of this social worker's strong objection to what he called "directive" contracts which were only "made to look as if they were the result of agreement" I was interested to know what he felt about the use of contracts with parents in legally-backed child care cases. Somewhat surprisingly, he was all in favour of contracts in this situation. As he saw it, it was important for the Social Work Department to give parents a contract to fulfil in order for them to receive their children back from care because this indicated the grounds on which the parents were being assessed. This was a matter of a person's right to know the basis on which decisions which affected them were being taken. The use of contract was to be understood as follows: the parents were telling the Social Work Department that they wanted their child back. The social worker was showing them how they could achieve this.

The opponents

The most antipathetic view of contract was expressed by a social worker who felt that the idea had been "rammed down her throat" during her training course. She saw contract as a method which she would only use with "desperate" cases as a measure of documenting the anticipated failure for a family (or client) unwilling to recognize their limitations. Three arguments were advanced against the value of using contracts more widely. Firstly, when contracts could not achieve the aims they were consciously designed to serve they risked obfuscating or sabotaging these very goals. This point was well captured by her claim that "If (social work) really relates to the things clients value, then they don't need something written down." Contract could easily become a short-cut obviating the need to ensure that the client really did understand what was being proposed—"If you are doing your job properly you shouldn't need to write it down." Contract could easily become tokenism—the mere appearance of understanding and consent. Moreover, contracts were notoriously open to differing interpretations by social workers and clients, so that each side would tend to read in different meanings to the requirements and tend to disagree on whether real improvements had been attained. This was easily seen if the parties were asked to say what the contract meant. And there was a logical and practical limit to how far meaning could be made transparent—"to spell out what contract means, it's a book not a contract you'd need."

As a result of all this, reliance on contracts could *conceal* the failure to get to grips with a client's problem. Persistence in drawing attention to the contract and using it as a weapon in the course of social work intervention might then make things go doubly wrong. Not only might problems be wrongly identified but the contract could then be used as a source of binding obligation to continue working on them even if progress was not being made. She illustrated this point with a case of community carers who felt that a placement was going wrong but were reminded by the social work department of their contractual obligations to persist with the child—with unfortunate results for the child concerned. Other alleged advantages of contracts were also questioned. Contracts would be unlikely to motivate or serve as a sign of achievement because frequently social work problems were so difficult to shift. Forced to monitor success in this way, both the client and the social worker could easily become depressed and demoralized. There was no easy substitute for the hard and uphill struggle of helping a client to change the way he or she functioned.

As this suggests, her second objection to contract harked back to the traditional conception of the case-work relationship in social work. She argued that it was just not possible to define at the outset which problems social work intervention should be designed to help. Nothing—including contract—could identify *the* problem because there were 100 different factors relevant to most social work cases. Such cases are best seen as "a constellation or interplay of emotions, forces and potentials" and it was unhelpful to reduce this complexity for the sake of fixing a specific problem in a contract. The job of the social worker was *to relate, not facilitate*—"she must stay in there and work with the client, renegotiating the nature of the problem as and when necessary." In her view any other approach ran a severe risk of bad faith especially where contracts in pursuance of statutory requirements were concerned. For the trouble with precise statements of social work problems is that they could easily be overtaken by events. The example she provided was of a worker telling parents, in a contract, that provided they improved the quality of their home conditions and paid off their debts, the Social Work Department would recommend that their child would be returned from care. She posed the following hypothetical question: What would happen if they dutifully did this but the worker later discovered some other problem, for example severe marital violence, which made her fear for the child's safety were he to be returned home? Could the social worker then honour her agreement? The existence of a contract would not help you deal with this dilemma; on the contrary, because it misidentified the problem, it would represent an obstacle to resolving it.

Her last criticism of contract work was also linked to her positive preference for a more psycho-dynamic view of social work. As opposed to the *future orientation* of work on tasks and problems, she stressed the importance of *backward-looking* work. For her, the goal of the social worker was to find out *why* problematic behaviour takes place. Unless and until this was understood, no real help was possible. To concentrate on ticking-off a number of particular achievements over the period of a contract was illusory if the causes of the behaviour were not uprooted.

This social worker was prepared to concede that there might be a limited role for contracts in certain types of work, such as community care schemes. She also saw the point of contracts when working with children who denied what they had promised unless you were able to confront them with the evidence of their agreement. In addition, she thought that contracts could be useful in the management of social work intervention—"if various workers dealing with a case all showed that contracts were not being kept by a family, then this would be justification for action." The limitations of contract work could also sometimes turn out to be a blessing too. They could provide restrictions on what social workers could demand from a client and help "get social workers out of families' homes." But overall she remained sceptical and uneasy about the value of using contracts to achieve social work goals.

Conclusion

My intentions in this pilot study of the use of contracts in social work were comparatively modest. I set out to find out something about the area of work in which contracts have come to be used, the reasons for their increasing popularity, the types of contracts which exist and the functions which they are expected to perform. In addition, I was particularly interested in the different attitudes which social workers and others are adopting towards this new method of working with clients. Even so a number of puzzles and problems are raised by these initial interviews (and by examination of the sample of contracts they provided). How far does the use of contract presuppose a previous basis of agreement? How far does the continuing success of the contract depend on the strength of the non-contractual relationship between the social worker and client?[30] How closely should contract requirements be specified? When is it appropriate to re-negotiate a contract and when should the contract be ended? What is to be done about supervening events? Under what circumstances, if any, is it legitimate for a social worker to set up a contract she knows the client will be unable to keep? It is possible that some of these problems can be illuminated by referring to the doctrine, jurisprudence and sociology of legal contracts. But it is even more likely that what is needed for both theoretical and practical purposes is a better appreciation of what is special about the use of contracts in social work rather than an effort to assimilate them to what is already known and understood.

Notes

[1] Although I have used the term contracts without quotation marks throughout this paper, it will be clear from the argument that this is not because I subscribe to the view that they are binding legal contracts.

[2] Although I have not yet been able to carry out systematic comparative research I have information that social work contracts are used extensively throughout Britain as well as in the United States, Scandinavia and France.

[3] See D. Nelken,, "Social Work Contracts and Social Control," in R. Mathews (ed.), *Reconstructing Criminal Justice* (Forthcoming).

[4] M. Foucault, *Discipline and Punish* (1977), J. Donzelot, *The Policing of Families* (1979).

[5] J. Corden, "Contracts in Social Work Practice" (1980) 10 *British Journal of Social Work* 143–161.

[6] S. Macaulay, "Non-Contractual Relations in Business: A Preliminary Study:" (1963) 28 Am.Soc.Rev. 55–67; H. Beale and T. Dugdale, "Contracts between

Businessmen: Planning and the use of Contractual Remedies;" (1975) 2 Brit.J. Law and Soc. 45–60.

[7] W. J. Reid and A. Shyne, *Brief and Extended Casework* (1969), p. 69; W. J. Reid and L. Epstein, *Task Centred Casework* (1972).

[8] B. Sheldon, "Making Contracts to Please" (1978) 24 *Community Care'*, and B. Sheldon, "The use of contracts in social work" *Practice Note Series 1*, B.A.S.W. (1980).

[9] A. T. Bottoms and R. McWilliams, "A Non-Treatment Paradigm for Probation Practice" (1979) 9 *British Journal of Social Work* 159.

[10] J. Collins, "A contractual approach to Social Work Intervention" *Social Work Today* February 8, 1977.

[11] A. Scull, *Decarceration* (1977).

[12] D. Nelken, "Community Involvement in Crime Control" (1985) 38 *Current Legal Problems* 239.

[13] N. Hazel, *A Bridge to Independence* (1978) 38–47.

[14] A. Smith and J. Corden, "The Introduction of Contracts in a Family Service Unit" (1981) *British Journal Social Work 11* 289.

[15] Z. Bankowski and D. Nelken, "Discretion as a social problem" in M. Alder and S. Asquith, *Discretion and Welfare* (1981), p. 247–268.

[16] See Sheldon, (1980) *op. cit.* n. 8.

[17] See, *e.g.* "Service Contracts" in Sheldon (1980), *ibid.*

[18] See, *e.g.* "Contingency Contracts" in Sheldon (1980), *ibid.* and the example in Smith and Corden, *op. cit.* n. 14.

[19] See A. Walter *Sent Away* (1978).

[20] R. Burgess *et. al.* "Working with Sex Offenders" (1980) 10 *British Journal of Social Work* 133.

[21] Smith and Corden *op. cit.* n. 14.

[22] S. Cohen in "The Punitive City: Notes on the Dispersal of Social Control" (1979) 3 *Contemporary Crises* 339 offers some examples, together with heavy critical commentary.

[23] See S. Reid, "The Community Care Scheme as perceived by some adolescents involved in it"; unpublished undergraduate thesis Edinburgh University 1983.

[24] The literature review was based on Burgess *op. cit.* n. 20, J. Butler *et. al.*. "Task-Centred Casework with Marital Problems" (1978) 8 *British Journal of Social Work*, 393 T. Campbell, "Discretionary Rights" in N. Timms and D. Watson (eds.), *Philosophy in Social Work* (1978): Cohen *op. cit.* n. 22; Collins *op. cit.* 10, Corden *op. cit.* n. 5, M. Goldberg *et. al.* "Exploring the task centred casework method" *Social Work Today* May 6, 1977, Hazel *op. cit.* n. 13; J. Hutton, "Short Term Contracts III" *Social Work Today* November 27, 1975; "Short Term Contracts IV *Social Work Today* Janurary 8, 1976; J. E. Mayer and N. Timms, *The Client Speaks* (1970); P. Parsloe, "The Use of 'Contracts' in a social work course" mimeo (n.d.) Pincus and Monaham, *Social Work Practice: Model and Method* (1975). Chap. 9. S. Rees, "No more than contact" (1974) 4 *British Journal of Social Work* p. 255 S. Rees and A. Wallace, *Verdicts on Social Work* (1982); Reid and Shyne *op. cit.* n. 7; Reid and Epstein *op. cit.* n. 7 and Smith and Corden *op. cit.* n. 21.

[25] This study of social workers in Scotland has since been followed up with intensive interviews of over one hundred social workers, lawyers and others in London and elsewhere in England. The data from this project, which was carried out with the assistance of Stewart Hughan, is currently being transcribed from the recorded interviews but results so far are consistent with the findings of the pilot study.

[26] I am grateful to Mrs Nancy Drucker of Edinburgh University Social Administration Department for help in arranging these interviews.

[27] Reid *op. cit.* n. 23.
[28] Reid *ibid*.
[29] *Cf.* Walter *op. cit.* n. 19.
[30] See Macaulay *op. cit.* n. 6.

Reservation of Title in the Construction Industry: Who Wants It?— Some Economic Perspectives on Risk-Allocation

ANTOINETTE WILLIAMS

Introduction

This paper explores the problem of risk-allocation which is implicit in disputes over the ownership of materials on a construction site where the main builder becomes insolvent between receiving payment for the goods from the client and passing the money on to the supplier. Before 1976, few lawyers would have thought that this question of ownership raised any difficult or controversial issues. According to the Sale of Goods Act 1893, the builder would acquire title to the goods well before delivery to the site. This could of course be varied by the contract between the builder and the supplier, but there did not seem to be any compelling reason to do so. As to the position between the client and builder, the building contract would normally stipulate that ownership passes to the client when she/he pays the builder for the goods. Thus before 1976, a dispute between client and supplier over ownership of goods on a construction site would have been resolved in favour of the client. However, in that year, the Court of Appeal decided *Aluminium Industrie Vaassen B.V.* v. *Romalpa Aluminium Ltd.*,[1] a dispute between a supplier of aluminium foil and a buyer which at the time of the writ, was on the brink of receivership. The court held that where a sales contract stipulates that a buyer of goods will become owner only when it has paid in full; requires the buyer to store the seller's goods apart from those which it has paid for; and defines the relationship between buyer and seller as "fiduciary," the seller owned, and therefore could retake possession of goods which it had delivered and the buyer had not paid for. In addition, the seller had a valid claim to the proceeds from resale of goods which the buyer had delivered to sub-purchasers before going into receivership where the sub-purchasers had paid the Receiver.

In short, by structuring the contract so that transfer of title is

233

conditional on receiving payment in full, a seller of goods could find itself at the front of the line of creditors awaiting distribution of the assets of an insolvent debtor.

Reaction to the decisions was dramatic and immediate. Cline reports that the lawyers involved in the dispute received an "unusual" number of enquiries.[2] It is clear from the report of *Re Bond Worth*[3] that the seller—Monsanto—had tried to modify its existing contract with Bond Worth to take advantage of the *Romalpa* decision before that case had been reported.[4] Slade J., when delivering judgment in *Bond Worth*, noted that "clauses purporting to reserve proprietary rights . . . to a vendor on a sale of goods are now in quite common use in this country."[5] By 1978, the Joint Contracts Tribunal[6]—the agency which drafts the principal standard form building contracts for non-government projects—thought it necessary to warn clients not to over-react to reservation of title clauses in contracts to supply materials to construction projects.[7]

At a general level, the debate over enforcement of reservation of title clauses illustrates conflicts between policies such as sanctity of contract and fair distribution of assets on insolvency. It also highlights the importance of careful planning of commercial relationships and reveals tensions between classical forms of contracting and the complexity of modern structures for organising economic activity. Attempting to resolve these issues by reference to concepts of agency, bailment, trusts, sale, charging, tracing and to canons of construction leads to technical knockouts, anomalies, complexity and unpredictability.[8]

The current uncertainty over the status of reservation of title clauses does make life difficult for business persons. The Report of the Review Committee of Insolvency Law and Practice (The Cork Report)[9] notes an overwhelming "cry for certainty"[10]:

> "Consultee after consultee has put to us, . . . a series of illus-trations of commercial circumstances in which the position regarding the competing claims of supplier, debenture-holder, liquidator and others in respect of goods supplied under a reservation of title clause is confused and unclear. The common refrain is that there must be certainty, since otherwise there will be interminable litigation resolving a host of nice and difficult points."[11]

But in the following paragraphs of the Report, the Committee rejects the plea arguing that "perplexing and difficult problems" are an inevitable consequence of "the wide variety of clauses imposing reservation of title which can be employed, the many different commercial circumstances in which goods can be supplied and used, and the present illogical and complex law relating to security in respect of goods."[12] This part of the Report concludes that certainty is probably unobtainable, but the Committee was optimistic that "contesting parties will be able to negotiate their way to a commercial settlement without incurring the expense of litigating abstruse legal points."[13]

What is lacking from the debate so far is systematic analysis of the implications of enforcing reservation of title clauses for activity in different sectors of the economy. That is to say, research into the consequences of enforcing these terms in particular commercial circumstances. This type of analysis would help to identify the nature and scope of problems created by such clauses. For instance, it might be shown that in some industries economic agents readily adapt to reservation of title clauses as just another contract term which defines the allocation of risk. On the other hand, the organisation of an industry might be such that these clauses have side-effects which are not found in other contexts. The reported cases to date suggest that the judges are beginning to formulate distinctions based on the nature of the buyer's business and what it intends to do with the goods.[14] However, as the scope for investigating the commercial context of a dispute before the court is limited, it is hard to know whether there is any rational, as opposed to conceptual, basis for the categories which are developing.

A conventional legal framework does create difficulties for analysing commercial justifications for, and implications of, contract terms. The common law approach focuses on reasons rather than effects. It tends to be inward-looking: concerned with the logic and consistency of a set of decisions as opposed to the impact of a decision. Of course, these comments refer to general tendencies, there are plenty of examples of judgments which regard an outcome as "good" because it is thought to enhance some value associated with that area of common law. The problem is that the current approach to resolution of commercial disputes does not attempt explicitly to weigh up the implications of alternative choices.

This paper considers the role which economic theory might play in resolving problems which arise from reservation of title clauses in contracts to supply input to a construction project. While economics cannot produce a definitive solution to all interest-conflicts created by this type of clause; by providing "a new metaphor"[15] this type of analysis does highlight issues which are obscured by the traditional legal approach. In particular, the techniques of economics supply tools for exploring some implications of choosing to protect one interest at the expense of another.

Part I sets the context for later discussion by outlining the basic structure of a construction project. It identifies the main participants; describes the network of contractual relationships; and sketches out the payment procedure under the main standard form of building contract for medium to large-scale projects. This section goes on to explain the general rules on passing of property in the context of a building project and how these might be affected by reservation of title clauses. Part II discusses economic theory and some of the analytical perspectives which form part of the economic approach to law. It also demonstrates how these models would tackle questions about allocation of the risk that a builder will go into liquidation before completing performance of its contracts. Used carefully, these economic insights help to explain why a problem exists; to clarify the objectives behind potential solutions; and to evaluate different methods of arriving at a solution. The final section interprets the responses of the Joint Contracts Tribunal (J.C.T.) to reservation of title clauses in the light of insights derived from the economic models.

Part I—The Construction Process

A. The organisation of a building project[16]

Construction is a complex production process. The list of participants in a medium to large-scale project includes: the client, an architect, a quantity surveyor, a general contractor, ordinary and specialist sub-contractors, ordinary and specialist suppliers and statutory utility suppliers. All except the last are linked to the project by a contract with the client or with the general contractor.

The client engages an architect to supply design and supervision services and to act as one of her/his representatives on the site. A large part of the role of the modern architect consists of operating complex contractual procedures. The quantity surveyor also contracts directly with the client. Her/his general function is to give cost advice at the start of the project and to maintain control over costs as work progresses. This will frequently include operating the payment procedures in conjunction with the architect.

In terms of building production, the central contractual bond is between the client and the general contractor (the general). The general undertakes to complete the Contract Works (the Works) for the sum agreed, the effect of which is that the general is fully responsible to the client for all labour and materials input to the project.[17]

An ordinary (domestic) sub-contractor supplies labour and materials input to the project under a contract with the general. The main contract usually stipulates that the general cannot engage a domestic sub-contractor unless the client (or the architect acting on behalf of the client) gives permission to sub-let that part of the Works, but this is normally a formality. Once the client or architect gives approval, all decisions about the sub-contract are for the general and domestic sub-contractor alone. Neither the client nor any of her/his representatives participates in decisions about selection of a sub-contractor or the terms of the sub-contract. Specialist (nominated) sub-contractors are selected by the client or the architect. The general usually has limited, contractually defined, rights to refuse to contract with the specialist chosen by the client,[18] but otherwise does not participate in decisions about selection, terms, or price. However, it is the general who contracts with a nominated sub-contractor, and again, is fully responsible to the client for labour and materials provided by the sub-contractor.[19]

There is a similar distinction between specialist and ordinary suppliers both of which contribute materials only. The architect acting on behalf of the client selects a nominated supplier, but neither she/he nor any other representative of the client participates in transactions with an ordinary supplier. Nominated suppliers are engaged for those parts of the Works where the client wants a particular input or "finish." As with nominated sub-contractors, the general has little control over the identity of the specialist, or the terms of its contract with the specialist.[20] An ordinary supplier contracts with the general to sell standard input—bricks, timber, slates, etc. The specification for the main contract usually describes these items in sufficiently broad terms that the general can select from a number of sources, and of course, the general is free to negotiate its own terms without reference to the client or her/his representatives.

B. *The procedure for payment*

Building contracts are traditionally classified as lump-sum entire contracts to supply work and materials.[21] As such, "substantial performance" by the general contractor is a condition precedent to a claim for any part of the contract sum.[22] Today, few construction firms could extend credit to a client for the entire production period, and the cost of borrowing would increase building costs dramatically.[23] Thus, standard form building contracts include a procedure for periodic payment. The usual practice is for the general contractor to meet current liabilities to sub-contractors and suppliers from this interim payment.

Clause 30 of the principal standard form contract produced by the Joint Contracts Tribunal (J.C.T.80) sets out the machinery for instalment payments under that contract. At the start of the transaction the client and the general contractor agree on the interval for payment.[24] Once the project is underway, the architect operates the procedure. She/he must draw up a schedule of all work and materials that qualify for payment at the intervals stated in the contract.[25] This schedule must include materials which are on the site and ready for incorporation into the Works.[26] After certifying the quantity of materials and labour which qualifies for payment, the architect must either price the input herself/himself, or call on the quantity surveyor to value it.[27] The client is contractually bound to pay the sum stated on the schedule within 14 days of the date of issue.[28] According to clause 16 of the main contract, property in materials on the site passes to the client when she/he pays the general the amount certified as due for that input. But this term does not of itself bind input suppliers who are not party to the main contract. As the payment goes directly to the general who has sole control over distribution of the sum, it is difficult for a client to ensure that the general passes the money on to sub-contractors and suppliers as intended.

C. *Reservation of title clauses and the construction process*

Most of the decisions about the validity of reservation of title clauses are concerned with a seller's rights against a receiver or liquidator of the insolvent buyer. The conflict is between a financial creditor who holds orthodox security—usually a floating charge—and a trade creditor who, without the contested clause would be just another unsecured creditor. Thus the main focus of the debate over validity is whether the law should permit reservation of title clauses to operate outside the registration requirements for conventional forms of security.[29]

Within the construction process, the more significant conflict is between an input supplier (either a sub-contractor or a supplier of materials only) who has delivered goods and not received payment, and a client who has paid the insolvent builder for the materials. Thus, the question is whether a claim to the goods which is based on a reservation of title clause should override a claim derived from possession together with actual payment to an intermediary. The underlying problem is to decide which of the two parties—client or supplier[30]—has assumed the risk of the general becoming insolvent before completing performance of its contracts. This may not be clear from the terms of the arrangements because the general who contracts with both client and input suppliers does not have a direct interest in rational allocation of the risk of its own liquidation. And, the absence of a contractual link between the client and input suppliers means that there is no forum for those parties to decide upon the appropriate allocation of the costs of that contingency. Thus it may be that the allocation of risk resulting from the two contracts (between client and general and between supplier and general) is indeterminate. In this situation, a dispute between client and supplier over ownership of materials on the site falls to be resolved in accordance with general rules of law. And the implicit question is which of the two parties "ought" to bear the risk of the general going into liquidation.

Assuming that in this context there is no relevant difference between a sub-contractor who supplies materials and labour and a supplier who sells materials only, the technical distinction between a sale of goods transaction and a contract to supply materials together with labour, potentially creates an obstacle to rational risk-allocation.

The contract between the general and a supplier of materials only, is an orthodox transaction for the sale of goods. Therefore, unless the parties to the contract agree to a specific term relating to transfer of title, property passes in accordance with the rules in section 18 of the Sale of Goods Act 1979. In fact, the structure of relationships within a construction project is such that any sales contract is likely to provide that title does not pass to the general until the supplier receives payment.[31] (A general contractor may be able to obtain goods more cheaply if a supplier has a reservation of title clause and it does not face the adverse consequences of accepting the term. To the extent that a general contractor can control the terms of its contracts with input suppliers, there is nothing to prevent it agreeing to include this type of term in any contract.) Where a reservation of title clause is valid between the general and supplier, it means that the general does not own the goods until the seller receives payment. Therefore, the general cannot pass title to its client unless the latter falls within the protection of section 25 of the Sale of Goods Act 1979. The effect of this section is that a buyer who has a seller's consent to possess goods which she/he has bought or agreed to buy, can pass good title to a purchaser who buys in good faith and without notice of any rights to the goods which the original seller retains. Thus, if a client can show that she/he bought materials in good faith and without knowledge of a supplier's reservation of title clause, she/he will have a complete defence to any claim from the supplier.

The decision in *Fourpoint Garage* v. *Carter*[32] illustrates the general point. The dispute concerned ownership of a car which the defendant had agreed to buy from a dealer. The dealer had arranged for the plaintiff to deliver the car to the defendant. For reasons which are unclear, the plaintiff did not realise that the dealer sold vehicles; it thought that the defendant was hiring the car rather than purchasing it. In turn, the defendant knew nothing of the plaintiff and assumed that the dealer had delivered the car. Inevitably, the contract of sale between the plaintiff and dealer contained a reservation of title clause. This formed the basis of the plaintiff's claim to repossess the vehicle when the dealer went into liquidation between receiving payment from the defendant and paying the plaintiff.

The plaintiff argued that the defendant was not protected by section 25 of the Sale of Goods Act 1979 because that defence requires an intermediary to take possesion of the goods and as it had delivered to the defendant, the car dealer had never obtained possession. The second argument was that the dealer did not have the right to sell the car to the defendant because it had neither title to the goods, nor authority to sell. There was no explicit authority stated in the contract between the plaintiff and the intermediary garage; and the plaintiff argued that authority to sell should not be implied because of its mistake about the nature of the dealer's business.

The Judge found for the defendant. He thought that in the context of the dispute, there was no significant distinction between direct delivery to a sub-purchaser and delivery to an intermediary who then transferred possession to a sub-purchaser. The quirk of fact that the plaintiff happened to take the car to the defendant could not affect the application of section 25. Simon Brown J. gave short shrift to the second argument. As there was no evidence that the dealer had attempted to mislead the plaintiff about the nature of its business there was no reason to refuse to apply the "*Romalpa* principle" of implied authorisation to resell.[33]

If, and it is a big if, this decision is followed in a dispute between supplier and client, it will mean that a supplier cannot enforce a reservation of title clause by making a direct claim against a client who has paid the general contractor.

The transaction between a general contractor and a sub-contractor is not a contract for the sale of goods but a contract to supply labour and materials.[34] Orthodox analysis would suggest that a general contractor does not at any point buy, or agree to buy, the materials which a sub-contractor supplies. Hence, the general does not at any stage acquire property in the goods and so it has nothing to pass on to the client. As there is no equivalent to section 25 for this type of transaction, the effect of the general rules is that an unpaid sub-contractor can reclaim the goods (or their value) at least until the materials become part of the building.[35] *Dawber Williamson Roofing Ltd.* v. *Humberside County Council*[36] illustrates this analysis. In January 1976, Humberside County Council (H.C.C.) entered into a building contract by which a firm called Taylor & Coulbeck (T.C.) undertook to build a school. The parties used a revised version of the 1963 edition of the J.C.T. standard form of building contract. In May 1976, T.C. sub-let the roof-work to Dawber Williamson (D.W.). The domestic sub-contract incorporated a J.C.T. standard form of sub-contract. This did not mention ownership of materials which were to be used to fulfil the sub-contract, but it did state that the sub-contractor is "deemed to have notice" of the terms of the main contract. Clause 14 of that contract stated that property in materials which had been delivered to the site passed to the client when it paid the value of the goods as certified by the architect.

In November 1976, D.W. delivered to the site the roofing slate which it intended to use to fulfil the sub-contract. It sent an invoice to H.C.C. at the end of November. On December 6 the architect issued an interim certificate which included the sum of £4500 for the slate. The client included this sum in a payment to T.C. which had not passed this on to D.W. by January 24, 1977 when it (T.C.) went into liquidation.

After some negotiation between H.C.C. and D.W., the sub-contractor agreed to complete the roof on a "fix-only" basis (a contract for labour only) because the client had refused to make an additional direct payment for the materials. D.W. then issued a writ claiming the value of the slates; damages for retention or conversion of the goods; and damages for the cost of labour and profit.

The Judge found for the plaintiff, reasoning that a sub-contract is a contract for the supply of work and materials, not for the sale of goods. Therefore, a general contractor does not acquire property rights in materials delivered to the site. If the general does not have title to the goods, it cannot pass ownership to its client, whatever the terms of the main contract. As it is usually possible for parties to contract around general rules of contract law, the Judge also considered whether there was anything in the sub-contract to show that the parties (T.C. and D.W.) had intended T.C. to acquire rights which it could pass to the client. On this point, Mais J., thought that the "deemed to have notice" stipulation was not sufficient to incorporate clause 14 (or any other term) of the main contract into the sub-contract; and the privity doctrine meant that the clause could not operate directly against D.W. Thus, H.C.C. was required to make an additional direct payment to the plaintiff with little prospect of recovering the money which it had previously paid to the insolvent builder.

To summarise, the general rules of law create a sharp distinction between the position of the sub-contractor, who supplies goods and labour and the supplier who supplies goods only. Where the general contractor goes into liquidation while goods are on site prior to incorporation, and the client has paid the general; a sub-contractor may bring a direct claim against the client without using a reservation of title clause. Under the same circumstance, a supplier of materials alone may bring such a claim only if it can show: that its contract with the general includes a reservation of title clause: and that the client falls outside the ambit of section 25 of the Sale of Goods Act 1979. This difference in treatment may be quite significant because it is frequently a matter of chance whether a particular input supplier is classified as a sub-contractor or supplier.[37] It seems unlikely that participants in the construction industry intend the label to make such a difference to the allocation of the risk that a general contractor will go into liquidation before completing its contracts.

However, it may be that the anomaly is more a matter of form than of substance. The decision in *Fourpoint Garage* v. *Carter*[38] is probably not a reliable guide for the construction industry. The Judge made no attempt to generalise from the facts before him. In the context of the particular dispute it was significant that the defendant was an individual consumer while the plaintiff operated in the same business and locality as the insolvent dealer.[39] It is by no means clear that in the very different context of the construction industry, a dispute between a client and a supplier of materials would have the same outcome. First of all, it is arguably the client or her/his representatives who have the closer link with the intermediary (at least for the duration of the project). Secondly, it is improbable that a client can remain ignorant of the terms on which suppliers deliver materials to the project. In most situations, a supplier would simply need to send the client a copy of its contract with the general to ensure that the client could not rely on section 25. If this analysis is correct, a supplier of materials alone who is not protected by general rules may shift the risk of the builder becoming insolvent during the period between delivery and incorporation of the goods, by informing the client that its contract with the builder contains a reservation of title clause.

Part II Economic Perspectives[40]

Economic anlaysis of law views legal rules as a system of incentives and constraints which influence the decisions of actors within a society. It is an *ex ante* approach; a perspective which explores the implications of rules for human behaviour. Thus economic analysis of common law regards potential litigants as more significant than the two parties before a court.

At a general level economics provides techniques for analysing the implications of scarcity. The fact that resources are scarce means that it is not possible for everyone to satisfy her/his wants from the resources available to society. One consequence of scarcity is that society develops mechanisms for rationing its available resources among competing claimants.

Neoclassical microeconomics explores the effects of rationing by individual decisions to trade property rights in the market. Whatever its purpose, whether the aim is explanation; definition of objectives; or predicting outcomes, the standard neoclassical model starts with the assumptions that markets are perfectly competitive and individuals who trade in markets are rational utility or profit maximisers. These assumptions do not pretend to describe accurately the real context of trade or the way that an individual acts when she/he makes a choice. Instead they are used to formulate generalisations about the behaviour of economic agents as a group. The economist's rational utility or profit maximiser is not a real person any more than is the lawyer's "reasonable man." While the reasonable person of negligence liability is a criterion for making normative decisions *ex post*, it sets the standard to whch the behaviour of a real person "ought" to have conformed; the rational utility or profit-maximiser establishes a basis for *ex ante* positive generalisations about decisions that economic agents will make.

A. Positive economics

Positive economic analysis enquires into the consequences of a change in some part of the economic system. The analyst starts by developing a model which she/he uses to generate a hypothesis that an alteration in one variable will have such an impact on aggregate decisions that the trading process will produce a different outcome to that before the change. This proposition is subject to an important limitation: that is, the predicted difference in outcome will occur only if all other things in the economic system remain as they were before the change. The next stage is to test the hypothesis by subjecting empirical observations to statistical analysis. Observing the predicted outcome does not prove that the model is true, rather that it has not been falsified and so can stand until it does not accurately predict responses to change as frequently as a competing model. It should be emphasised that this type of analysis is always partial in the sense that it focuses on the relationship between one factor and another, rather than on how a change affects the full decision-making calculus. The purpose of simplifying in this way is to identify those factors which are significant to human choice.

1. The market for credit terms. As positive economics lacks the analytical equipment to assess the merits of a policy choice, its main role in evaluating law is to provide a framework for examining the impact of a change in the law on something that can be measured. Thus, positive economics cannot "prove" that reservation of title clauses are good for society or bad for society; but, it can provide some insights into the credit implications for a particular industry of moving from validity to invalidity or vice versa.

A change from blanket non-enforceability to universal use and enforcement of reservation of title clauses could be modelled as a move from a position where the right to the income stream from materials to be used in a building passes to a client when a supplier delivers the goods (and the parties cannot vary this rule); to a situation where that right passes when the supplier receives payment (and again the parties cannot vary this rule)[41] one effect of such a change is that clients realise at the start of a project that they may be required to pay twice for goods which are delivered on credit terms. For suppliers, the change reduces the risk that they will not receive any payment for goods which they supply on credit terms. Thus altering the rule shifts the risk of the general contractor becoming insolvent from suppliers to clients.[42] Assuming for the moment that it is cheaper for suppliers to bear this risk,[43] the change means that it costs the client more to obtain supplies on credit terms than it did previously. That expenditure which used to buy her/him an absolute right to the asset, must now also cover the expected cost of the general going into liquidation before it pays its suppliers. Because the change requires clients to pay more to obtain the same quantity of goods on credit terms, positive economics would predict that they will react by buying fewer of the goods on credit terms than they did previously.[44]

Conversely, suppliers will derive greater benefit from selling materials on credit terms at the old price. The profit maximising price before the change would have covered both production (and delivery) costs and the expected cost of the general contractor becoming insolvent without paying for the goods. As the supplier no longer bears this risk, that part of the price which was intended to protect against the contingency becomes part of the profit from the transaction. So if suppliers could sell the same quantity of goods on the same credit terms (including price) as before the change, they would make greater profit. However, it is unlikely that suppliers would be able to sell the same quantity of goods at the old price. First of all, the model also predicts that clients would demand fewer goods because the change means a rise in price for that side of the market. Secondly, the quantity that they used to sell will no longer be the level of output which produces the greatest possible profit. It would be more profitable for suppliers to expand the quantity that they produce until the cost of producing and delivering the last unit of the good on credit terms is equal to the revenue that they would make from selling that last unit. But increasing the quantity of the goods means that it is not as scarce as before the change and so the theory would predict that the price would fall.

If, contrary to the initial assumption, the cost to the client of assuming the risk of the general contractor becoming insolvent were the same as the cost to the supplier of bearing this risk, the switch from invalidity to enforcement may cause a fall in market price but not affect the quantity of goods supplied on credit terms. The interaction of demand and supply would cause the original price (which included the expected cost to suppliers of a general contractor becoming insolvent) to fall by the amount which clients must "pay" to protect themselves against that risk. If these two amounts are the same, the model would predict that the market will stabilise at a point where the original quantity of goods are supplied at a lower credit price.

This description of positive economics is of course very crude. It is intended only to outline: the type of question that the analyst would ask—"how will the market for construction materials sold on credit terms react to a change which shifts a particular risk from suppliers to buyers?"; and the method of arriving at some answers. A complete economic model of this issue would also take account of the competitive structure of the market; the sensitivity of each side of the market to changes in costs; and the time frame for the analysis.

Traditionally, this type of positive analysis provides techniques for comparing two stable positions. The models aim to evaluate the impact of a change. Thus they start by predicting what will happen once the smoke clears and the economic system settles into equilibrium (however temporary) after the change. A developing use of positive economics in analysis of private law is to predict the responses of economic agents to a rule or legal institution. Thus the focus shifts from comparing the predicted stable outcome of a change in the law with the previous situation, to predicting the reactions of economic actors to the existing position and exploring why those reactions will occur. This approach might model the problem of rational allocation of the risk that a general contractor will become insolvent as a "creditors' bargain." The aim of the analysis is to predict when a client and supplier would agree that the client will make an additional direct payment to the supplier if the general becomes insolvent.

2. The "creditors' bargain."[45] Suppose that a legal regime allocates to a client the right to the income stream from an asset from the date of delivery to the construction site, but leaves clients and suppliers free to change this allocation. Assuming that the processes of bargaining, maintaining and enforcing contracts do not consume resources,[46] positive economic analysis predicts that rational profit maximising parties will change the official allocation of rights when each perceives the alteration to be in its best interests. For a client to agree to relinquish her/his right, she/he must believe herself/himself to be better off if she/he bears the risk of the general contractor becoming insolvent than if the supplier bears that risk. This will be the case where the cost to a client of bearing the risk is less than the reduction in price that the supplier would offer in exchange for the right to make a direct claim. In this situation the benefit to the client from a lower price outweighs this part of the expected costs of the general contractor going into liquidation.[47] Turning to the supplier, it will want the right to make a direct claim where it believes that the cost of securing the right (the discount from the price it can charge) is less than the benefit of knowing that it will not lose out if the general contractor becomes insolvent before paying for the goods. The crucial issue is to decide when clients and suppliers will hold these beliefs and so, in the absence of transaction costs, would negotiate for a reservation of title clause.

As the perspective is *ex ante*, an economist would look for reasons why at the start of a project, the expected costs of the same contingency might differ between clients and suppliers. One possibility is that the two parties have different attitudes to risk so that any uncertainty about the future is more harmful to one of them and thus is regarded as more costly by that party than by the other.[48] A second explanation is that although both have the same attitude to risk, one party estimates that the event is less likely to occur than the other believes. The expected cost of a contingency is lower for the party who believes the event to be less likely than for the person who thinks that the event is more probable. For example, suppose that a client believes that there is a 1 in 1000 chance of the general contractor becoming insolvent so that if a supplier has a reservation of title clause, she/he will have to make a direct payment of £5000 after having paid that sum to the general. And the supplier believes that the probability is 1 in 500, so that if it does not have a reservation of title clause, it will lose £5000.[49] At the start of the project, the client estimates this part of the expected costs of the general becoming insolvent to be £5 (£5000 × 0.001) and the supplier believes the expected cost to be £10 (£5000 × 0.002). If the structure of the market is such that the full expected cost must be borne either by the client or by the supplier, it would be rational for the client to agree to assume the risk. The cost to the client of assuming the risk is half of the amount which she/he would pay the supplier to bear the risk. Therefore, when viewed *ex ante*, the cost of producing the building(s) will be lower if the client agrees that she/he will pay twice if the general goes into liquidation.

A further consideration which might influence the outcome of the creditor's bargain is the extent to which one party is better able to "cover" against the risk of insolvency. That is to say, how far one person is in a better position to spread the expected cost of liquidation of the general over a range of transaction. The effect of distributing the loss is to reduce the actual expected cost of an event.

Suppose that a supplier 'S' has one hundred contracts to supply timber to construction sites and that for each transaction it is to supply timber worth £5000. Further assume that for all contracts except that involving client 'A,' S knows that it will receive payment because the price is payable on delivery. The only risky transaction is that with the general engaged by 'A.' If 'S' believes that there is a 1 in 500 chance of that builder becoming insolvent before it pays for the timber, the nominal expected cost of the contingency is £10. However, 'S' can cover all of that loss by charging each customer an extra ten pence. Of course, if 'A's' general contractor does go into liquidation before paying 'S,' the supplier will not recover ten pence from that customer. Thus the real expected cost of the event to 'S' is ten pence. If the expected cost to 'A' were again £5 (£5000 x 0.001), positive economics would predict that 'S' will not want to negotiate a reservation of title clause. The supplier would have to "pay" (discount its price by) £5 for the client to assume the risk. But having the clause would make the supplier only ten pence better off than it is without the term. Therefore, 'S' would suffer a net loss of £4.90 if it did bargain for the right to make a direct claim against 'A.'

As the creditors' bargain aims only to identify those factors which affect decisions about risk-allocation, it cannot by itself determine whether enforcement of reservation of title clauses is desirable. However, an important initial assumption of the model is that bargaining and enforcing contracts does not consume resources—the assumption that transaction costs are zero. Failure to observe the ideal creditors' bargain in the "real-world" might mean either that the model is falsified or that there are costs to transacting which prevent parties achieving the profit-maximising allocation of risks. The dominant approach to normative economic analysis of law builds the latter explanation into its framework for evaluating rules. Applied to the "current legal problem" under discussion, this argument suggests that reservation of title clauses ought to be enforced where client and supplier would have agreed to the term if transaction costs had been zero.

B. Normative economic analysis

Normative economic analysis is concerned with developing criteria for comparing situations by reference to their impact on social welfare.[50] One situation is better than another if it produces a greater amount of social welfare when both are measured on the same index. The dominant criterion in economic analysis of common law is allocative efficiency. This marks the point at which every resource is put to the most productive use possible or enjoyed by the person who values it most highly. The two main definitions of what it means to say that resources are allocated efficiently are 'Pareto' efficiency[51] and 'Kaldor-Hicks' efficiency.[52]

Pareto efficiency rests on the twin premises that: each individual is the only judge of her/his welfare; and the welfare of society depends on the welfare of each member of that society. An allocation of resources is 'Pareto efficient' if it is not possible to increase the welfare of one individual without decreasing the welfare of another. According to this test a change in the law is an improvement only if it benefits at least one person and no-one is worse off after the change than she/he was before. The 'Kaldor-Hicks' test regards a change as an improvement in social welfare if those who benefit gain so much that they *could* compensate those who lose and still be better off than in the previous situation.

The hypothetical perfectly competitive market produces allocative efficiency as measured by the Pareto criterion. So where the
outcome of "real-world" markets diverges from that predicted by
the model, it means that one or more of the restrictive assumptions
does not hold true. As a result, too great a proportion of society's
resources are devoted to some activities and insufficient resources
are allocated to others. In this situation the economist aims to
identify reasons for failure in the market and to devise correctives.
The 'Kaldor-Hicks' test provides a method for evaluating
responses to market failure.

Modern interest in common law enforcement of private rights as
a corrective technique started with R.H. Coase's seminal analysis
of social costs.[53] Coase argued that private bargaining could in
theory correct resource misallocation caused by external costs—the
situation where someone does not take full account of harmful
effects which follow from her/his activity. The specific focus of his
analysis is the situation where one person's use of her/his property
interferes with another's use of her/his own property.[54] The standard economic response to the presence of an externality was to
impose a tax that is equivalent to the costs borne by other members
of society, in order to force the producer to pay the "social cost" of
her/his activity. The purpose of the tax was not to compensate those
who were harmed but to reduce the amount of the harmful activity
and thus correct the misallocation of resources to that use.

Coase began by reformulating the problem. He argued that the
source of harm was not the activity but competing claims to use the
same resource. Each claim must be satisfied from one bundle of
resources which is insufficient to satisfy both fully. By removing
either claim on the resource, society would remove the harm. In
other words, loss or damage has reciprocal causes; the presence of
the injured person and the presence of the active person. This
model suggested that both lawyers and economists were misguided
in their traditional focus on the active person.

The next stage of the argument considered how society might
decide which claim should prevail. At this point Coase suggests
that regarding this question as one for "society" is misleading.
Administrative bodies or other state agencies are not necessarily
the best institutions for making decisions about resource allocation. An alternative approach would be to leave the decision to
those most intimately affected by it. If the active person values the
activity more than the other values her/his freedom from interference, it is better for society that the former uses the resource and
the other gives up her/his claim to freedom from interference. The
"Coase theorem" asserts that so long as rights are well-defined;

there are only two claimants and each is perfectly informed; markets are competitive and there are no transaction costs, the parties will reach a privately and socially efficient bargain whatever the initial assignment of property rights. In other words, when these assumptions hold, efficient resource use is unaffected by the initial allocation of property rights. Of course, the other side of the coin is that where any of the restrictive assumptions fail, the original assignment of property rights does matter. In particular, where transaction costs are significant,[55] the parties may find that it is too costly to bargain their way to a privately efficient outcome and so will not be able to correct resource misallocation. In these circumstances, private law could neutralise the impact of transaction costs if it were able to structure liability rules so that they replicated the outcome of the optimal private bargain.

The main reason why suppliers want to use reservation of title clauses—and clients resist them—is lack of information about the chances of the general contractor surviving its contracts. Failure of the general's business is an event which cannot be controlled by clients or suppliers, thus neither can be sure whether or when it will occur. As a result, privately rational transactions between client and general and between supplier and general may not be socially optimal when viewed together.

As neither client nor supplier can prevent the general contractor going into liquidation before it completes the contracts, the main thrust of attempts to minimise the expected costs of the contingency will be devoted to precautionary strategies. The individually rational reaction is for each to engage in precautionary measures until the cost of an additional unit of protection (to that person) is the same as the increase in benefit from having that unit of protection. But to the extent that clients and suppliers act independently, it is likely that they will duplicate investment in precautions (and so duplicate the cost) without any corresponding increase in protection. Thus, uncertainty as to the probability of a general contractor surviving to complete its contracts could mean that too great a proportion of society's resources is devoted to precautionary measures.

For example, one reaction to the knowledge that some general contractors become insolvent before fully performing their contracts is for clients and suppliers (acting separately) to acquire more information about the likelihood of a potential co-contractor becoming insolvent during the contract period. Clients might engage in a thorough investigation of the financial health of tenderers. This could involve examining accounts; seeking references from banks and other financial institutions; and contacting previous clients. Suppliers might try to find out from other local trade creditors whether there is any reason to be wary of extending credit to this particular builder.

This type of precautionary measure is inevitably costly. It requires clients and suppliers to set up administrative procedures for collecting, sorting and evaluating information. While it is rational for each to invest in acquiring information until the point where the benefit from an additional item is equal to the cost of acquiring that piece of information; it is wasteful for both to invest in gathering the same information. In the context of construction, the potential for duplication of search costs is exacerbated by the degree of specialisation in the industry the main effect of which is that every building project uses input from several independent suppliers.

Another private response to uncertainty whether a general contractor will remain solvent is for clients and suppliers to insure against the expected costs of default. Assuming that most transactions are completed successfully, a client or supplier could recoup the expected loss on one contract by adding a small percentage of that loss to the price of every other contract.[56] This response is most obviously available to a supplier of standard material input to a project—someone who makes a large number of virtually identical contracts. However, specialist suppliers, subcontractors and clients who may not have the same volume of transactions could achieve the same end by purchasing market insurance. Again the fragmentation of the construction industry means that this reaction creates the possibility of waste; using either type of insurance mechanism consumes resources which could be deployed elsewhere.

Where independent action by suppliers and clients means that the aggregate cost of an additional unit of protection is greater than the benefit from that unit, it would be better for social efficiency if fewer resources were devoted to precautionary measures. One method of achieving this reduction is to allocate the expected costs of the contingency to one person (preferably the one who belongs to the group which can take precautions most cheaply). It is at this point that the creditors' bargain of positive economics may play a role in deciding what the law should be.

The privately efficient creditors' bargain is socially efficient if it reduces the total costs of investment in precautions to a level which is justified by the risk of insolvency. As the main effect of one party paying the other to bear the risk of liquidation of a general contractor is that the payor does not need to expend resources on protection; the creditors' bargain will reduce duplication and so tend to lower investment in precautions. Thus, so long as the configuration of transaction costs and market conditions is such that clients and suppliers are able to negotiate a creditors' bargain, the primary role for law is to reinforce the arrangement by upholding the bargain. Imposing a legal sanction on attempts to renege from the creditors' bargain adds to the reliability of the transaction. Therefore, enforcement should further the objective of reducing wasteful duplication of investment in protection. In those circumstances, where transaction costs create such severe obstacles to exchange that clients and suppliers cannot arrange for the optimal allocation of risk. The law would enhance the efficiency index of social welfare if it were able to reproduce the outcome of a hypothetical creditor bargain. Specifically, normative economic analysis suggests that suppliers to a building project should have a direct claim against a client where at the start of the project the expected cost to the client of making additional payments is less than the aggregate cost of each supplier taking precautions.

This type of normative economics may be used to set objectives for the law and to evaluate general rules or specific private provisions in the light of those objectives.[57]

Part III Rational Risk-Allocation and the J.C.T.: Responses to the Implicit Creditors' Bargain

The arguments in Part I suggest that the creditors' bargain implicit in general rules depends upon whether an input supplier is classified as a sub-contractor or a supplier of materials alone, but that this difference is not necessarily fatal to rational allocation of the risk of liquidation of a general contractor. The structure of contractual relationships within a construction project is such that a supplier of materials alone may put itself in the same position as a sub-contractor by ensuring that its contract with the general includes an effective reservation of title clause. However, there remains the question whether it is efficient for a client to bear the risk during the period between delivery of materials to the site and incorporation of those materials into the building. Two responses from the J.C.T. give some indication of the construction industry's view on this matter.

In 1978 the J.C.T. published a formal notice explaining why it was not necessary to amend the standard form contracts to take account of suppliers who had recently discovered reservation of title clauses.[58] The formal notice was a response to information that some clients and professional advisers had reacted to the threat of reservation of title clauses by refusing to pay the general contractor for materials delivered to the site unless the general could prove that it owned the goods. This practice was a clear breach of existing contractual payment procedures. It also appeared that some potential clients were attempting to amend the standard forms so as to make evidence of ownership a condition precedent to the architect certifying payment to the general.

The J.C.T. considered the pros and cons of altering the standard forms and concluded that the costs of trying to nullify reservation of title clauses by requiring the general to prove ownership of the goods far outweighed the benefits which would follow such an amendment. Costs were likely to be high because it would often be very difficult for a general contractor to prove legal ownership of goods delivered to the site. Even if it were willing and able to ensure that the immediate supplier did not retain title, the general would have little control where the immediate supplier was a distributor. For the general to unravel each distribution chain in order to prove ownership of goods delivered to the site would be a costly and complex exercise. Furthermore clients and their professional advisers would also face the administration costs of verifying evidence of ownership. The J.C.T. also argued that a "proof of ownership" requirement, would mean that general contractors could not be sure when they would be paid for materials delivered to the site. A rational response to this uncertainty would be for general contractors to increase their prices. Thus the Tribunal concluded that an effective amendment to the standard form would be likely to increase building costs quite significantly.

On the question whether such a rise in building costs might be justified by an increase in protection for clients, the J.C.T. concluded that the probability of suppliers successfully making a direct claim against a client was low. First of all liquidation of a general contractor during a project was regarded as a very unusual event. Secondly, the creditors' bargain implicit in general rules limited a supplier's claim to goods which it could physically repossess and recycle at low cost—goods had not been incorporated into the building. Therefore in the highly unlikely event of a general contractor going into liquidation during a project, a reservation of title clause could only be enforced where the materials were on the site in their original form. Finally, the Tribunal suggested that a supplier's claim to materials on the site would last only until they were sold to the client. After that point, any claim would be against the proceeds of resale held by the insolvent general. For these reasons the J.C.T. concluded that clients would not in fact gain very much from any attempt to nullify the effect of reservation of title clauses in contracts between general contractors and their supliers.

The J.C.T. was far less sanguine about the implicit creditor's bargain between clients and sub-contractors. In 1984, the Tribunal attempted to reverse the effect of the *Dawber Williamson* decision.[59] The amendment to the standard form contract[60] requires the general contractor to ensure that any sub-contract provides that ownership of materials delivered to the site passes to the client when she/he pays the general for the goods.[61] In addition the sub-contract must include a term to the effect that property in materials delivered to the site passes to the general contractor if it pays the sub-contractor before receiving money from the client.[62]

At first sight this reaction seems a little bizarre. After all, *Dawber Williamson* simply makes it clear that sub-contractors are in the same position as suppliers who use a valid reservation of title clause. Surely the arguments which suggested that it was not necessary to amend the standard form contracts to deal with those who supply materials on terms which include a reservation of title clause apply with equal force where a sub-contractor supplies materials together with labour?

One explanation is that the 1984 amendment establishes the industry's preferred apportionment of the risk of a general contractor becoming insolvent during a project, and that this allocation is optimal no matter what the classification of an input supplier. As sub-contractors are more directly involved in a construction project than suppliers of materials alone, and this involvement is reflected by their membership of the Joint Contracts Tribunal[63]; it is possible to draft a standard form contract so that it incorporates the efficient allocation of risk. By contrast the position between clients and suppliers of materials alone is such that the cost of achieving the optimal allocation is very high.

The difference between the J.C.T.'s two responses might also be explained by a change in circumstances which altered its perception of the expected costs to clients of making additional direct payments to input suppliers. In 1978, the Tribunal noted that very few general contractors become insolvent during a building project. Just two years later the construction industry went into a steep decline.[64] This would suggest that a number of firms dropped out of the industry. Given the production cycle for construction it is unlikely that those firms had no work at all at the time of exit. It may be that by 1984 liquidation of a general contractor during a project was thought to be a more probable event and so pose a greater threat to clients. Thus the J.C.T. felt that some modification to the allocation of this risk was called for.

Finally, it is possible that there are rational grounds for distinguishing between suppliers of labour and materials and suppliers of materials alone. And that the former are in a better position to guard against insolvency of the general contractor than is the client. While as between clients and suppliers of materials alone, it is the client who has the advantage. If this is true, both creditors' bargains implicit in general rules of law allocate the risk of insolvency to the wrong party. Enforcement of reservation of title clauses is then desirable because it provides a simple mechanism which participants in the construction industry can use to re-allocate the risk of insolvency. And the 1984 amendment could be interpreted as an attempt to reverse the other misallocation. More detailed economic analysis of the position of sub-contractors and suppliers relative to clients would enable this hypothesis to be tested.

Concluding Remarks

In any situation where performance of contractual obligation is projected into the future, the parties will lack vital information at the start of the transaction. Thus long-term commercial contracts are largely concerned with risk-management. Within a construction project this task is made more difficult by the number of independent economic agents, each with autonomy over the terms of its participation. An organisation such as the J.C.T. may ameliorate the problem by providing a forum for negotiations between representatives of different interest groups. The outcome of these discussions is reflected in the standard form contracts. However, with respect to the specific risk of a builder going into liquidation after receiving (but not paying) money for delivery of goods to the site by a supplier of materials alone, there remains the problem of deciding which of two inconsistent contracts should prevail. The difficulty arises because there is no direct contractual link between client and supplier and so no *ex ante* apportionment of the risk. In these circumstances economic theory may inform a decision as to who *ought* to bear the risk. A model might suggest how a decision will affect price; how the parties themselves would manage the risk if they had the opportunity to do so; or some objective which a decision-maker might pursue. The question which remains, but which must be left for another occasion, is how far it is appropriate to use these criteria as a basis for making and evaluating decisions?

Notes

¹ [1976] 1 W.L.R. 676.

² (1976) 73 Law Society Gazette 281.

³ [1980] 1 Ch. 228.

⁴ *Aluminium Industrie Vaassen B.V.* v. *Romalpa Aluminium Ltd.*, *supra*, n. 1 was decided in January 1976, but not reported until July 1976. Monsanto wrote to Bond Worth on June 30, 1976 purporting to change the contract so as to include a reservation of title clause [1980] 1 Ch. 228 at 235E–236A.

⁵ *Op.cit.*, at 232G.

⁶ The Joint Contracts Tribunal (J.C.T.) is a representative agency which draws its membership from organisations and trade associations to which most of the major participants in the construction industry belong. Its sole function is to draft, revise and amend standard form contracts. As the Tribunal includes representatives from public sector clients, architects, contractors and sub-contractors; its contracts are regarded as documents which balance the needs of different groups within the industry and as such should be classified as negotiated rather than adhesive standard forms.

⁷ *Retention of Title (Ownership) by Suppliers of Building Materials and Goods* 1978 R.I.B.A. publications. See text at n. 58.

⁸ Iwan Davies, "Reservation of title clauses: a legal quagmire?" [1984] L.M.C.L.Q. 49 provides a detailed account of the conceptual complexities of debates over enforcement of reservation of title clauses. See also Davies, " 'Romalpa' clauses: further developments" [1984] I.M.C.L.Q. 280; Goodhart and Jones , "The Infiltration of Equitable Developments into English Commercial Law" (1980) 43 M.L.R. 489; Garry A. Muir, "Recent Developments in Reservation of Property Clauses" (1985) 13 A.B.L.R. 3.

⁹ Cmnd. 8558 (1982).

¹⁰ *Op.cit.*, para. 1627.

¹¹ *Ibid.*

¹² *Op.cit.*, para. 1628.

¹³ *Op.cit.*, para. 1629.

¹⁴ Where the buyer is a distributor, the seller's reservation of title clause (if adequate) will give it a right to repossess goods on the buyer's premises at the time of receivership or insolvency. And to the proceeds of resale if these are readily identifiable in a separate bank account *Aluminium Industrie Vaassen B.V.* v. *Romalpa Aluminium Ltd. supra*, n. 1. Similarly, where the buyer incorporates the goods into a different product, but the seller's goods can be readily separated from the new product, an adequate reservation of title clause gives the seller a right to repossess its own goods and to the proceeds of sale if these can be identified, *Hendy Lennox (Industrial Engines) Ltd.* v. *Grahame Puttick Ltd.* [1984] 1 W.L.R. 485. Where the buyer uses the goods in a manufacturing process during which the seller's goods lose their original identity, a claim which is based on reservation of title clause alone is lost once the goods are used in the manufacturing process. Any purported rights to the manufactured goods constitute a charge which is void against third parties unless registered. Companies Act 1985, s.395; *Re Bond Worth supra*, n. 3, and *Borden (U.K.) Ltd.* v. *Scottish Timber Products Ltd.* [1981] 1 Ch. 25; see also Matthews (1981) 34 C.L.P. 159.

¹⁵ A. K. Klevorick, "Law and Economic Theory: An Economist's View" (1975) 65 Am.Econ.Rev. 237, 243.

¹⁶ This section describes the traditional set of contractual relationships where the construction project is a response to the demands of a particular client. The princi-

pal standard form contract produced by the J.C.T. is based on this organisational framework.

[17] This obligation relates to the quantity and quality of materials and workmanship. The general is also responsible for the timing of the project. The main objective is to organise the project in such a way that the liability of different input suppliers is channelled through the general contractor.

[18] *E.g.* J.C.T. 80 forbids the nomination of anyone against which the general makes reasonable objection cl. 35.4.1.

[19] Although the general is responsible to the client for the quantity and quality of a nominated sub-contractor's input, J.C.T. 80 includes a mandatory collateral warranty between the client and nominated sub-contractor under which the nominated sub-contractor assumes primary responsibility for delay which it causes.

[20] Again, the general usually has contractually defined rights to reject a particular nomination. Cl. 36.4 of J.C.T. 80 provides that the general may reject a nominated supplier who is not willing to include certain terms in the sales contract.

[21] *Sumpter* v. *Hedges* [1898] 1 Q.B. 673.

[22] *Hoenig* v. *Isaacs* [1952] 2 All E.R. 176.

[23] It will usually be cheaper for the client to borrow money to finance a building contract than for a builder to finance its work by borrowing. Firstly, clients may be able to use the building as security for the loan and so face a lower interest rate than the builder. Secondly, a builder who has a programme of work would need to borrow more money than a client who is only involved in one project at a time.

[24] Cl. 30.1.3. The interval agreed should be recorded in the Appendix to the main contract. J.C.T. 80 includes a default period of one month which will apply to those contracts where the client and general do not make their own provision.

[25] Cl. 30.1.1.1. This is just one of many terms which purports to impose duties on someone who is not a party to the main contract.

[26] Cl. 30.2.1.2.

[27] Cl. 30.1.2. The certificates have a cumulative effect. The architect or quantity surveyor values to total quantity of work on the site and deducts from this total the amount paid on previous certificates. Thus, it is usually possible to correct under-/over-certification as the work progresses. See *Sutcliffe* v. *Thackrah* [1974] A.C. 727 for analysis of the architects liability where she/he cannot correct a mistaken valuation before liquidation of the general contractor.

[28] Cl. 30.1.1.1.

[29] An effective reservation of title clause does not constitute a charge on the buyer's property because the seller does not pass ownership to the buyer, thus the reservation of title clause is outside the scope of the Companies Act 1985, s.395. The Cork Report, *supra*, n. 9 recommended that reservation of title clauses should be treated as a form of security and that a notice filing system analogous to Art. 9 of the Uniform Commercial Code should be established (paras. 1638–1640). This recommendation has not yet been implemented.

[30] "Supplier" is used here as a generic term to encompass sub-contractors and suppliers of materials only. This usage is maintained unless the context suggests otherwise.

[31] The effect of the general rules in the Sale of Goods Act 1979, s.18 is that property would usually pass the general contractor well before delivery to the construction site. However, the Sale of Goods Act 1979, s.19 expressly preserves a seller's freedom to make passing of property conditional on a stipulated event.

[32] [1985] 3 All E.R. 12.

[33] In *Aluminium Industrie Vaassen B.V.* v. *Romalpa Aluminium Ltd.*, *supra*, n. 1 the buyer had argued against validity of the reservation of title clause by reasoning that the natural inference to be drawn from such a clause was that the

buyer would not be able to use the goods for its own business purposes, specifically resale, until it had paid the seller. The Court of Appeal managed to avoid the problem by implying a term giving the buyer authority to resell as principal with respect to sub-purchasers and as agent with respect to the plaintiff in that case, see especially Roskill L.J., *supra* n. 1 at 690.

³⁴ *Young & Marten Ltd.* v. *McManus Childs Ltd.* [1969] 1 A.C. 454.

³⁵ The general rule is that once materials become part of a structure and lose their separate identity ownership of the materials is subsumed into ownership of the building. *Holland* v. *Hodgson* (1872) L.R. 7 C.P. 328.

³⁶ (1979) 14 Building Law Reports 90.

³⁷ Compare *Gloucestershire County Council* v. *Richardson* [1969] 1 A.C. 480 where a nominated *supplier* was engaged to design, deliver and fix concrete columns and *Sauter Automation Ltd.* v. *H. C. Goodman (Mechanical Srvices) Ltd. The Financial Times*, May 14, 1986 where the plaintiff was a *sub-contractor* but was required only to manufacture and deliver the equipment. It was not responsible for installation.

³⁸ *Supra*, n. 32.

³⁹ This was an important factor in rejecting the plaintiff's second line of attack—that its mistake as to the nature of the dealer's business should preclude implication of a term giving the dealer authority to sell, *supra*, n. 32 at 16g.

⁴⁰ See generally P. Burrows and C. G. Veljanovski (eds.) *The Economic Approach to Law*, Butterworths (1981) especially Chap. 1; A. I. Ogus and C. G. Veljanovski (eds.) *Readings in the Economics of Law and Regulation* O.U.P. 1984; *The New Law-and-Economics A Research Review* C. G. Veljanovski SSRC 1982.

⁴¹ The model is not intended to be a realistic description of the legal position. In most circumstances parties can vary a rule by agreement. The purpose of the model is to abstract from reality in order to highlight fundamental relationships.

⁴² "Risk" is used interchangeably with "expected cost" of a contingency. These terms are defined as the product of the probability of insolvency and the loss if it does occur. Altering the rule does not affect the probability of the event but it does change the magnitude of the loss to clients and suppliers.

⁴³ See discussion of the "creditors' bargain" text at n. 45, *infra*.

⁴⁴ It is a fundamental proposition of microeconomics that for normal goods there is an inverse relationship between price and the quantity demanded.

⁴⁵ Jackson has developed the model of the "creditors' bargain" to provide the basis of a normative theory which he uses to evaluate bankruptcy law in the United States of America. See T. H. Jackson "Bankruptcy, Non-Bankrupty Entitlements, and the Creditors' Bargain" (1982) 91 Yale Law Journal.

⁴⁶ This assumption of no transaction costs is fundamental to economic analysis of law. Again it is not intended to describe reality; rather it is used to build a model against which to compare the "real-world."

⁴⁷ Liquidation of a general contractor is an enormously costly contingency. Other costs which a client might face include delay to the project retaining consultants for a longer period; finding new input suppliers; protecting the partially completed building; servicing loans over a longer period.

⁴⁸ The usual assumption is that economic agents are risk averse. See A. J. Culyer, *Economics* Blackwell (1985) at 350–353 for a clear account of risk-profiles and their significance in economics.

⁴⁹ Such a difference in belief might arise because clients and suppliers do not have the same information about the general contractor's financial standing.

⁵⁰ See Veljanovski, *The New Law-and-Economics supra* n. 40 at pp. 24–25.

⁵¹ Vilfredo Pareto *Manuel d'Economie Politique* (1909).

⁵² See N. Kaldor, "Welfare Propositions of Economics and Interpersonal Com-

parisons of Utility" (1939) 40 Econ.J. 549 and J. R. Hicks, "The Valuation of Social Income" (1940) 7 Economica 105.

[53] "The Problem of Social Cost" (1960) 3 J. Law and Economics 1.

[54] See A. I. Ogus and G. M. Richardson, "Economics and the Environment: A Study of Private Nuisance" (1977) 36 Camb.L.J. 284 for a valuable analysis of the English law of nuisance in the light of allocative efficiency and other ojectives.

[55] Mishan describes transaction costs as "all costs connected with negotiations between the interested parties" and includes among his examples the costs of protecting private property and of enforcing contracts. E. Mishan, *Introduction to Political Economy* (Butterworths, 1982), p. 48.

[56] See discussion at pp. 247–48 *supra*.

[57] See Ogus and Veljanovski, *supra*, n. 40 for examples of scholarship which argues that the law should pursue efficiency or attempts to assess how far legal rules can be rationalised in terms of efficiency.

[58] *Supra*, n. 7.

[59] *Supra*, n. 36.

[60] Amendment 1984 replaces cl. 19.4 of the main contract.

[61] Cl. 19.4.2.2.

[62] Cl. 19.4.2.3.

[63] Both the Committee of Associations of Specialist Engineering Contractors (C.A.S.E.C.) and the Federation of Associations of Specialists and Sub-Contractors (F.A.S.S.) are members of the J.C.T.

[64] See Patricia M. Hillebrandt, *Analysis of the British Construction Industry* (MacMillan, 1984) Chaps. 2 and 4 for a careful account of the reasons for volatility in the construction industry.

The author wishes to thank Iain Ramsay and Sue McLaughlin for their valuable comments on the draft of this paper.

1836 and All That: Laws in the University of London 1836–1986

WILLIAM TWINING*

Introduction

One hundred and fifty years ago the University of London Mark II was born. That is how Negley Harte,[1] in his splendid illustrated history, characterises this celebration. Last week saw the birth of the latest child of the Faculty of Laws: *Law and Morals: Warnock, Gillick and Beyond* by Simon Lee of King's. I have undertaken to give a comprehensive history, analysis, evaluation, evocation and celebration of the story of Laws in London between these auspicious events. I shall try to deliver on this rash promise. Michael Thompson, the impresario for this series, has made the task a little less impossible by wisely imposing some taboos: no attempt at connected institutional history; no parade of famous, notorious or eccentric men and women; no cataloguing of educational programmes or listing of individual achievements. This may not be Art, but it is a licence for almost data-free history.

I must confess that in moments of anguished insomnia I have been tempted to rebel. Once at 4.00 a.m. I started to assemble an A–Z of personalities in rhyming couplets. I was rather pleased with the start:

A is for Amos—Sheldon, Maurice and Andy;
A is also for Austin, who was no Tristram Shandy.
B is for Bentham who sits in a box—

and so on up to Zander, for whom I had some promising possible rhymes. However, when I reached G, I ran into a spot of trouble:

G is Gower, there were David and Jim;
Jim was sharp as a razor; but David . . .
. . . well David was no intellectual and his batting average for
England somewhat exceeded his score in Roman Law.

Parodying Ogden Nash is a confession of failure. I have decided to conform. So my subject is the contributions of our discipline in the University of London to intellectual, social and legal life. This

261

involves considering a good many institutions. The most important are these:

The Faculty of Laws in University College, which could be said to have begun life in 1826, (becoming a "Faculty" in 1908).

The Faculty of Laws at King's, which began with the introductory lecture by Professor Park in 1831.

The Department of Law at L.S.E., which was fully recognised in 1921; however, law was taught at the school since its inception in 1895.

The Department of Law at S.O.A.S., founded in 1947/8, but preceded by some teaching of law from at least 1932.

The Faculty of Laws at Q.M.C., founded in 1965.

Several Institutes and Centres, the most important of which is the Institute of Advanced Legal Studies, established in 1946.

I shall also deal briefly with the system of External Degrees and Special Relationships, as they have affected Law.[2]

The National Context

A comprehensive history of legal education in England has yet to be written.[3] The story is complex and could be constructed in a number of ways. On almost any interpretation it would make depressing reading. One outstanding feature, which Max Weber and others have emphasised, is the very minor role played by the universities both in the formation of the legal profession and in the development of the common law. Weber treated this as the distinguishing characteristic between the modes of thought of civil law and common law systems.[4]

The standard overview—as presented by Gower, irreverently glossed by Abel-Smith and Stevens, and given respectability by the Ormrod Report of 1971[5]—can be briefly restated as follows: civil law was studied at Oxford and Cambridge from an early date, but the study of English Law did not become firmly established in the universities until the late nineteenth century. Systematic study of law was never accepted by those in power as a necessary preparation for practice; indeed its desirability was often questioned. Today a law degree is the normal first stage for qualification as a barrister or solicitor, but we remain one of the few countries in the world in which a law degree is not a necessary qualification for practice. We are not here concerned with the history of entry to the legal profession; however, in assessing the contributions of the University of London in the field of law, it is worth remembering the limited and ambiguous role that university law faculties play in preparation for practice and in professional life. They have never

had a monopoly, or anything approaching one, over legal education. Law schools run by the professions, private crammers and,
more recently, polytechnic law schools (some of which, unlike the
universities, are directly involved in professional training) all play
a significant part. Similarly, unlike the continent of Europe, legal
scholars have made an extremely modest impact on legal development.[6]

In this standard account, the foreshortened history of the discipline of law in the universities emerges as a series of false starts
and disappointed expectations. From the Middle Ages until the
late sixteenth century the Inns of Court were the only centres for
the study of English law. In their heyday they were vigorous intellectual communities, which served to provide a general education
as well as professional training. But the educational functions of
the Inns atrophied, especially after the Civil War, and for a long
time such legal education as there was rested on apprenticeship
and self-education.

Blackstone's lectures, and the creation of the Vinerian Chair, in
the period 1753–65 failed to institutionalise the teaching of English
law at Oxford. So did the establishment of the Downing Chair at
Cambridge in 1800. The Faculty of Arts and Laws at University
College, founded in 1826, is sometimes said to be England's first
modern law school. But, as we shall see, the story of law in London in the nineteenth century is a rather sad tale of missed opportunities and promise unfulfilled.

1846 rather than 1836 is often treated as the start of modern
legal education in England.[7] In that year a Select Committee on
Legal Education was set up by the House of Commons and produced a remarkable report in three months.[8] What it found
amounted to an almost total vacuum:

> "It revealed that there was virtually no institutional law
> teaching of any kind in England, with the exception of Pro-
> fessor Amos's teaching at University College, London [which
> had stopped in 1834]. At Oxford, Dr Phillimore, the Pro-
> fessor of Civil Law, had ceased to lecture because there were
> 'few or no attendants.' The Vinerian professor had at most 38
> students because there were no degrees in Common Law. The
> Downing Professor of Law at Cambridge informed the Com-
> mittee that 'there are at present no lectures given, and no
> attendance whatever.'[9] The Regius Professor of Civil Law at
> Cambridge continued to lecture because attendance to his lec-
> tures was a necessary requirement for a degree in Civil Law,
> but there were no examinations. Apart from attendance at

these lectures, the only qualification for a degree was lapse of time, seven years for a Bachelor's and 12½ years for a Doctor's degree. At the Inns of Court, there was no formal instruction, and no test of proficiency of any kind before Call to the Bar."[10]

The examination which intending solicitors were required to pass under the 1843 Act served "merely as a guarantee against absolute incompetency"[11]; and the Committee had almost nothing good to say about the operation of articles.

In the Committee's view, the consequences of this situation were serious: there was no guarantee of minimum competence in either branch of the profession; there was "a hypercritical attention to the technicalities"[12] and a lack of concern for general principle; there was no class of jurists of eminence concerned with the systematic exposition and reform of the law[13]; and there was inadequate provision for the study of law for "the unprofessional student."[14]

The Committee saw the solution in the institutionalisation of legal education. It put forward three main proposals:

(i) a great expansion of university legal education in England and Ireland through the creation of new chairs and a proper system of examination for law degrees; systematic law teaching should be revived in Oxford and Cambridge and extended in London.[15]

(ii) the Inns of Court should combine to form "a special institution," a College or "Law University" analogous to the College of Surgeons or Physicians. There should be an examination on entry to the Inns, a formal system of lectures and a public qualifying examination for call to the Bar.[16]

(iii) intending solicitors should be stringently examined both prior to admission to Apprenticeship and by a final examination that should be "conducted more in reference to general principles than technicalities."[17] There should be separate provision for classes suited to the needs and situation of articled clerks, to supplement articles, but with some provision for attendance at certain classes in the Inns of Court and for exemption on the basis of attendance at University lectures.

In 1971 the Ormrod Committee commented: "The history of legal education in England over the past 120 years is largely an account of the struggle to implement the recommendations of the 1846 Committee and the effects of that struggle."[18] This oversimplifies the story and, read out of context, exaggerates the significance of the 1846 Report in respect of both originality and influence.[19] Nevertheless, the Report was prophetic in a number of ways, including anticipating exemptions, stringent Law Society Finals, and some common training for barristers and solicitors. Its more immediate significance was two-fold: First, it made a sharp distinction between "the practical and mechanical side" of legal study and "the higher and doctrinal" side and argued strongly that the role of university law faculties was to concentrate on the latter.[20]

Secondly, it accepted that some aspects of the practical side could be the subject of formal instruction and examination, but recommended that these should be the responsibility of separate institutions. As the Ormrod Committee observed, the most striking difference between our system of education and training and that of most other countries (and, one might add, other professions) is "the existence of independent law schools run by the profession itself" which play a part in the education of future professional lawyers (particularly of solicitors).[21]

Such thinking had three interrelated consequences: first, it institutionalised some extremely dubious distinctions between theory and practice; education and training; and knowledge, understanding and skill. Secondly it further marginalised the contribution of the universities not only to professional formation, but also to legal practice and the operation of the legal system. We now have a four-stage structure of legal education and training: the academic stage, the vocational stage, apprenticeship (articles and pupillage) and continuing legal education.[22] The universities produce a significant, but not overwhelming, majority of those who satisfy the requirements of the academic stage[23]; unlike the polytechnics they play almost no part in conversion courses for non-law graduates and in the vocational stage; their contribution to the rapidly developing field of continuing legal education is growing, but uneven.

Thirdly, questions about the educational objectives of law degrees, the role of law schools and the identity of academic lawyers are endemic matters of controversy in most countries. The structure of our system has excluded a number of options: it rules out the possibility that university law faculties can emulate English medical schools, German law faculties or the Harvard Law School—all of which have been put forward as models in the past 150 years. On the other hand, legal education is largely demand-led and a significant percentage of students sees the law degree as a passport to a professional qualification, though not necessarily to practice. Thus the influence of the legal profession is mediated through students' expectations, some of which are unrealistic or unsuited to a university environment. Accordingly, despite the yearnings of some law teachers, it is virtually impossible for a law faculty to seek to be an institution which is single-mindedly devoted to pure science or liberal education or systematic law reform or to serve as a guerrilla base. The market pressures against this are too strong. Yet, at least since the rise of full-time teaching, academic lawyers have consistently rejected "the trade school model." They have also regularly insisted that a law degree can serve equally well as a general education and as a foundation for law practice. University law schools, especially since World War II, have been hybrid institutions serving a variety of constituencies and uneasily juggling with competing purposes. Similarly the individual law teacher has to struggle with often irreconcilable demands to be an Expositor, Craftsman, Liberal Intellectual, Scientist or Censor. Pessimists call this falling between stools[24]; optimists call it creative tension. This is the situation of the London Law Faculties.

The Benthamite Vision and the Austinian Gloss

Once upon a time there was a man named Henry Tonks, who was Slade Professor of Fine Art at University College from 1917 to 1930. In 1922 he painted an enormous canvas depicting Jeremy Bentham in the foreground, considering the architect's plans for University College, watched by Henry Brougham, Thomas Campbell and Crabb Robinson who are very much in the background.[25] An irreverent wag once said of the picture that its "lack of artistic distinction is overshadowed by historical inaccuracy." For Bentham is about twice the size of the others; yet he is not officially recognised as a founder of the College and played a minor and rather obscure role in its establishment. He took, as it were, a back seat. For many years the painting hung at ground level in the North Cloister. Unfortunately in 1985 it was vandalised—whether by an historian, an aesthete or a common or cloistered vandal is likely to remain a mystery.

I confess that I was that irreverent commentator[26]; but not, I hasten to add, the vandal. I hereby retract my judgment. For in preparing this lecture I have learned that the curious perspective of the painting was due, not to incompetence, but because it was intended to hang under the dome of the Flaxman gallery and to be viewed from below.[27] In short, for years we have been looking at it from the wrong angle. There may be a moral there. Furthermore, like this lecture, the picture is a celebration, which should not be judged by conventional standards of either History or Art. Indeed, only in a naively literal sense is it true that Bentham was not among the founders of University College. In spirit the institution was, and in important respects still is, Bentham's College.[28] He departed in 1832, but he has never left us. Much the same is true of John Austin. Seen from a narrow institutional angle, his tenure of the Chair of Jurisprudence was a disaster. But in the perspective of intellectual history, Austin's ideas, even more than Bentham's, were the single most important force in academic law for nearly 150 years—not only in the University of London, but also in England and much of the common law world.

The story, in my opinion, is a sad one: Austin narrowed down Bentham; the followers of Austin narrowed down Austin and the opportunity was lost to create a genuinely systematic, interdisciplinary, critical intellectual tradition in academic law. It is only recently that Bentham, rather than Austin has belatedly been recognised as the true "Father of English Jurisprudence" and that what passed as the Austinian Expository approach to the study of law is acknowledged to be a sadly impoverished interpretation of the vision of that tragic figure.[29]

In assessing the contribution of a great University one must, of course, take account of the achievements of successful individuals—teachers, scholars, alumni and even administrators and entrepreneurs. One must also try to make some assessment of its contributions to national life—a much more elusive form of enquiry. I shall touch on these. But a University is above all a house of intellect; its currency is ideas. So I make no apology in placing the ideas of our two leading thinkers in the foreground and in inviting you to consider Bentham's and Austin's visions of law and of its study, as it were, from below. Then continuing the allegory, let us consider an alternative model—that of Austin's brilliant and engaging colleague, Andrew Amos, our first Professor of English Law. I shall present these as symbolising three different visions of what might have been.

First then, Jeremy Bentham. Whether one loves or hates him, accepts or rejects his ideas—or like most Bentham scholars one is caught in a posture of deep ambivalence[30]—one cannot ignore him. He is there, larger than life and more persistent. He presented a vision of a science of law and of its potential that is clear, comprehensive, coherent and intellectually ambitious. The composition is classical and its outline can be sketched quite simply.

The foundation is a theory of value—utility—by which all human institutions, practices, designs and actions are to be judged. It is opposed not only to deontological moral theories (especially all versions of natural law and natural rights), but also to intuitionist, irrationalist and sceptical theories of value. It underpins and suffuses all of Bentham's work.

The second element is an epistemology and a theory of language, embodied in his theory of fictions. This was the basis of Bentham's method of classification and precise conceptual analysis, characterised by John Stuart Mill as "the method of detail."[31] The theory of fictions had its roots in English empiricism, but has subsequently been recognised as anticipating to a remarkable degree, developments in analytical philosophy associated with, for example, Russell, Wittgenstein and J. L. Austin.[32] It is no coincidence and highly significant that Bentham's approach to conceptual analysis was explicitly the starting-point of the work of our greatest contemporary legal philosopher, Herbert Hart.[33]

Thirdly, Bentham had a somewhat mechanistic view of the nature of man and of man in society. In the eyes of many, the Achilles heel of his general approach lies in his psychology and social theory.[34] This may indeed make him vulnerable to criticism from the perspective of the sociology of law; yet psychology and social theory are widely acknowledged to be among the least developed aspects of the discipline of law today.

Fourthly, in politics Bentham was—especially in later life—a genuine radical, who tried to steer a clear path between reaction and piecemeal reform on the one hand and violent revolution and anarchy on the other.[35] It is a curious feature of secondary juristic discourse that legal positivism, of which he is one of the leading exponents, is still often treated as inherently amoral and conservative. Yet, if the term "critical" is to be given other than a narrow and contingent meaning, Bentham must surely count as a critical theorist.

All of these ingredients underpin Bentham's theory of law and legislation. This was positivist, instrumentalist and normative.[36] It was positivist in two important senses: first, he insisted that laws are human artefacts, created by the will of men with the power to impose that will (the sovereign). Laws are posited by man (*nomos*) rather than immanent in nature (φυσι). Secondly, he insisted on a sharp distinction between law as it is and law as it is ought to be—a distinction he considered to be essential for clarity of thought in the service of utility. His main concern was normative: one needs to have a language for accurately expounding, describing and analysing actual laws (and their context and their consequences) in order to criticize, evaluate and improve them. The science of legislation is a technology concerned with the design, creation, and evaluation of institutions and laws as instruments of utility.[37]

The story of poor John Austin, the first Professor of Jurisprudence in London, has recently been retold in no less than three books.[38] There are several interpretations. In nutshell form, the one that I favour, can be restated as follows. Austin was a committed utilitarian, but his followers played down or overlooked this aspect of his thought. He shared Bentham's concern for conceptual analysis, but his epistemology and his conception of language were both closer to common sense and cruder than those of his master. Politically he was a strange mixture of reformist and reactionary; but, more important, his primary concern in Jurisprudence was scientific rather than critical. Austin's command theory of law was in general outline and structure very similar to Bentham's; but it was also much simpler and more vulnerable to criticism. For over a hundred years it was the chief target of critics both within and outside the positivist tradition. It was Austin's simple command theory, rather than Bentham's, that was the target of Hart's *Concept of Law* that in 1961 launched the most important modern version of English legal positivism.[39]

In this view, Austin was a poor man's Bentham and, if the commentators are to be believed, the first Professor of law at King's, the ill-fated J. J. Park, was an inferior version of Austin (Park is said to have been appointed *because* he was an opponent of Bentham).[40] Yet it was Austin rather than Bentham who came to be called the "Father of English Jurisprudence" and whose received ideas not only dominated the teaching of Jurisprudence, but provided the theoretical justification—such as it was—for our dominant tradition of academic law.[41]

There are two crucial distinctions that are relevant to interpreting this aspect of our intellectual tradition. The first is the distinction between Expository and Censorial Jurisprudence.[42] In a *Fragment on Government* Bentham wrote: "To the province of the *Expositor* it belongs to explain to us what, as he supposes the Law *is*; to that of the *Censor* to observe to us what he thinks it *ought to be*."[43] Bentham gave a central place in his science to exposition; but he made it clear that he cast himself in the role of censor: "[T]he business of simple *exposition* is a harvest in which there seemed no likelihood of there being any want of labourers; and into which, therefore, I had little ambition to thrust my sickle."[44] Furthermore, unlike Austin and many later law teachers, Bentham did not insist that systematic exposition of the "is" must always *precede* criticism.[45]

Strikingly absent from this dichotomy, is a third character, the ordinary legal practitioner—let us call him the craftsman—concerned to advise on, apply, manipulate, and argue about and within the law as it is. As we shall see, the biggest deviation from the Benthamic model, is that academic law in London—and indeed in England—has concentrated almost entirely on exposition and craft; academics have sporadically been involved in criticism and reform, but *systematic* intellectual criticism and design, along the lines of Bentham's Science of Legislation, or some functional equivalent, have been neglected, sometimes explicitly rejected.

A second important distinction, to be found in Bentham but more fully articulated by Austin, is between General and Particular Jurisprudence.[46] Particular jurisprudence is concerned with a single system or body of law. General jurisprudence is, according to Austin, "the science concerned with the exposition of the principles, notions, and distinctions which are common to (maturer) systems of law"—including notions and distinctions and principles which are necessary to any system.[47] For Bentham, "the *Expositor* is always the citizen of this or that particular country: the *Censor* is, or ought to be the citizen of the world."[48] Both Bentham and Austin, therefore, in different ways, saw the scientific study of law as transcending the study of particular systems. Bentham chose the role of Censor, Austin that of Expositor. Both were mainly concerned with General Jurisprudence.

In this regard, the cosmopolitan spirit of Bentham and Austin has always been part of the London tradition. So far as I can tell, at every point in our history there has been firm resistance to pressures to confine legal studies to a parochial concern with English law.[49] The particulars have changed, but at different times London has emphasised, and has been in the forefront of General Analytical Jurisprudence, International Law, Roman Law, Modern Civilian Systems, Socialist Legal Systems, Oriental and African Laws, Laws of the European Community, and International Trade. Intellectually as well as institutionally ours has been a cosmopolitan tradition. Yet I think that it is fair to say that often in the treatment of those subjects, the significance of the distinction between general and particular expository jurisprudence has been obscured. For Austin, the foundation for all study of law and its claim to be a science lie in general jurisprudence. Bentham proposed a School of Legislation; Austin argued for a School of Law; what we have are Faculties of Laws.

Bentham's views on legal education were never published and need not concern us.[50] Austin's were set out in his well-known prefatory lecture on "The Uses and Study of Jurisprudence."[51] Using the Prussian system as a model, he suggested that the preparation of a "theoretico-practical" lawyer should be divided into two stages—what we would now call the academic and the vocational. The first stage should take place in a Law Faculty, the second in lawyers' offices. The Law Faculty would provide a systematic grounding both for intending practitioners and for those destined for public life in legislation or administration. London would be a particularly suitable place for this, because teaching would either be carried out by practitioners or under their supervision. "In England, theory would be moulded to practice."[52]

The emphasis would be on General Expository Jurisprudence— with logic as a necessary foundation and a strong emphasis on Roman Law. Austin was prepared to concede some place to the study of English Law, but it occupied a restricted and subordinate place in his curriculum. This would include logic, the general principles of jurisprudence and of legislation (the two involving ethics generally), international law and the history of English law. Significantly, he pointed out that: "In the Prussian Universities, little or no attention is given by the Law Faculty to the actual law of the country."[53]

Austin narrowed down Bentham by giving a subordinate place to the normative, critical science of legislation; by down-playing the idea that understanding law is essentially an inter-disciplinary endeavour; and above all by putting exposition of the law as it is at the core of the academic enterprise. Austin's followers and successors diluted and narrowed his vision in some crucial respects: they substituted the detailed study of English law (particular jurisprudence) for Austin's more rigorous and scientific general jurisprudence.[54] The study of logic dropped out of the curriculum and, insofar as Austinian analytical jurisprudence survived, it was banished to separate courses labelled "Jurisprudence," which became increasingly seen as a subject apart, rather than being the necessary foundation and starting point of all particular study, providing both a map of the discipline of law and a methodology for systematic exposition of principles.

Andrew Amos: An Alternative Model?[55]

The first Professor of English Law, and Austin's only colleague, was Andrew Amos, a successful barrister with a rising reputation. He was by all accounts a brilliant and engaging figure. Shelley's friend at Eton; a wrangler at Cambridge, a keen classical scholar, a lively and conscientious teacher, he could not be accused either of anti-intellectualism or of indifference to education. Yet he can usefully be made to symbolise a significantly different approach to the study of law. John Baker has vividly evoked the image:

> "He loved the fire and thunder of actual litigation, and felt the intellect most usefully engaged when exploring problems casually thrown up in the course of forensic warfare. Order and analysis and deep reflection were necessary for writers of books; but there was no more place for them in the classroom than in the courtroom. . . . The very first lecture (1828) gave sufficient foretaste: opening with the law of maritime accretion—by any reckoning an odd way to begin a general survey of English Law—he proceeded to tenures, followed by a discussion of contingent remainders and executory devises and conveyancing problems associated therewith; then finally, presumably somewhat late at night, he outlined the history of the forms of action, illustrated (doubtless to gasps of amazement) by the writs *de ventre inspiciendo* and *de pipa vini carianda.*"[56]

What is significant here is not the contrasts in personality and teaching styles of Amos and Austin, but rather the differences and the similarities in their conceptions of legal education: Austin was concerned with the patient, systematic search for general principles and universal truths. The approach was abstract, dry and analytical. Amos's objective was "emphatically practical"[57]; his presentation was anecdotal, unsystematic, even disorderly and his subject-matter was largely based on first-hand experience, "such as no person is competent to teach but a barrister familiar with the practice of the Courts."[58] In his lack of concern for systematic theory and for general principle, Amos may have mirrored the prevailing attitude of barristers of his day. Yet his enterprise was an exercise in intellect. He invited students to argue with him about difficult points of law. It has been suggested that his approach was a forerunner of the American case method. It would be more accurate to say that it anticipated the problem method—for the focus was on problems rather than on the texts of reported cases. And the problems were derived from, and presented in the context of, actual practice. Austin's central focus was General Jurisprudence, his model product was the scientifically educated lawyer; Amos was particularistic, his model the courtroom advocate.

It is tempting to set up Austin and Amos as symbols of the difference between "theoretical" and "practical" approaches. But here they merely illustrate the inadequacy of such distinctions. For the similarities between them are as important as the differences. The Utilitarians and University College were concerned with "useful knowledge" and Austin, no less than Amos, saw his enterprise as a preparation for practice. They also shared the same arena, the classroom; both saw their enterprise as laying a foundation rather than providing a substitute for apprenticeship. Furthermore, Amos may have taught a few tricks of the trade *en passant*, but his aim was to stretch the minds of his students intellectually. His problems were exercises in argument and analysis based on logic. Both were concerned to develop *skills* of analysis rather than to purvey *information*. This is particularly significant in the light of subsequent developments, especially since Amos, the practitioner, was even less concerned than his colleague with "coverage"—the unfortunate obsession, which through the medium of the professional examinations was to blight both academic and practical legal education.[59]

Thus we have four possible models or ideal types for the role of the law teacher: Bentham's Censor, whose subject is the Science of Legislation; Austin's Scientific Expositor, whose subject is General Analytical Jurisprudence; the more modest Particular Expositor, concerned to describe accurately (with or without systematic search for underlying principle) the law as it is in a given legal system; and the Craftsman, symbolised perhaps imperfectly by Amos, whose aim is to develop even within the University the intellectual and other skills of the practitioner. A fifth, largely more recent role, is the External Observer whose concern is to understand law in society from an external point of view, which may involve the perspective of Sociology or Political Economy or some kind of History.

It is, of course, artificial to suggest that these perspectives are mutually exclusive or necessarily in competition with each other. Are they not complementary and should not a balanced system include all of them? Should not one Faculty contain latterday Benthams, Austins and Amoses—and others besides? But these are useful concepts for analysing many of the tensions and conflicts over priorities within academic law. They are certainly more illuminating than the crude distinction between "academic" and "practical."

In the University of London, three of these five perspectives have been generally excluded completely or at best treated as marginal. Thus at no time has Bentham's Censorial (Jurisprudence or) Science of Legislation nor some non-utilitarian counterpart provided the basis for systematic instruction on a significant scale. Much of what passes for criticism or policy analysis would have been rejected by Bentham as caprice.[60] The formal teaching of practical skills has been almost entirely confined to the professional law schools and then only recently and in a rudimentary form. The marginality of Historical Jurisprudence and Sociology of Law throughout the history of English legal education gives the lie to the claim that the primary objective of some degree programmes is the understanding of law in society.[61] All of these have from time to time had a place in our academic culture, and L.S.E. in particular has consistently emphasised the links between law and the social sciences.[62] But by and large the discipline of law has been concerned with two types of exposition: at the lowest end, has been the acquisition of particular detailed information of the kind that has been traditionally tested in professional examinations; at the higher end, the central concern has been with digging out, analysis and application of the more abstract concepts and the general principles that are thought to provide coherence and system in legal doctrine—what might be called applied particular jurisprudence. Even at L.S.E., leading proponents of broader, critical approaches, scholars such as Kahn-Freund and Wedderburn, have insisted—unlike Bentham—that exposition and analysis of the law as it is must *precede* criticism or sociological study.[63]

Laws in London 1836–1908[64]

1836 is not a very auspicious moment at which to begin our story. By then, the two stars of University College, Amos and Austin, had both resigned; in 1833 Professor Park of King's had died at a young age. They had been replaced by competent, but uninspiring part-timers.[65] More important, law teaching was revived at the Inns of Court in 1833 and it soon became apparent that neither University College nor King's was able to compete with them in attracting students. The first degree in English Law in the country was instituted on the foundation of the University, but the first graduating class with LL.B. in 1839 totalled only three.[66] All were from University College and none from King's. Brave efforts were made to keep the enterprises going with very few students, but the 1846 Committee on Legal Education was rather generous in suggesting that University College was the only institution in the country to provide "any considerable facilities for legal education."[67] At that time there were only two part-timers and a handful of students.

Throughout the second half of the nineteenth century, Law in London languished for lack of students. Reforms in the 1860s and

1870s and beyond enabled University College to attract some men of distinction, such as Sheldon Amos, Bund, Bolland, Hunter, Murison, Scrutton, Pollock, Taswell-Langmead and, later, Holdsworth—but they failed to attract students and few lasted long. For example, at U.C.L. in 1867–9 the largest class in any subject (Roman Law) had eight students[68]; in 1890–1 there were only 13 students attending classes. Baker reports that in the 14 years prior to 1909 the College had produced a total of only nine graduates in law.[69] For most of this period the situation at King's was no better and was often worse. Hearnshaw, the often acerbic author of King's centenary house history, paints a depressing picture of repeated failures to form viable courses; and for long periods the Chair of Law was perceived as a sinecure. Law was not the only subject in difficulties in this period. For example, Hearnshaw reports: "In February 1854 the Reverend Richard Jones, who had slept in the Chair of Political Economy since 1833, woke up and announced his wish to retire. The Council placed no obstacle in his path and expressed no thanks for his inactivities."[70]

Hale Bellot attributes this unhappy situation to the lack of full-time teachers: "In law, as in history and economics, in fact, the professors were little more than visiting lecturers whose emoluments were not sufficient to procure a greater share of their services, and whose activities were inadequate to the creation of a flourishing school of studies in any of their several departments."[71] Others emphasise the competition from the professional schools, despite or because of their poor quality: for, says Baker, in the days before local authority grants, they offered a quicker and cheaper crash course than a law degree.[72] Perhaps more fundamental than those inter-related factors was the point that academic law had failed to find any recognisable role: academic legal education was not seen as a serious form of general education nor as a valuable preparation for practice nor, as Austin envisaged, as a preparation for public life.

Thus we must be careful to set some claims in perspective. London rightly boasts the first degree in English Law, but University College produced only 135 LL.B.s in the nineteenth century; the number for King's is substantially less.[73] A majority of those who earned LL.B.'s studied privately. Again one of the proudest claims of the University is that it provided opportunities for many classes of students who had previously been denied access to University education, especially Jews, Catholics, Protestant dissenters and women. Women were first allowed to study Jurisprudence at University College in 1873, but the first woman law graduate took her degree in 1917.[74] It is advisable not to make both boasts in the same sentence.

1908–1965 The Inter-Collegiate Heyday[75]

The situation was transformed after the Haldane reforms of 1898 that launched the University of London Mark III.[76] The turning-point in law came in 1906–1908 when, under the aegis of the University of London, King's, University College, and the recently formed London School of Economics agreed to pool their resources in a tripartite scheme of lectures leading to an LL.B. degree of the University of London. This inter-collegiate system of teaching lasted until the 1960s and survives today at postgraduate level in the Master of Laws.

Numbers picked up after the introduction of the tripartite system, very rapidly at King's—mainly among evening students; more gradually at U.C.L., which attracted mainly day students. During this period, L.S.E. law students began to be treated as internal students and L.S.E. academics began to make their distinctive contribution to law teaching. To start with nearly all of the teaching was done by part-timers. Only at L.S.E. were there any full-time posts at all. After World War I student demand for law increased significantly and between 1919 and 1931 a great advance was made by the establishment of five new full-time chairs and three full-time readerships, mainly financed through the U.G.C.[77] They were filled by some notable scholars.[78] Part of the stimulus for this "revolutionary change,"[79] as Keeton called it, appears to have come from Sir William Beveridge, who in the late twenties proposed that all law teaching should be transferred to L.S.E.[80] The case was a strong one: L.S.E. had by far the best law library and almost the only full-time teachers; the tripartite system of lectures made life difficult for students who had to move continuously between the three centres. It also upset college time-tables. However, not surprisingly, King's and U.C.L. resisted—after all, each had been teaching law for almost exactly a hundred years, (whenever they had students to teach) and U.C.L., in particular, could point to an extremely distinguished list of names, even if the incumbents had been paid almost nothing and most had not stayed for very long. The outcome was that the need for full-time teachers was accepted at King's and U.C.L. as well as at L.S.E.

Professor George Keeton remembers the period 1930–39 as the happiest years of the Inter-Collegiate system.[81] For the first time there was a body of full-time scholar-teachers of law who were dedicated to the enterprise. They were young, keen, proud of what they were doing and determined to work within the Inter-Collegiate system. Until the late thirties the enterprise was quite small (averaging about 50 students a year for the full-time degree), but in respect of both teaching and scholarship the quality was outstandingly high. There were inevitably conflicts, but the three Heads of Department—of whom Hughes Parry was the acknowledged leader—worked as a team and managed to resolve them amicably. By modern standards teaching loads were heavy, especially in respect of spread of subjects.[82] In 1931 Keeton recalls being asked by Jolowicz to teach Equity and Trusts, and both the newly introduced course on English legal system and Evidence, which he had never studied, to the evening students. He was also asked to "look after" U.C. students in English Law—a further six subjects. In 1938 Gower resigned his position at University College, partly because he was expected to cover six or seven subjects.[83]

Others who were students and teachers during this era confirm Keeton's picture of harmonious cooperation, of a generally high level of teaching and some remarkable achievements in scholarship, exemplified by the establishment of the *Modern Law Review* and by the publications of individuals such as Jennings, Jolowicz, Keeton, Lauterpacht Plucknett, Potter and Robson.[84] No doubt a great deal of this story of unpretentious institutional development and individual excellence is attributable to the work of some outstanding long-serving Heads of Department: Sir David Hughes Parry was Head of Department at L.S.E. for nearly 30 years; George Keeton controlled U.C.L. from 1939–69; and Harold Potter who was Head of Department at King's from 1930 until his untimely death in 1950, in the words of the College History, "worked to build up the Faculty virtually from nothing into one which by the time of his death was more than pulling its weight in the life of the College."[85]

In retrospect four features of this period stand out. First, the genuinely inter-collegiate nature of the enterprise. Secondly, given its modest scale it was remarkable what was achieved in both scholarship, teaching and public influence. Thirdly, by 1939 most of the work had been taken over by full-time teachers. Yet the number of full-time teachers responsible for teaching day and evening classes in the internal LL.B., and for the LL.M., (as well as evening external students) never exceeded 15 before 1939.[86] Fourthly, throughout this period the LL.B. degree catered uniformly for several very different constituencies: full-time day students who usually came straight from school; and internal evening students, (including articled clerks, a few admitted solicitors, and members of the legal staffs of government departments and private sector enterprises). There were also three classes of external students: students in University Colleges in the United Kingdom; students in Law Schools overseas that were in a special relationship with the University of London; and independent external students.[87] I shall return to deal in more detail with the story of the External LL.B. and special relationships— for it is in this area perhaps more than any other that the University of London made a distinctive contribution to legal education.

During World War II the London law schools were dispersed: initially L.S.E. went to Peterhouse, Cambridge, U.C.L. to Aberystwyth and K.C.L. to Bristol. Harold Potter nobly kept his evening class for students from the Estate Duty Office going in London.[88] After a year U.C.L. moved to Cambridge and King's followed in 1941. Technically speaking the Inter-Collegiate system did not operate during the war; naturally resources were pooled, and some lectures were shared with the diminished Cambridge Law Faculty, but this was an emergency arrangement rather than a continuation of the system.[89] During this period servicemen, prisoners-of-war and others were able to read for the external LL.B. and a significant number succeeded.[90]

After the War, the three Heads of Department Parry, Keeton and Potter were keen to revive and develop the Inter-Collegiate system. But, largely because of an increase in numbers of students and staff and the need to give younger teachers opportunities to teach their own courses, the system came increasingly under strain.[91] More and more parallel lecture courses developed. At the same time, the common undergraduate syllabus and examinations required approval of all three departments in regard to any change in curriculum and methods of assessment. This provided a rigidity that was increasingly resented. Eventually, following the reforms in the University, associated with the Saunders Committee of 1965–66, the present system of Special Regulations was introduced in the mid-sixties. This allows each College Law Faculty to have its own curriculum and methods of assessment in the LL.B., although they are all under the aegis of the University of London. This granting of "Dominion status"[92] to the colleges allowed much greater flexibility in a time of rapid expansion, and facilitated the establishment of a new Faculty of Laws at Q.M.C. in 1965 and the introduction of a distinctive undergraduate course in law at S.O.A.S. (B.A. 1975, LL.B. 1976).

1965–1975. The Modern Period

The last 21 years have seen an enormous expansion and diversification of Laws in London. Many flowers have bloomed and each School has developed its own distinctive programme and strengths. In 1983 a committee of the Heads of University Law Schools listed 14 important changes and trends in the discipline of law in the previous 15 years.[93] The University of London, mainly through its five law schools, has both participated in and contributed to nearly all of these changes.[94] For example:

a. the *scale* of the enterprise increased at both undergraduate and post-graduate levels; (i)[95]
b. there was a trend towards *diversification* within and between undergraduate law degrees; (ii)[96]
c. there has been increased emphasis on *European Law*; (iii)[97]
d. the range of *standard* subjects has greatly expanded (for example, Administrative Law, Family Law, Labour Law, Revenue Law and Planning Law are found in nearly all London degrees.) (iv)[98]
e. there has been an increased involvement in *continuing legal education*, especially in the last three years; (v)
f. the *computer* has begun to make an impact; (vi)
g. some *four year* degrees have been introduced; (ix)[99]
h. there have been several new institutes and research centres.[1]

The same committee projected a series of likely developments in the next 10 to 15 years.[2] It is difficult to believe that all or most of the London law schools will not be involved in all of them. The H.U.L.S.C. Report painted a picture of a discipline in the process of rapid expansion and change that started in the mid-nineteen sixties and continues today. Change has been uneven and not as radical nor as systematic as some of us would wish. The economic climate has slowed and frustrated, but not entirely halted, expansion. For law is currently one of the most buoyant of disciplines. Considerable damage has recently been done to libraries and to the age-structure of the law-teaching profession, yet it is probably true to say that at no stage in its history has the overall picture of legal education and training in the United Kingdom presented such a vibrant diversity of activities or such a range of opportunities.

What is true of our discipline nationally applies to the University of London and its five constituent law schools. Nearly all of the teaching and research, grumping and trumpeting, innovation and reaction take place within these loosely confederated institutions. Any attempt by a member of one of them to give an account of the present and recent past of the others would be invidious; if it were even tinged with honesty, it would invite the kind of ridicule and calumny that have been heaped on the U.G.C. in its recent clumsy exercise in purporting to evaluate the research of university departments. We are celebrating the sesquicentennial of the University; so, leaving the individual schools to beat their own drums, I shall confine myself to a brief consideration of three distinctive features of our joint enterprise at University level: the External System; the LL.M. and the Institute of Advanced Legal Studies.

The External System[3]

From its inception until 1900 the University was only an examining and degree conferring body. The sharp separation of teaching and examining functions paved the way for what is arguably London's most important contribution to higher education: the external system. In 1985–1986 there were 24,500 students registered for external degrees in six main subject areas. It is estimated that about 75 per cent. of these were actively studying. Law is by far the biggest subject, with about 75 per cent. of all enrolments. In 1985 358 LL.B.s were awarded to internal students; in the same year 298 graduated with External LL.B.s.[4] Given a rather high wastage rate, there are overall many more candidates (at undergraduate level) in the external programme than in the five London Law Schools.[5]

The scale of the enterprise is not, of course, the main reason for the significance of the External System. At different stages in history, it has served a variety of functions, both for individuals and for other educational institutions. For example, for long periods it met needs that today are largely catered for by such admirable institutions as the C.N.A.A., the Open University and the Common Professional Examination. During World War II hundreds of servicemen and prisoners of war were able to continue their studies by reading for External Degrees.[6] Today, at least, three very different categories of students avail themselves of the opportunities offered by the external LL.B.: "(a) well-qualified people, often graduates, seeking to advance already established careers or to change career or more generally to pursue an academic interest in law; (b) educationally disadvantaged people, often with minimum qualifications, who see the degree (based, as it is, on the principles of open entry and freedom in respect of methods of study) as providing opportunities denied by conventional institutions; (c) school leavers, in several countries in the Far East and Africa, who have been unable to obtain a university place in their own country."[7] The LL.B. is not only by far the most popular external degree, but "Laws has been the pioneer for the rest of the External programme"—especially in the last few years.[8]

Perhaps even more significant than provision for individual students has been the contribution of the external system to institution-building. Between 1849 and 1949 "all university colleges created in England and Wales . . . automatically spent their apprentice years under the aegis of the London External Degree System."[9] From 1850 students of institutions in the British Empire were eligible to register for London degrees and from 1858 this facility was extended to students anywhere in the world. After the Report of the Asquith Committee in 1945, London created a scheme of special relationships with eight colleges in Africa and the West Indies, which proved to be one of the great success stories of the late colonial period. So far as law is concerned the actual numbers of students who graduated with the External LL.B. under this scheme were quite modest, but law faculties in four countries spent their formative years in special relationships and several others, formally outside the scheme, were heavily influenced by the London model.[10]

During the period of decolonisation the scheme of special relationships gradually ran down as university colleges became fully independent universities. The external degree system, however, continued to flourish, with registrations reaching a peak of 34,198 in 1970.[11]

This rise in numbers led to the conclusion that the University was over-reaching itself. During the early seventies it was decided to wind down and severely limit the system. First, it was decided to cease to register home students enrolled in full-time courses in public educational institutions and to abdicate this role to the C.N.A.A. and the Open University. Private External students were still enrolled in the United Kingdom, but the degree was no longer actively promoted. Later it was announced that, starting in 1977, the University would cease to register overseas students.

It is hardly surprising, given the continuing demand, that these decisions caused consternation in a number of quarters, especially overseas. Subsequently it was acknowledged that "While necessary at the time, the decision to cease overseas registration seemed ungenerous retrospectively in the light of the University's long history of work in the Commonwealth, and of the [Government's] decision in 1980 to raise overseas student fees for those studying in Britain."[12] Accordingly in 1982–1983 the process of winding-down was reversed and a brand new policy was formulated. This period of retrenchment provided an opportunity for a fundamental re-thinking of the system. The new scheme differs from the old one in several key respects. For example, the new External System is entirely self-financing; London University teachers are involved in providing instruction for external students; revision of syllabuses has been institutionalised; the academic support provided by the University is being significantly enhanced in a number of ways; there is to be a greater emphasis on continuing education and dis-tance learning; and the way has been opened for a measure of exchange between school-sponsored degrees on the one hand, and External Syllabus and modes of study on the other.[13]

Clearly all of these new developments have particular signifi-cance for law which, as I have said, has by far the largest, indeed a disproportionate, share of enrolments for external degrees. It is impossible to do justice to this large and immensely important sub-ject here. But it is far too important to say nothing about it. So let me venture a few personal comments from a broad historical per-spective.

Special Relations

My very first examiners' meeting was a direct experience of a special relationship. It was 1959 and I was a lecturer at the Univer-sity of Khartoum, which two years previously had become an inde-pendent university. This was to be one of the first occasions on which our students would be given a Khartoum degree.

The Sudanese were ambivalent: they were proud to be indepen-dent of London, but they were fearful for the prestige of their own degree—at home as well as abroad. A few facts stick out in my memory about the occasion. The examiners' meeting was held in London, at K.C.L. Nearly all of the External Examiners were well-known London law teachers: Coulson, Crane, De Smith, Gower, Graveson, Grunfeld, Keeton, Lloyd, Nokes, Schwarzen-berger.[14] I had not met most of them before. Nearly all had taken the trouble to turn up and were very gracious. I was dazzled. The meeting lasted less than an hour, largely because the internal examiners' marks and judgements were accepted almost without question. Then we recessed to drink champagne at the retirement party for a 30 year old lecturer who had inherited an estate in

Scotland. I decided on the spot to emulate him—and I left Africa and duly retired to the United Kingdom shortly after my 30th birthday. Like me, he is still teaching.

Later, in 1961, I was involved in negotiations with the University of London over the syllabus for the London LL.B. in the new Law Faculty in Dar-es-Salaam—which this month is celebrating its 25th anniversary. We were more concerned in Dar to innovate and to localise and we tended to grumble about the constraints of the special relationship. But, in looking through my old papers I find that nearly everything we proposed was accepted—including a course on the Constitutions and Legal Systems of East Africa and a general mandate to study local law where this was feasible.

Sir Eric (later Lord) Ashby has said that "the link with the University of London was one of partnership, not merely of patronage."[15] Under the special relationship, a fair degree of leeway was given in adapting course content to local conditions, but London "was uncompromising in resisting any departure from the pattern of the degree."[16] The foundation of this attitude was a concern to maintain "standards"; but, as Ashby points out, there was a tendency to lump together under the idea of "standards" three quite separate ideas: academic excellence or quality; the particular methods and criteria by which such quality was assessed; and curriculum (the structure and pattern of degrees—notably with emphasis on single subject Honours).[17] The outcome was that concern for quality—largely supported by nationalist leaders and public opinion—at times resulted in a somewhat rigid "consolidation of orthodoxy."[18] Nevertheless, Ashby concludes, the system of special relationship avoided what were seen to be historic mistakes in the development of Indian unversities, and the "supreme merit" of enabling the Asquith colleges to be accepted as full members of "the international family of universities."[19]

Generally speaking, my experience in Africa—especially in Khartoum and Dar-es-Salaam—confirms Ashby's analysis.[20] We chafed at some of the constraints that we felt were imposed by London, but the students in particular were concerned with the international and local recognition of their degrees. Moreover, it is striking that when the university colleges became independent universities relatively few changes in structure, methods of assessment and, to a lesser extent, course content were introduced. Even Dar-es-Salaam, by far the most radical of the new African law faculties, did not deviate far from the London model in respect of course structure, quality and methods of assessment; insofar as it did, it pioneered adjustments that became quite commonplace in English law faculties after 1968—such as half-courses and continuous assessment.[21] No doubt in the early stages there were some inhibitions about making too radical a break for fear of jeopardising the reputation of the degree; but I suspect that a far greater constraint was the limits of the imagination and expertise of the innovators. Writing of the early days of Ibadan in Nigeria, its first Principal, Dr Kenneth Melanby, summed up why relatively few modifications were ever requested of London:

> "First we had to use existing textbooks. Secondly, many courses (e.g. mathematics, chemistry) are of universal applications and there is no specific 'African' version. Thirdly, most of our staff, both African and European, had insufficient experience of Africa to be competent at the outset to modify their courses."[22]

In the case of law, the special relationship system did not so much serve to put a brake on localisation—inevitably a slow process—as to limit American influence, which was much more pronounced in countries outside the special relationship system, such as Ethiopia and Liberia.

The institutional history of the system of special relations has been relatively well-researched and proclaimed.[23] The more complex human story of individual candidates for external degrees—both the successes and the failures—remains largely unexplored; it deserves more attention from social historians and students of education.

There can be no doubt at all of the historical and contemporary importance of the external system in providing educational opportunity, in institution building, and in meeting a variety of specific needs and demands. From a purely intellectual and educational point of view the merits of the system have not been so clear-cut. Consistent attempts have been made to maintain standards in all three senses distinguished by Ashby. The external LL.B. has gained widespread international recognition, but there have been costs: for example, a certain rigidity and conservatism; painfully high failure and wastage rates; few Upper Seconds and almost no Firsts—though I am pleased to say that one First was awarded in 1986—the first for many years.

The revival and reform of the external system provides a great opportunity to make external degrees more interesting, flexible and up to date. For its potential to be realised it must be adequately funded, so that its operation can be properly monitored, new forms of distance learning and educational technology can be fully used and, above all, that it should be adapted to the human and educational needs of students of different kinds. As an outside observer, I see two dangers which, are both associated with the "London disease" of spreading academic resources too thinly and making a virtue of parsimony. The External System is too important to be left entirely to a handful of dedicated administrators and the voluntary efforts of academics who contribute over and above their ordinary duties as full-time scholar-teachers in the various Law Schools.[24] The new external system also needs active support, financial as well as professional, not only from law teachers, but also from any body concerned with improving access to legal education and the legal profession, both in this country and elsewhere.[25]

A Prose Poem in Praise of the LL.M.

Once upon a time, long, long, ago the LL.M. was a quiet gentlemanly affair: a handful of academically promising students working largely on their own and meeting occasionally with their tutors. Over the years it growed and growed and became internationalised. Student numbers increased, new courses developed—often as an outlet for individual teachers seeking a less constricting forum than the three year LL.B. for the development of their interests and ideas. Despite this expansion, for many years it was seen as a side-show, a hangover from the days of the inter-collegiate system—at best a pleasing avocation, at worst a diversion from the serious enterprise of teaching undergraduates.

Then the LL.M. was privatised. From a marginal sideshow it has developed into a Juristic Bazaar with nearly 500 students from over 50 countries; there are at present over 80 courses on the books ranging from Child Law and Juvenile Justice to Chinese, Islamic and African Law—and, indeed, Space Law. It has been said that according to present projections, the rate of growth of numbers of lawyers in the United States relative to population is such that by about 2050 there will be more lawyers than people in that country. Some fear that, according to present trends, there will be more courses than students in the LL.M. by the year 2000. Others see this as evidence of the vitality of Laws in London.

As most of you will know, the main impetus for reform has come from the imposition by Government of a requirement to charge differential fees for overseas (non-EEC) students. Within a relatively short time those who had opposed differential fees on principle found themselves, largely by economic necessity, acting as sales persons and recruiters for their own institutions. As one who has consistently opposed this provision, I have to admit that one good result of the policy—perhaps the only one—is that it has led to an enormous improvement in the LL.M. Decaying courses that had sat untouched on stalls for 20 years were revised or dropped; brand new glossy products—some produced not far from here—come off the presses almost weekly. Finance officers tremble when students, quite rightly, demand value for money. Tutors prepare proper reading-lists and course materials; teaching in the LL.M. counts as part of one's teaching load; the Institute of Advanced Legal Studies buys books; British Council Representatives complain that their time is taken up by over-eager sales persons claiming to represent well over 100 British institutions of higher education. It is rumoured that in one of the fringe subjects students are wooed with beer in the Jeremy Bentham; yet down the road, the story goes, a lecturer stands on the table in front of a packed room and tries to deter people by saying: "Go away—if all you want is to get rich quick" . . . to which the students reply: "So we do and so do you." For it is widely, though erroneously, believed that the LL.M. is a profit-making enterprise.

It would not be appropriate on a celebratory occasion to pursue some of the more controversial aspects of this matter here. For whatever reason, it is clear that in recent years the LL.M. has been enriched and tightened up into one of the largest, most varied and most genuinely cosmopolitan postgraduate programmes in the world. For better or worse, it *is* a bazaar—an extraordinarily diverse group of clients in search of a variety of wares and services from a pretty diverse group of stall-holders. In the first few weeks of term, new postgraduates are advised to shop around and sample what is on offer, before committing themselves. The record is said to be held by one keen student, who starting at 10 a.m. on Monday managed to attend 45 lectures and tutorials by Friday evening, including three different courses on Intellectual Property, a private tutorial on Mongolian Law and a small seminar discussing the meaning of the auto-icon.

Like all bazaars, the fascination lies in the diversity of the customers and of the wares on offer. In time, one hopes that most people find something to suit their needs. There are, of course, some carpers who would homogenize the enterprise by creating a monopolistic superstore along the lines of Sainsbury's or Marks and Spencer. To my mind this is a mistake. Rather we should celebrate the LL.M. for what it is: five law schols, over a hundred academics and practitioners, and students from all over the world jostling together—often in friendly competition—in a great big, booming, buzzing marketplace of ideas and information, lightly regulated in an incomprehensible way by the invisible hand of that great poker player of academia, Senate House.

The Institute of Advance Legal Studies[26]

In 1986 the University of London has eight Institutes and Centres devoted wholly or partly to the advancement of our discipline. These are:

Institute of Advanced Legal Studies
Centre of European Law (K.C.L.)
Centre of Law, Medicine and Ethics (K.C.L.)
Institute for Economics and Related Disciplines (L.S.E.)
Centre for Labour Economics (L.S.E.)
Centre for African Studies (S.O.A.S.)
Centre for Commercial Law Studies (Q.M.C.)
Centre for the Study of Socialist Legal Systems (U.C.L.).

Few will contest the proposition that the most important of these is the Institute of Advanced Legal Studies, which celebrated its 40th birthday last week with a visit from the Chancellor. In 1934 one of the two conclusions of the very disappointing Atkin Committee on Legal Education was that there was a need for an institution which would be a national headquarters for academic research and would promote the advancement of knowledge of the law in the most general terms. "The natural organ for this purpose will be found in the establishment of an Institute of Advanced Legal Studies."[27] This proposal was all that remained of the more ambitious plans for a Legal University of London, which had been revived by Harold Laski who was a member of the Atkin Committee. The Government took no action on the recommendation, but after the War Professor David Hughes Parry persuaded the University of London to set up such an Institute. This was in 1946.[28]

Forty years on the Institute is well-established as an important centre both nationally and internationally. Within the University of London it plays an absolutely pivotal role, both symbolically and practically, in sustaining inter-collegiate cooperation in our discipline. It houses the best Law Library in the University and one of the three best in the country. It is the headquarters for many visiting scholars from all over the world, for approximately 700 graduate students, for the Board of Studies, and for all law teachers in the University.[29]

Without the Institute Laws in London would be fragmented and drastically impoverished. It is also fair to say that the significance of the Institute lies as much in its future potential as in its past achievements. For, it is a widely held view, which I share, that it has a long way to go before it fulfills its promise. For much of its history, the Institute has not had funds to match its aspirations.[30] Only in respect of its building—which was given to the University by Sir Charles Clore—can it be said that it has ever have been adequately provided for. Its greatest achievement is the Library; yet, in 1983–84 approximately 60 law schools in the United States (and several in Canada) were reported to have more books than are at present in the Institute Library. Harvard has nearly one-and-a-half million volumes; the Bodleian Law Library about 290,000; I.A.L.S. has 174,000 slightly fewer than Emory University Law School, and slightly more than Hofstra.[31] Allowance must be made for the crudity of such statistics; also for "rationalisation," which is Newspeak for cutting costs. This prevents wasteful, necessary and useful duplication. It also creates or obscures vacuums of responsibility, especially in interdisciplinary areas such as Law and Psychology, Law and Social History, American Legal History, Legal Education and Training, Forensic Science, Access to Justice, and many other areas where legal practice intersects with broader worlds of practical affairs. This is just not good enough for what aspires to be the second best academic law library in the country.[32] There is no point in allocating blame—indeed there are many individual heroes and heroines in the Institute's history: but this clearly represents a collective failure of imagination and of will on the part of both the academic and the legal communities over a period of 50 years.

The Institute organises or hosts many valuable academic activities, but it has never quite achieved the aim of becoming the national headquarters for academic law.[33] In this respect we could still learn a lot from our neighbours in the Institute of Historical Research. The I.A.L.S. is both inter-collegiate and international; it has some way to go before it is a centre for sustained interdisciplinary research. Again, it has long been recognised that the Institute has great potential for strengthening the ties between the academic and practising branches of the legal profession. This is reflected in the composition of the Committee of Management and in some valuable occasional seminars; but what has been achieved to date falls far short of what could be.

This is not captious carping by a disgruntled academic. For much the same assessment was made in a report of a Policy Review Sub-committee chaired by Sir Robert Megarry in 1986. This concluded that the Institute "has yet to develop into what it should be and was originally intended to be, the national centre for research with a wide spectrum of scholarly activities."[34] This remarkable document, which represented an unexpected *volte face* from an essentially pessimistic and defensive approach, was unanimously and enthusiastically endorsed by the Committee of Management and the Board of Studies and, despite the chill economic and political climate, steps are currently being taken to implement its recommendations.

I will add only one personal coda to this report. One of the most important recommendations of the Ormrod Committee that has yet to be implemented, is that there should be an Institute of Professional Legal Studies, which would be a means by which universities and other institutions could be involved in professional education and training in a co-ordinated way.[35] It is a constant source of amazement to visitors from abroad that in England the university law schools are almost totally uninvolved in professional training after the academic stage. As I have argued elsewhere, there is also an unmet need for research in and systematic development of the direct teaching of professional skills.[36] The Institute of Advanced Legal Studies, in addition to aspiring to be an excellent Library and centre of research, can perform a vital role in strengthening links with the practising profession. Twelve years after the Atkin Report the University of London implemented a recommendation that had been ignored by Government. Fifteen years after Ormrod seems a good time to revive another idea that has not yet found official favour.

Conclusion

When proper histories of legal education in England and in this University come to be written, three themes ought to be treated as central.

The first is economic: during the past 150 years academic law has been perceived and treated as a low-cost enterprise. For the first hundred years in London nearly all teaching was left to parsimoniously remunerated part-time teachers. A major change came with the shift to full-time teachers. But staff-student ratios have always been among the worst, research funding has been almost non-existent, and professional training today is Ormrod-on-the-cheap. Some heroic feats have been achieved with minimal resources; but the potential of our discipline is far from being realised. Recently the climate of opinion has begun to change. In 1983 the Heads of University Law Schools argued that while law remains one of the most cost-effective subjects, nearly all recent developments in our rapidly changing discipline involve at least some increases in unit costs. This message has been reiterated in 1986 by a forceful report of Australian Law School Deans, by the Policy Review Committee of the I.A.L.S. and, in more muted terms, even by the U.G.C.

The second theme is political. The often dismal history of legal education and training in England has been in part a story of failures of cooperation. At crucial points—for example, in 1846; in 1900; in the series of abortive attempts to establish a great Legal University in London and, more recently, in the Ormrod and Benson exercises, the main interest groups—the Inns of Court, the Solicitors and the academic community—refused to cooperate. One result was that Government was freed from sustained pressure to provide public funding on the same scale as for other professional subjects, such as Medicine or Engineering.

The uneven history of Laws in the University of London illustrates a converse pattern. For some of the main success stories— the inter-collegiate system, especially in the inter-war years; the External system; the Institute of Advanced Legal Studies; and the recent strengthening of the LL.M.—are all instances where the constituent colleges, while maintaining their distinct identities, have been able to sink their differences and engage in joint enterprises of the University of London. The twin factors of our geographical location and the opportunity to pool the resources of five law schools remain our greatest source of potential strength.

Perhaps the most important lesson of history is that legal education, in this country and in most parts of the world, has tended to be demand-led. The scale and nature of the enterprise of academic law are largely determined by the popularity of the subject, rather than by the ideas of planners or academics or governments. Legal education in London in the nineteenth century languished for lack of students. Today the high demand for legal education is a remarkable international phenomenon. In this country Law is better protected than most disciplines by the buoyancy of demand, both at home and overseas. There is, of course, a constant tension between what students want, or think they want, and what their teachers think they ought to want or want to offer them. But an institution such as ours is well-placed to resolve many of these tensions if we stand firm on a single principle. Over time law lecturers can exert proper control over their situation only if they have imagination, the will and the persistence to reiterate an uncompromising message to colleagues and administrators, to the legal profession, to providers of funds—both public and private—and, above all, to our students: "We demand excellence."

Today this may sound like crying in the wilderness. We are living in a period of cuts, and of official incomprehension, hostility and ineptitude. Morale is low. The legal profession is experiencing what may prove to be an historic series of traumas. We have been damaged, but largely because of bouyant demand we have not been maimed. Indeed never in our history have Laws in London

been stronger. Nevertheless, the last 15 years have been very painful, for all of us. Students, younger teachers and libraries have
been among the main victims. There are two main responses to
this kind of adversity: one can stonewall: or, like Gooch playing
Hadlee, one can counter-attack. The revival of the External System and the recent report on the Institute of Advanced Legal
Studies represent the latter approach. They deserve our full support. In this regard I am reminded of two precepts of Lord Butter-
worth, one of the most successful Vice-Chancellors in recent
years. In the seventies, he used to say to me "My boy, in a period
of stop-go, stop-go, always be ready to go." Later, when the cuts
came, he said to us "When everyone else has their heads beneath
the parapet, that is the time to CHARGE!"[37]

Notes

This is a revised version of a lecture delivered at Queen Mary College on
October 28, 1986 as part of the sesquicentennial celebrations of the University of
London. In the course of preparing the lecture I have benefited from help and
advice of numerous individuals and institutions. Professor Michael Thompson,
Negley Harte and Andrew Lewis provided invaluable advice and material. David
Sugarman joined me in interviewing Professors Albert Kiralfy, L. C. B. Gower, Sir
Jack Jacob, George Keeton and Lord Wedderburn, all of whom provided invalu-
able information insights and correctives. Professors Antony Allott, Francis
Jacobs, Jeffrey Jowell, Michael Zander and Graham Zellick supplied me with a
mass of information about the five London law schools. Members of the External
Division and Judith Maynard, Secretary of the Board of Studies in Law, provided
invaluable assistance. Among others to whom I am indebted are Dr John Baker,
Professor F. R. Crane, Jacky Gorringe and Professor Robert Stevens. This lecture
is a celebration, interpretation and commentary, rather than a descriptive history.
However, in the course of its preparation, I acquired sufficient material to form a
small archive. This will in due course be deposited in the Institute of Advanced
Legal Studies in the hope that it will be of help to real historians.
*Quain Professor of Jurisprudence

[1] Negley Harte, *The University of London 1836–1986* (London, 1986).
[2] Courses in Law have, from time to time, been offered by other schools and
institutions of the University. For example, evening classes were regularly offered
by Birkbeck College before World War II; the Department of Extra-Mural Studies
offers courses on Criminology and is planning a Certificate in Legal Method. Law
has feature in a modest way in other degrees, such as the B.Sc. (Engineering).
[3] Standard accounts include: L. C. B. Gower, "English Legal Training" (1950)
13 M.L.R. 137, B. Abel-Smith and R. Stevens, *Lawyers and the Courts* (London,
1967); *Report of the Committee on Legal Education* Cmnd. 4595 (1971), (Ormrod
Report). The modern history of legal education in England 1800–1980 is currently
being re-interpreted by David Sugarman, see especially "The Legal Boundaries of
Liberty: Dicey, Liberalism and Legal Science" (1983) 46 M.L.R. 102 and "Legal

Theory and the Common Law Mind: The Making of the Textbook Tradition" in
W. L. Twining (ed.), *Legal Theory and Common Law* (Oxford, 1986). There are,
of course, many particular studies, too numerous to mention here.

[4] Max Weber, *Law in Economy and Society* (ed. M. Rheinstein) (Cambridge,
Mass., 1954), Chap. VII.

[5] Above n. 3.

[6] Their influence has increased in recent years but, as Brian Simpson remarked:
"Any attempt by the academics to displace the higher judiciary from their central
place as expounders and modifiers of the law seems to me to have always been fore-
doomed to failure. In the absence of some quite radical scheme of modification the
judges, and in particular the members of the Court of Appeal and the House of
Lords, are hardly likely to abdicate their status in favour of the professors. Why
should they?" A. W. B. Simpson, "The Survival of the Common Law System" in
Then and Now, 1799–1974, (London, 1974), 63–64.

[7] *E.g.* Ormrod, 5.

[8] *Report from the Select Committee on Legal Education* August 25, 1846 B.P.P.
Vol. X, p. 1.

[9] iv.

[10] Ormrod, 5. This contains a useful, and generally accurate, summary of the
Report.

[11] 1846 Report, xvi.

[12] *Id.* xxxix (quoting R. Bethell Q.C.).

[13] *Ibid.* lvii.

[14] *Ibid.* lviii. The Committee concluded: "That the present state of Legal Education in England and Ireland, in reference to the classes professional and unprofessional concerned, to the extent and nature of the studies pursued, the time
employed, and the facility with which instruction may be obtained, is extremely
unsatisfactory and incomplete, and exhibits a striking contrast and inferiority to
such education, provided as it is with ample means and a judicious system for their
application, at present in operation in all the more civilised States of Europe and
America" (lvi).

[15] *Ibid.* lviii–lix.

[16] *Ibid.* lix–lx.

[17] *Ibid.* lxi.

[18] Ormrod, 8.

[19] For details see Abel-Smith and Stevens, Gower, and A. H. Manchester,
Modern Legal History, (London, 1980), 54–66.

[20] The contrast between "higher" and "technical" studies pervades the Report;
see, *e.g.* xlvii–xlviii.

[21] Ormrod, 3.

[22] See further W. Twining, "The Benson Report and Legal Education: A Personal View" in *Law in the Balance* (ed. P. A. Thomas), (Oxford, 1982), Chap. 8.

[23] The most comprehensive figures are to be found in J. F. Wilson and S. B.
Marsh, *A Second Survey of Legal Education in the United Kingdom* (I.A.L.S.,
London, 1981). On the basis of projected intake quotas for 1983/84 Wilson and
Marsh predicted that the output of law graduates in England and Wales would be
Universities 2455 (66 per cent.), Polytechnics 1238 (34 per cent.) (Table 43 at
p. 45). These figures did not take account of the revival of the External LL.B., the
License of the University of Buckingham, graduates with mixed degrees who pro-
ceed to a professional qualification and non-law graduates who take the Common
Professional Examination.

[24] L. C. B. Gower, "The Future of the Legal Profession" (1946) 9 M.L.R. 211,
at p. 218.

[25] N. Harte and J. North, *The World of University College 1828–1978* at pp. 8–9, 108–112.

[26] W. Twining, "Why Bentham?" *The Bentham Newsletter*, No. 8, 1984, at p. 36.

[27] Harte and North, 67. The picture has recently been returned to its intended place in the Flaxman Gallery.

[28] Professor J. L. Montrose, one of the most imaginative pioneers of modern attempts to broaden the study of law, entitled his Presidential Address to the Bentham Club in 1950, "Return to Austin's College." No irony seems to have been intended.

[29] W. Twining, "Academic Law and Legal Philosophy: The Significance of Herbert Hart" 95 L.Q.R. 557–60.

[30] Twining, (1984), 44–47, *op.cit.* n.26.

[31] J. S. Mill, "Bentham" *10 Collected Works of John Stuart Mill* (ed. Robson), (Toronto, 1969), 75.

[32] *E.g.* H. L. A. Hart, *Essays on Bentham* (Oxford, 1982), 11, 128; Ross Harrison, *Bentham* (London, 1983), Chap. 3.

[33] See especially Hart's inaugural lecture H. L. A. Hart, "Definition and Theory in Jurisprudence" (1954) 70 L.Q.R. 37, reprinted in H. L. A. Hart, *Essays in Jurisprudence and Philosophy* (Oxford, 1983).

[34] For a defence of Bentham's Psychology see Mary Mack, *Jeremy Bentham: An Odyssey of Ideas 1748–1832* (London, 1962).

[35] *Op. cit.* n. 24.

[36] See generally H. L. A. Hart, *Essays on Bentham* (Oxford U.P., 1982).

[37] *Ibid.*

[38] W. Morison, *John Austin* (London, 1982); W. E. Rumble, *The Thought of John Austin: Jurisprudence, Colonial Reform and the British Constitution* (London, 1985); L. and J. Hamburger, *Troubled Lives, John and Sarah Austin*, (Toronto, 1985).

[39] H. L. A. Hart, *The Concept of Law* (Oxford, 1961).

[40] R. Cocks, *Foundations of the Modern Bar* (1983) 42–43, 50.

[41] *E.g.* Sugarman, (1986), 37–44.

[42] The *locus classicus* is J. Bentham, *A Fragment on Government* (ed. J. H. Burns and H. L. A. Hart), *Collected Works* (1977, Preface).

[43] *Fragment*, 397.

[44] *Id.* 404.

[45] Below n. 63.

[46] J. Austin, *The Province of Jurisprudence Determined* (ed. H. L. A. Hart), (London, 1954); J. Bentham, *Introduction to Principles of Morals and Legislation* (ed. J. H. Burns and H. L. A. Hart) CW., (1970), 294–95 (*Jurisprudence Local-Universal*). These recent reappraisals bring out the fact that Austin was more concerned than Bentham to develop an empirical science that was close to the facts of legal practice and based on political economy. His successors both obscured this distinctive emphasis and, more strikingly, down-played or ignored Austin's broader political and moral concerns. Rumble and others have also shown how Austin's enterprise departed much further from Blackstone's than did Bentham's (*e.g.* Rumble, 227 n. 101). I am grateful to David Sugarman for this point.

[47] Austin, 367.

[48] *Fragment*, 398.

[49] *E.g.* G. W. Keeton, "University College, London, and the Law" (1939) 51 *Juridical Review*, 118; A. N. Allott, A Short History of the Teaching and Investigation of Law at the School of Oriental and African Studies (unpublished manuscript, May 1986).

[50] The most important source for Bentham's views is: "Proposal for a School of Legislation" Bentham Mss, U.C. CVII, (c. 1794).

[51] Above n. 44.

[52] Austin, 390.

[53] Austin, 381.

[54] See generally, Morison Chap. 5.

[55] This section draws heavily on John Baker's admirable paper "University College and Legal Education 1826–1976" (1977) *Current Legal Problems* 1–13 and Hale Bellot, *University College London 1826–1926* (1926). A collection of Andrew Amos's papers survives: UC Ms Add. 90 (seven boxes). A clear summary of Amos's approach, based on his evidence to them, is given by the 1846 Select Committee of Legal Education, *op. cit.* at p. viii.

[56] Baker, 2–4, citing Amos's "Introductory Lecture."

[57] A. Amos, An Introductory Lecture Upon the Study of Law, delivered in the University of London, November 2, 1829.

[58] Cited Baker, 3.

[59] There is, admittedly, a marked contrast between Amos's accounts of his intentions and practice and the markedly pedestrian factual questions that he set in examinations. Examples of the latter were appended to his Introductory Lecture.

[60] J. Bentham, *Introduction to the Principles of Morals and Legislation* (ed. Hart and Burns), CW, 1970, 21–22n.

[61] It is beyond the scope of this lecture to explore controversial questions about the extent and the nature of the relative marginalization of broader approaches to legal education in our intellectual tradition. Suffice to say that the story is a complex one and at no stage did more extreme versions of the Expository Orthodoxy go unchallenged.

[62] John Griffith, "Law at L.S.E." *L.S.E.*, June 1979; Cyril Grunfeld, "Reflections of a Convenor" (1978).

[63] *E.g.* O. Kahn-Freund, "Reflections on Legal Education" (1966) 29 *Modern Law Review*, 121 at 129; Confirmed by Professor Lord Wedderburn (Interview, October, 1986). Compare the more cautious statement by Kahn-Freund and Wedderburn in the Editorial Foreword to the first book in the "Law in Society Series," D. W. Elliott and H. Street *Road Accidents* (1968). For a different view, see W. Twining and D. Miers, *How To Do Things With Rules* (2nd, ed., 1982), Chap. 2, (attacking the fallacy of The Way of the Baffled Medic—prescription before diagnosis).

[64] The main sources for this section are for UCL:— Baker (1977), Bellot (1926), Keeton (1939); for King's:— F. J. C. Hearnshaw, *The Centenary History of King's College, London 1828–1928* (1928); Gordon Huelin, *King's College London 1828–1978* (1978); Cocks, (1983). It is fair to say that the history of Laws at King's is less well-documented than that of U.C.L.

[65] For details, see Bellot Chap. 4 (and Charts); Hearnshaw at 98 *et seq.*

[66] For details see Harte, (1986) 106; Baker 5–6.

[67] At vii.

[68] Bellot, 327.

[69] Baker, 8. Figures for the period 1838–1900 are set out in Harte, (1986) at 106 and 139. The bulk of LL.B. graduates before the Inter-Collegiate system was established seems to have been external students.

[70] Hearnshaw, 243.

[71] Bellot, 331.

[72] Baker, 7.

[73] Personal details of the Law Graduates of U.C.L. are collected in a valuable

unpublished document by Dr J. H. Baker, *University College London: Faculty of Laws, List of Graduates 1839–1930* (1969–70) (Copy on file at I.A.L.S.).

[74] Baker, 7. Women were first admitted to the legal profession in 1922, Abel-Smith and Stevens, 192–94.

[75] The main published sources for this section are Keeton, (1939), Gower, (1950), Edward Jenks, "English Legal Education" 1885–1935; (1935) 51 *Law Quarterly Review*, 162. In addition I am greatly indebted to Professor George Keeton for permission to draw on a personal memoir (September, 1985) and an extended interview in August, 1986.

[76] Harte, 158.   [77] Jenks, 171–72.

[78] The incumbents of the Chairs were: 1919 Commercial and Industrial Law—H. Gutteridge; 1924 English Law—E. Jenks; 1920 International Law—E. P. Higgins; 1930 Legal History—T. F. T. Plucknett; 1931 Roman Law—H. F. Jolowicz. In addition, three Readerships in English Law were established in this period: U.C.L.—G. W. Keeton; K. C. L.—H. Potter; L.S.E.—W. I. Jennings. Other notable pre-1939 appointments included: R. S. T. (later Lord) Chorley; H. (later Sir Hirsch) Lauterphacht; A. T. (later Lord) McNair; D. (later Sir David) Hughes Parry; and W. A. Robson.

[79] Keeton, (1939) at 133.

[80] G. W. Keeton (interview); Professor A. Kiralfy (interview).

[81] G. W. Keeton, letter to author (17.9.85). Interview.

[82] *Id.*

[83] Professor L. C. B. Gower (interview).

[84] *E.g.* Professor A. Kiralfy (interview), Professor F. R. Crane ("A Note on the London Law Faculty, 1930–85" communication to author); Professor Sir Jack Jacob Q.C. (interview).

[85] Huelin, (1978) at 112.

[86] These figures are approximate, partly because the distinction between "part-time" and "full-time" teachers was not always a sharp one.

[87] G. W. Keeton "The Revision of Courses for the LL.B. in London" (1948) 1 *Jo Soc Pub Teachers of Law* (NS.) 189.

[88] G. W. Keeton (interview).

[89] Keeton (interview).

[90] Harte, 238–41.

[91] Keeton (letter to author, *op. cit.* n. 79), Kiralfy (interview).

[92] Harte, 264–65. One of the most significant results of the introduction of Special Regulations was that internal and external candidates no longer took examinations that were common to all students.

[93] Heads of University Law Schools, *Law as an Academic Discipline*: A reponse to the Leverhulme Report and the U.G.C. Letter on a Strategy for Higher Education into the 1990s (March, 1984). An abbreviated version was published in The Society of Public Teachers of Law *Newsletter*, Summer, 1984.

[94] Material on the history of the five London Law Schools is collected in the "archive" mentioned in the introductory note, above.

[95] Some indication of the changes can be obtained from the following figures for the University of London:

(a) *LL.B.* (internal):
   Intake: 1965/6 309; total undergraduate law students; 755
              1983/4 441; total undergraduate law students: 1186
   (Source: *Law as an Academic Discipline*, Appendix).

(b) *LL.M.* (internal)	*Candidates*	*Passes*
1974	237	171
1985	419	289

(c) *Institute of Advanced Legal Studies*
Students registered for postgraduate work in the University of London. (Law in brackets).

1965/66	337 (312)	1984/85	573 (531)

(I.A.L.S. *Annual Reports*)

⁹⁶ Some examples of diversification are as follows:

(a) Each of the five schools has its own curriculum for the three year LL.B. (London) (internal) (for details, see the prospectus of each law school). These have diverged both from each other and, even more strikingly, from the curriculum as it stood at the end of the inter-collegiate period.

(b) In addition to the three year LL.B., there are several distinctive undergraduate degree programmes offered by individual schools. For example:

    (i) *King's*: joint four year programme in English and French Law leading to both the LL.B. (London) and the Maitrise en Droit of the University of Paris I.

    (ii) *L.S.E.* Degree of Bachelor of Laws with French Law (for which candidates are eligible to enter for a Diplome d'études juridiques of the University of Strasbourg) and Degree of Bachelor of Laws with German Law (which includes a certifying Examination of the University of Hamburg).

    (iii) *Queen Mary College* has a joint B.A. in Law and Politics and particular strengths in Commercial Law and Intellectual Property.

    (iv) *U.C.L.* has recently introduced a provision enabling undergraduates to opt for a four year programme leading to the LL.B.

    (v) *S.O.A.S.* has a number of distinctive undergraduate degrees with a unique emphasis on oriental, African and Comparative laws and connections with other disciplines, including anthropology, languages, religious studies and economics.

(c) Perhaps the most significant diversification has taken place in the LL.M. (internal). In 1965 30 options were listed in the Regulations; in 1986 82 options were listed, of which 71 were examined (source, Senate House).

⁹⁷ All five programmes leading to the LL.B. (internal) include at least one course relating to the E.E.C. The majority also contain at least one course on Foreign or Comparative Law related to Europe. In 1986–87 there were courses in the internal LL.M. relating to E.E.C. and Laws of particular European countries.

⁹⁸ The main exceptions in 1985–86 were (a) the S.O.A.S. LL.B., which has more emphasis on Oriental and African Laws and less on specialised English Law subjects and (b) Planning Law, which received more emphasis at L.S.E. (a full option on Land Development and Planning Law) than in the other LL.B. curricula.

⁹⁹ See above n. 96. ¹ See below, text at 287.

² The HULSC Report stated: "Significant developments in legal education in the next 10–15 years are likely to include:

    (i) continuing pressure to expand the range of subjects and to adopt broader approaches within the LL.B.;

    (ii) similar pressure at postgraduate level, especially in respect of inter-disciplinary work, research training and expanding fields such as foreign law in relation to commerce, trade and economic development;

    (iii) possibly, an expansion of mixed two-subject honours degrees;

    (iv) possibly, a more substantial legal input into other general, non-vocational degree courses;

    (v) a continuing increase in the demand from other disciplines for legal inputs into vocationally oriented courses;

    (vi) more emphasis on computer applications to legal education and research, not solely in respect of information retrieval, but also, for example, in the development of "expert systems";

(vii) a rapid expansion of continuing legal education and of part-time studies, for the legal profession and for a great variety of other groups; it is particularly significant that from 1985 continuing legal education for solicitors in England and Wales will be compulsory for the first three years of practice;

(viii) developments in teaching of practical skills, simulation exercises and clinical legal education.

(ix) changes in the nature and environment of legal practice including increasing complexity, shifts in markets for legal services and the varying impacts of information technology will continue to exert pressure on the legal education system to anticipate and adapt to changing conditions."

Law as an Academic Discipline (1984), para. 6.

[3] I am grateful to members of the External Division of the University of London, especially Andrea Kelly, Sam Crooks and Jenny Shelburne for help with this section. Other sources relied on include: Bruce Pattison, *Special Relations: The University of London and New Universities Overseas* (University of London, 1984); The University of London: *The University's Policy for the External System* (Policy Statement, July 1983); The University of London: *The External System: A Background Paper* (unpublished policy statement, 1986). A. M. Carr-Saunders, *New Universities Overseas* (London, 1961); Eric Ashby, *Universities: British, Indian, African* (London, 1966); I. C. M. Maxwell, *Universities in Partnership* (Edinburgh, 1980).

[4] Figures supplied by Senate House.

[5] In June, 1985 the figures for *candidates* for the LL.B. were as follows: Intermediate: Internal: 415 (including eight absent); External: (a) Home: 894 (168 absent); (b) Overseas 1292 (399 absent).

Part I: Internal: 374 (eight absent); External: Home: 472 (90 absent); Overseas: 291 (78 absent).

Part II: Internal: 331 (two absent); External: Home: 288 (28 absent); Overseas 105 (13 absent).

These figures exclude mixed degrees. (Figures supplied by Senate House).

[6] A note supplied by Senate House reads:

Examinations in Prisoner of War Camps, 1942–45

"The University of London provided 1,305 different examination papers to prisoner of war camps—over a fifth of the total. Only 11 other Examination Boards exceeded 100 papers, the next largest being the Royal Society of Arts with 324 papers.

Examination papers were sent by air mail via Lisbon from May 1942 to March 1944, when the arrangements had to be suspended owing to the plans for D-Day. The Lisbon air-route was resumed in July 1944 but did not prove satisfactory under the different conditions and a new quicker air-route via Sweden was begun on 9 September 1944 and continued until the last despatch on 7 April 1945 when the scheme came to its anticipated end with the victorious advance of the Allied Armies and the over-running of the prisoner-of-war Camps in Germany." See further, Harte, (1986) at 238–41.

[7] Andrea Kelly (letter to author 17/10/86, cited with permission).

[8] *Ibid.*

[9] "The External System: A Background Paper" *op. cit.* n. 3.

[10] The law schools directly affected were: Gordon College, Khartoum (later University of Khartoum); University College. Gold Coast/Ghana (later University of Ghana, Legon); University College, Dar-es-Salaam (via Makerere College, Uganda; subsequently Dar-es-Salaam became a constituent college of the University of East Africa and then the independent University of Dar-es-Salaam). Law

Faculties developed after the attainment of University status in the University of the West Indies, and in a more complicated way, at the institutions that became Makerere University, Kampala and the University of Nairobi. The Law Faculties of Hong Kong, Singapore, Malaya (Kuala Lumpur), Malawi and the first generation of Nigerian Law Faculties could be said to have belonged to the same family of law schools, without having been part of the special relationship system. For details, see Pattison, (1984) 133–36; L. C. B. Gower, *Independent Africa: The Challenge to the Legal Profession* (Cambridge, Mass. 1966); J. Bainbridge, *The Study and Teaching of Law in Africa* (South Hackensack, New Jersey 1972).

[11] "The External System: A Background Paper," *op. cit.*

[12] S. B. Crooks paper on "External Fund-Raising" for the Working-Party on the Development of the External System (1986), (quoted with permission).

[13] See references in nn. 1, 9 and 10 above.

[14] The names of the External Examiners for 1958 are listed in the University of Khartoum *Calendar* (1959).

[15] Ashby, (1966) at 235.

[16] *Id.* 238.

[17] *Id.* 259–60.

[18] *Id.* 258.

[19] *Id.* 259.

[20] For details, see William Twining, "Legal Education within East Africa" in (1966) *East African Law Today* 115. British Institute of Int. and Comp. Law, London; and "The Camel in the Zoo" in Issa Shivji (ed.) *The Limits of Legal Radicalism*, Dar-es-Salaam (1986).

[21] For details, see Twining, (1966).

[22] Minerva I (1963), 153 cited Pattison (1984) at 162. Professor Gower suggests that "increasingly in the Post-War period the failure of Commonwealth Universities to adapt to local conditions was due to their reluctance to put forward proposals rather than London's reluctance to accept suggestions" (letter to author, January 6, 1987).

[23] Especially Ashby, Carr-Saunders, Maxwell and Pattison *op. cit.* n. 3.

[24] Professor F. R. Crane points out that the involvement of senior London law teachers declined significantly after the introduction of Special Regulations (letter to author, December, 1986). Individuals who teach or examine for external degrees are paid *pro rata*, but participation is not part of their contractual duties and normally no allowance is made in respect of their duties in their respective schools. What is surely needed is a small group of full-time academic staff (perhaps on temporary secondment) who can devote themselves single-mindedly to this important enterprise.

[25] The Commonwealth Legal Education Association is currently engaged in a study of Access to Legal Education and the Legal Profession in the Commonwealth.

[26] The main sources for this section are Institute of Advanced Legal Studies *Annual Reports*; I.A.L.S., *Report of the Policy Review Sub-Committee* (Chairman Sir Robert Megarry) (May, 1986); Sir David Hughes-Parry, "The Institute of Advanced Legal Studies" J.S.P.T.L. (N.S.) I, 183 (1949); Lord MacMillan, *A Man of Law's Tale* (1952) at 217–18; Aubrey Diamond, "Willi Steiner and the Institute of Advanced Legal Studies" (1989) 15 *The Law Librarian* 46–47; *Report of the Legal Education Committee* (Atkin Report) Cmd 4663 (1934); Gower, "English Legal Training" (1950) *op. cit.* n. 3 above. I am grateful to Professor Aubrey Diamond, Professor Sir Jack Jacob Q.C., Muriel Anderson and Barbara Tearle for information used in this section; the opinions expressed are my own.

[27] Atkin Report, *op. cit.* n. 26 at 13.

[28] The Institute celebrated its 40th birthday in October, 1986. Some historians give its date of birth as 1947 (*e.g.* Harte, (1986) 247) or 1948 (Abel-Smith and Stevens, 1967, at 185). The University of London formally decided to establish it in 1946; it began work in 1947 and was formally opened by the Lord Chancellor on June 11, 1948. The phenomenon of a person celebrating their 39th birthday in several successive years is quite familiar; on a generous interpretation of history the Institute has a unique opportunity to celebrate its 40th birthday for three years in succession.

[29] Other achievements of the Institute include *The Index of Foreign Legal Periodicals* (1960–83); *List of Current Legal Research Topics*; the annual W. G. Hart Workshop; the *University of London Legal Series* and miscellaneous bibliographical and special publications (for details, see *Annual Reports*).

[30] Many of the constraints were foreseen by Sir David Hughes-Parry in 1947 (*op. cit.* n. 26).

[31] The main sources for these figures are David A. Thomas, "1983–84 Statistical Survey of Law School Libraries and Libraries' " (1984–85) 77 *Law Library Journal* 575; I.A.L.S. *Report of the Policy Review Sub-Committee* (1986).

[32] The modesty of our national aspirations can be guaged by comparing the latest S.P.T.L., "Statement of Minimum Holdings for Law Libraries in England and Wales" (revised 1986) (1986) 6 *Legal Studies* 195–215 with equivalent documents in other common law countries.

[33] On "rationalization" within London see Megarry Report, *op. cit.*, Appendix A.

[34] *Id.* 5. Unlike some London Institutes, the I.A.L.S. does not register research students; it provides services to postgraduates registered in the various schools, but does not itself earn any income from fees.

[35] Ormrod Report, *op. cit.* n. 1, at pp. 88, 98, discussed in Twining, (1982) *op. cit.* n. 22 at 209–13.

[36] "Taking Skills Seriously" *Commonwealth Legal Education Newsletter* No. 44 (1986), Appendix.

[37] Reconstructed and cited with permission.

INDEX